TECHNOLOGY, ORGANIZATION, AND
COMPETITIVENESS

TECHNOLOGY, ORGANIZATION, AND COMPETITIVENESS

Perspectives on Industrial and Corporate Change

Edited by

GIOVANNI DOSI, DAVID J. TEECE, AND JOSEF CHYTRY

OXFORD UNIVERSITY PRESS

OXFORD

UNIVERSITY PRESS

Great Clarendon Street, Oxford OX2 6DP

Oxford University Press is a department of the University of Oxford.
It furthers the University's objective of excellence in research, scholarship,
and education by publishing worldwide in

Oxford NewYork

Athens Auckland Bangkok Bogotá Buenos Aires Calcutta
Cape Town Chennai Dar es Salaam Delhi Florence Hong Kong Istanbul
Karachi Kuala Lumpur Madrid Melbourne Mexico City Mumbai
Nairobi Paris São Paulo Singapore Taipei Tokyo Toronto Warsaw

with associated companies in Berlin Ibadan

Oxford is a registered trade mark of Oxford University Press
in the UK and in certain other countries

Published in the United States
by Oxford University Press Inc., New York

First published 1998

British Library Cataloguing in Publication Data
Data available

Library of Congress Cataloging in Publication Data
Data available
ISBN 0-19-829098-5
ISBN 0-19-829096-9 (Pbk)

3 5 7 9 10 8 6 4 2

Printed in Great Britain by
Bookcraft Ltd., Midsomer Norton, Somerset

PREFACE

This is the first of what we hope will be a series of books based on articles published in *Industrial and Corporate Change*. Our purposes are threefold. First, as editors of *ICC*, we would like to showcase some of the excellent scholarship appearing in *ICC*. Second, we wish to display some of the common themes which run through much of the new literature on technological and organizational innovation. Third, we would like to bring together in one volume important articles that would assist the teaching enterprise in universities and companies throughout the world. Indeed, we suggest that this book could complement instruction in graduate and advanced undergraduate courses in economics, business, innovation studies, and business history. The materials assembled draw on all of the above disciplines, and in turn inform important issues in each of the identified fields.

The authors are drawn from many different universities around the world, but nevertheless coexist and interact in an invisible college of scholars committed to understanding the foundations of firm level and national competitiveness, and ultimately the wealth of nations. All authors tacitly take for granted certain legal prerequisites, such as the existence of property rights and contract law, and a judicial system able to enforce agreements among individuals and business entities. That put to one side, the study of wealth creation through innovation becomes the study of the development of new technologies and their successful commercialization. It is aspects of this process at work in the advanced industrial economies which are the focus of this volume. Organization becomes the key. Indeed, it is the middle word in the title of this book, flanked by technology to the left and competitiveness to the right. This almost stands as a metaphor for the basic thesis of this book: *organization systems mediate the impact of technology on competitiveness*. Absent robust and adaptable organizational systems in firms, among firms, and between firms and external institutions, the fruits of technology will become dissipated. Conversely, well-designed organization structures and effective management are the handmaidens of competitive advantage, economic development, and growth.

Giovanni Dosi, David J. Teece, and Josef Chytry

CONTENTS

LIST OF CONTRIBUTORS

Clayton M. Christensen
Associate Professor of Business
 Administration
Graduate School of Business Administration
Harvard University
Soldiers Field
Boston, MA 02163
tel 617-495-6295
fax 617-495-0355

Josef Chytry
Senior Lecturer in the History of World
 Cultures
California College of Arts and Crafts
5212 Broadway
Oakland, CA 94618
tel 510-643-1631
fax 510-642-2826

Giovanni Dosi
Professor of Economics
Department of Economic Sciences
University of Rome 'La Sapienza'
Via Andrea Cesalpino 12/14
Rome 00161, Italy
tel 39-6-442-84232
fax 39-6-440-4572

Robert C. Feenstra
Professor of Economics & Chairperson
Department of Economics
1113 Social Sciences and Humanities
 Building
University of California
Davis, CA 95616-8692
tel 916-752-0741

Martin Fransman
Institute for Japanese-European Technology
 Studies
University of Edinburgh
25 Buccleuch Place
Edinburgh EH8 9KN
United Kingdom

Mark Granovetter
Professor of Sociology
Department of Sociology
Northwestern University
Evanston, IL 60208-1330
tel 708-491-5415
fax 708-491-9907

Gary G. Hamilton
Professor of Sociology
Department of Sociology
University of Washington
202 Savery
Box 353340
Seattle, WA 98195
tel 206-534-5883
fax 206-543-2516

William Lazonick
Codirector
Center for Industrial Competitiveness
University of Massachusetts Lowell
One University Avenue
Lowell, MA 01854
tel 508-934-2720
fax 508-934-3021

Richard R. Nelson
Professor of International and Public Affairs
School of International and Public Affairs
Columbia University
420 West 118th Street
New York, NY 10027
tel 212-854-8720

Parimal Patel
Fellow
Science Policy Research Unit
University of Sussex
Mantell Building
Falmer, Brighton
East Sussex BN1 9RF
United Kingdom
fax 44-1273-685865
tel 44-1273-6867-6865

Keith Pavitt
R. M. Phillips Professor of Science Policy &
  Director of Research
Science Policy Research Unit
University of Sussex
Mantell Building
Falmer, Brighton
East Sussex BN1 9RF
United Kingdom
fax 44-1273-685865
tel 44-1273-6867-6865

Gary Pisano
Associate Professor of Business
Graduate School of Business
Soldiers Field
Harvard University
Boston, MA 02163
fax 617-496-5265
tel 617-495-6562

Richard S. Rosenbloom
David Sarnoff Professor of Business
  Administration
Graduate School of Business Administration
Soldiers Field
Harvard University
Boston, MA 02163
tel 617-495-6295
fax 617-495-0355

David J. Teece
Mitsubishi Bank Professor in International
  Business and Finance
Institute of Management, Innovation and
  Organization F402
Haas School of Business #1930
University of California
Berkeley, CA 94720-1930
tel 510-642-1075
fax 510-642-2826

Jonathan West
Assistant Professor of Technology and
  Operations Management
Graduate School of Business Administration
Soldiers Field
Harvard University
Boston, MA 02163
tel 617-495-5492
fax 617-496-4072

Oliver E. Williamson
Edgar F. Kaiser Professor of Business
  Administration
Haas School of Business #1930
University of California
Berkeley, CA 94720-1930
tel 510-642-8697
fax 510-642-2826

Introduction

GIOVANNI DOSI, DAVID J. TEECE, AND JOSEF CHYTRY

> Civilization means that you must allow the possibility of change without ceasing to be totally dedicated to—and ready to die for—your ideals so long as you believe in them.
>
> Isaiah Berlin[1]

The hallmark of modern market economies has always been change. Technological and organizational innovation are in turn the primary driver of change, shaping, reshaping, and sometimes completely overturning the existing order. The classical economists, in particular Adam Smith and Karl Marx, were keenly interested in innovation and its transforming effects on enterprises, markets, institutions, and, more broadly, society. However, much of the richness in economics provided by the classical economists withered with the advent of 'modern economic analysis', particularly in the economic neoclassical synthesis which progressively came to dominate the intellectual scene from the 1950s onwards. While interest in the interplay of markets, institutions, and industrial structure never died, there has been a resurgence during the 1980s and 1990s of interest in the firm and in markets, in the coevolution of business firms and institutions. This collection of essays brings together some of the more interesting and provocative papers from *Industrial and Corporate Change* during its early years of publication (1992–5) which deal with issues lying at the intersection of the theory of the firm, industrial dynamics, and innovation.

For expository convenience, we have grouped the contributions which follow into a first part focused primarily on firms (Part A)—including their nature, internal organization, patterns of change, and relationships with each other—and a second part (Part B) with relatively more emphasis on topics like industrial dynamics, institutions, and interactions between corporate characteristics and rational determinants of competitiveness. However, that distinction is largely arbitrary since a few common themes run through most of the chapters.

---

[1] Berlin (1991), 108.

First, there is a concerted effort by all authors to understand firms as specific organizational forms whose behaviours and performances are largely shaped by institutional arrangements which govern what their members do, how they interact with each other and, ultimately, the collective outcomes in terms of corporate performances. All chapters endeavour to grapple with the firm as something other than a blackbox into which inputs are sucked and from which outputs are ejected; indeed, one begins to see promising complementarities between efforts to open up the 'technological black box'—as Rosenberg (1982) puts it—and attempts to disentangle the properties of different organizational structures and dynamics.

In this respect, *forms of organizational governance* are a crucial object of analysis. And, as Oliver E. Williamson in 'Transaction Cost Economics and Organization Theory' argues, governance analysis needs to be *comparative* in nature. This is a *second* major theme. One simply cannot determine the merit of an organizational form by comparing it to some theoretical ideal. It is only by comparing it with available institutional alternatives that meaningful assessment can occur. This might seem like an obvious point, but a good deal of contemporary theorizing is done in a quite different vein.

Williamson's discussion of the transaction-cost foundations of a comparative theory of organizations is certainly a forceful point of departure. After a helpful summary of the main tenets of transaction cost economics and its emergence out of the tradition of institutional economics, Williamson surveys the range of its exchange with organization theory and considers some implications of the relations that are presently taking place, including areas of lively tension.

Organization theory and transaction cost economics have exercised a significant influence on each other through their common agreement on the behavioural assumptions of bounded rationality and potential microeconomic conflicts of interest and, hence, under asymmetric information, opportunism—as well as the general proposition that organization matters. Williamson surveys interorganizational comparisons touching on areas such as control demands, identity/ capabilities, and bureaucratization as well as organization theory work applied to discrete structural analysis. His central claim is that transaction cost theory provides the appropriate unit of analysis—i.e., the nature of transactions themselves—which is able to account for the very evidence of economic organizations and their structural differences. This early Coasian conjecture (Coase (1993)) is thus refined and made analytically operational by mapping transaction features onto discretely different forms of governance of contractual relations—with organizations *stricto sensu* being an institutional setup combining contractual incompleteness with farsighted contracting and forbearance of the contracting partners within hierarchical arrangements.

The idea that organizations are much more than a 'veil' or a collective name for otherwise identical contractual relations (including those analyzed by equilibrium contract theories in the principal-agent mode) seems to be implicitly or explicitly shared by all contributors to this volume. However, it is much more controversial how far one can go with one form or another of 'economic reasoning' in interpreting the observed variety of organizational arrangements. This is the *third* major theme, broadly speaking, of the *institutional embeddedness* of economic organizations (with possible broader controversies on the nature and origins of societal institutions implicit in the background).

In this respect, Williamson's view is that one may indeed go quite far just by exploring cost economizing, and especially the *transaction* cost properties of different organizational structures, conditional upon the available transaction-cost technologies. Hence, even notions like those of power and trust, when appropriately interpreted, can be parsimoniously understood as transaction governance arrangements. Conversely, both Mark Granovetter in 'Coase Revisited: Business Groups in the Modern Economy' and Gary G. Hamilton and Robert C. Feenstra in 'Varieties of Hierarchies and Markets: An Introduction' set much stricter limits to the scope of efficiency-based interpretations of the observed variety of organizational forms, and symmetrically place much more emphasis upon the institutional structure within which firms are embedded.

An enlightening example considered by both the Granovetter and the Hamilton and Feenstra chapters is that of interfirm relationships. Business groups—the authors note—are all but invisible in the analytical literature in industrial organization. Indeed, fascination seems to be with cartels and price-fixing arrangements with most other more subtle and at least equally important phenomena being relegated to footnotes. Granovetter's departure is the Coasian (and Williamsonian) question ('Why do firms exist?') in terms of groups, i.e. why do firms coalesce into identifiable social structures. In every known capitalist economy, he maintains, firms do not conduct business as isolated units, but rather from cooperative relations with other firms. Despite the fact that firms are typically bound together into groups in some formal or informal way—creating keiretsu, chaebols, and grupos economicos—business groups become invisible in the analytical literatures of economics and sociology. Unfortunately this tendency is abetted by official data collections, which most often take the firm as the unit of analysis, whereas in many cases the business groups may be more fundamental.

Taking issue with strictly economic explanations of the existence of business groups (e.g. based on market failures or sheer transaction-cost minimization), Granovetter argues that the necessary conditions for their sustainability rest on social structures and related 'axes of solidarity', including geographical and social proximity, political party, ethnicity, kinship, and relation. An important dimension of how business groups function is what he calls the extent of 'moral economy' for business groups. The moral economy question is the degree to which a group's operations presuppose a moral community in which trustworthy behaviour can be expected, normative standards understood, and opportunism foregone. Thus cartels are unlikely to succeed, Granovetter observes, unless their members partake of some moral community.

In this respect, the Hamilton and Feenstra chapter is in many ways complementary to Granovetter's and argues—in a Weberian reading of the market vs. hierarchies distinction—that one of the key elements in economic organization is the nature of the authority relations that hold people together. Hierarchy is not only concerned with the integration of economic activities within organizations (in turn floating in a sea of market relations) but includes specific authority structures and their bases for legitimacy. This applies—the authors argue—also to interfirm relations. In looking at interfirm networks, embedded in normative social structures, Hamilton and Feenstra compare the examples of South Korea and Taiwan, two industrializing economies with ostensibly similar economic 'initial conditions' and available transaction-governance 'technologies'. This notwithstanding, the authors show, the two economies display remarkably different networking patterns. South Korea is characterized by highly vertical, authoritatively controlled networks, tending to sustain large power inequalities. Taiwan, in contrast, shows business networks operating with distinctly lower vertical integration and power asymmetries.

Such differences, Hamilton and Feenstra hold, are to be explained not so much in terms of the timing of industrialization or state action, as from differences in social structures related to the character of family property which gave rise to the particular network hierarchies at play. Hierarchy, such case studies suggest, may be described as the manner of organizing groups on the basis of authoritatively enforced rules of conduct which may *create* (*ex post*) transactional efficiency in the courses of their interactions with the broader market environment.

Behind this discussion on institutional embeddedness and history-driven specificities of organizational arrangement lies the question concerning the nature and degrees of path-dependency of observed organizational forms and competitive outcomes—the *fourth* major issue running across the chapters that follow. Williamson's chapter argues in favour of explanations of the observed variety of organizational structures in terms of efficiency-driven (transaction-cost minimizing) selection among a discrete set of alternatives. The boundaries of the set might well be history-determined, but—Williamson suggests—at any time the *irremediability* of historical constraints supports an interpretation of the evidence primarily in terms of (historically-bounded) efficiency considerations. Hence, the implication is that in a first approximation at least, path-dependency should not come as a central tenet of any theory about why organizations are what we observe them to be.

Conversely, Granovetter's and Hamilton-Feenstra's view is that such an argument tends to be either tautological or dangerously teleological ('Something exists because it was meant to perform with a certain function, given irremediable historically inherited constraints'). Since institutions are the carriers of history—as Paul David (1993) has put it—and they reproduce quite inertially possibly well beyond any economically useful function for which they emerged (if any), institutional and cultural path-dependency should appear prominently in the theory. At different levels, the argument reappears with respect to corporate competences and strategies and also broader patterns of national specialization and competitiveness.[2]

Fifth, yet another perspective from which to open up the 'organizational black-box' and map organizational arrangement and rules of behaviour into revealed performances is to comparatively analyze the ways different organizations manage the uneasy integration of potentially conflictual interests (and by doing so shape the learning and competitive patterns of the organization). In 'Organizational Integration and Competitive Advantage: Explaining Strategy and Performance in American Industry', William Lazonick and Jonathan West address this point, with reference to the purported decline of US competitiveness in global markets since the 1960s.

As a process of ongoing relationships that socializes individuals or groups into an organization in the achievement of common aims, organizational integration highlights the capacity to learn and the potential to innovate in market competition. By this standard, the authors find Japanese business enterprises to have been far more successful in their adoption of organizational integration. Japanese corporations have developed organizationally integrated relations with shop-floor workers and with vertically related enterprises to such a degree that Japanese managers can plan and coordinate specialized divisions of labour and innovative investment strategies. Nonetheless, even in industries facing formidable Japanese challenges, select US firms have managed to remain competitive through innovative strategies that incorporate organizational integration into the social structure of their enterprise. Discrete examples of innovative policies undertaken by Motorola and IBM (with some question marks on the more recent evidence) confirm the authors' confidence in the US capacity to successfully organize complex divisions of labour planned and coordinated to utilize new technology by bringing strategic decision-makers directly into the organizational structure.

Activities underlying organizational integration help develop the tacit knowledge which enables enterprises to function by making organizational routines dynamically fruitful. In general, Lazonick and West regard organizational

---

[2] Cf. in particular the chapters by Teece and Pisano, Rosenbloom and Christensen, Patel and Pavitt, and Nelson.

structure as both cause and effect of strategic decisions. Their argument runs against the exclusive importance of market-driven mechanisms of coordination (and the related incentive structures). On the contrary, the authors argue, what are conventionally considered 'market imperfections'—such as sticky labour market relations, running all the way to lifetime employment—may well turn out to be powerful conditions for organizational learning and competitiveness (whenever matched by consistent institutional arrangements and intra-organizational incentive rules).[3]

Sixth, a theme central to many chapters is to approach *organizations* as learning *entities*, whose behaviours and competitive success is shaped, together, by (a) what the organization is 'capable of doing well', (b) the directions toward which it is able to change, and (c) the (partly overlapping) orientation of its strategic management.

Of course, a *knowledge-focused* appraisal of firms adds considerably to any view centred exclusively on incentive-governance considerations. In this vein, Martin Fransman in 'Information, Knowledge, Vision and Theories of the Firm' critically reviews theories of the firm based on the notion that firms are best understood as organizational arrangements to deal with principal agent distortions and unbridled opportunism associated with market type arrangements. Instead, Fransman takes the position that the firm is a repository of knowledge (broadly on the lines of Nelson and Winter (1982)). Thus agent theoretic views of the firm miss an essential point. Knowledge is distanced from information and information is part of the 'raw material' that goes into knowledge-based problem solving.

Many individuals may have access to the same information, but what they do with it is something different. Fransman appeals to Herbert Simon and bounded rationality (see the pioneering Simon (1976) and March and Simon (1993)) but makes the important distinction that bounded rationality does not stem so much from sheer physiological limits (e.g. related to memory) as from organizational ones. Administrative limits are also set by social and organizational forces. Firms are a way for people, through cooperation, to pool their limited-rationality capacities to achieve collectively what cannot be accomplished individually. Thus, firms may indeed economize on bounded rationality as Williamson suggests, but Fransman argues that what is economizing and what is not is often unclear, because individuals and organizations weigh analysis information differently. Indeed, organizational routines are what enable firms to interpret information.

The way forward, Fransman proposes, is to distinguish information from knowledge. Knowledge is influenced by processed information, but this also

---

[3] For more detailed analysis on these points, cf. e.g. Aoki (1988), Coriat and Dosi (1994), and Odagiri (1981).

involves insight, creativity, and routine. Vision is the dominant set of beliefs a firm has about its internal circumstances and external environment. It explains how a firm appraises its circumstances and decides the action it should take (which in turn might well be partly inconsistent with its operational routines and thus also with the actual capabilities of the organization at any one time).

As Fransman stresses the knowledge-building aspect of business firms,[4] David J. Teece and Gary Pisano in 'The Dynamic Capabilities of Firms: An Introduction' endeavour to reconceptualize some basic building blocks of the theory of the firm itself. Firms are not seen primarily as arrangements to fulfil incentive and agency problems, but *in primis* as structures to solve complex coordination, recombination and accumulation of *competences* to meet *and anticipate* changing technological and market circumstances. Given the positioning on the market of any firm (historically inherited) and the technological opportunities ahead (specific to its knowledge bases and 'paradigms' (cf. Dosi (1982)) it can effectively master), its learning and competitive potential is path-dependently constrained by its portfolio of *technological and problem-solving assets and capabilities* (e.g. the 'legacy software' of a software company).

Strategic management may and does orient market positioning and learning trajectories in the longer term. However, the subtle balance between what have to be taken as 'state variables' inevitably inherited from the past and what should be considered 'control variables' (cf. Winter (1987)) is precisely one of the trickiest challenges to managerial strategies. Teece and Pisano advance the 'dynamic capabilities' framework to analyze the sources and methods of wealth creation and capture by private enterprise firms operating in environments of rapid technological change. The competitive advantage of firms is regarded as resting on distinctive processes (ways of coordinating and combining), positions (the firm's portfolio of difficult-to-trade knowledge assets and complementary assets), and paths (the firm's prior history and experience). The importance of path dependencies is amplified where conditions of increasing returns exist. Whether and how a firm's competitive advantage is eroded depends on the stability and structure of market demand, and their ease of replicability (expanding internally) and imitativeness (replication by competitors).

If correct, the framework suggests that private wealth creation in regimes of rapid technological change depends less on strategizing and more on honing internal technological, organizational, and managerial processes inside the firm. In short, identifying new opportunities and organizing effectively and efficiently to embrace them are more fundamental to private wealth creation than is strategizing, if by strategizing one means engaging in business conduct that keeps competitors off balance, raises the costs of rivals, and excludes new entrants.

---

[4] See also Teece, Rumelt, Dosi and Winter (1994), Dosi and Malerba (1996), Dosi and Marengo (1992), and Winter (1987) and (1993).

Strategic discretionality vs. *path-dependency* in both competences and corporate orientations is the *seventh* major issue addressed in the following, vividly illustrated by Richard S. Rosenbloom and Clayton M. Christensen in 'Technological Discontinuities, Organizational Capabilities, and Strategic Commitments'. The starting point is the familiar assumption that it is new firms which often pioneer radically new technologies. According to this viewpoint, despite advantages deriving from superior established resources, incumbents suffer from inertias associated with an organizational structure geared to the old technology, whereas newcomers can take full advantage of radical changes in technology to institute the 'creative' phase of 'Schumpeterian creative destruction'. While not challenging the conjecture that major discontinuities in knowledge bases (or 'paradigms') might indeed be matched by somewhat similar disruptions in the corporate identities of the major players in any one industry, the authors in fact explore the puzzling evidence of (relatively) unchanged knowledge bases associated with a rather striking turnover of leading firms.

Rosenbloom and Christensen stress the diverse ability of firms to elicit flexibility to new generations of products and production processes (even within a knowledge devoid of significant ruptures). The crucial variables here appear to be whether existing routines and 'value networks' are consonant with the requirements of the new generations of the technology. 'Value network' refers to the system of producers and markets which serve the ultimate users of the products and services to which a given innovation contributes. In these terms any value inherent in new technology is a function of the characteristics of the ultimate 'systems-in-use' in which products or services based on that technology will be employed. Thus a given firm's position in a value network strongly influences incentives and, together, 'strategic perceptions' of technological innovation. Incumbents which have been successful in the network in which they compete may well become less suited to compete in other networks.

The authors' detailed account of competition in the disk drive industry connects this notion of value network *a fortiori* with technological innovation that is 'radical', i.e. marks a substantial departure from the direction of 'normal' technological progress in a given industrial field. They argue that newcomers have advantages in innovations that redefine the overall direction of progress of an established technological trajectory, since the new technological paradigm calls upon a set of performance parameters valued in a different value network. Entrants could develop emerging market applications found in these value networks, whereas incumbents lack the incentive to undertake innovations unconnected with the needs of known customers. The issue turns out to be not so much a matter of technology as of strategy.

A remarkable implication of the argument is that while various sorts of path-dependencies (related to production competences, organizational routines, and strategic 'visions') do matter a lot, in the longer term it is not just paths and positions that matter, it is also the underlying process of dynamic adaptation and discovery. Recently, a few sources of path-dependent development of individual firms and whole industries have indeed been analyzed. One is the emergence of commonly shared bodies of knowledge ('paradigms'). Largely overlapping, dominant designs and standards often become watersheds in the patterns of evolution of industries (cf. Afuah and Utterback (1997) and Klepper (1997)). Relatedly, standard developers or sponsors become reinforced by the emergence of such designs.

Moreover, complex (i.e. nonlinear and rather opaque) correlations among many behavioural and technological traits within organizations tend to foster 'lock-in' within particular technological trajectories and operational repertoires (Levinthal (1992) and Levinthal and Warglien (1997)). A pertinent example is the importance for innovation of access to, or control over, complementary assets. As indicated in Teece (1986), technological innovation often requires the services of complementary assets either inside or outside the firm to deliver to the end user. Sometimes the 'assets' are other technologies. For example, instant photography required both new cameras and new films, while the commercialization of electricity required the development of long-lasting light-bulb filaments plus innovation in generation and transmission. Likewise, the sewing machine required Singer to put into place a sales and service operation to facilitate the development of a mass market for sewing machines.

The other side of the coin is the large set of unexploited opportunities which most incumbent organizations for *good evolutionary reasons* tend to neglect. For example, the inability of incumbents to quickly respond to market changes is often cited. So too are various forms of 'institutional inertias'. But, at least to some extent, the exploration of new technological and organizational trajectories is precisely the role played by both new entrants within particular markets and 'outliers' among incumbents. Indeed, the potential for strategic directionality and, in a sense, for 'institutional de-locking', is illustrated also in the Lazonick and West chapter which describes the 'first mover' strategies of Motorola implemented through purposeful accumulation of capabilities derived at least in part from its integrated approach, with *de facto* lifetime employment, proactive management, proactively engaging in production cannibalization when necessary, and proactively migrating first in the 1960s from car radios to television and other equipment, then in the 1970s from consumer electronics to semiconductors, then in the 1980s from commodity semiconductors to specialty semiconductors. Note also that, despite the general US institutional environment which is not conducive to such types of practices, the benefits of 'integration' are that the activities and relationships which support it generate the tacit knowledge that enables the enterprise to function as a cohesive and coherent system.

Eighth, another major theme concerns the *co-evolution of technologies, social communities of practitioners, industrial organizations, and institutions.* It is a theme which also links firm-level properties with country-level performances. In 'Uneven (and Divergent) Technological Accumulation among Advanced Countries: Evidence and a Framework of Explanation', Parimal Patel and Keith Pavitt argue that although technology gaps have been recognized by (a growing minority of) economists as central to the pattern of growth of different economies, it has been generally assumed that the decline of US technological superiority after World War II, supposedly due largely to the increasing international openness of markets and the rise of highly educated, and the international nature of, technological communities, would be followed by the gradual disappearance of a technology gap among industrially advanced countries.

The authors find however that deliberate acquisition of the tacit knowledge that underlies ability to cope with complexity and ever-changing technologies has in fact led to persistent international technological gaps even among OECD countries. The cumulative evidence they present indicates that such differences are most striking in the volume of change-generating activities, including R&D expenditures, that are supported by business firms, and in the skills of the workforce they train. Nor do the authors expect that the global activities of larger corporations will lessen differences of technological accumulation in the future. Firms continue to concentrate much of their technological activities in those locations which help them mobilize tacit skills and handle uncertainties. Hence also conditions in the home country strongly affect the technological performance of large firms, and, in turn, strategies of major domestic firms are likely to affect the long-term technological and competitive performance of the whole country.

There is here an illuminating illustration of *positive feedbacks* between geographically (and/or institutionally) local externalities and corporate strategies (see also Cantwell (1989)). Take the international disparities in education and workforce skills as an example. 'Globalized' firms are likely to respond to any initial distribution by tapping what appears to be the best on the international markets (e.g. Silicon Valley PhDs; German mechanical skilled workers; Singaporean disciplined and cheap assemblers). But in so doing, they might well reinforce disparities rather than convergence.

Distinctive systems of finance and management—the authors argue—also influence not only the size of overall commitment of resources to technological accumulation, but also the capacity to exploit competences in core technologies that might hold a promise of future product opportunities. Patell and Pavit draw on Alfred Chandler's studies of US and UK corporations (Chandler (1977) and (1990)) to highlight the latters' failures and they discuss the greater effectiveness—at least in some sectors—of German and Japanese financial systems for promoting business activities, their methods of management of large firms in R&D-intensive sectors, and their systems of education and training.

Among the various local inducement mechanisms that the localized nature of technological accumulation imposes on differences in patterns of technological accumulation, Patel and Pavitt especially mark out the directions of persistent investment, and the cumulative mastery of core technologies along with the latters' knowledge bases. Hence, rather than an expected productivity convergence, they foresee continued disparities among OECD countries in the 1990s and possibly, even in the longer term a sustained condition of uneven and divergent technological development over time.

Richard R. Nelson's chapter, 'The Co-Evolution of Technology, Industrial Structure, and Supporting Institutions', endeavours to close the gap between formal and 'appreciative' theorizing on growth in an evolutionary perspective. Technical advance, while characterized by uncertainty as to its outcomes, is by no means an entirely random process. While market environments provide systematic selection among diverse outcomes of such efforts, the 'mutations' are shaped by the knowledge bases which firms can master, their interactions with customers, and the broader institutional context. This combined dynamic of learning and selection provides direction to technological advance, which is itself often highly cumulative. In many cumulative technologies, *technological trajectories* tend to appear, with the paths being shaped both by what entrepreneurs believe customers will buy, and by what technologists understand is achievable. As already mentioned, technological paradigms or regimes can be thought of as the cognitive aspects of such dynamics.

Technological development often seems to change in character as it matures, possibly suggesting a life cycle. The point of discontinuity is often the emergence of a 'dominant design'. Nelson identifies three different possible ways in which a dominant design comes into existence: (1) one variant is better than the others, and with time and experimentation, the best design becomes identified and wins. (2) When technologies are cumulative, an early advantage, sometimes obtained by chance, leads to the adoption of one design over the other. Competing designs get left behind, even though they might prove superior if given an equal footing. (3) Network externalities may arise when consumer learning under interdependent user demand turns out to be critical. This may likewise cause an early 'lock' onto a design/standard which need not have been optimal in any fundamental sense.[5]

Nelson is not convinced that this dominant design story is universal, and questions whether it fits such cases as the chemical products industry where

[5] Points (2) and (3) are those emphasized in the historical and theoretical literature of path-dependency. Cf. David (1985).

often a variety of quite different products is produced for similar uses, or pharmaceuticals, where customer needs are divergent and specialized. Note also that the dominant design theories (2) and (3) cast doubt on the notion that market forces produce efficient outcomes, and even as regards what one precisely means by market forces. In fact, early stochastic fluctuations can decisively influence long-term collective outcomes, especially when in the presence of dynamic increasing returns of some sort (e.g. as mentioned, those associated with cumulative learning and with the externalities embodied in particular users/producers networks). Similarly, institutional and political structures can of course influence market outcomes.

There is also now a body of illuminating work on how firm and industry structure changes as technology matures.[6] The basic propositions are that during the early period of technological evolution, where there is experimentation and flux, but before dominant design emerges, there are no particular incumbency advantages. Market demand is fragmented, and entry and exit are frequent. Model changes are frequent and producers tend to be small. However, after the dominant designs emerge, learning by incumbent firms becomes more cumulative, and new entrants must enter at a larger scale to succeed (although the evidence also shows relatively high rates of entry *and* mortality across all industries). Firms try to exploit latent scale and scope economies, and entry costs increase. Cumulative organizational learning and competency building proceed in tandem with industry evolution, but they really cannot get started until dominant designs and/or dominant paradigms emerge.

While the evolutionary processes discussed above proceed in a market setting, empirical studies suggest that the institutional environment also shapes outcomes, and is shaped by outcomes. Collective action by private parties and government matters. Even technical societies, journals, spring up to provide support. New technologies often drive scientific discovery, as when metallurgy comes into existence to better understand the properties of steel. Such developments simply exemplify the general proposition that institutions coevolve with technology, rarely leading, often impairing: a good example among many is the wide range of legal and regulatory matters that needed to be decided before electric power could go forward strongly. Airplanes required airports, and the automobile better roads. Interest group conflict is often involved in public responses, and as Douglass North has taught us (Alston, Eggertsson, North (1996)), outcomes depend importantly on political structures and processes.

An additional set of issues arises when radical technological development strikes a mature industry. Incumbents are on the vanguard only in circumstances where the new technology employs roughly the same competences. Otherwise,

---

[6] More on this in Klepper (1997) and Afuah and Utterback (1997).

new firms frequently enter, and the failure rate among incumbents may be high. Supporting institutions often do not adjust well either. Indeed, also at a more macroeconomic level Thorstein Veblen has argued that Germany eclipsed Britain as an economic power in large measure because British institutions and past investment stultified adjustment and ability to change (Veblen (1939)), and a more general argument along similar lines is put forward by Perez and Soete (1988), according to which different (Schumpeterian) epochs are punctuated by different techno-economic paradigms—involving broad 'meta-technologies' (e.g. electricity, synthetic chemistry, information technologies) as well as institutions which ought to match them. Nelson's chapter, while somewhat sceptical on the generality of this 'Schumpeterian punctuation' of modern economic development, does indeed emphasize the importance of 'matching'/'mismatching' between technologies and institutions as a crucial factor which might either support innovation and growth or thwart them.

A key concept running through many of the chapters that follow is indeed the notion that competing in changing environments requires the ability to reconfigure basic organizational processes and systems, while achieving close coordination throughout with complementary assets and institutions external to the firm. Symmetrically, the institutional environment must adapt as well.

The complexity and systematic nature of value enhancing change is thus starkly apparent. It means that the study of industrial and corporate change must be first and foremost the study both of the firm (because the firm is the organizational site for the largest share of technological innovation in modern market economics), and of the institutional structure in which the firm is embedded. The way thar organizational systems evolve, and the manner in which firms transform themselves and deliver innovation, lies at the heart of firm-level and national competitiveness.

References

Afuah, A. N. and J. M. Utterback (1977), 'Responding to Structural Industry Changes: A Technological Evolution Perspective', *Industrial and Corporate Change*, 6:1.

Alston, Lee J., Thrainn Eggertsson, and Douglass C. North (1996), *Empirical Studies in Institutional Change*. Cambridge University Press: New York and Cambridge, MA.

Aoki, M. (1988), *Information, Incentive and Bargaining in the Japanese Economy*. Cambridge University Press: Cambridge.

Arthur, Brian (1988), 'Competing Technologies: An Overview', in Giovanni Dosi, Christopher Freeman, Richard Nelson, Gerald Silverberg, and Luc Soete (eds.), *Technical Change and Economic Theory*. Pinter Publishers: London and Columbia University Press: New York, 590–607.

Berlin, Isaiah (1991), *Conversations with Isaiah Berlin: Isaiah Berlin and Ramin Johanbegloo*. Charles Scribner's: New York.

Cantwell, J. (1989), *Technological Innovation and Multinational Corporations*. Blackwell: New York.

Chandler, A. J., Jr. (1977), *The Visible Hand: The Managerial Revolution in American Business*. Harvard University Press: Cambridge, MA.

Chandler, A. J., Jr. (1990), *Scale and Scope: The Dynamics of Industrial Capitalism*. Harvard University Press: Cambridge, MA.

Coase, R. J. (1993), 'The Nature of the Firm' (1937), in E. O. Williamson and S. G. Winter (eds.), *The Nature of the Firm: Origin, Evolution, and Development*. Oxford University Press: New York and Oxford.

Coriat, B. and G. Dosi (1994), 'Learning How to Govern and Learning How to Solve Problems: On the Co-Evolution of Competences, Conflicts and Organizational Routines', Prince Bertil Symposium, Stockholm School of Economics: Stockholm; and IIASA Working paper, IIASA, Laxenburg, Austria.

David, P. A. (1985), 'Clio and the Economics of QWERTY', *American Economic Review*, 75:2, 332–7.

David, P. A. (1993), 'Why are Institutions the Carriers of History? Notes on Path-Dependence and the Evolution of Conventions, Organizations and Institutions', *Structural Change and Economic Dynamics*.

Dosi, G. (1982), 'Technological Paradigms and Technological Trajectories: A Suggested Interpretation of the Determinants and Directions of Technical Change', *Research Policy*.

Dosi, G. and F. Malerba (1996), *Organization and Strategy in the Evolution of the Enterprise*. Macmillan: London.

Dosi, G. and L. Marengo (1992), 'Towards a Theory of Organizational Competences', in R. W. England (ed.), *Evolutionary Concepts in Contemporary Economics*. Michigan University Press: Ann Arbor, MI.

Granovetter, M. S. (1985), 'Economic Action and Social Structure: The Problem of Embeddedness', *American Journal of Sociology*, 51, 481–510.

Klepper, S. (1997), 'Industry Life Cycles', *Industrial and Corporate Change*, 6:1.

Levinthal, D. (1992), 'Surviving Schumpeterian Environments: An Evolutionary Perspective', *Industrial and Corporate Change*, 1:3.

Levinthal, D. and Warglien, M. (1997), 'Landscape Design: Designing for Local Action in Complex Worlds', University of Pennsylvania, Wharton School, mimeo: Philadelphia, PA.

Nelson, R. R. and S. G. Winter (1982), *An Evolutionary Theory of Economic Change*. Harvard University Press: Cambridge, MA.

Odagiri, H. (1981), *The Theory of Growth in a Corporate Economy: Management Preferences Research and Development, and Economic Growth*. Cambridge University Press: New York.

Perez, C. and L. Soete (1988), 'Catching Up on Technology: Entry Barriers and Windows of Opportunity', in G. Dosi, C. Freeman, G. Silverberg, and L. Soete (eds.), *Technical Change and Economic Theory*. Pinter: London and Cambridge University Press: New York.

Rosenberg, N. (1982), *Inside the Black Box*. Cambridge University Press: New York and Cambridge, MA.

Simon, H. (1976), *Administrative Behavior: A Study of Decision-Making Processes in Administrative Organization*. The Free Press: New York.

Simon, H. and J. G. March (1993), *Organizations*. 2nd edn. Basil Blackwell: Oxford and Cambridge, MA.

Teece, D. J. (1986), 'Profiting from Technological Innovation', *Research Policy*, 15:6.

Teece, D. J., R. Rumelt, G. Dosi, and S. G. Winter (1994), 'Understanding Corporate Coherence: Theory and Evidence', *Journal of Economic Behavior and Organization*, 23:1.

Veblen, T. (1939), *Imperial Germany and the Industrial Revolution*. Viking: New York.

Winter, S. G. (1987), 'Knowledge and Competence as Strategic Assets', in D. J. Teece (ed.), *The Competitive Challenge: Strategies for Industrial Innovation and Renewal*. Harper and Row: New York.

Winter, S. G. (1993), 'On Coase, Competence and the Corporation' (1988), in O. E. Williamson and S. G. Winter (eds.), *The Nature of the Firm: Origin, Evolution, and Development*. Oxford University Press: New York and Oxford.

PART A

THE FIRM

Transaction Cost Economics and Organization Theory

OLIVER E. WILLIAMSON*

(University of California, Berkeley, Berkeley, CA 94720, USA)

1. Introduction

Economic and sociological approaches to economic organization have reached a state of healthy tension. That is to be contrasted with an earlier state of affairs in which the two approaches were largely disjunct, hence ignored one another, or described each other's research agendas and research accomplishments with disdain (Swedberg, 1990, p. 4). Healthy tension involves genuine give-and-take. Neither the obsolescence of organization theory, to which Charles Perrow has recently alluded (1992, p. 162), nor the capitulation of economics, to which James March (tongue-in-cheek) remarks,[1] is implied.

A more respectful relation, perhaps even a sense that economics and organization are engaged in a joint venture, is evident in W. Richard Scott's remark that 'while important areas of disagreement remain, more consensus exists than is at first apparent' (1992, p. 3), in game theorist David Kreps's contention that 'almost any theory of organization which is addressed by game theory will do more for game theory than game theory will do for it' (1992, p. 1), and in my argument that a science of organization is in progress in which law, economics, and organization are joined.[2]

* The author is Transamerica Professor of Business, Economics, and Law at the University of California, Berkeley. This paper has benefitted from oral presentations to the Macro Organization Behavior Society at the October 1992 meeting at Northwestern, the Stanford Center for Organizational Research, the Institutional Analysis Workshop at the University of California, Berkeley, and the 'Handbook of Economic Sociology Conference' at the Russell Sage Foundation in February 1993. Helpful comments by James Baron, Paul DiMaggio, David Levine, Neil Smelser, and Richard Swedberg are gratefully acknowledged.

I am also grateful to the conference organizers and to the Russell Sage Foundation for permission to publish this version of the paper here. (A somewhat revised version will appear in the *Handbook*.)

[1] James March advised the Fourth International Conference of the Society for the Advancement of Socio-Economics that economics had been so fully reformed that the audience should 'declare victory and go home' (Coughlin, 1992, p. 23).

[2] Richard Posner comes out differently. He argues that 'organization-theory . . . [adds] nothing to economics that the literature on information economics had not added years earlier' (1993, p. 84).

Joint ventures sometimes evolve into mergers and sometimes unravel. I do not expect that either will happen here. That merger is not in prospect is because economics, organization theory, and law have separate as well as combined agendas. A full-blown merger, moreover, would impoverish the evolving science of organization—which has benefitted from the variety of insights that are revealed by the use of different lenses. I expect that the joint venture will hold until one of the parties has learned enough from the others to go it alone. Progress attended by controversy is what I project for the remainder of the decade.

This paper focuses on connections between transaction cost economics and organization theory and argues that a three-part relation is taking shape. The first and most important of these is that transaction cost economics has been (and will continue to be) massively influenced by concepts and empirical regularities that have their origins in organization theory. Secondly, I sketch the key concepts out of which transaction cost economics works to which organization theorists can (and many do) productively relate. But thirdly, healthy tension survives—as revealed by an examination of phenomena for which rival interpretations have been advanced, remain unsolved, and provoke controversy.

I begin this paper with some background on institutional economics, both old and new. A three-level schema for studying economic organization is proposed in section 3. Some of the more important ways in which transaction cost economics has benefitted from organization theory are examined in section 4. The key concepts in transaction cost economics are sketched in section 5. Empirical regularities, as discerned through the lens of transaction cost economics, that are pertinent to organization theory are discussed in section 6. Contested terrain is surveyed in section 7. Concluding remarks follow.

2. *Institutional Economics*

Older traditions

Leading figures in the older institutional economics movement in the United States were Wesley Mitchell, Thorstein Veblen, and John R. Commons. Although many sociologists appear to be sympathetic with the older tradition, there is growing agreement that the approach was 'largely descriptive and historically specific' (DiMaggio and Powell, 1991, p. 2) and was not cumulative (Granovetter, 1988, p. 8).

Criticisms of the old institutional economics by economists have been scathing. Thus George Stigler remarks that 'the school failed in America for a very simple reason. It had nothing in it except a stance of hostility to the standard theoretical tradition. There was no positive agenda of research' (Stigler, 1983, p. 170). Similar views are expressed by R. C. O. Matthews (1986, p. 903). Ronald Coase concurs: the work of American institutionalists 'led to nothing. . . . Without a theory, they had nothing to pass on except a mass of descriptive material waiting for a theory or a fire. So if modern institutionalists have antecedents, it is not what went immediately before' (Coase, 1984, p. 230).

My general agreement with these assessments notwithstanding, I would make an exception for John R. Commons. Not only is the institutional economics tradition at Wisconsin still very much alive (Bromley, 1989), but also the enormous public policy influence of Commons and his students and colleagues deserves to be credited. Andrew Van de Ven's summary of Commons's intellectual contributions is pertinent to the first of these (1993, p. 148):

> Especially worthy of emphasis [about Commons] are his (a) dynamic views of institutions as a response to scarcity and conflicts of interest, (b) original formulation of the transaction as the basic unit of analysis, (c) part-whole analysis of how collective action constrains, liberates, and expands individual action in countless numbers of routine and complementary transactions on the one hand, and how individual wills and power to gain control over limiting or contested factors provide the generative mechanisms for institutional change on the other, and (d) historical appreciation of how customs, legal precedents, and laws of a society evolve to construct a collective standard of prudent reasonable behavior for resolving disputes between conflicting parties in pragmatic and ethical ways.

Albeit in varying degree, transaction cost economics is responsive to Commons in *all four of these respects*.[3]

Commons and his colleagues and students were very influential in politics during and after the Great Depression—in shaping social security, labor legislation, public utility regulation, and, more generally, public policy toward business. Possibly because of its public policy successes, the Wisconsin School was remiss in developing its intellectual foundations. The successive operationalization—from informal into preformal, semiformal, and fully formal modes of analysis—that I associate with transaction cost economics

---

[3] Briefly, the transaction cost economics responses are: (i) institutions respond to scarcity as economizing devices, (ii) the transaction is expressly adopted as the basic unit of analysis, (iii) conflicts are recognized and relieved by the creation of credible commitments/*ex post* governance apparatus, and (iv) the institutional environment is treated as a set of shift parameters that change the comparative costs of governance. Although these may be incomplete responses, the spirit of the transaction cost economics enterprise nevertheless makes serious contact with Commons's prescription.

(Williamson, 1993a) never materialized. Instead, the institutional economics of Commons progressed very little beyond the informal stage.

There is also an older institutional economics tradition in Europe. Of special importance was the German Historical School. [Interested readers are advised to consult Terrence Hutchison (1984) and Richard Swedberg (1991) for assessments.] And, of course, there were the great works of Karl Marx.

A later German School, the Ordoliberal or Freiburg School, also warrants remark. As discussed by Heinz Grossekettler (1989), this School was inspired by the work of Walter Eucken, whose student Ludwig Erhard was the German Minister of Economics from 1949 to 1963, Chancellor from 1963 to 1966, and is widely credited with being the political father of the 'economic miracle' in West Germany. Grossekettler describes numerous parallels between the Ordoliberal program and those of Property Rights Theory, Transaction Cost Economics, and especially Constitutional Economics (1989, pp. 39, 64–67).

The Ordoliberal program proceeded at a very high level of generality (Grossekettler, 1989, p. 47) and featured the application of lawful principles to the entire economy (Grossekettler, 1989, pp. 46–57). Its great impact on postwar German economic policy notwithstanding, the influence of the School declined after the mid-1960s. Although Grossekettler attributes the decline to the 'wide scale of acceptance of the Keynesian theory . . . [among] young German intellectuals' (1989, pp. 69–70), an additional problem is that the principles of Ordoliberal economics were never given operational content. Specific models were never developed; key trade-offs were never identified; the mechanisms remained very abstract. The parallels with the Wisconsin School—great public policy impact, underdeveloped conceptual framework, loss of intellectual influence—are striking.

The New Institutional Economics

The new institutional economics comes in a variety of flavors and has been variously defined. The economics of property rights—as developed especially by Coase (1959, 1960), Armen Alchian (1961), and Harold Demsetz (1967)—was an early and influential dissent from orthodoxy. An evolutionary as opposed to a technological approach to economic organization was advanced, according to which new property rights were created and enforced as the economic needs arose, if and as these were cost effective.

The definition of ownership rights advanced by Eirik Furubotn and Svetozar Pejovich is broadly pertinent: 'By general agreement, the right of ownership of an asset consists of three elements: (a) the right to use the asset . . . ,

(b) the right to appropriate the returns from the asset . . . , and (c) the right to change the asset's form and/or substance' (174, p. 4). Strong claims on behalf of the property rights approach to economic organization were set out by Coase as follows (1959, p. 14):

> A private enterprise system cannot function unless property rights are created in resources, and when this is done, someone wishing to use a resource has to pay the owner to obtain it. Chaos disappears; and so does the government except that a legal system to define property rights and to arbitrate disputes is, of course, necessary.

As it turns out, these claims overstate the case for the property rights approach. Not only is the definition of property rights sometimes costly— consider the difficult problems of defining intellectual property rights— but also court ordering can be a costly way to proceed. A comparative contractual approach—according to which court ordering is often (but selectively) supplanted by private ordering for purposes of governing contractual relations (Macneil, 1974, 1978; Williamson, 1979, 1991a)—rather than a pure property rights approach, therefore has a great deal to recommend it.

Although the earlier property rights approach and the more recent comparative contractual approach appear to be rival theories of organization, much of that tension is relieved by recognizing that the new institutional economics has actually developed in two complementary parts. One of these parts deals predominantly with background conditions (expanded beyond property rights to include contract laws, norms, customs, conventions, and the like) while the second branch deals with the mechanisms of governance. The two-part definition proposed by Lance Davis and Douglass North (1971, pp. 5–6; emphasis added) is pertinent:

> The *institutional environment* is the set of fundamental political, social and legal ground rules that establishes the basis for production, exchange and distribution. Rules governing elections, property rights, and the right of contract are examples. . . .
>
> An *institutional arrangement* is an arrangement between economic units that governs the ways in which these units can cooperate and/or compete. It . . . [can] provide a structure within which its members can cooperate . . . or [it can] provide a mechanism that can effect a change in laws or property rights.

Interestingly, these two parts correspond very closely with the much earlier division of effort between 'economic sociology' and 'economic theory' described by Joseph Schumpeter—where economic sociology was expected to study the institutional environment and economic theory was concerned principally with the mechanisms of governance (1989, p. 293). As it turns out, a large number of economists have productively worked on issues relating to the institutional environment. These include a prodigious amount of research by North, who defines institutions as 'the humanly devised constraints that structure political, economic, and social interactions. They consist of both informal constraints (sanctions, taboos, customs, traditions, and codes of conduct), and formal rules (constitutions, laws, property rights)' (1991, p. 97). Elsewhere he argues that 'institutions consist of a set of constraints on behavior in the form of rules and regulations; a set of procedures to detect deviations from the rules and regulations; and, finally, a set of moral, ethical behavioral norms which define the contours and that constrain the way in which the rules and regulations are specified and enforcement is carried out' (1984, p. 8). Relatedly, Allan Schmid defines institutions as 'sets of ordered relationships among people which define their rights, exposures to the rights of others, privileges, and responsibilities' (1972, p. 893); Daniel Bromley contends that institutions fall into two classes: conventions, and rules or entitlements (1989, p. 41); and Andrew Schotter defines institutions as 'regularities in behavior which are agreed to by all members of a society and which specify behavior in specific recurrent situations' (1981, p. 9). According to Eirik Furubotn and Rudolf Richter, 'Modern institutional economics focuses on the institution of property, and on the system of norms governing the acquisition or transfer of property rights' (1991, p. 3), although they subsequently make significant provision for governance.

This emphasis on property rights, customs, norms, conventions and the like is especially pertinent for purposes of doing intertemporal, international, or cross-cultural comparisons. What the economics of organization is predominantly concerned with, however, is this: holding these background conditions constant, why organize economic activity one way (e.g. procure from the market) rather than another (e.g. produce to your own needs: hierarchy)? That is the Coasian question (Coase, 1937), is the focus of transaction cost economics, and explains much of the interest of organization theorists and the sociology of organization with the New Institutional Economics. Not only does the study of governance raise different issues, but also much of the predictive content and most of the empirical research in institutional economics has been at the governance level (Matthews, 1986, p. 907).

3. A Three-Level Schema

Transaction cost economics is mainly concerned with the governance of contractual relations. Governance does not, however, operate in isolation.

The comparative efficacy of alternative modes of governance varies with the institutional environment on the one hand and the attributes of economic actors on the other. A three-level schema is therefore proposed, according to which the object of analysis, governance, is bracketed by more macro features (the institutional environment) and more micro features (the individual). Feedbacks aside (which are underdeveloped in the transaction cost economics set-up), the institutional environment is treated as the locus of shift parameters, changes in which shift the comparative costs of governance, and the individual is where the behavioral assumptions originate.

Roger Friedland and Robert Alford also propose a three-level schema in which environment, governance, and individual are distinguished, but their emphasis is very different. They focus on the individual and argue that the three levels of analysis are 'nested, where organization and institution specify progressively higher levels of constraint and opportunity for individual action' (1991, p. 242).

The causal model proposed here is akin to and was suggested by, but is different from, the causal model recently proposed by W. Richard Scott (1992, p. 45), who is also predominantly concerned with governance. There are three main effects in my schema (see Figure 1). These are shown by the solid arrows. Secondary effects are drawn as dashed arrows. As indicated, the institutional environment defines the rules of the game. If changes in property rights, contract laws, norms, customs, and the like induce changes in the comparative costs of governance, then a reconfiguration of economic organization is usually implied.

The solid arrow from the individual to governance carries the behavioral

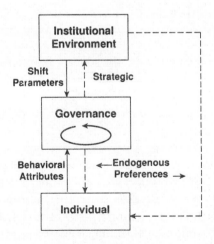

FIGURE 1. A layer schema.

assumptions within which transaction cost economics operates, and the circular arrow within the governance sector reflects the proposition that organization, like the law, has a life of its own. The latter is the subject of section 3.

Although behavioral assumptions are frequently scanted in economics, transaction cost economics subscribes to the proposition that economic actors should be described in workably realistic terms (Simon, 1978; Coase, 1984). Interestingly, 'outsiders', especially physicists, have long been insistent that a better understanding of the actions of human agents requires more self-conscious attention to the study of how men's minds work (Bridgeman, 1955, p. 450; Waldrop, 1992, p. 142). Herbert Simon concurs (1985, p. 303):

> Nothing is more fundamental in setting our research agenda and informing our research methods than our view of the nature of the human beings whose behavior we are studying. It makes a difference, a very large difference, to our research strategy whether we are studying the nearly omniscient *Homo economicus* of rational choice theory or the boundedly rational *Homo psychologicus* of cognitive psychology. It makes a difference to research, but it also makes a difference for the proper design of political institutions. James Madison was well aware of that, and in the pages of the *Federalist Papers* he opted for this view of the human condition (*Federalist*, No. 55):
>
> > As there is a degree of depravity in mankind which requires a certain degree of circumspection and distrust, so there are other qualities in human nature which justify a certain portion of esteem and confidence.
>
> —a balanced and realistic view, we may concede, of bounded human rationality and its accompanying frailties of motive and reason.

Transaction cost economics expressly adopts the proposition that human cognition is subject to bounded rationality—where this is defined as behavior that is 'intendedly rational, but only limitedly so' (Simon, 1957a, p. xxiv)—but differs from Simon in its interpretation of the 'degree of depravity' to which Madison refers.

Whereas Simon regards the depravity in question as 'frailties of motive and reason', transaction cost economics describes it instead as opportunism—to include self-interest seeking with guile. The former is a much more benign interpretation, and many social scientists understandably prefer it. Consider, however, Robert Michels's concluding remarks about oligarchy: 'nothing but a serene and frank examination of the oligarchical dangers of democracy will enable us to minimize these dangers' (1962, p. 370). If a serene and frank reference to opportunism alerts us to avoidable dangers which the more benign reference to frailties of motive and reason would not, then there are real hazards in adopting the more benevolent construction. As discussed in section 5, below, the mitigation of opportunism plays a central role in transaction cost economics.

Opportunism can take blatant, subtle, and natural forms. The blatant form is associated with Niccolò Machiavelli. Because he perceived that the economic agents with whom the Prince was dealing were opportunistic, the Prince was advised to engage in reciprocal and even pre-emptive opportunism—to breach contracts with impugnity whenever 'the reasons which made him bind himself no longer exist' (1952, p. 92). The subtle form is strategic and has been described elsewhere as 'self-interest seeking with guile' (Williamson, 1975, pp. 26–37; 1985, pp. 46–52, 64–67). The natural form involves tilting the system at the margin. The so-called 'dollar-a-year' men in the Office of Production Management, of which there were 250 at the beginning of World War II, were of concern to the Senate Special Committee to Investigate the National Defense Program because (McCullough, 1992, p. 265):

> Such corporate executives in high official roles were too inclined to make decisions for the benefit of their corporations. 'They have their own business at heart,' [Senator] Truman remarked. The report called them lobbyists 'in a very real sense,' because their presence inevitably meant favoritism, 'human nature being what it is.'

Michel Crozier's treatment of bureaucracy makes prominent provision for all forms of opportunism, which he describes as 'the active tendency of the human agent to take advantage, in any circumstances, of all available means to further his own privileges' (1964, p. 194).

Feedback effects from governance to the institutional environment can be either instrumental or strategic. An example of the former would be an improvement in contract law, brought about at the request of parties who find that extant law is poorly suited to support the integrity of contract. Strategic changes could take the form of protectionist trade barriers against domestic and/or foreign competition. Feedback from governance to the level of the individual can be interpreted as 'endogenous preference' formation (Bowles and Gintis, 1993), due to advertising or other forms of 'education'. The individual is also influenced by the environment, in that endogenous preferences are the product of social conditioning. Although transaction cost economics can often relate to these secondary effects, other modes of analysis are often more pertinent.

More generally, the Friedland and Alford scheme, the Scott scheme, and the variant that I offer are not mutually exclusive. Which to use when depends on the questions being asked. To repeat, the main case approach to economic organization that I have proposed works out of the heavy line causal relations shown in Figure 1, to which the dashed lines represent refinements.

4. *The Value Added of Organization Theory*

Richard Swedberg (1987, 1990), Robert Frank (1992), and others have described numerous respects in which economics has been influenced by sociology and organization theory. The value added to which I refer here deals only with those aspects where transaction cost economics has been a direct and significant beneficiary.

The behavioral assumptions to which I refer in section 3 above—bounded rationality and opportunism—are perhaps the most obvious examples of how transaction cost economics has been shaped by organization theory. But the proposition that organization has a life of its own (the circular arrow in the governance box in Figure 1) is also important. And there are yet additional influences as well.

Intertemporal Process Transformations

Describing the firm as a production function invites an engineering approach to organization. The resulting 'machine model' of organization emphasizes intended effects to the neglect of unintended effects (March and Simon, 1958, chapter 3). But if organizations have a life of their own, and if the usual economic approach is unable to relate to the intertemporal realities of organization, then—for some purposes at least—an extra-economic approach may be needed.

Note that I do not propose that the economic approach be abandoned. Rather, the 'usual' or orthodox economic approach gives way to an augmented or extended economic approach. That is very different from adopting an altogether different approach—as, for example, that of neural networks.

As it turns out, the economic approach is both very elastic and very powerful. Because it is elastic and because increasing numbers of economists have become persuaded of the need to deal with economic organization 'as it is', warts and all, all significant regularities whatsoever—intended and unintended alike—come within the ambit. Because it is very powerful, economics brings added value. Specifically, the 'farsighted propensity' or 'rational spirit' that economics ascribes to economic actors permits the analysis of previously neglected regularities to be taken a step further. Once the unanticipated consequences are understood, those effects will thereafter be anticipated and the ramifications can be folded back into the organizational design. Unwanted costs will then be mitigated and unanticipated benefits will be enhanced. Better economic performance will ordinarily result.

Unintended effects are frequently delayed and are often subtle. Deep knowledge of the details and intertemporal process transformations that attend organization is therefore needed. Because organization theorists have wider and deeper knowledge of these conditions, economists have much to learn and ought to be deferential. Four specific illustrations are sketched here.

Demands for control. A natural response to perceived failures of performance is to introduce added controls. Such efforts can have both intended and unintended consequences (Merton, 1936; Gouldner, 1954).

One illustration is the employment relation, where an increased emphasis on the reliability of behavior gives rise to added rules (March and Simon, 1958, pp. 38–40). Rules, however, serve not merely as controls but also define minimally acceptable behavior (Cyert and March, 1963). Managers who apply rules to subordinates in a legalistic and mechanical way invite 'working to rules', which frustrates effective performance.

These unintended consequences are picked up by the wider peripheral vision of organization theorists. In the spirit of farsighted contracting, however, the argument can be taken yet a step further. Once apprised of the added consequences, the farsighted economist will make allowance for them by factoring these into the original organizational design. (Some organization theorists might respond that this last is fanciful and unrealistic. That can be decided by examining the data.)

Oligarchy. The Iron Law of Oligarchy holds that 'It is organization which gives birth to the dominion of the elected over the electors, of the mandatories over the mandators, of the delegates over the delegators. Who says organization, says oligarchy' (Michels, 1962, p. 365). Accordingly, good intentions notwithstanding, the initial leadership (or its successors) will inevitably develop attachments for the office. Being strategically situated, the leadership will predictably entrench itself by controlling information, manipulating rewards and punishments, and mobilizing resources to defeat rivals. Even worse, the entrenched leadership will use the organization to promote its own agenda at the expense of the membership.

One response would be to eschew organization in favor of anarchy, but that is extreme. The better and deeper lesson is to take all predictable regularities into account at the outset, whereupon it may be possible to mitigate foreseeable oligarchical excesses at the initial design stage.[4]

Identity/capability. The proposition that identity matters has been featured in transaction cost economics from the outset. As developed in section 6, below, identity is usually explained by some form of 'asset specificity'. The 'capabilities' view of the firm (Penrose, 1959; Selznick, 1975; Wernerfelt, 1984; Teece *et al.*, 1992) raises related but additional issues.

One way to unpack the 'capabilities' view of the firm is to ask what—in addition to an inventory of its physical assets, an accounting for its financial assets, and a census of its workforce—is needed to describe the capabilities of a firm. Features of organization that are arguably important include the following: (i) the communication codes that the firm has developed (Arrow, 1974); (ii) the routines that it employs (Cyert and March, 1963; Nelson and Winter, 1982); (iii) the corporate culture that has taken shape (Kreps, 1990). What do we make of these?

One response is to regard these as spontaneous features of economic organization. As interpreted by institutional theory in sociology, 'organizational structures, procedures, and decisions are *largely ritualistic and symbolic*, especially so when it is difficult or impossible to assess the efficacy of organizational decisions on the basis of their tangible outcomes' (Baron and Hannan (1992), p. 57; emphasis added).

If, of course, efficiency consequences are impossible to ascertain, then intentionality has nothing to add. Increasingly, however, some of the subtle efficiency consequences of organization are coming to be better understood, whereupon they are (at least partly) subject to strategic determination. If the benefits of capabilities vary with the attributes of transactions, which arguably they do, then the cost effective thing to do is to *shape* culture, *develop* communication codes, and *manage* routines in a deliberative (transaction specific) way. Implementing the intentionality view will require that the microanalytic attributes that define culture, communication codes, and routines be uncovered, which is an ambitious exercise.

---

[4] Oligarchy is usually applied to composite organization, but it applies to subdivisions as well. Whether a firm should make or buy is thus a matter for which oligarchy has a bearing. If the decision to take a transaction out of the market and organize it internally is attended by subsequent information distortions and subgoal pursuit, then that should be taken into account at the outset (Williamson, 1975, chapter 7; 1985, chapter 6). Not only do operating costs rise but also a constituency develops that favors the renewal of internal facilities. An obvious response is to demand high hurdle rates for new projects, thereby to protect against the unremarked but predictable distortions (added costs; advocacy efforts) to which internal (as compared with market) procurement is differentially subject.

The argument applies to public sector projects as well. Because of the deferred and undisclosed but nevertheless predictable distortions to which 'organization' is subject, new projects and regulatory proposals should be required to display large (apparent) net gains.

Bureaucratization. As compared with the study of market failure, the study of bureaucratic failure is underdeveloped. It is elementary that a well-considered theory of organization will make provision for failures of all kinds.

Albeit underdeveloped, the bureaucratic failure literature is vast, partly because purported failures are described in absolute rather than comparative terms. Unless, however, a superior and feasible form of organization to which to assign a transaction (or related set of transactions) can be identified, the failure in question is effectively irremediable. One of the tasks of transaction cost economics is to assess purported bureaucratic failures in comparative institutional terms.

The basic argument is this: it is easy to show that a particular hierarchical structure is beset with costs, but that is neither here nor there if all feasible forms of organization are beset with the same or equivalent costs. Efforts to ascertain bureaucratic costs that survive comparative institutional scrutiny are reported elsewhere (Williamson, 1975, chapter 7; 1985, chapter 6), but these are very provisional and preliminary. Although intertemporal transformations and complexity are recurrent themes in the study of bureaucratic failure, much more concerted attention to these matters is needed.

Adaptation

The economist Friedrich Hayek maintained that the main problem of economic organization was that of adaptation and argued that this was realized spontaneously through the price system. Changes in the demand or supply of a commodity give rise to price changes, whereupon '*individual* participants . . . [are] able to take the right action' (1945, p. 527; emphasis added). Such price-induced adaptations by individual actors will be referred to as autonomous adaptations.

The organization theorist Chester Barnard also held that adaptation was the central problem of organization. But whereas Hayek emphasized autonomous adaptation of a spontaneous kind, Barnard was concerned with co-operative adaptation of an intentional kind. Formal organization, especially hierarchy, was the instrument through which the 'conscious, deliberate, purposeful' cooperation to which Barnard called attention was accomplished (1938, p. 4). Barnard's insights, which have had a lasting effect on organization theory, should have a lasting effect on economics as well.

Transaction cost economics (i) concurs that adaptation is the central problem of economic organization; (ii) regards adaptations of both autonomous and cooperative kinds as important; (iii) maintains that whether adaptations to disturbances ought to be predominantly autonomous, cooperative, or a mixture thereof varies with the attributes of the transactions (especially on the degree to which the investments associated with successive stages of activity are bilaterally or multilaterally dependent); and (iv) argues that each generic form of governance—market, hybrid, and hierarchy—differs systematically in its capacity to adapt in autonomous and cooperative ways. A series of predicted (transaction cost economizing) alignments between transactions and governance structures thereby obtain (Williamson, 1991a), which predictions invite and have been subjected to empirical testing (Joskow, 1988; Shelanski, 1991; Masten, 1992).

Politics

Terry Moe (1990) makes a compelling case for the proposition that public bureaucracies are different. Partly that is because the transactions that are assigned to the public sector are different, but Moe argues additionally that public sector bureaucracies are shaped by politics. Democratic politics requires compromises that are different in kind from those posed in the private sector and poses novel expropriation hazards. Added 'inefficiencies' arise in the design of public agencies on both accounts.

The inefficiencies that result from compromise are illustrated by the design of the Occupational Safety and Health Administration (OSHA) (Moe, 1990, p. 126):

> If business firms were allowed to help design OSHA, they would structure it in a way that it could not do its job. They would try to cripple it.
>
> This is not a hypothetical case. Interest groups representing business actually did participate in the design of OSHA, . . . [and] OSHA is an administrative nightmare, in large measure because some of its influential designers fully intended to endow it with structures that would not work.

To be sure, private sector organization is also the product of compromise. Egregious inefficiency in the private sector is checked, however, by competition in both product and capital markets. Note with reference to the latter that the voting rules in the private and public sectors are very different. The private rule is one share one vote, and shares may be concentrated through purchase. The public rule is one person one vote, and the 'purchase' of votes is much more cumbersome. Because, moreover, the gains that result from improved efficiency accrue (in the first instance, at least) to private sector owners in proportion to their ownership, private incentives to concentrate ownership and remove inefficiency are greater.

Even setting voting considerations aside, however, there is another factor that induces politicians to design agencies inefficiently. Incumbent politicians who create and design bureaus are aware that the opposition can be expected to win a majority and take control in the future. Agencies will therefore be designed with reference to both immediate benefits (which favors responsive mechanisms) and possible future losses (which often favors crafting inertia into the system). A farsighted majority party will therefore design some degree of (apparent) inefficiency into the agency at the outset—the effect of which will be to frustrate the efforts of successor administrations to reshape the purposes served by an agency.[5]

Embeddedness and Networks

Gary Hamilton and Nicole Biggart take exception with the transaction cost economics interpretation of economic organization because it implicitly assumes that the institutional environment is everywhere the same; namely, that of Western democracies, and most especially that of the United States. They observe that large firms in East Asia differ from United States corporations in significant respects and explain that 'organizational practices . . . are fashioned out of preexisting interactional patterns, which in many cases date to preindustrial times. Hence, industrial enterprise is a complex modern adaptation of pre-existing patterns of domination to economic situations in which profit, efficiency, and control usually form the very conditions of existence' (1988, p. S54).

The evidence that East Asian corporations differ is compelling. The argument, however, that transaction cost economics does not have application to East Asian economies goes too far.

The correct argument is that the institutional environment matters and that transaction cost economics, in its preoccupation with governance, has been neglectful of that. Treating the institutional environment as a set of shift parameters—changes in which induce shifts in the comparative costs of governance—is, to a first approximation at least, the obvious response (Williamson, 1991a). That is the interpretation advanced above and shown in Figure 1.

The objection could nevertheless be made that this is fine as far as it goes, but that comparative statics—which is a once-for-all exercise—does not go far enough. As Mark Granovetter observes, 'More sophisticated . . . analyses of cultural influences . . . make it clear that culture is not a once-for-all

---

[5] That is an interesting and important argument. Politics really is different. But it is not as though there is no private sector counterpart. The more general argument is this: weak property rights regimes— both public and private—invite farsighted parties to provide added protections. The issues are discussed further in conjunction with remediableness (see section 5.5, below).

Note, as a comparative institutional matter, that secure totalitarian regimes can, according to this logic, be expected to design more efficient public agencies. That is neither here nor there if democratic values are held to be paramount—in which event the apparent inefficiencies of agencies under a democracy are simply a cost of this form of governance.

influence but an *ongoing process*, continuously constructed and reconstructed during interaction. It not only shapes its members but is also shaped by them, in part for their own strategic reasons' (1985, p. 486).

I do not disagree, but I would observe that 'more sophisticated analyses' must be judged by their value added. What are the deeper insights? What are the added implications? Are the effects in question really beyond the reach of economizing reasoning?

Consider, with reference to this last, the embeddedness argument that 'concrete relations and structures' generate trust and discourage malfeasance of non-economic or extra-economic kinds (Granovetter, 1985, p. 490):

> Better than a statement that someone is known to be reliable is information from a trusted informant that he has dealt with that individual and found him so. Even better is information from one's own past dealings with that person. This is better information for four reasons: (1) it is cheap; (2) one trust one's own information best—it is richer, more detailed, and known to be accurate; (3) individuals with whom one has a continuing relation have an economic motivation to be trustworthy, so as not to discourage future transactions; and (4) departing from pure economic motives, continuing economic relations often become overlaid with social content that carries strong expectations of trust and abstention from opportunism.

This last point aside, the entire argument is consistent with, and much of it has been anticipated by, transaction cost reasoning. Transaction cost economics and embeddedness reasoning are evidently complementary in many respects.

A related argument is that transaction cost economics is preoccupied with dyadic relations, whereupon network relations are given short shrift. The former is correct,[6] but the suggestion that network analysis is beyond the reach of transaction cost economics is too strong. For one thing, many of the network effects described by Ray Miles and Charles Snow (1992) correspond very closely to the transaction cost economics treatment of the hybrid form of economic organization (Williamson, 1983, 1991a). For another, as the discussion of Japanese economic organization (see section 6.4, below) reveals, transaction cost economics can be and has been extended to deal with a richer set of network effects.

Discrete Structural Analysis

One possible objection to the use of maximization/marginal analysis is that 'Parsimony recommends that we prefer the postulate that men are reasonable

---

[6] Interdependencies among dyadic contracting relations and the possible manipulation thereof have, however, been examined (Williamson, 1985, pp. 318–319). Also see the discussion of appropriability in section 5, below.

to the postulate that they are supremely rational when either of the two assumptions will do our work of inference as well as the other' (Simon, 1978, p. 8). But while one might agree with Simon that satisficing is more reasonable than maximizing, the analytical toolbox out of which satisficing works is, as compared with maximizing apparatus, incomplete and very cumbersome. Thus if one reaches the same outcome through the satisfying postulate as through maximizing, and if the latter is much easier to implement, then economists can be thought of as analytical satisficers: they use a short-cut form of analysis that is simple to implement. Albeit at the expense of realism in assumptions, maximization gets the job done.

A different criticism of marginal analysis is that this glosses over first-order effects of a discrete structural kind. Capitalism and socialism, for example, can be compared in both discrete structural (bureaucratization) and marginal analysis (efficient resource allocation) respects. Interestingly, Oskar Lange (1938, p. 109) conjectured that, as between the two, bureaucratization posed a much more severe danger to socialism than did inefficient resource allocation.

That he was sanguine with respect to the latter was because he had derived the rules for efficient resource allocation (mainly of a marginal cost pricing kind) and was confident that socialist planners and managers could implement them. Joseph Schumpeter (1942) and Abram Bergson (1948) concurred. The study of comparative economic systems over the next fifty years was predominantly an allocative efficiency-exercise.

Bureaucracy, by contrast, was mainly ignored. Partly that is because the study of bureaucracy was believed to be beyond the purview of economics and belonged to sociology (Lange, 1938, p. 109). Also, Lange held that 'monopolistic capitalism' was beset by even more serious bureaucracy problems (p. 110). If, however, the recent collapse of the former Soviet Union is attributable more to conditions of waste (operating inside the frontier) than to inefficient resource allocation (operating at the wrong place on the frontier), then it was cumulative burdens of bureaucracy—goal distortions, slack, maladaptation, technological stagnation—that spelt its demise.

The lesson here is this: always study first-order (discrete structural) effects before examining second-order (marginalist) refinements. Arguably, moreover, that should be obvious: waste is easily a more serious source of welfare losses than are price induced distortions [cf. Harberger (1954) with Williamson (1968)].

Simon advises similarly. Thus he contends that the main questions are (1978, p. 6):

> Not 'how much flood insurance will a man buy?' but 'what are the structural conditions that make buying insurance rational or attractive?'

> Not 'at what levels will wages be fixed' but 'when will work be performed
> under an employment contract rather than a sales contract?'

Friedland and Alford's recent treatment of institutions is also of a discrete structural kind. They contend that 'Each of the most important institutional orders of contemporary Western societies has a central logic—a set of material practices and symbolic constructions—which constitutes its organizing principles and which is available to organizations and individuals to elaborate' (1991, p. 248). Transaction cost economics concurs. But whereas Friedland and Alford are concerned with discrete structural logics between institutional orders—capitalism, the state, democracy, the family, etc.— transaction cost economics maintains that distinctive logics within institutional orders also need to be distinguished. Within the institutional order of capitalism, for example, each generic mode of governance—market, hybrid, and hierarchy—possesses its own logic and distinctive cluster of attributes. Of special importance is the proposition that each generic mode of governance is supported by a distinctive form of contract law.

As developed elsewhere (Williamson, 1991a), transaction cost economics holds that classical contract law applies to markets, neoclassical contract law applies to hybrids, and forbearance law is the contract law of hierarchy. As between these three concepts of contract, classical contract law is the most legalistic, neoclassical contract law is somewhat more elastic (Macneil, 1974, 1978), and forbearance law has the property that hierarchy is its own court of ultimate appeal. But for these contract law differences, markets and hierarchies would be indistinguishable in fiat respects.

Recall in this connection that Alchian and Demsetz introduced their analysis of the 'classical capitalist firm' with the argument that (172, p. 777): 'It is common to see the firm characterized by the power to settle issues by fiat. . . . This is delusion. The firm . . . has no power of fiat, no authority, no disciplinary action any different in the slightest degree from ordinary market contracting.' That is a provocative formulation and places the burden on those who hold that firm and market differ in fiat respects to show wherein those differences originate.

The transaction cost economics response is that courts treat interfirm and intrafirm disputes differently, serving as the forum of ultimate appeal for interfirm disputes while refusing to hear identical technical disputes that arise between divisions (regarding transfer prices, delays, quality, and the like). Because hierarchy is its own court of ultimate appeal (Williamson, 1991a), firms can and do exercise fiat that markets cannot. Prior neglect of the discrete structural contract law differences that distinguish alternative modes of governance explains earlier claims that firms and markets are indistinguishable in fiat and control respects.

5. *Transaction Cost Economics, the Strategy*

The transaction cost economics program for studying economic organization has been described elsewhere (Williamson, 1975, 1981, 1985, 1988a, 1991a; Klein *et al.*, 1978; Alchian and Woodward, 1987; Davis and Powell, 1992). My purpose here is to sketch the general strategy that is employed by transaction cost economics, with the suggestion that organization theorists could adopt (some already have adopted) parts of it.

The five-part strategy that I describe entails (i) a main case orientation (transaction cost economizing), (ii) choice and explication of the unit of analysis, (iii) a systems view of contracting, (iv) rudimentary trade-off apparatus, and (v) a remediableness test for assessing 'failures'.

The Main Case

Economic organization being very complex and our understanding being primitive, there is a need to sort the wheat from the chaff. I propose for this purpose that each rival theory of organization should declare the *main case* out of which it works and develop the *refutable implications* that accrue thereto.

Transaction cost economics holds that economizing on transaction costs is mainly responsible for the choice of one form of capitalist organization over another. It thereupon applies this hypothesis to a wide range of phenomena— vertical integration, vertical market restrictions, labor organization, corporate governance, finance, regulation (and deregulation), conglomerate organization, technology transfer, and, more generally, to any issue that can be posed directly or indirectly as a contracting problem. As it turns out, large numbers of problems which on first examination do not appear to be of a contracting kind turn out to have an underlying contracting structure—the oligopoly problem (Williamson, 1975, chapter 12) and the organization of the company town (Williamson, 1985, pp. 35–38) being examples. Comparisons with other—rival or complementary—main case alternatives are invited.

Three of the older main case alternatives are that economic organization is mainly explained by (i) technology, (ii) monopolization, and (iii) efficient risk bearing. More recent main case candidates are (iv) contested exchange between labor and capital, (v) other types of power arguments (e.g. resource dependency), and (vi) path dependency. My brief responses to the first three are that (i) technological non-separabilities and indivisibilities explain only small groups and, at most, large plants, but explain neither multiplant organization nor the organization of technologically separable groups/ activities (which should remain autonomous and which should be joined), (ii) monopoly explanations require that monopoly preconditions be satisfied, but most markets are competitively organized, and (iii) although differential risk aversion may apply to many employment relationships, it has much less applicability to trade between firms [where portfolio diversification is more easily accomplished and where smaller firms (for incentive intensity and economizing, but not risk bearing, reasons) are often observed to bear inordinate risk]. Responses to the last three are developed more fully below. My brief responses are these: (iv) the failures to which contested exchange refers are often irremediable, (v) resource dependency is a truncated theory of contract, and (vi) although path dependency is an important phenomenon, remediable inefficiency is rarely established.

To be sure, transaction cost economizing does not always operate smoothly or quickly. Thus we should 'expect [transaction cost economizing] to be most clearly exhibited in industries where entry is [easy] and where the struggle for survival is [keen]' (Koopmans, 1957, p. 141).[7] Transaction cost economics nevertheless maintains that later, if not sooner, inefficiency in the commercial sector invites its own demise—all the more so as international competition has become more vigorous. Politically imposed impediments (tariffs, quotas, subsidies, rules) can and have, however, delayed the reckoning;[8] and disadvantaged parties (railroad workers, longshoremen, managers) may also be able to delay changes unless compensated by buyouts.

The economizing to which I refer operates through weak-form selection—according to which the fitter, but not necessarily the fittest, in some absolute sense, are selected (Simon, 1983, p. 69).[9] Also, the economizing in question works through a private net benefit calculus. That suits the needs of positive economics—What's going on out there?—rather well, but public policy needs to be more circumspect. As discussed below, the relevant test of whether public policy intervention is warranted is that of remediableness.

These important qualifications notwithstanding, transaction cost economics

[7] The statement is a weakened variant on Tjalling Koopmans. Where he refers to 'profit maximization', 'easiest', and 'keenest', I have substituted transaction cost economizing, easy, and keen.

[8] Joe Mokyr observes that resistance to innovation 'occurred in many periods and places but seems to have been neglected by most historians' (1990, p. 178). He nevertheless gives a number of examples in which established interests, often with the use of the political process, set out to defeat new technologies. In the end, however, the effect was not to defeat but to delay machines that pressed pinheads, an improved slide rest lathe, the ribbon loom, the flying shuttle, the use of arabic numerals, and the use of the printing press (Mokyr, 1990, pp. 178–179). That, of course, is not dispositive. There may be many cases in which superior technologies were in fact defeated—of which the typewriter keyboard (see Section 7, below) is purportedly an example. Assuming, however, that the appropriate criterion for judging superiority is that of remediability (see below), I register grave doubts that significant technological or organizational efficiencies can be delayed indefinitely.

[9] The Schumpeterian process of 'handing on'—which entails 'a fall in the price of the product to the new level of costs' (Schumpeter, 1947, p. 155) and purportedly works whenever rivals are alert to new opportunities and are not prevented by purposive restrictions from adopting them—is pertinent. The efficacy of handing on varies with the circumstances. When are rivals *more* alert? What are the underlying information assumptions? Are there other capital market and/or organizational concerns?

maintains that economizing is mainly determinative of private sector economic organization and, as indicated, invites comparison with rival main case hypotheses. Nicholas Georgescu-Roegen's views on the purpose of science and the role of prediction are pertinent: 'the purpose of science in general is not prediction, but knowledge for its own sake,' yet prediction is 'the touchstone of scientific knowledge' (1971, p. 37). There being many plausible accounts from which to choose, it is vital that each be prepared to show its hand (offer its predictions).

Unit of Analysis

A variety of units of analysis have been proposed to study economic organization. Simon has proposed that the *decision premise* is the appropriate unit of analysis (1957a, pp. xxx–xxxii). '*Ownership*' is the unit of analysis for the economics of property rights. The *industry* is the unit of analysis in the structure–conduct–performance approach to industrial organization (Bain, 1956; Scherer, 1970). The *individual* has been nominated as the unit of analysis by positive agency theory (Jensen, 1983). Transaction cost economics follows John R. Commons (1924, 1934) and takes the *transaction* to be the basic unit of analysis.

Whatever unit of analysis is selected, the critical dimensions with respect to which that unit of analysis differs need to be identified. Otherwise the unit will remain non-operational. Also, a paradigm problem to which the unit of analysis applies needs to be described. Table 1 sets out the relevant comparisons.

As shown, the representative problem with which transaction cost economics deals is that of vertical integration—when should a firm make rather than buy a good or service? The focal dimension on which much of the predictive content of transaction cost economics relies, moreover, is asset

TABLE 1. Comparison of Units of Analysis

Unit of Analysis	Critical Dimensions	Focal Problem
Decision premise	Role; information; idiosyncratic[a]	Human problem solving[b]
Ownership	'Eleven characteristics'[c]	Externality
Industry	Concentration; barriers to entry	Price–cost margins
Individual	Undeclared	Incentive alignment
Transaction	Frequency; uncertainty; asset specificity	Vertical integration

[a] Simon (1957a, pp. xxx–xxxi).
[b] Newell and Simon (1972).
[c] Bromley (1989, pp. 187–190).

specificity, which (as discussed in section 6, below) is a measure of bilateral dependency. More generally, transaction cost economics is concerned with the governance of contractual relations (which bears a resemblance to the 'going concerns' to which Commons referred). As it turns out, economic organization—in intermediate products markets, labor markets, capital markets, regulation, and even the family—involves variations on a few key transaction cost economizing themes. The predictive action turns on the following proposition: transactions, which differ in their attributes, are aligned with governance structures, which differ in their costs and competence, in a discriminating—mainly, transaction cost economizing—way.

The arguments are familiar and are developed elsewhere. Suffice it to observe here that empirical research in organization theory has long suffered from the lack of an appropriate unit of analysis and the operationalization, which is to say, dimensionalization, thereof.

Farsighted Contracting

The preoccupation of economists with direct and intended effects to the neglect of indirect and (often delayed) unintended effects is widely interpreted as a condition of myopia. In fact, however, most economists are actually farsighted. The problem is one of limited peripheral vision.

Tunnel vision is both a strength and a weakness. The strength is that a focused lens, provided that it focuses on core issues, can be very powerful. The limitation is that irregularities which are none the less important will be missed and/or, even worse, dismissed.

Transaction cost economics relates to these limitations by drawing on organization theory. Because organization has a life of its own, transaction cost economics (i) asks to be apprised of the more important indirect effects, whereupon (ii) it asks what, given these prospective effects, are the ramifications for efficient governance. A joinder of unanticipated effects (from organization theory) with farsighted contracting (from economics) thereby obtains.

Lest claims of farsightedness be taken to hyper-rationality extremes, transaction cost economics concedes that all complex contracts are unavoidably incomplete. That has both practical and theoretical significance. The practical lesson is this: all of the relevant contracting action cannot be concentrated in the *ex ante* incentive alignment but some spills over into *ex post* governance. The theoretical lesson is that differences among organization forms lose economic significance under a comprehensive contracting set-up because any form of organization can then replicate any other (Hart, 1990).

Transaction cost economics combines incompleteness with farsighted contracting by describing the contracting process as one of 'incomplete contracting in its entirety'. But for incompleteness, the above-described significance of *ex post* governance would vanish. But for farsightedness, transaction cost economics would be denied access to one of the most important 'tricks' in the economist's bag, namely the assumption that economic actors have the ability to look ahead, discern problems and prospects, and factor these back into the organizational/contractual design. 'Plausible farsightedness', as against hyper-rationality, will often suffice.

Consider, for example, the issue of threats. Threats are easy to make, but which threats are to be believed? If A says that it will do X if B does Y, but if after B does Y, A's best response is to do Z, then the threat will not be perceived to be credible to a farsighted B. Credible threats are thus those for which a farsighted B perceives that A's *ex post* incentives comport with its claims, because, for example, A has made the requisite kind and amount of investment to support its threats (Dixit, 1980).

Or consider the matter of opportunism. As described above, Machiavelli worked out of a myopic logic, whereupon he advised his Prince to reply to opportunism in kind (get them before they get you). By contrast, the farsighted Prince is advised to look ahead and, if he discerns potential hazards, to take the hazards into account by redesigning the contractual relation— often by devising *ex ante* safeguards that will deter *ex post* opportunism. Accordingly, the wise Prince is advised to give and receive 'credible commitments'.

To be sure, it is more complicated to think about contract as a triple (p, k, s), where p refers to the price at which the trade takes place, k refers to the hazards that are associated with the exchange, s denotes the safeguards within which the exchange is embedded, and price, hazards, and safeguards are determined simultaneously—than as a scalar, where price alone is determinative. The simple schema shown in Figure 2 nevertheless captures much of the relevant action.[10]

It will facilitate comparisons to assume that suppliers are competitively organized and are risk neutral. The prices at which product will be supplied therefore reflect an expected break-even condition. The break-even price that is associated with Node A is p_1. There being no hazards, $k = 0$. And since safeguards are unneeded, $s = 0$.[11]

Node B is more interesting. The contractual hazard here is $\bar{k}$. If the buyer is unable or unwilling to provide a safeguard, then $s = 0$. The corresponding break-even price is $\bar{p}$.

Node C poses the same contractual hazard, namely $\bar{k}$. In this case,

---

[10] The remainder of this subsection is based on Williamson (1993a).

[11] Another way of putting it is that (transition problems aside), each party can go its own way without cost to the other. Competition provides a safeguard.

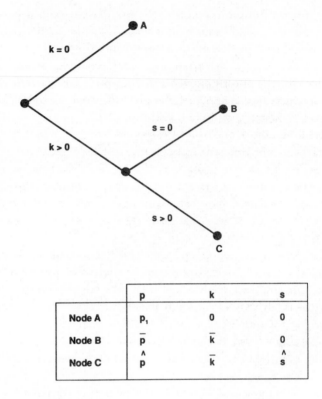

	p	k	s
Node A	p_1	0	0
Node B	$\bar{p}$	$\bar{k}$	0
Node C	$\hat{p}$	$\bar{k}$	$\hat{s}$

FIGURE 2. Simple contractual schema.

however, a safeguard in amount $\hat{s}$ is provided. The break-even price that is projected under these conditions is $\hat{p}$. It is elementary that $\hat{p} < \bar{p}$.

Note that Jeffrey Bradach and Robert Eccles contend that 'mutual dependence [i.e. $k > 0$] between exchange partners . . . [promotes] trust, [which] contrasts sharply with the argument central to transaction cost economics that . . . dependence . . . fosters opportunistic behavior' (1989, p. 111). What transaction cost economics says, however, is that because opportunistic agents will not self-enforce open-ended promises to behave responsibly, efficient exchange will be realized only if dependencies are *supported* by credible commitments. Wherein is trust implicated if parties to an exchange are farsighted and reflect the relevant hazards in terms of the exchange? [A better price ($\hat{p} < \bar{p}$) will be offered if the hazards ($k > 0$) are mitigated by cost-effective contractual safeguards ($\hat{s} > 0$).]

As it turns out, the farsighted approach to contracting has pervasive ramifications, some of which are developed below.

Trade-offs

The ideal organization adapts quickly and efficaciously to disturbances of all kinds, but actual organizations experience trade-offs. Thus whereas more decentralized forms of organization (e.g. markets) support high-powered incentives and display outstanding adaptive properties to disturbances of an autonomous kind, they are poorly suited in cooperative adaptation respects. Hierarchy, by contrast, has weaker incentives and is comparatively worse at autonomous adaptation but is comparatively better in cooperative adaptation respects.

Simple transactions (for which $k = 0$)—in intermediate product markets, labor, finance, regulation, and the like—are easy to organize. The requisite adaptations here are preponderantly of an autonomous kind and the market-like option is efficacious (so firms buy rather than make, use spot contracts for labor, use debt rather than equity, eschew regulation, etc.). Problems with markets arise as bilateral dependencies, and the need for cooperative adaptations, build up. Markets give way to hybrids which in turn give way to hierarchies (which is the organization form of last resort) as the needs for cooperative adaptations ($k > 0$) build up.

More generally, the point is this: informed choice among alternative forms of organization entails trade-offs. Identifying and explicating trade-offs is the key to the study of comparative economic organization. Social scientists—economists and organization theorists alike—as well as legal specialists, need to come to terms with that proposition.

Remediability

Related to this last is the concept of remediability. If all feasible forms of organization are flawed (Coase, 1964), then references to benign government, costless regulation, omniscient courts, and the like are operationally irrelevant. That does not deny that hypothetical ideals can be useful as a reference standard, but standards are often arbitrary. Is unbounded rationality the relevant standard? How about perfect stewardship, in which event opportunism vanishes?

Lapses into ideal but operationally irrelevant reasoning will be avoided by (i) recognizing that it is impossible to do better than one's best, (ii) insisting that all of the finalists in an organization form competition meet the test of feasibility, (iii) symmetrically exposing the weaknesses as well as the strengths of all proposed feasible forms, and (iv) describing and costing out the mechanisms of any proposed reorganization. Such precautions seem to be reasonable, transparent, even beyond dispute; yet all are frequently violated.

Note in this connection that 'inefficiency' is unavoidably associated with contractual hazards. The basic market and hierarchy trade-off that is incurred upon taking transactions out of markets and organizing them internally sub-stitutes one form of inefficiency (bureaucracy) for another (maladaptation). Other examples where one form of inefficiency is used to patch up another are (i) decisions by firms to integrate into adjacent stages of production (or distribution) in a weak intellectual property rights regime, thereby to mitigate the leakage of valued know-how (Teece, 1986), (ii) decisions by manufacturers' agents to incur added expenses, over and above those needed to develop the market, if these added expenses strengthen customer bonds in a cost-effective way, thereby to deter manufacturers from entering and expropriating market development investments (Heide and John, 1988), and (iii) the use of costly bonding to deter franchisees from violating quality norms (Klein and Leffler, 1981). Organization also has a bearing on the distribution of rents as well as asset protection. Concern over rent dissipation influenced the decision by the United States automobile industry firms to integrate into parts (Helper and Levine, 1992) and also helps to explain the resistance by oligopolies to industrial unions.

To be sure, any sacrifice of organizational efficiency, for oligopolistic rent protection reasons or otherwise, poses troublesome public policy issues.[12] A remediability test is none the less required to ascertain whether public policy should attempt to upset the oligopoly power in question. The issues are discussed further in relation to path dependency in section 7, below.

6. *Added Regularities*

It is evident from the foregoing that the comparative contractual approach out of which transaction cost economics works can be and needs to be informed by organization theory. Transaction cost economics, however, is more than a mere user. It pushes the logic of self-interest seeking to deeper levels, of which the concept of credible commitment is one example. More generally, it responds to prospective dysfunctional consequences by proposing improved *ex ante* designs and/or alternative forms of governance. Also, and what concerns me here, transaction cost has helped to discover added regular-ities that are pertinent to the study of organization. These include (i) the Fundamental Transformation, (ii) the impossibility of selective intervention, (iii) the economics of atmosphere, and (iv) an interpretation of Japanese economic organization.

---

[12] This has public policy ramifications. As between two oligopolies, one of which engages in rent-protective measures while the other does not, and assuming that they are identical in other respects, the dissolution of the rent-protective oligopoly will yield larger welfare gains.

The Fundamental Transformation[13]

The Fundamental Transformation is the principal transaction cost economics way of demonstrating that 'identity matters'. It helps to explain how firms take on distinctive identities and why identity matters.

Economists of all persuasions recognize that the terms upon which an initial bargain will be struck depend on whether non-collusive bids can be elicited from more than one qualified supplier. Monopolistic terms will obtain if there is only a single highly qualified supplier, while competitive terms will result if there are many. Transaction cost economics fully accepts this description of *ex ante* bidding competition but insists that the study of contracting be extended to include *ex post* features.

Contrary to earlier practice, transaction cost economics holds that a condition of large numbers bidding at the outset does not necessarily imply that a large numbers bidding condition will obtain thereafter. Whether *ex post* competition is fully efficacious or not depends on whether the good or service in question is supported by durable investments in transaction specific human or physical assets. Where no such specialized investments are incurred, the initial winning bidder realizes no advantage over non-winners. Although it may continue to supply for a long period of time, this is only because, in effect, it is continuously meeting competitive bids from qualified rivals. Rivals cannot be presumed to operate on a parity, however, once substantial investments in transaction specific assets are put in place. Winners in these circumstances enjoy advantages over non-winners, which is to say that parity at the renewal interval is upset. Accordingly, what was a large numbers bidding condition at the outset is effectively transformed into one of bilateral supply thereafter. The reason why significant reliance investments in durable, transaction specific assets introduce contractual asymmetry between the winning bidder on the one hand and non-winners on the other is because economic values would be sacrificed if the ongoing supply relation were to be terminated.

Faceless contracting is thereby supplanted by contracting in which the pairwise identity of the parties matters. Not only would the supplier be unable to realize equivalent value were the specialized assets to be redeployed to other uses, but also a buyer would need to induce potential suppliers to make similar specialized investments were he to seek least-cost supply from an outsider. Such parties therefore have strong incentives to work things out rather than terminate. More generally, farsighted agents will attempt to craft Node C safeguards *ex ante*. As previously indicated, that entails a progression

[13] This subsection is based on Williamson (1985, pp. 61–63).

from markets to hybrids and, if that does not suffice, to hierarchies. Given its bureaucratic disabilities, hierarchy is the organizational form of last resort.

The Impossibility of Selective Intervention

Large established firms purportedly have advantages over smaller potential entrants because (Lewis, 1983, p. 1092):

> . . . the leader can at least use [inputs] exactly as the entrant would have . . . , and earn the same profit as the entrant. But typically, the leader can improve on this by coordinating production from his new and existing inputs. Hence [inputs] will be valued more by the dominant firm.

That argument has the following implication: if large firms can everywhere do as well as a collection of smaller firms, through replication, and can sometimes do better, through selective intervention, then large firms ought to grow without limit. That is a variant of the Coasian puzzle 'Why is not all production carried on in one big firm?' (1937, p. 340).

The simple answer to that query is that replication and/or selective intervention are impossible. But that merely moves the argument back one stage. What explains these impossibilities?

The underlying difficulty is this: the integrity of rule governance is unavoidably compromised by allowing discretion (Williamson, 1985, chapter 6). Accordingly, any effort to combine rule governance (as in markets) with discretionary governance (hierarchy) experiences trade-offs. The proposal to 'Implement the rules with discretion' is simply too facile.

That comes as no surprise to those who approach the study of governance in discrete structural terms—whereupon each generic form of governance possesses distinctive strengths and weaknesses and movements between them entail trade-offs. The puzzle of limits to firm size none the less eluded an answer for fifty years and more (Williamson, 1985, pp. 132–135) and still occasions confusion.

Atmosphere[14]

The unintended effects described in 4 above are of a more local kind than the atmospheric effects examined here. Atmosphere refers to interactions

[14] This subsection is based on Williamson (1993a).

between transactions that are technologically separable but are joined attitudinally and have systems consequences.

Thus suppose that a job can be split into a series of separable functions. Suppose further that differential metering at the margin is attempted with reference to each. What are the consequences?

If functional separability does not imply attitudinal separability, then piecemeal calculativeness can easily be dysfunctional. The risk is that pushing metering at the margin everywhere to the limit will have spillover effects from easy-to-meter on to hard-to-meter activities. If cooperative attitudes are impaired, then transactions that can be metered only with difficulty, but for which consummate cooperation is important, will be discharged in a more perfunctory manner. The neglect of such interaction effects is encouraged by piecemeal calculativeness, which is to say by an insensitivity to atmosphere.

A related issue is the matter of externalities. The question may be put as follows: ought all externalities to be metered which, taken separately, can be metered with net gains? Presumably this turns partly on whether secondary effects obtain when an externality is accorded legitimacy. All kinds of grievances may be 'felt', and demands for compensation made accordingly, if what had hitherto been considered to be harmless byproducts of normal social intercourse are suddenly declared to be compensable injuries. The transformation of relationships that will ensue can easily lead to a lower level of satisfaction felt among the parties than prevailed previously—at least transitionally and possibly permanently.

Part of the explanation is that filing claims for petty injuries influences attitudes toward other transactions. My insistence on compensation for *A* leads you to file claims for *B*, *C*, and *D*, which induces me to seek compensation for *E* and *F*, etc. Although an efficiency gain might be realized were it possible to isolate transaction *A*, the overall impact can easily be negative. Realizing this to be the case, some individuals will be prepared to overlook such injuries. But everyone is not similarly constituted. Society is rearranged to the advantage of those who demand more exacting correspondences between rewards and deeds if metering at the margin is everywhere attempted. Were the issue of compensation to be taken up as a constitutional matter, rather than on a case-by-case basis, a greater tolerance for spillover would commonly be obtained (Schelling, 1978).

Also pertinent is that individuals keep informal social accounts and find the exchange of reciprocal favors among parties with whom uncompensated spillovers exist to be satisfying (Gouldner, 1954). Transforming these casual social accounts into exact and legal obligations may well be destructive of atmosphere and lead to a net loss of satisfaction between the parties. Put differently, pervasive pecuniary relations impair the quality of 'contracting'—even if the metering of the transactions in question were costless.[15]

The argument that emerges from the above is not that metering ought to be prohibited but that the calculative approach to organization that is associated with economics can be taken to extremes. An awareness of attitudinal spillovers and non-pecuniary satisfactions serves to check such excesses of calculativeness.

Japanese Economic Organization

Transaction cost economics deals predominantly with dyadic contractual relations. Viewing the firm as a nexus of contracts, the object is to prescribe the best transaction/governance structure between the firm and its intermediate product market suppliers, between the firm and its workers, between the firm and finance, etc. Japanese economic organization appears to be more complicated. Employment, banking, and subcontracting relations need to be examined simultaneously.

The banking, employment, and subcontracting differences between Japanese and United States economic organization have been explicated by Masahiko Aoki (1988, 1990), Banri Asanuma (1989), Erik Berglof (1989), Ronald Dore (1983), Michael Gerlach (1992), James Lincoln (1990), Paul Sheard (1989), and others. I am not only persuaded that these three are joined but believe that transaction cost economics can help to explicate the complementarities (Williamson, 1991b).

Figures 3A and B display the nature of the complementarities. Figure 3A depicts the contractual hazards that are posed by lifetime employment. These are (i) economic adversity—due, say, to periodic decreases in demand—which makes it costly to offer lifetime employment; (ii) workers who enjoy lifetime employment may treat it as a sinecure and shirk; (iii) workers who are induced by promises of lifetime employment to specialize their assets to a firm are exposed to a breach of contract hazard; (iv) equalitarian pressures develop within firms, whereupon the offer of lifetime employment to key workers (where the justification is strong) spreads to all workers (to include those for whom the justification is weak). Although each of these can be addressed separately, the systems solution shown by Figure 3A is (arguably) more effective still.

[15] The buying of 'rounds' in English pubs is an example. Would a costless meter lead to a superior result? Suppose that everyone privately disclosed a willingness to pay and that successive bids were solicited until a breakeven result was projected. Suppose that the results of the final solicitation either are kept secret or posted, depending on preferences, and that rounds are thereafter delivered to the table on request. Monthly bills are sent out in accordance with the breakeven condition. How is camaraderie effected?

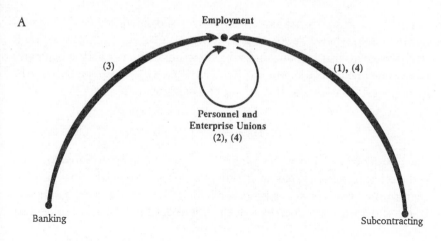

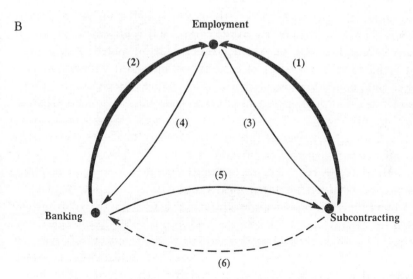

FIGURE 3. (A) Supports for life-time employment against the hazards of (1) adversity, (2) shirking, (3) breach, (4) equalitarianism. Subcontracting reduces (1) and (4), the personnel office and enterprise unions reduce (2) and (4), and banking reduces (3). (B) Japanese corporate connectedness through contracting, where ⟶ denotes strong support; → denotes support; – – → denotes weaker support. Benefits are (1) greater homogeneity; (2) greater contract stability; (3) feedback stability; (4) reliably responsive to adversity; (5) financial planning (convergent expectations); (6) no surprises.

Figure 3B is somewhat more complicated and interested readers are referred to discussions elsewhere (Williamson, 1991b; Aoki, 1992). Suffice it to observe here that banking and subcontracting (i) are not only supports for the employment relation in the core firm but (ii) are supported by the employment relation and (iii) are supports for each other.

7. *Unresolved Tensions*

The healthy tension to which I referred at the outset has contributed to better and deeper understandings of a variety of phenomena. The matters that concern me here—power, path dependence, the labor managed enterprise, trust, and tosh—are ones for which differences between transaction cost economics and organization theory are great.

Power/Resource Dependence

That efficiency plays such a large role in the economic analysis of organization is because parties are assumed to consent to a contract and do this in a relatively farsighted way. Such voluntarism is widely disputed by sociologists, who 'tend to regard systems of exchange as embedded within systems of power and domination (usually regarded as grounded in a class structure in the Marxian tradition) or systems of norms and values' (Baron and Hannan, 1992, p. 14).

The concept of power is very diffuse. Unable to define power, some specialists report that they know it when they see it. That has led others to conclude that power is a 'disappointing concept. It tends to become a tautological label for the unexplained variance' (March, 1988, p. 6).

Among the ways in which the term power is used are the following: the power of capital over labor (Bowles and Gintis, 1993); strategic power exercised by established firms in relation to extant and prospective rivals (Shapiro, 1989); special interest power over the political process (Moe, 1990); and resource dependency. Although all are relevant to economic organization, the last is distinctive to organization theory.[16] I examine it.

Two versions of resource dependency can be distinguished. The weak version is that parties who are subject to dependency will try to mitigate it. That is unexceptionable and is akin to the safeguard argument advanced in 5, above. There are two significant differences, however: (i) resource dependency nowhere recognizes that price, hazards, and safeguards are determined simultaneously; (ii) resource dependency nowhere remarks that asset

---

[16] Friedland and Alford (1991, p. 235) identify resource dependency as one of the two dominant theories of organization (the other being population ecology).

specificity (which is the source of contractual hazard) is intentionally chosen because it is the source of productive benefits.

The strong version of resource dependency assumes myopia. The argument here is that myopic parties to contracts are victims of unanticipated and unwanted dependency. Because myopic parties do not perceive the hazards, safeguards will not be provided and the hazards will not be priced out.

Evidence pertinent to the myopic versus farsighted view of contract includes the following. (i) Are suppliers indifferent between two technologies that involve identical investments and have identical (steady state) operating costs, but one of which technologies is much less redeployable than the other? (ii) Is the degree of non-redeployability evident *ex ante* or is it revealed only after an adverse state realization (which induces defection from the spirit of the agreement) has materialized? (iii) Do added *ex ante* safeguards appear as added specificity builds up? (iv) Does contract law doctrine and enforcement reflect one or the other of these concepts of contract? Transaction cost economics answers these queries as follows: (i) the more generic (redeployable) technology will always be used whenever the cetera are paria; (ii) non-redeployability can be discerned *ex ante* and is recognized as such (Masten, 1984; Palay, 1984, 1985; Shelanski, 1993); (iii) added *ex ante* safeguards do appear as asset specificity builds up (Joskow, 1985, 1988); (iv) because truly unusual events are unforeseeable and can have punitive consequences if contracts are enforced literally, various forms of 'excuse' are recognized by the law, but excuse is granted sparingly.[17]

Path Dependency

Transaction cost economics not only subscribes to the proposition that history matters but relies on that proposition to explain the differential strengths and weaknesses of alternative forms of governance. The Fundamental Transformation, for example, is a specific manifestation of the proposition that history matters. (Transactions that are not subject to the Fundamental Transformation are much easier to manage contractually.) The bureaucracy

---

[17] Because contracts are incomplete and contain gaps, errors, omissions, and the like, and because the immediate parties may not be able to reconcile their differences when an unanticipated disturbance arises, parties to a contract will sometimes ask courts to be excused from performance. Because, moreover, literal enforcement can pose unacceptably severe contractual hazards—the effects of which are to discourage contracting (in favor of vertical integration) and/or to discourage potentially cost-effective investments in specialized assets—some relief from strict enforcement recommends itself. How much relief is then the question. Were excuse to be granted routinely whenever adversity occurred, then incentives to think through contracts, choose technologies judiciously, share risks efficiently, and avert adversity would be impaired. Accordingly, transaction cost economics recommends that (i) provision be made for excuse but (ii) excuse should be awarded sparingly—which it evidently is (Farnsworth, 1968, p. 885; Buxbaum, 1985).

problems that afflict internal organization (entrenchment; coalitions) are also the product of experience and illustrate the proposition that history matters. Were it not that systems drifted away from their initial conditions, efforts to replicate markets within hierarchies (or the reverse) and selectively intervene would be much easier—in which event differences between organization forms would diminish.

The benefits that accrue to experience are also testimony to the proposition that history matters. Tacit knowledge and its consequences (Polanyi, 1962; Marschak, 1968; Arrow, 1974) attest to that. More generally, firm-specific human assets of both spontaneous (e.g. coding economies) and intentional (e.g. learning) kinds are the product of idiosyncratic experience. The entire institutional environment (laws, rules, conventions, norms, etc.) within which the institutions of governance are embedded is the product of history. And although the social conditioning that operates within governance structures [e.g. corporate culture (Kreps, 1990)] is reflexive and often intentional, this too has accidental and temporal features.

That history matters does not, however, imply that only history matters. Intentionality and economizing explain a lot of what is going on out there. Also, most of the path dependency literature emphasizes technology (e.g. the QWERTY typewriter keyboard) rather than the organizational consequences referred to above, Paul David's recent paper (1992) being an exception. I am not persuaded that technological, as against organizational, path dependency is as important as much of that literature suggests. Many of the 'inefficiencies' to which the technological path dependency literature refers are of an irremediable kind.

Remediable inefficiencies.   As described in section 5 above, transaction cost economics emphasizes remediable inefficiencies; that is, those conditions for which a feasible alternative can be described which, if introduced, would yield net gains. That is to be distinguished from hypothetical net gains, where the inefficiency in question is judged by comparing an actual alternative with a hypothetical ideal.

To be sure, big disparities between actual and hypothetical sometimes signals opportunities for net gains. But a preoccupation with hypotheticals comes at a cost (Coase, 1964, p. 195; emphasis added):

> Contemplation of an optimal system may provide techniques of analysis that would otherwise have been missed and, in certain special cases, it may go far to providing a solution. But in general its influence has been pernicious. It has directed economists' attention away from the main question, which is how *alternative arrangements will actually work in practice.*

Consider Brian Arthur's (1989) numerical example of path dependency in which the pay-offs to individual firms upon adopting either of two technologies (A or B) depend on the number of prior adoptions of each. Technology A has a higher pay-off than B if there are few prior adoptions, but the advantage switches to technology B if there have been many prior adoptions. The 'problem' is that if each potential adopter consults only its own immediate net gain, then each will select A and there will be 'lock-in' to an inferior technology. A tyranny of micromotives thereby obtains (Schelling, 1978).

As S. J. Liebowitz and Stephen Margolis observe of this argument, however, whether choice of technology A is inefficient or not depends on what assumptions are made about the state of knowledge (1992, p. 15). Also, even if individual parties could be assumed to know that technology B would become the more efficient choice after thirty or fifty adoptions, the added costs of collective action to deter individuals from choosing technology A would need to be taken into account. If it is unrealistic to assume that individuals possess the relevant knowledge that a switchover (from A to B) will occur upon thirty or fifty adoptions, or if, given that knowledge, the costs of orchestrating collective action are prohibitive, then the inefficiency in question is effectively irremediable through private ordering.

Sometimes, however, public ordering can do better. The issues here are whether (i) the public sector is better informed about network externalities, (ii) the requisite collective action is easier to orchestrate through the public sector (possibly by fiat), and/or (iii) the social net benefit calculus differs from the private in sufficient degree to warrant a different result. Absent *plausible* assumptions that would support a prospective net gain (in either private or social respects), the purported inefficiency is effectively irremediable.

That is regrettable, in that society would have done better if it had better knowledge or if a reorganization could have been accomplished more easily. Hypothetical regrets—the 'nirvana economics' to which E. A. G. Robinson (1934) and Harold Demsetz (1969) refer—are neither here nor there. Real costs in relation to real choices is what comparative institutional economics is all about.

Quantitative significance.   Path dependency, remediable or not, poses a greater challenge if the effects in question are large and lasting rather than small and temporary. It is not easy to document the quantitative significance of path dependency. Arthur provides a series of examples and emphasizes especially the video cassette recorder [where VHS prevailed over the Beta technology (1990, p. 92)] and nuclear power [where light water reactors prevailed over high-temperature, gas-cooled reactors (1990, p. 99)]. But while both are interesting examples of path dependency, it is not obvious that the 'winning' technology is significantly inferior to the loser, or even, for that matter, whether the winner is inferior at all.

Much the most widely cited case study is that of the typewriter keyboard. The QWERTY keyboard story has been set out by Paul David (1985, 1986). It illustrates 'why the study of economic history is a necessity in the making of good economists' (David, 1986, p. 30).

QWERTY refers to the first six letters on the top row of the standard typewriter keyboard. Today's keyboard layout is the same as that which was devised when the typewriter was first invented in 1870. The early mechanical technology was beset by typebar clashes, which clashes were mitigated by the QWERTY keyboard design.

Subsequent developments in typewriter technology relieved problems with typebar clashes, but the QWERTY keyboard persisted in the face of large (reported) discrepancies in typing speed between it and later keyboard designs. Thus the Dvorak Simplified Keyboard (DSK), which was patented in 1932, was so much faster than the standard keyboard that, according to United States Navy experiments, the 'increased efficiency obtained with DSK would amortize the cost of retraining a group of typists within the first ten days of their subsequent full-time employment' (David, 1986, p. 33). More recently, the Apple IIC computer comes with a built-in switch which instantly converts its keyboard from QWERTY to DSK: 'If as Apple advertising copy says, DSK "lets you type 20–40% faster," why did this superior design meet essentially the same resistance . . . ?' (David, 1986, p. 34).

There are several possibilities. These include non-rational behavior, conspiracy among typewriter firms, and path dependency (David, 1986, pp. 34–46). David makes a strong case for the last, but there is a fourth possibility, subsequently raised and examined by Liebowitz and Margolis (1990): neither the Navy study nor Apple advertising copy can support the astonishing claims made on their behalf. Upon going back to the archives and examining the data, Liebowitz and Margolis conclude that 'the standard history of QWERTY versus Dvorak is flawed and incomplete. . . . [The] claims of superiority of the Dvorak keyboard are suspect. The most dramatic claims are traceable to Dvorak himself, and the best documented experiments, as well as recent ergonomic studies, suggest little or no advantage for the Dvorak keyboard' (1990, p. 21). If that assessment stands up, then path dependence has had only modest efficiency effects in the QWERTY keyboard case. Such effects could easily fall below the threshold of remediable inefficiency.

Recent studies of the evolution of particular industries by sociologists also display path dependency. Population ecologists have used the ecological model of density-dependent legitimation and competition to examine the evolutionary process—both in particular industries [e.g. the telephone industry (Barnett and Carroll, 1993)] and in computer simulations. Glenn Carroll and Richard Harrison conclude from the latter that 'chance can play a major role in organizational evolution' (1992, p. 26).

Although their simulations do suggest that path dependency has large and lasting effects, Carroll and Harrison do not address the matter of remediability. Until a feasible reorganization of the decision process for choosing technologies can be described, the effect of which is to yield expected net private or social gains, it seems premature to describe their experiments as a test of the 'relative roles of chance and rationality' (Carroll and Harrison, 1992, p. 12). Large but irremediable inefficiencies nevertheless do raise serious issues for modelling economic organization.[18]

Perspectives. David contends and I am persuaded that 'there are many more QWERTY worlds lying out there' (1986, p. 47). An unchanged keyboard layout does not, however, strike me as the most important economic attribute of typewriter development from 1870 to the present. What about improvements in the mechanical technology? What about the electric typewriter? What about personal computers and laser printers? Why did these prevail in the face of path dependency? Were other 'structurally superior' technologies (as defined by Carroll and Harrison) bypassed? If, with lags and hitches, the more efficient technologies have regularly supplanted less efficient technologies, should not that be featured? Possibly the response is that 'everyone knows' that economizing is the main case: 'It goes without saying that economizing is the main case to which path dependency, monopolizing, efficient risk bearing, etc. are qualifications.'

The persistent neglect of economizing reasoning suggests otherwise. Thus the 'inhospitality tradition' in antitrust proceeded with sublime confidence that non-standard and unfamiliar business practices had little or no efficiency rationale but mainly had monopoly purpose and effect. Similarly, the vast inefficiencies that brought down the economies of the Soviet Union and Eastern Europe may now be obvious, but that could never have been gleaned from the postwar literature on comparative economic systems or from CIA intelligence estimates. The preoccupation in the area of business strategy with clever 'plans, ploys, and positioning' to the neglect of economizing is likewise testimony to the widespread tendency to disregard efficiency (Williamson, 1991b). And the view that the 'effective organization is (1) *garrulous*, (2) *clumsy*, (3) *superstitious*, (4) *hypocritical*, (5) *monstrous*, (6) *octopoid*,

---

[18] I have argued that dominant firm industries in which chance plays a role do warrant public policy intervention (Williamson, 1975, chapter 11), but whether net gains would really be realized by implementing that proposal (especially as international competition becomes more intensive) is problematic.

(7) *wandering*, and (8) *grouchy*' (Weick, 1977, pp. 193–194; emphasis in original) is reconciled with economizing only with effort. More recent 'social construction of industry' arguments reduce economizing to insignificance.[19]

If economizing really does get at the fundamentals, then that condition ought to be continuously featured. Some progress has been made (Zald, 1986), but there is little reason to be complacent.

Worker-managed Enterprises[20]

John Bonin and Louis Putterman define a worker-managed firm as (1987, p. 2):

> . . . a productive enterprise the ultimate decision-making rights over which are held by member-workers, on the basis of equality of those rights regardless of job, skill grade, or capital contribution. A full definition would state that no non-workers have a direct say in enterprising decisions, and that no workers are denied an equal say in those decisions. This definition does not imply that any particular set of decisions must be made by the full working group, nor does it imply a particular choice rule, such as majority voting. It says nothing about financing structures other than that financiers are not accorded direct decision-making powers in the enterprise by virtue of their non-labor contributions, and it does not say anything about how income is distributed among workers. On all of these matters, all that is implied is that ultimate decision-making rights are

---

[19] The 'new sociology of organization' holds that 'even in identical economic and technical conditions, outcomes may differ dramatically if social structures are different' (Granovetter, 1992, p. 9). The 'social construction of industry' argument is developed in a major book by Patrick McGuire, Mark Granovetter, and Michael Schwartz on the origins of the American electric power industry. That book has been described as follows (McGuire *et al.*, 1992, pp. 1–2):

> Building on detailed historical research, . . . this book treats the origins of the electrical utility industry from a sociological perspective. The idea that industries, like other economic institutions, are 'socially constructed,' derives from Granovetter's work on 'embeddedness' (1985) and presents an alternative to the new institutional economics, which contends that economic institutions should be understood as the efficient solutions to economic problems. . . .
>
> We believe that the way the utility industry developed from its inception in the 1880s was not the only technologically practical one, nor the most efficient. It arose because a set of powerful actors accessed certain techniques and applied them in a highly visible and profitable way. Those techniques resulted from the shared personal understandings, social connections, organizational conditions, and historical opportunities available to these actors. This success, in turn, triggered pressures for uniformity across regions, even when this excluded viable and possibly more efficient alternative technologies and organizational forms.
>
> Our argument resembles that made by economists Paul David and Brian Arthur on the 'lock-in' of inefficient technologies (such as the QWERTY keyboard . . .), but draws on the sociology of knowledge and of social structure.

[20] This subsection is based on Williamson (1989, pp. 41–43).

vested in the workers, and only in the workers. Thus, the basic definition centers on an allocation of governance rights, and is simultaneously economic and political.

This definition does not preclude hierarchical structure, specialized decision-making, a leadership élite, or marginal product payment schemes. It merely stipulates that finance can have no decision rights in the labor-managed enterprise. The question is whether these financial restrictions come at a cost. Putterman evidently believes that they do not, since he elsewhere endorses Roger McCain's proposal that the labor-managed enterprise be financed in part by 'risk participation bonds', where these purportedly differ from 'ordinary equity' only in that 'its owner can have no voting control over enterprise decisions, or over the election of enterprise management' (Putterman, 1984, p. 189). Since 'the labor-managed firm whose objective is to maximize profit-per-worker, having both ordinary and "risk participation" bonds at its disposal, would "attain the same allocation of resources as would a capitalist corporation, under comparable circumstances and informationally efficient markets"' (1984, p. 189), Putterman concludes that the labor-managed firm is on a parity.

The argument illustrates the hazards of addressing issues of economic organization within a framework that ignores, hence effectively suppresses, the role of governance. Operating, as he does, out of a firm-as-production-function framework, McCain (1977) is only concerned with examining the marginal conditions that obtain under two different set-ups, under both of which the firm is described as a production function.

Governance issues never arise and hence are not amenable to analysis within this orthodox framework. If, however, a critical—indeed, I would say, the critical—attribute of equity is the ability to exercise contingent control by concentrating votes and taking over the board of directors, then McCain's demonstration that allocative efficiency is identical under standard equity and risk participation bonds is simply inapposite.

Indeed, if risk participation finance is available on more adverse terms than standard equity because holders are provided with less security against mismanagement and expropriation, then the constraints that Bonin and Putterman have built into the worker-managed firm come at a cost. To be sure, the worker-managed firm may be able to offset financial disabilities by offering compensating advantages. If those advantages are not uniform but vary among firms and industries, then the net gains of the worker-managed firm will vary accordingly.

I submit that firms that can be mainly financed with debt are the obvious candidates for worker-management. Thus, if there is little equity-like capital at stake, then there is little reason for equity to ask or expect that pre-emptive control over the board of directors will be awarded to equity as a contractual safeguard. The question then is what types of firms best qualify for a preponderance of debt financing?

As discussed elsewhere, peer group forms of organization can and do operate well in small enterprises where the membership has been carefully screened and is committed to democratic ideals (Williamson, 1975, chapter 3). Also, the partnership form of organization works well in professional organizations, such as law and accounting firms, where the need for firm-specific physical capital is small (Hansmann, 1988). There being little need for equity capital to support investment in such firms, the control of these firms naturally accrues to those who supply specialized human assets (Williamson, 1989, pp. 24–26). These exceptions aside, 'third forms' experience serious incentive disabilities.[21]

Trust

There is a growing tendency, among economists and sociologists alike, to describe trust in calculative terms: both rational choice sociologists (Coleman, 1990) and game theorists (Dasgupta, 1988) treat trust as a subclass of risk. I concur with Granovetter that to craft credible commitments (through the use of bonds, hostages, information disclosure rules, specialized dispute settlement mechanisms, and the like) is to create functional substitutes for trust (Granovetter, 1985, p. 487). Albeit vitally important to economic organization, such substitutes should not be confused with (real) trust.[22]

That calculativeness plays a larger role in economics than in the other social sciences is evident from my discussion of farsighted contracting. But calculativeness can also be taken to excesses, which is the main point in my discussion of atmosphere (*see* above). Sometimes, however, an altogether different orientation is needed. Thus whereas the response to excesses of monitoring is to *be more sophisticatedly calculative* (take the dysfunctional

[21] The limits of third forms for organizing *large* enterprises with *variegated* membership are severe in both theory and fact. To be sure, some students of economic organization remain sanguine (Horvat, 1991). The evidence from Eastern Europe has not, however, been supportive. Maciej Iwanek (1991, p. 12) remarks of the Polish experience that 'except [among] advocates of workers' management, nobody believes that the . . . governance scheme of state-owned enterprises [by workers' management] creates strong incentives'; Manuel Hinds (1990, p. 28) concludes that 'absenteeism, shirking, and lack of initiative are pervasive in the self-managed firm'; Janos Kornai (1990, p. 144) counsels that 'it would be intellectually dishonest to hide the evidence concerning the weakness of third forms'.

[22] Note that the trust that Granovetter ascribes to ongoing relations can go either way—frequent suggestions to the contrary notwithstanding. That is because experience can be either good (more confidence) or bad (less confidence), which, if contracts of both kinds are renewed, will show up in differential contracting (Crocker and Reynolds, 1993).

effects into account), there are other circumstances where the response is to *avoid being calculative*.

As I have argued elsewhere (Williamson, 1993a), relations that are subject to continuous Bayesian updating of probabilities based on experience are thoroughly calculative. And because commercial relations are invariably calculative, the concept of calculated risk (rather than calculated trust) should be used to describe commercial transactions.

Continuous experience rating need not obtain everywhere, however. Indeed, because some personal relations are unique and because continuous updating, even if only of a low-grade kind, can have corrosive effects,[23] certain personal relations are treated in a nearly non-calculative way. That is accomplished by a discrete structural reclassification, according to which personal relations are dealt with on an all-or-none, rather than a continuous updating, basis.

The upshot is that personal trust relations and commercial/calculative risk relations differ in kind. Commercial relations are in no way denigrated as a result (Robbins, 1933, pp. 179–180).

Tosh

The legal philosopher, Lon Fuller, distinguished between 'essentials' and 'tosh', where the former involves an examination of the 'rational core' (1978, pp. 359–362) and tosh is preoccupied with 'superfluous rituals, rules of procedure without clear purpose, [and] needless precautions preserved through habit' (1978, p. 356). According to Fuller, to focus on the latter would 'abandon any hope of fruitful analysis' (1978, p. 360).

I think that this last goes too far: a place should be made for tosh, but tosh should be kept in its place.[24] Consider in this connection the Friedland and Alford interpretation of Clifford Geertz's description of Balinese cockfights (1991, pp. 247–248; emphasis added):

> Enormous sums of money can change hands at each match, sums that are *irrational* from an individualistic, utilitarian perspective. The higher the sums, the more *evenly matched* the cocks are arranged to be, and the more likely the odds on which the bet is made are even. The greater the sum of

---

[23] Not only can intendedly non-calculative relations be upset by type I error, according to which a true relation is incorrectly classified as false, but calculativeness may be subject to (involuntary) positive feedback. Intendedly non-calculative relations that are continuously subject to being reclassified as calculative are, in effect, calculative.

[24] The evolution of cooperation between opposed armies or gangs that are purportedly engaged in 'deadly combat' is illustrated by Robert Axelrod's examination of 'The Live-and-Let-Live System in Trench Warfare in World War I' (1984, pp. 73–87). Interesting and important as the live-and-let-live rituals were, these non-violent practices should not be mistaken for the main case. Rather, these rituals were the exception to the main case, which was that British and German troops were at war.

money at stake, the more the decision to bet is not individualistic and utilitarian, but collective—one bets with one's kin or village—and status-oriented.

That there are social pressures to support one's kin or village is a sociological argument. Absent these pressures, the concentration of bets on evenly matched cocks would be difficult to explain. It does not, however, follow that it is 'irrational' to bet enormous sums on evenly matched cocks. Given the social context, it has become non-viable, as a betting matter, to fight unevenly matched cocks.

Thus suppose that the objective odds for a proposed match are 4:1. Considerations of local pride may reduce the effective odds to 3:2. Such a match will not attract much betting because those from the village with the lesser cock who view it from an individualistic, acquisitive perspective will make only perfunctory bets. Accordingly, the only interesting matches are those *where social pressures are relieved by the even odds.*[25] The 'symbolic construction of reality' to which Friedland and Alford refer thus has real consequences. It delimits the feasible set within which rationality operates; but rationality is fully operative thereafter.

One interpretation of this is that tosh has discrete structural effects and that rationality, operating through the marginal calculus, applies thereafter. Indeed, that seems to fit the Balinese cockfight rather well. Whether the social construction of reality has such important consequences more generally is then the question. My sense is that it varies with the circumstances.

Tosh is arguably more important in non-commercial circumstances—state, family, religion—than in the commercial sector, although the Hamilton and Biggart (1988) examination of differences in corporate forms in Far East Asia might be offered as a contradiction. Hamilton and Biggart, however, go well beyond tosh (as described by Fuller) to implicate the institutional environment—to include property rights, contract law, politics, and the like.

Thus although both tosh (superfluous rituals) and the institutional environment refer to background conditions, the one should not be confused with the other. Tosh is a source of interesting variety and adds spice to life. Core features of the institutional environment, as defined by North (1986,

----

[25] Richard M. Coughlin contends that the 'essence' of the socio-economic approach proposed by Amitai Etzioni is that (1992, p. 3):

> Human behavior must be understood in terms of the fusion of individually-based and communally-based forces, which Etzioni labels the *I and We*. The *I* represents the individual acting in pursuit of his or her own pleasure; the *We* stands for the obligations and restraints imposed by the collectivity.

That is close to the interpretation that I advance here to interpret the Balinese cock fights.

1991) and others (Sundaram and Black, 1992), are arguably more important, however, to the study of comparative economic organization.[26]

8. *Conclusions*

The science of organization to which Barnard made reference (1938, p. 290) over fifty years ago has made major strides in the past ten and twenty years. All of the social sciences have a stake in this, but none more than economics and organization theory.

If the schematic set out in Figure 1 is an accurate way to characterize much of what is going on, then the economics of governance needs to be informed both from the level of the institutional environment (where sociology has a lot to contribute) and from the level of the individual (where psychology is implicated). The intertemporal process transformations that take place within the institutions of governance (with respect to which organization theory has a lot to say) are also pertinent. The overall schema works out of the rational spirit approach that is associated with economics.[27]

This multilevel approach relieves some, perhaps much, of the strain to which Baron and Hannan refer: 'we think it important to understand the different assumptions and forms of reasoning used in contemporary sociology versus economics. . . . These disciplinary differences . . . represent major barriers to intellectual trade between economics and sociology' (1992, p. 13). If, however, deep knowledge at several levels is needed and is beyond the competence of any one discipline, and if a systems conception can be devised in which intellectual trade among levels can be accomplished, then some of the worst misunderstandings of the past can be put behind us.

I summarize here what I see to be some of the principal respects in which the healthy tension to which I referred at the outset has supported intellectual trade, of which more is in prospect.

Organization Theory Supports for Transaction Cost Economics

Behavioral assumptions. Organization theory's insistence on workably realistic, as opposed to analytically convenient, behavioral assumptions is a

---

[26] This is pertinent, among other things, to the study of the multinational enterprise. As Anant Sundaram and J. Stewart Black observe, MNEs 'pursue different entry/involvement strategies in different markets and for different products at any given time' (1992, p. 740). Their argument, that transaction cost economics 'is inadequate for explaining simultaneously different entry modes because . . . asset specificity . . . [is] largely the same the world over' (1992, p. 740) assumes that the governance level operates independently of the institutional environment under a transaction cost set-up. That is mistaken.

[27] I borrow the term 'rational spirit' from Kenneth Arrow (1974, p. 16). The rational spirit approach holds that there is a *logic* to organization and that this logic is mainly discerned by the relentless application of economic reasoning (subject, however, to cognitive constraints). The rational spirit approach is akin to but somewhat weaker (in that it eschews stronger forms of utility maximization) than the 'rational choice' approach associated with James Coleman (1990).

healthy antidote. Transaction cost economics responds by describing economic actors in terms of bounded rationality and opportunism.

Adaptation.   The cooperative adaptation emphasized by Barnard is joined with the autonomous adaptation of Hayek, with the result that transaction cost economics makes an appropriate place for both market and hierarchy.

Unanticipated consequences.   The subtle and unintended consequences of control and organization need to be uncovered, whereupon provision can be made for these in the *ex ante* organizational design.

Politics.   Because property rights in the public arena are shaped by democratic politics, provision needs to be made for these in the *ex ante* organizational design of public sector bureaus.

Embeddedness.   The first-order response to the proposition that embeddedness matters is to regard the institutional environment as a locus of shift parameters, changes in which change the comparative costs of governance.

Discrete structural analysis.   Each generic form of organization is described as a syndrome of attributes and possesses its own logic. These discreteness features need to be discovered and explicated both within and between sectors.

Transaction Cost Economics Supports for Organization Theory

Unit of analysis.   Any theory of organization that fails to name the unit of analysis out of which it works and thereafter identify the critical dimensions with respect to which that unit of analysis varies is non-operational at best and could be bankrupt.

The main case.   All rival theories of organization are asked to nominate the main case, develop the refutable implications that accrue thereto, and examine the data. Economizing on transaction costs is the transaction cost economics candidate.

Farsighted contracting.   Looking ahead, recognizing hazards, and folding these back into the design of governance is often feasible and explains a very considerable amount of organizational variety.

Trade-offs.   Because each mode of governance is a syndrome of attributes, the move from one mode to another involves trade-offs. The key trade-offs need to be stated and explicated.

Remediability. Relevant choices among feasible forms of organization are what the analysis of comparative economic organization is all about.

References

Alchian, A. (1961), *Some Economics of Property*. RAND D-2316. RAND Corporation: Santa Monica.

Alchian, A. and H. Demsetz (1972), 'Production, Information Costs, and Economic Organization,' *American Economic Review*, 62 (December), 777–795.

Alchian, A. and S. Woodward (1987), 'Reflections on the Theory of the Firm,' *Journal of Institutional and Theoretical Economics*, 143 (March), 110–136.

Aoki, M. (1988), *Information, Incentives, and Bargaining in the Japanese Economy*. Cambridge University Press: New York.

Aoki, M. (1990), 'Toward an Economic Model of the Japanese Firm,' *Journal of Economic Literature*, 28 (March), 1–27.

Aoki, M. (1992), 'The Japanese Firm as a System of Attributes: A Survey and Research Agenda,' unpublished manuscript.

Arrow, K. J. (1974). *The Limits of Organization*, 1st edn. W. W. Norton: New York.

Arthur, B. (1989), 'Competing Technologies, Increasing Returns, and Lock-In by Historical Events,' *Economic Journal*, 99 (March), 116–131.

Arthur, B. (1990), 'Positive Feedbacks in the Economy,' *Scientific American* (February), 92–99.

Asanuma, B. (1989), 'Manufacturer-Supplier Relationships in Japan and The Concept of Relationship-Specific Skill,' *Journal of Japanese and International Economies*, 3, 1–30.

Axelrod, R. (1984), *The Evolution of Cooperation*. Basic Books: New York.

Bain, J. (1956), *Barriers to New Competition*. John Wiley & Sons: New York.

Barnard, C. (1938). *The Functions of the Executive*. Harvard University Press (fifteenth printing, 1962): Cambridge, MA.

Barnett, W. and G. Carroll (1993), 'How Institutional Constraints Affected the Organization of the Early American Telephone Industry,' *Journal of Law, Economics, and Organization*, 9 (April).

Baron, J. and M. Hannan (1992), 'The Impact of Economics on Contemporary Sociology,' unpublished manuscript.

Becker, G. (1976), *The Economic Approach to Human Behavior*. University of Chicago Press: Chicago.

Berglof, E. (1989), 'Capital Structure as a Mechanism of Control—A Comparison of Financial Systems,' in M. Aoki, B. Gustafsson, and O. Williamson (eds), *The Firm as a Nexus of Treaties*. Sage: London, pp. 237–262.

Bergson, A. (1948), 'Socialist Economies,' in Howard Ellis (ed.), *Survey of Contemporary Economies*. Philadelphia: Blakiston, pp. 430–458.

Bonin, J. and L. Putterman (1987), *Economics of Cooperation and Labor Managed Economies*. Cambridge University Press: New York.

Bowles, S. and H. Gintis (1993), 'The Revenge of Homo Economicus: Contested Exchange and the Revival of Political Economy,' *Journal of Economic Perspectives* (Winter).

Bradach, J. and R. Eccles (1989), 'Price, Authority, and Trust,' *American Review of Sociology*, 15, 97–118.

Bridgeman, P. (1955), *Reflections of a Physicist*, 2nd edn. Philosophical Library: New York.

Bromley, D. (1989), *Economic Interests and Institutions*. Basil Blackwell: New York.

Buxbaum, R. (1985), 'Modification and Adaptation of Contracts: American Legal Developments,' *Studies in Transnational Law*, 3, 31–54.

Carroll, G. and J. R. Harrison (1992), 'Chance and Rationality in Organizational Evolution,' unpublished manuscript.

Coase, R. H. (1937), 'The Nature of the Firm,' *Economica*, 4, 386–405.

Coase, R. H. (1959), 'The Federal Communications Commission,' *Journal of Law and Economics*, 2 (October), 1–40.

Coase, R. H. (1960), 'The Problem of Social Cost,' *Journal of Law and Economics*, 3 (October), 1–44.

Coase, R. H. (1964), 'The Regulated Industries: Discussion,' *American Economic Review*, 54 (May), 194–197.

Coase, R. H. (1972), 'Industrial Organization: A Proposal for Research,' in V. R. Fuchs (ed.), *Policy Issues and Research Opportunities in Industrial Organization*. National Bureau of Economic Research: New York, pp. 59–73.

Coase, R. H. (1984), 'The New Institutional Economics,' *Journal of Institutional and Theoretical Economics*, 140 (March), 229–231.

Coleman, J. (1982). *The Asymmetric Society*. Syracuse University Press: Syracuse, NY.

Coleman, J. (1990), *The Foundations of Social Theory*. Harvard University Press: Cambridge, MA.

Commons, J. R. (1924), *Legal Foundations of Capitalism*. Macmillan: New York.

Commons, J. R. (1934), *Institutional Economics*. University of Wisconsin Press: Madison.

Coughlin, R. (1992), 'Interdisciplinary Nature of Socio-Economics,' unpublished manuscript.

Crocker, K. and K. Reynolds (1993), 'The Efficiency of Incomplete Contracts: An Empirical Analysis of Air Force Engine Procurement,' *Rand Journal of Economics* (Spring).

Crozier, M. (1964), *The Bureaucratic Phenomenon*. University of Chicago Press: Chicago.

Cyert, R. M. and J. G. March (1963), *A Behavioral Theory of the Firm*. Prentice-Hall: Englewood Cliffs, NJ.

Dasgupta, P. (1988), 'Trust as a Commodity,' in D. Gambetta (ed.), *Trust: The Making and Breaking of Cooperative Relations*. Basil Blackwell: Oxford, pp. 49–72.

David, P. (1985), 'Clio in the Economics of QWERTY,' *American Economic Review*, 75 (May), 332–337.

David, P. (1986), 'Understanding the Economics of QWERTY: The Necessity of History,' in W. N. Parker (ed.), *Economic History and the Modern Economist*. Basil Blackwell: New York.

David, P. (1992), 'Heroes, Herds, and Hysteresis in Technological History,' *Industrial and Corporate Change*, 1, 129–180.

Davis, G. F. and W. W. Powell (1992), 'Organization-Environment Relations,' in M. Dunnette (ed.), *Handbook of Industrial and Organizational Psychology*, Vol. 3 (2nd edn). Consulting Psychologists Press: New York, pp. 315–375.

Davis, L. E. and D. C. North (1971), *Institutional Change and American Economic Growth*. Cambridge University Press: Cambridge.

Demsetz, H. (1967), 'Toward a Theory of Property Rights,' *American Economic Review*, 57 (May), 347–359.

Demsetz, H. (1969), 'Information and Efficiency: Another Viewpoint,' *Journal of Law and Economics*, 12 (April), 1–22.

DiMaggio, P. and W. Powell (1991), 'Introduction,' in Walter Powell and Paul DiMaggio (eds), *The New Institutionalism in Organizational Analysis*. University of Chicago Press: Chicago, pp. 1–38.

Dixit, A. (1980), 'The Role of Investment in Entry Deterrence,' *Economic Journal*, 90 (March), 95–106.

Dore, R. (1983), 'Goodwill and the Spirit of Market Capitalism,' *British Journal of Sociology*, 34 (December), 459–482.

Farnsworth, E. A. (1968), 'Disputes Over Omissions in Contracts,' *Columbia Law Review*, 68 (May), 860–891.

Frank, R. (1992), 'Melding Sociology and Economics,' *Journal of Economic Literature*, 30 (March), 147–170.

Friedland, R. and R. Alford (1991), 'Bringing Society Back In: Symbols, Practices, and Institutional Contradictions,' in Walter Powell and Paul DiMaggio (eds), *The New Institutionalism in Organizational Analysis*. University of Chicago Press: Chicago, pp. 232–266.

Fuller, L. L. (1978), 'The Forms and Limits of Adjudication,' *Harvard Law Review*, 92, 353–409.

Fuller, L. L. (1981), 'Human Interaction and the Law,' in Kenneth I. Winston (ed.), *The Principles of Social Order: Selected Essays on Lon L. Fuller*. Duke University Press, Durham, NC, pp. 212–246.

Furubotn, E. and S. Pejovich (1974), *The Economics of Property Rights*. Ballinger: Cambridge, MA.

Furubotn, E. and R. Richter (1991), *The New Institutional Economics*. Texas A&M University Press: College Station, TX.

Georgescu-Roegen, N. (1971), *The Entropy Law and Economic Process*. Harvard University Press: Cambridge, MA.

Gerlach, M. (1992), *Alliance Capitalism*. University of California Press: Berkeley, CA.

Gouldner, A. W. (1954), *Industrial Bureaucracy*. Free Press: Glencoe, IL.

Granovetter, M. (1985), 'Economic Action and Social Structure: The Problem of Embeddedness,' *American Journal of Sociology*, 91 (November), 481–501.

Granovetter, M. (1988), 'The Sociological and Economic Approaches to Labor Market Analysis,' in George Farkas and Paula England (eds), *Industries, Firms, and Jobs*. Plenum: New York, pp. 187–218.

Granovetter, M. (1990), 'The Old and the New Economic Sociology: A History and an Agenda,' in Roger Friedland and A. F. Robertson (eds), *Beyond the Marketplace*. Aldine: New York.

Granovetter, M. (1992), 'Economic Institutions as Social Constructions: A Framework for Analysis,' *Acta Sociologica*, 35, 3–11.

Grossekettler, H. (1989), 'On Designing an Economic Order: The Contributions of the Freiburg School,' in Donald Walker (ed.), *Perspectives on the History of Economic Thought, Vol. II*. Edward Elgar: Aldershot, pp. 38–84.

Hamilton, G. and N. Biggart (1988) 'Market, Culture, and Authority,' *American Journal of Sociology* (Supplement), 94, S52–S94.

Hansmann, H. (1988), 'The Ownership of the Firm,' *Journal of Law, Economics, and Organization*, 4, 267–303.

Harberger, A. (1954), 'Monopoly and Resource Allocation,' *American Economic Review*, 44 (May), 77–87.

Hart, O. (1990), 'An Economist's Perspective on the Theory of the Firm,' in Oliver Williamson (ed.), *Organization Theory*. Oxford University Press: New York, pp. 154–171.

Hayek, F. (1945), 'The Use of Knowledge in Society,' *American Economic Review*, 35 (September), 519–530.

Hechter, M. (1987), *Principles of Group Solidarity*. University of California Press: Berkeley, CA.

Heide, J. and G. John (1988), 'The Role of Dependence Balancing in Safeguarding Transaction-Specific Assets in Conventional Channels,' *Journal of Marketing*, 52 (January), 20–35.

Helper, S. and D. Levine (1992), 'Long-Term Supplier Relations and Product-Market Structure,' *Journal of Law, Economics, and Organization*, 8 (October), 561–581.

Hinds, M. (1990), 'Issues in the Introduction of Market Forces in Eastern European Socialist Economies,' The World Bank. Report No. IDP-0057.

Horvat, B. (1991), 'Review of Janos Kornai, The Road to a Free Economy,' *Journal of Economic Behavior and Organization*, 15 (May), 408–410.

Hutchison, T. (1984). 'Institutional Economics Old and New,' *Journal of Institutional and Theoretical Economics*, 140 (March), 20–29.

Iwanek, M. (1991), 'Issues of Institutions Transformations and Ownership Changes in Poland,' *Journal of Institutional and Theoretical Economics*, 147, 83–95.

Jensen, M. (1983), 'Organization Theory and Methodology,' *Accounting Review*, 50 (April), 319–339.

Joskow, P. L. (1985), 'Vertical Integration and Long-Term Contracts,' *Journal of Law, Economics, and Organization*, 1 (Spring), 33–80.

Joskow, P. L. (1988), 'Asset Specificity and the Structure of Vertical Relationships: Empirical Evidence,' *Journal of Law, Economics, and Organization*, 4 (Spring), 95–117.

Klein, B., R. A. Crawford, and A. A. Alchian (1978), 'Vertical Integration, Appropriable Rents, and the Competitive Contracting Process,' *Journal of Law and Economics*, 21 (October), 297–326.

Koopmans, T. (1957), *Three Essays on the State of Economic Science*. McGraw-Hill Book Company: New York.

Kornai, J. (1990), 'The Affinity Between Ownership Forms and Coordination Mechanisms: The Common Experience of Reform in Socialist Countries,' *Journal of Economic Perspectives*, 4 (Summer), 131–147.

Kreps, D. M. (1990), 'Corporate Culture and Economic Theory,' in James Alt and Kenneth Shepsle (eds), *Perspectives on Positive Political Economy*. Cambridge University Press: New York, pp. 90–143.

Kreps, D. M. (1992), '(How) Can Game Theory Lead to a Unified Theory of Organization?' unpublished manuscript.

Lange, O. (1938), 'On the Theory of Economic Socialism,' in Benjamin Lippincott (ed.), *On the Economic Theory of Socialism*. University of Minnesota Press: Minneapolis, pp. 55–143.

Lewis, T. (1983), 'Preemption, Divestiture, and Forward Contracting,' *American Economic Review*, 73, (December), 1092–1101.

Liebowitz, S. J. (1992), 'Path Dependency, Lock-In, and History,' unpublished manuscript.

Liebowitz, S. J. and S. Margolis (1990), 'The Fable of the Keys,' *Journal of Law and Economics*, 33 (April), 1–26.

Lincoln, J. (1990), 'Japanese Organization and Organization Theory,' *Research in Organizational Behavior*, 12, 255–294.

Llewellyn, K. N. (1931), 'What Price Contract? An Essay in Perspective,' *Yale Law Journal*, 40 (May), 704–751.

McCain, R. (1977), 'On the Optimal Financial Environment for Worker Cooperatives,' *Zeitschrift für Nationalekonomie*, 37, 355–384.

McCullough, D. (1992), *Truman*. Simon & Schuster: New York.

McGuire, P., M. Granovetter, and M. Schwartz (1992), 'The Social Construction of Industry' (a book prospectus).

Machiavelli, N. (1952), *The Prince*. New American Library: New York.

Macneil, I. R. (1974), 'The Many Futures of Contracts,' *Southern California Law Review*, 47 (May), 691–816.

Macneil, I. R. (1978), 'Contracts: Adjustments of Long-Term Economic Relations Under Classical, Neoclassical, and Relational Contract Law,' *Northwestern University Law Review*, 72, 854–906.

March, J. G. (1988), *Decisions and Organizations*. Basil Blackwell: Oxford.

March, J. G. and H. A. Simon (1958), *Organizations*. John Wiley & Sons: New York.

Marschak, J. (1968), 'Economics of Inquiring, Communicating, Deciding,' *American Economic Review*, 58 (May), 1–18.

Masten, S. (1984), 'The Organization of Production: Evidence from the Aerospace Industry,' *Journal of Law and Economics*, 27 (October), 403–418.

Masten, S. (1992), 'Transaction Costs, Mistakes, and Performance: Assessing the Importance of Governance,' *Management and Decision Sciences*, in press.

Matthews, R. C. O. (1986), 'The Economics of Institutions and the Sources of Economic Growth,' *Economic Journal*, 96 (December), 903–918.

Merton, R. (1936), 'The Unanticipated Consequences of Purposive Social Action,' *American Sociological Review*, 1, 894–904.

Michels, R. (1962), *Political Parties*. Free Press: Glencoe, IL.

Miles, R. and C. Snow (1992), 'Causes of Failure in Network Organizations,' *California Management Review*, 34 (Summer), 53–72.

Moe, T. (1990), 'Political Institutions: The Neglected Side of the Story: Comment,' *Journal of Law, Economics, and Organization*, 6 (Special Issue), 213–254.

Mokyr, J. (1990), *The Lever of Riches*. Oxford University Press: New York.

Nelson, R. R. and S. G. Winter (1982), *An Evolutionary Theory of Economic Change*. Harvard University Press: Cambridge, MA.

Newell, A. and H. Simon (1972), *Human Problem Solving*. Prentice-Hall: Englewood Cliffs, NJ.

North, D. (1986), 'The New Institutional Economics,' *Journal of Institutional and Theoretical Economics*, 142, 230–237.

North, D. (1991), 'Institutions,' *Journal of Economic Perspectives*, 5 (Winter), 97–112.

Palay, T. (1984), 'Comparative Institutional Economics: The Governance of Rail Freight Contracting,' *Journal of Legal Studies*, 13 (June), 265–288.

Palay, T. (1985), 'The Avoidance of Regulatory Constraints: The Use of Informal Contracts,' *Journal of Law, Economics, and Organization*, 1 (Spring).

Parsons, T. and N. Smelser (1956), *Economy and Society*. New York: The Free Press.

Penrose, E. (1959), *The Theory of Growth of the Firm*. New York: John Wiley & Sons.

Perrow, C. (1992), 'Review of the New Competition,' *Administrative Science Quarterly*, 37 (March), 162–166.

Pfeffer, J. (1981), *Power in Organizations*. Marshfield, MA: Pitman Publishing.

Polanyi, M. (1962), *Personal Knowledge: Towards a Post-Critical Philosophy*. Harper & Row: New York.

Posner, R. (1993), 'The New Institutional Economics Meets Law and Economics,' *Journal of Institutional and Theoretical Economics*, 149 (March), 73–87.

Putterman, L. (1984). 'On Some Recent Explanations of Why Capital Hires Labor,' *Economic Inquiry*, 22, 171–187.

Robbins, Lionel (ed.) (1933), *The Common Sense of Political Economy, and Selected Papers on Economic Theory*, by Philip Wicksteed. G. Routledge and Sons, Ltd.: London.

Robinson, E. A. G. (1934), 'The Problem of Management and the Size of Firms,' *Economic Journal*, 44 (June), 240–254.

Schelling, T. C. (1978), *Micromotives and Macrobehavior*. Norton: New York.

Scherer, F. M. (1970), *Industrial Market Structure and Economic Performance*. Rand McNally & Company: Chicago.

Schotter, A. (1981), *The Economic Theory of Social Institutions*. Cambridge University Press: New York.

Schmid, A. (1972), 'Analytical Institutional Economics,' *American Journal of Agricultural Economics*, 54, 893–901.

Schumpeter, J. A. (1942), *Capitalism, Socialism, and Democracy*. Harper & Row: New York.

Schumpeter, J. A. (1947), 'The Creative Response in Economic History,' *Journal of Economic History*, 7 (November), 149–159.

Schumpeter, J. A. (1989), *Essays on Entrepreneurs, Innovations, Business Cycles, and the Evolution of Capitalism*. New Brunswick: Transaction Publishers.

Scott, W. R. (1992), 'Institutions and Organizations: Toward a Theoretical Synthesis,' unpublished manuscript.

Selznick, P. (1949), *TVA and the Grass Roots*. University of California Press: Berkeley, CA.

Selznick, P. (1957), *Leadership in Administration*. Harper & Row: New York.

Shapiro, C. (1989), 'The Theory of Business Strategy,' *Rand Journal of Economics*, 20 (Spring), 125–137.

Sheard, P. (1989), 'The Main Bank System and Corporate Monitoring in Japan,' *Journal of Economic Behavior and Organization*, 11 (May), 399–422.

Shelanski, H. (1991), 'Empirical Research in Transaction Cost Economics: A Survey and Assessment,' unpublished manuscript, University of California, Berkeley.

Shelanski, H. (1993), 'Transfer Pricing,' unpublished Ph.D. Dissertation, University of California, Berkeley.

Simon, H. (1957a), *Administrative Behavior*. Macmillan: New York, 2nd edn.

Simon, H. (1957b), *Models of Man*. John Wiley & Sons: New York.

Simon, H. (1978), 'Rationality as Process and as Product of Thought,' *American Economic Review*, 68 (May), 1–16.

Simon, H. (1983), *Reason in Human Affairs*. Stanford University Press: Stanford.

Simon, H. (1985), 'Human Nature in Politics: The Dialogue of Psychology with Political Science,' *American Political Science Review*, 79, 293–304.

Simon, H. (1991), 'Organizations and Markets,' *Journal of Economic Perspectives*, 5 (Spring), 25–44.

Stigler, G. J. (1968), *The Organization of Industry*. Richard D. Irwin: Homewood, IL.

Stigler, G. J. (1983), Comments in Edmund Kitch (ed.), 'The Fire of Truth: A Rembrance of Law and Ecpnomics at Chicago, 1932–1970,' *Journal of Law and Economics*, 26 (April), 163–234.

Sundaram, A. and J. S. Black (1992), 'The Environment and Internal Organization of Multinational Enterprise,' *Academy of Management Review*, 17 (October), 729–757.

Swedberg, R. (1987), 'Economic Sociology: Past and Present,' *Current Sociology*, 35, 1–221.

Swedberg, R. (1990), *Economics and Sociology: On Redefining Their Boundaries*. Princeton University Press: Princeton, NJ.

Swedberg, R. (1991), 'Major Traditions of Economic Sociology,' *Annual Review of Sociology*, 17, 251–276.

Teece, D. J. (1986), 'Profiting From Technological Innovation,' *Research Policy*, 15 (December), 285–305.

Teece, D. J., G. Pisano, and A. Shuen (1990), 'Firm Capabilities, Resources, and the Concept of Strategy' (unpublished manuscript, University of California, Berkeley).

Van de Ven, A. (1993), 'The Institutional Theory of John R. Commons: A Review and Commentary,' *Academy of Management Review*, 18 (January), 139–152.

Waldrop, M. M. (1992), *Complexity*. New York: Simon & Schuster.

Weick, K. E. (1977), 'Re-Punctuating the Problem,' in Paul S. Goodman, Johannes M. Pennings (eds), *New Perspectives on Organizational Effectiveness*. Jossey-Bass: San Francisco, pp. 193–225.

Wernerfelt, B. (1984). 'A Resource-Based View of the Firm,' *Strategic management Journal*, 5, 171–180.

Williamson, O. E. (1968), 'Economies as an Antitrust Defense: The Welfare Tradeoffs,' *American Economic Review*, 58 (March), 18–35.

Williamson, O. E. (1975), *Markets and Hierarchies: Analysis and Antitrust Implications*. Free Press: New York.

Williamson, O. E. (1979), 'Transaction-Cost Economics: The Governance of Contractual Relations,' *Journal of Law and Economics*, 22 (October), 233–261.

Williamson, O. E. (1981), 'The Economics of Organization: The Transaction Cost Approach,' *American Journal of Sociology*, 87 (November), 548–577.

Williamson, O. E. (1983), 'Credible Commitments: Using Hostages to Support Exchange,' *American Economic Review*, 73 (September), 519–540.

Williamson, O. E. (1985), *The Economic Institutions of Capitalism*. Free Press: New York.

Williamson, O. E. (1988a), 'The Logic of Economic Organization,' *Journal of Law, Economics, and Organization*, 4 (Spring), 65–93.

Williamson, O. E. (1988b), 'The Economics and Sociology of Organization: Promoting a Dialogue,' in G. Farkas and P. England (eds), *Industries, Firms, and Jobs*. Plenum: New York, pp. 159–185.

Williamson, O. E. (1989), 'Internal Economic Organization,' in O. E. Williamson, S.-E. Sjostrand, and J. Johanson (eds), *Perspectives on the Economics of Organization*. Lund University Press: Lund, Sweden, pp. 7–48.

Williamson, O. E. (1991a), 'Comparative Economic Organization: The Analysis of Discrete Structural Alternatives,' *Administrative Science Quarterly*, 36 (June), 269–296.

Williamson, O. E. (1991b), 'Economic Institutions: Spontaneous and Intentional Governance,' *Journal of Law, Economics, and Organization*, 7 (Special Issue), 159–187.

Williamson, O. E. (1991c), 'Strategizing, Economizing, and Economic Organization,' *Strategic Management Journal*, 12, 75–94.

Williamson, O. E. (1993a), 'Calculativeness, Trust, and Economic Organization,' *Journal of Law and Economics* 36 (April), 221–270.

Williamson, O. E. (1993b). 'The Evolving Science of Organization,' *Journal of Institutional and Theoretical Economics*, 149 (March), 36–63.

Zald, M. (1987), 'Review Essay: The New Institutional Economics,' *American Journal of Sociology*, 93 (November), 701–708.

Coase Revisited: Business Groups in the Modern Economy

MARK GRANOVETTER

(Department of Sociology, Northwestern University, Evanston, IL 60208-1330, USA)

Ronald Coase's celebrated query as to why economic actors typically aggregate into entities called 'firms' rather than transacting as individuals in a market has engendered a vigorous stream of research. This paper asks a parallel question: why is it that in all modern economies, firms themselves aggregate into larger entities, often more stable than any literature predicts, which are here referred to as 'business groups'? After establishing some working definitions, and discussing the curious conjunction of empirical importance and analytical invisibility of business groups, an attempt is made to establish the most significant dimensions along which such groups vary. We end with some speculations on the role of these groups in economic development.

1. Coase Encounters of the Second Kind[1]

In 1937, Ronald Coase began a quiet revolution in economic theory, by asking the innocuous question: why do firms exist? Coase wondered why if, as competitive market theory suggested, the price system perfectly coordinated the provision of goods and services, we would have units called firms and individuals called managers, supplying still more coordination.[2] His now-famous answer, greatly elaborated by Oliver Williamson in his 'markets and hierarchies' research program (1975, 1985), was that firms existed because in the presence of transaction costs, the price system could not in fact provide all the coordination required to transact business anew for each project and enterprise, across a 'market' boundary. Coase pointed to the

> costs of using the pricing mechanism. What the prices are have to be
> discovered. There are negotiations to be undertaken, contracts have to be

---

[1] Credit (or blame) for this subtitle goes to Charles Tilly.

[2] See Coase (1993) for an account of how this question occurred to him.

drawn up, inspections have to be made, arrangements . . . to settle disputes
. . . It was the avoidance of the costs of carrying out transactions through
the market that could explain the existence of the firm in which the allocation
of factors came about as a result of administrative decisions . . . (Coase,
1993, p. 230).

Coase's question was pathbreaking because it recognized that among the
fictions of classical economics, the depiction of economic agents as always
acting alone rather than cooperating with others in a defined social unit was
especially misleading. I suggest that parallel to Coase's 1937 question is
another of at least equal significance, which asks about firms what Coase
asked about individual economic actors: why do they coalesce into identifiable
social structures? That is, why is it that in every known capitalist economy,
firms do not conduct business as isolated units, but rather form cooperative
relations with other firms. In no case do we observe an economy made up
of atomized firms doing business at arm's length with other firms across a
market boundary any more than we observe individuals trading with one
another to the exclusion of firms. It is collections of cooperating firms that
I refer to as 'business groups'. In drawing this analogy between the original
and the second 'Coasian' question, I imply that 'business group' is to firm
as firm is to individual economic agent. This obvious oversimplification is
meant to cut through a series of issues usually discussed separately.

Yet, such questions as why firms or business groups exist are not entirely
appropriate. The difficulty is that these 'why' questions are syntactically
disposed to teleological or functionalist answers — that firms exist in order
to reduce transaction costs, for example. In the case of firms, it is urgent to
add the 'how' question: 'how is it that in circumstances where profits could
be made from the formation of a firm, actors are in fact able to construct
one?'. Once this question is posed, we are alerted to the fact that the
assembling of economic elements into a firm is a formidable act of organization;
it is a good example of what Schumpeter defined as 'entrepreneurship' — the
pulling together of previously unconnected elements for an economic purpose
(Schumpeter, 1926). Historically, the discipline of economics has been weak
on theories and empirical accounts of entrepreneurship (cf. Blaug, 1986),
because of its assumption that profitable activities automatically take place,
as summed up in the aphorism that 'you will not find money lying in the
street'. But in fact, empirical studies make clear that there are many circumstances where although it would profit actors to construct firms, social
structural difficulties — especially the absence of trust in the relevant social
group — make this difficult or impossible (see Granovetter, 1992).

For business groups, where the task of construction is even larger than
for firms, the 'how' question must also be asked: what makes *possible* the

agglomeration of firms into some more or less coherent social structure, and what determines the kind of structure that results? The 'why' question has in fact been addressed several times in the literature. Four answers to why firms might want to connect with one another are: (i) resource dependence — firms are rarely self-sufficient and may form alliances or connections with other firms upon whom they regularly depend for resources (Pfeffer and Salancik, 1978); (ii) the need for 'strategic alliances' among firms which is said to derive from the changing nature of markets and of consumer demand (Piore and Sabel, 1984); (iii) the need asserted by Marxist analysts for coalitions of capitalists to form against other societal interests, or for one sector of capitalist firms (typically finance) to ally against others (Mintz and Schwartz, 1985); and (iv) the desire of firms to extract 'rents' from the economy or the government through coalitions, over and above those that could be gotten in a properly competitive economy (Olson, 1982).

Like the transaction cost account of why firms exist, all these focus on what motives economic actors have to be linked, or on how their economic outcomes will be improved by such linkage. Knowing such motives is certainly a crucial part of understanding the origins of business groups, but stops short of illuminating the likelihood that such linkages will occur; to achieve an understanding of the scale at which economic cooperation occurs requires us to move beyond the comparative statics of economic environments in equilibrium to consider how economic actors construct these alliances, and this task require a serious examination of how actors mobilize resources. Only the combined analysis of incentives and possibilities will yield a satisfactory account.

2. A Working Definition of Business Groups

At the descriptive level, the question of business groups can be posed as one of what the structure of all linkages among firms would look like from an 'aerial' view; it is mainly from such an aerial perspective, rarely taken, that business groups would come into sharp focus. One can consider as business groups those collections of firms bound together in some formal and/or informal ways, characterized by an 'intermediate' level of binding. This means that we exclude, on the one hand, a set of firms bound merely by short-term strategic alliances, and on the other, a set of firms legally consolidated into a single entity.

There is necessarily some arbitrariness in the definition. Conglomerate firms, in which a single firm has diversified into many industries by acquisition of controlling shares, are a marginal case. Strachan (1976) makes an important distinction by noting that in the typical conglomerate, a 'common parent owns the subsidiaries but generally few operational or personal ties exist among the sister subsidiaries. On the other hand, within business groups, . . . there are generally personal and operational ties among all the firms' (Strachan, 1976, p. 20). Most American conglomerates fit the first description, and do so in part because component companies are acquired and divested mainly on financial grounds, so that the set is likely to be reshuffled as financial outcomes dictate. Indeed, Davis *et al.* (1994) chronicle the 1980s wave of 'deconglomeration' in the United States, arguing that American-style conglomerates are inherently unstable, as they eliminate the identity of the core firm as a sovereign actor, opening the way for shareholders and raiders to disassemble the parts. Other conglomerates, however, such as the Korean *chaebol*, are quite stable and fit the profile of a business group, because they are the outcome of investments by a single family or small number of allied families who, once having acquired the component companies, keep them together as a coherent group among which personnel and resources may be shifted as needed (Steers *et al.*, 1989). Yet, the individual companies continue to keep some separate identity.[3]

Holding companies and trusts are another marginal case, and here I wish to include them in the definition of 'business groups' insofar as their constituent firms keep their own management and identity, but to exclude cases where those firms have become nothing more than units of the parent company, so that the character of a federation is lost.

Stable cartels might also be profitably classified as business groups. On the whole I would exclude trade associations on the grounds that their activity has to do less with operations and more with negotiating and affecting the institutional and governance arrangements under which their industry proceeds.[4]

Finally, many business groups are stable but quite loose coalitions of firms which have no legal status and in which no single firm or individual holds controlling interests in the other firms. Some Latin American groups and Japanese intermarket groups (such as Mitsubishi) fit this description. Although mutual stockholding and frequent meetings of top executives serve to bind such groups together, they are the most loosely bound of the collections of firms I discuss here (see Gerlach, 1992).

Thus included under the heading of 'business groups' are sets of firms that

[3] The power of the *chaebol* is great enough that political demands for dismantling them are common. Periodically, pledges are made, as recently by Hyundai, that many units will be spun off and the entire structure downsized (see *Business Week*, 7 June 1993, p. 48). It remains to be seen to what extent this will actually occur.

[4] I believe that this is typically a reasonable account of what trade associations do. But under some circumstances, they may become involved in day-to-day operations and thus take on somewhat of the character of a business group; see, for example, Herrigel (1993).

are integrated neither completely nor barely at all; many such groups operate in the middle range of coalitions and federations—forms that some business historians such as Alfred Chandler (1977, 1990) have treated as transitional and unstable, at least in capital intensive industries, where, in his accounts, they must give way to the greater efficiency of large, integrated firms. It is in this middle range of organization among firms that I believe a theoretical treatment is most needed and least available.

So defined, the business group is in fact a very widespread phenomenon, known in many countries under various names: the old *zaibatsu* and their modern successors, the *keiretsu*, in Japan; the *chaebol* in Korea; the *grupos economicos* in Latin America; the 'twenty-two families' of Pakistan; and so on. Though there are some analyses of such groups in particular countries and regions, they have received far less attention than one might expect given their economic significance, and there has been even less sustained analysis of the phenomenon as a whole, or realization of its centrality to modern capitalism.

3. *The Invisible Problem of Business Groups*

Before plunging into the details and arguments about such groups, it is worth pausing to address the perplexing question of how, at the level of national economies, this important subject has received so little attention for so long. Business groups have been all but invisible in the analytical literature of economics and sociology, even more neglected as a research topic than the elusive subject of entrepreneurship (see Baumol, 1968; Blaug, 1986).

For many countries, authors mention in passing how crucial these groups are for their own particular economy, but then move on to their main interest. These main interests are always then at some level below or above that of the business group. Below are concerns about entrepreneurship, management of individual firms and labor relations. Above are the many treatments of how national economic policy is formulated, how foreign direct investment is managed, what is the relation between business elites and government officials, and to what extent the new economic liberalism of many countries will lead to privatization, 'shock therapy' or other movement toward 'free markets'.

At the middle level of studying what formal and informal structures connect firms in the economy, however, there is remarkably little attention, even in countries where business groups are known to dominate the economy. In one important study of Thai business groups, for example, Phipatseritham and Yoshihara (1983) refer to the most comprehensive study of Thai business groups, commenting that this work 'sells for a few thousand dollars, and only a small number of copies are available and difficult to obtain' (p. 1n). Even for Mexico, which is almost the type-case of a country dominated by business groups, the literature is extremely sparse, with almost the entire published corpus being on the Monterey group because of its dominance by a series of colorful families (see the references in Camp, 1989, p. 290).

Only for East Asia is this situation different—here there are many excellent studies of Japanese *keiretsu*, Korean *chaebol* and Taiwanese business groups. These have been followed with great interest because of the immense success of these Asian economies, and the consequent search for any characteristics that distinguish their brand of capitalism from ours, on the supposition that this would explain the so-called Asian 'miracle'. Thus there was a trend, perhaps now on the wane, for the American business press to trumpet tirelessly the need for American firms to learn how to form alliances like the Japanese *keiretsu* if they were to compete in the world economy.

Such accounts are reminiscent of the studies of the (now forgotten) turn-of the-century criminologist, Cesare Lombroso, who linked criminal behavior to the facial features of prison inmates he observed but neglected to check the distribution of these features in the general population, where, it turned out, they were about as frequent as in prisons. Linking business groups to efficient economic outcomes builds in a severe selection bias since one has studied only the successful cases. In fact, because business groups are so widespread, they can be found in highly inefficient as well as highly efficient economic systems. This has been obscured by the lack of any general account.

Why, then, have we found it so hard to see this level of analysis? One reason is that in some settings, although participants are well aware of its importance, it is relatively invisible to others. Thus, Encaoua and Jacquemin (1982), in their study of 319 important business groups in France, defined by the direct or indirect holding of a majority of stock by a parent company in a series of other companies, noted that these groups 'have no legal existence and are not identified in official censuses. Each subsidiary maintains its legal autonomy and keeps separate accounts. It is therefore not surprising that there have been very few quantitative studies of this phenomenon' (p. 26). Here the point is that official data collection procedures take as a given that the firm is the proper unit of analysis, and by collecting data with this bias reinforce this assumption. The point has been made quite generally that preconceptions about the economy shape data collection that then supports these preconceptions, as in Reddy's (1984) study of the French textile industry in the 18th and 19th centuries.

Zeitlin and Ratcliff (1988), in their detailed account of Chile in the 1960s, emphasize how extremely difficult it may be to uncover the actual family control of groups of businesses, since this control is disguised by pyramiding—controlling corporations even without holding any of their stock, by holding stock in corporations which hold stock in other corporations, and so on, until control is achieved at some number of removes (pp. 35–38). Some of the arrangements are so intricate that they can be uncovered only with great difficulty, as detailed further below when ownership and control and discussed.

But in many countries, business groups are quite visible. Harry Strachan, for example, whose book, *Family and Other Business Groups in Economic Development*, is one of the best sources in English for groups in Latin America, comments that in his fieldwork in Nicaragua,

> There have been around 20 to 30 social or semi-social occasions at which I was introduced to a businessman by one of his close friends. At some point in the conversation which followed, I have smiled the smile of an insider and asked 'And what group do you belong to?' The replies, often with the same smile, have been direct, 'Oh, I don't belong to any group', or 'I suppose I am a member of the Banco Nicaraguense Group', or in cases indirect and evasive. Never, however, has that question drawn a blank stare and the reply 'What do you mean by group?' And survey respondents had no doubt which firms belonged to which group, even though groups were informal coalitions without legal standing (Strachan, 1976, pp. 26–29).

Why then have analysts made so little of what is so transparent to so many participants? On the economics side, an obvious comment is that the neoclassical theory of the firm has had little to say about such matters; indeed, until Coase asked his famous 1937 question, it had scarcely wondered why firms existed—and even this query had to await Williamson's *Markets and Hierarchies* in 1975 for a thorough account.

Sociologists have also contributed little to this subject, in part because until recently they hardly studied business at all, but also because, like economists, they concentrate their theories and empirical work at either the micro- or macro-level, giving short shrift to the difficult and unsettled meso-level that provides the crucial link between the two. And historically, most organization theory concerned the functioning of single organizations, with interactions and linkages among them coming into play only since the late 1960s. Thus the complexity of this middle level and the paucity of concepts available to deal with it helped bias critics of the standard theory of the firm such as Chandler (1977, 1990) and the early Williamson (1975) toward assuming the instability of organizational forms between markets and hierarchies.

4. *Background and Critique of the Existing Literature*

One reason why we have been ill-prepared to see the importance of business groups is that while standard accounts of industrial organization offer no reason to expect it, critics of this literature have been dominated by influential theories suggesting that complex interactions among firms must lead to amalgamation, if efficiency is to be served.

Among the most influential of these critics has been Alfred Chandler, who in three major books has argued that under certain conditions, it has paid firms, especially in manufacturing, to become large, diversified and professionally managed. The conditions are a technology and market demand affording substantial economies of scale and/or scope, where 'scope' refers to making different products in the same production unit. Because these economies pertained also to distribution, firms needed not only to invest in new production facilities, but also to integrate forward into distribution and backward into purchasing (Chandler, 1990, p. 28). Chandler argues that in industries where 'owing to their technology, the optimal size of plant was small, where mass distribution did not require specialized skills and facilities, and where the coordination of flows was a relatively simple task—manufacturers had much less incentive to make the three-pronged investment in production, distribution and management. In the more labor-intensive industries . . . the large integrated firm had few competitive advantages' (Chandler, 1990, p. 45). Subsequent to integration, many firms discover that the most efficient organizational form to cope with the diseconomies of the large scale they have adopted is what he calls the 'multidivisional form', in which a general office is responsible for overall planning and coordination, and a series of profit centers, usually defined by product-line but sometimes by region (as with large retailers such as Sears), operate with substantial autonomy.[5]

Chandler does not argue that firms always end up at optimal scale or form, but suggests that when they do not, it is the result of a failure of managers to see the situation clearly or because of incentives other than profit-maximizing, and is therefore predictive of a declining firm or economy; he has no general account of such failure, but specific arguments for particular settings. He asserts, for example, that 'in Britain a large and stable income

[5] For a persuasive argument that Chandler's account does not logically imply the need for divisions defined by region, see Stinchcombe (1990, Ch. 4).

for the family was more of an incentive than the long-term growth of the firm . . . Thus British entrepreneurs lost out in many of the most dynamic new industries of the Second Industrial Revolution' (Chandler, 1990, pp. 390–391).[6]

Chandler's argument implies instability for organizational forms such as the federations and loose coalitions that characterize many business groups. In particular, he argues for Great Britain that such federations were wholly inadequate to the economic situation they faced, and for efficiency's sake had to give way to large, integrated firms.

Oliver Williamson (1975, 1985) gives a more abstract account, based less on technology and consumer demand and more on the nature of transactions firms must engage in. He suggests that transactions that are uncertain in outcome, recur frequently and require substantial transaction-specific invest-ments of, for example, money, time or energy not easily transferred to other uses, are more likely to lead to hierarchically organized firms and vertical integration. Those that are straightforward, one-time and require no particu-lar investment, such as the one-time purchase of standard equipment, will be more likely to occur between independent firms—that is, across a market interface. This is said to be so because the combination of bounded ration-ality and opportunism makes complex transactions difficult to manage be-tween separate independent firms. Although Williamson's 1975 account pays little attention to organizational forms between markets and hierar-chies, his later work is at great pains to set out conditions under which such intermediate forms may be viable (cf. Williamson, 1985, 1991).[7]

The Chandler and Williamson accounts are at variance with standard economic argument, and it may thus not be surprising that they have met some scepticism from those quarters. Much of Chandler's argument is premised, for example, on his casual assertions about the 'minimum efficient scale' of operations for firms in particular industries. But in a detailed review of the literature and concepts surrounding these issues, Scherer and Ross (1990) argue that many ambiguities surround the idea of 'minimum efficient scale'; they summarize considerable empirical evidence that efficiency in an

---

[6] The causes of British failure, and whether the British did in fact fail in any meaningful way, given the conditions they faced, is a favorite topic of economic historians, though Chandler gives little hint of the depth of controversy. For arguments against the 'failure' hypothesis, and some vigorous debate, see McCloskey (1981); a set of essays is presented by Elbaum and Lazonick (1986). A similar argument about family values leading to an inappropriately small size for many French firms, and thereby inhibiting economic growth, was made in 1951 by Landes (1965), but has subsequently been embarrassed by the remarkable growth of the French economy since that period. Several analysts have suggested that the small size of firms was actually quite appropriate under the circumstances. See Levy-Leboyer (1976), Nye (1987) and Adams (1989).

[7] For an extended discussion of Williamson's 'markets and hierarchies program', as presented in his writings before 1985, see Granovetter (1985).

industry is similar over a wide range of firm sizes, and tentatively conclude that 'actual concentration in U.S. manufacturing industry appears to be considerably higher than the imperatives of scale economies require' (p. 141). They note that empirical studies are equivocal as to the economic success of the multidivisional form (Scherer and Ross, 1990, p. 105 n. 17), and point out that one of the main exemplars of this form described by Chandler, General Motors, has faced difficulties at least since the 1940s that may be associated with rigidities of organizational form (Chandler, 1990, pp. 105–106).[8]

Indeed, one line of argument on industrial organization takes its point of departure precisely from these rigidities, and suggests that under modern conditions there may be substantial advantage in small, flexible firms bound together with similar other firms in networks of cooperation that characterize some business groups. The most influential such account is Piore and Sabel's sweeping treatment of industrial history in *The Second Industrial Divide* (1984), in which they argue that large mass production firms may have represented only a temporary interlude in industrial organization, brought on by a series of economic and political conditions that have now changed in a way that favors 'flexible specialization'.

Their argument is comparable to those of Chandler and Williamson in stressing contingency,[9] and is also reminiscent of the work of Joan Woodward (1980), who asserted that small, flexible, non-hierarchical organizations are especially well suited for making products as units or small batches: they assert that only under conditions where consumers will accept highly uniform goods can we expect to see large, integrated industrial units. But such acceptance is not guaranteed, but rather is historically situated, as in early nineteenth century America, where 'an affluent yeomanry—whose ancestral diversity of tastes had been erased by transplantation to the New World—was willing and able to purchase the crude standard products that early special-purpose machine tools turned out' (Piore and Sabel, 1984, p. 41). The modern world, in their view, now faces a saturation of mass production markets: 'By the late 1960's, domestic consumption of the goods that had led the postwar expansion had begun to reach its limits' (p. 184), and consumers, for a variety of reasons, began to crave highly differentiated

---

[8] It is worth mentioning that Sears, Roebuck, making up with General Motors two of the four cases discussed in Chandler's classic 1962 treatment of the advantages of the multidivisional form, has also been widely criticized for its cumbersome organizational structure and slow response to problems, leading to increasingly lackluster performance.

[9] But their full argument differs sharply from that of other contingency theorists in the loose coupling they see between external conditions and organizational form, mediated by the actions of political institutions and by complex strategies of decision-makers trying to find their way among constraints, and to re-shape those constraints. This distance from contingency theory is even clearer in the recent paper by Sabel and Zeitlin (1992) than in the Sabel and Piore volume.

products that could only with difficulty be made by the mass-production behemoths that dominated the previous scene but for which networks of cooperating small units, as in the 'Third Italy's' textile industry, provide just the needed flexibility (Piore and Sabel, 1984, Chs 8–11).

Chandler, Williamson and Piore–Sabel, despite their differences, are contingency theorists in that they predict the balance between federations of firms and single amalgamated units to derive from the need to adapt to variations in technology, consumer demand and market structure. But in most countries, this balance responds not only to these factors but also to a political and legal situation that results in part from the emotional and symbolic significance of firm size.

Thus, the Sherman Antitrust Act in the United States was originally framed as part of a political campaign against bigness. The impact of legislation is often unanticipated, however, and the Sherman Act can be argued to have led to a merger wave because it forbade most coordination mechanisms among firms short of merger (Fligstein, 1990, Ch. 2).[10] Similarly, the Celler–Kefauver Act of 1949, intended to prevent concentration within particular markets, ended up encouraging conglomerate mergers because these did not fall within the purview of its logic (Fligstein, 1990).

Though some scholars treat legislative differences among countries as inscrutably linked to historical common law and differences in national culture (e.g. Chandler, 1977, 1992), historical investigations of legislation usually reveal a more complex picture. In the United States, where some forms of cooperation among firms that are legal elsewhere are prohibited, this outcome is often taken as a measure of American cultural exceptionalism, a rugged individualism leading to a preference for small units in competitive markets. But Sanders (1986) shows that support had to be mobilized for such legislation, as it is in social movements, and argues that most successful attempts to produce government antitrust activity resulted from regional conflicts, in which one region felt especially aggrieved by the economic power of large firms centered in others. Before the 1930s, antitrust was the policy of the non-industrial states Sanders calls 'peripheral', as indicated by support from legislators in Congress. The general resentment of bigness as an Eastern establishment plot against the heartland was especially captured by the Populists, and is reflected in William Jennings Bryan's 1896 'cross of gold' speech, initiating his unsuccessful bid for the Presidency. By the 1970s, Sanders suggests, the tables had turned, and antitrust was supported by the old industrial states against the oil and gas behemoths of the emerging

[10] Fligstein (1990) points out that the 'language of the Sherman Act caused the Justice Department to focus on *conspiracies* in restraint of trade. Thus, actions that took place between firms were much easier to prosecute than actions involving only one firm' (p. 94).

Sunbelt regions. In both cases, to the extent that cooperation among independent firms was legislatively discouraged, this resulted from the ability of certain regions to mobilize support in a political system where a disciplined region can dominate the legislative process through careful building of alliances in the legislative branch, highly unlikely in most other democratic parliamentary systems (Sanders, 1986, pp. 213–214).

It has been common in different periods and places for the size of firms to acquire symbolic value that elicits strong political action. In the United States, from the late 1930s to the passage of the Celler–Kefauver Antitrust Act in 1950, there was considerable discussion of the evils of bigness in the economic sphere. The Roosevelt-appointed Temporary National Economic Commission in the late 1930s argued strongly that large firms had too much control and threatened basic democratic institutions. By the late 1940s the 'issue of "bigness" was firmly on the political agenda' (Fligstein, 1990, p. 167), and Harry Truman and his allies campaigned against it, identifying it with the evils of Fascism and Communism.

At times, the emphasis shifts away from the evils of the large to the virtues of the small. The symbolic imagery here relies on the ideas that 'small is beautiful' (Schumacher, 1973) and that we should strive for 'appropriate technology' (Lovins, 1977). Democratic theorists in the 1960s stressed the salutary political implications of radical decentralization, and some of this flavor persists in the more analytical work by Piore, Sabel and their colleagues and students on networks of flexible small producers. Smallness is not of interest, however, only to those with communitarian aims; under some circumstances it can become the program of businesses as well. Their purpose, however, is not to restore democracy or local decision-making, but to restore lumbering giant firms to profitability. Thus, the initial interest in 'downsizing' of firms has been accompanied by rhetorical flourishes such as the quest to be 'lean and mean' and to accomplish the process of 'right-sizing'. Vonk's empirical study (1992) of thirty-one large American corporations indicates that their reductions in workforce do not appear to be tailored to any calculation of the marginal costs of labor in production or to targeting particularly expensive parts of the labor process; instead, the cuts seem to be carried out in similar ways across large numbers of firms in quite different circumstances, suggesting a process of imitation or 'institutional isomorphism' (DiMaggio and Powell, 1983) in which firms adopt practices that become standard in their reference group so as not to appear backward or out-of-touch (see Meyer and Rowan, 1977). Similarly, Fligstein (1990) argues that once a strategy takes hold in the organizational field surrounding a firm, that strategy becomes highly legitimate and likely to be pursued; he suggests that vertical integration, diversification and the move to product-unrelated (i.e. 'conglomerate') mergers were all affected by having become dominant strategies that appeared successful for some leading actors and were therefore adopted by followers with much less careful analysis than by the first-movers.

But it is not only analysts such as Chandler and Williamson who favor bigness in firms; at times, especially those of perceived national economic decline, there have been clearly identifiable social movements in favor of large scale. Thus, a severe economic downturn in Britain in the early 1920s led to a strong emphasis on the need to increase the average firm size, an emphasis that came to be part of the 'rationalization' movement. Leslie Hannah notes that the

> implication of rationality in the term 'rationalization' emphasized that industry could conform to ideas and values whose proponents were growing in confidence and strength in contemporary society, and in particular to the growing awareness of, and faith in, things scientific at the level of popular philosophy. Businessmen and statesmen accepted the common popular theme that advances in science and technology were giving men a growing control over the natural environment and pleaded for a greater recognition that the methods of scientific enquiry could solve social and economic difficulties also (Hannah, 1983, p. 32).

By the 1930s, these ideas were a staple of discussion in many circles, and a 'program of merger, inter-firm agreements and "scientific" management (in short of "rationalization") thus became the common currency not only of a metropolitan elite of intellectuals . . . but also of businessmen who like to picture themselves as successful and hard-headed' (Hannah, 1983, p. 34). In the 1960s a similar view again gained currency, and the 'vogue for "restructuring", a term now widely used to denote mergers and the concentration of output in fewer firms, was popularized and was strongly reminiscent of the rationalization movement of the 1920's, both in the arguments used and in the oversimplifications to which its less intelligent advocates succumbed' (Hannah, 1983, p. 147). Both Hannah and Fligstein indicated that, despite the vogues for increasing size, the evidence does not support any particular advantages for it (Hannah, 1983, 153 ff.; Fligstein, 1990, Ch. 8). Scherer and Ross (1990) suggested that 'statistical evidence supporting the hypothesis that profitability and efficiency increase following mergers is at best weak. Indeed, the weight of the evidence points in the opposite direction' (p. 174).

The use of such highly charged terms as 'rationalization' and 'restructuring' should signal that much of the content that will follow is symbolic, as emphasized by scholars of the 'institutional' school of organizations. Whatever the symbolism and its aims, there seems to be good evidence that the choice between federation and consolidation is affected not only by economic contingencies, but also by symbolic discussions that are best analyzed as involving resource mobilization in social movements.

All this research on factors influencing the balance between federation and amalgamation of firms is highly relevant in understanding the circumstances under which business groups will thrive, rather than collapsing into single large firms. But because of the general neglect of the amorphous middle level of structured alliances of firms, little of this work has explicitly addressed the subject.

The explicit literature on business groups is small. In the first and probably still the best general treatment, Harry Strachan defines a business group as a 'long-term association of a great diversity of firms and the men who own and manage these firms' (Strachan, 1976, p. 2). He suggests that three characteristics distinguish them from other types of associations: (i) the great diversity of enterprises in a group; (ii) pluralism: the groups consist of a coalition of several wealthy businessmen and families; and (iii) an atmosphere of loyalty and trust 'normally associated with family or kinship groups. A group member's relation to other group members is characterized by a higher standard of fair dealings and disclosure than that which generally is found in arm's length commerce' (Strachan, 1976, p. 3).[11]

Economists who have studied business groups have generally interpreted them in one or another functionalist way as responses to economic problems. Leff, for example, suggests that the 'group pattern of industrial organization is readily understood as a microeconomic response to well-known conditions of market failure in the less developed countries' (Leff, 1978, p. 666), especially imperfect markets in capital and intermediate products. The general argument here is that business groups take up the slack in LDCs that lack well-functioning capital markets (Leff, 1976, 1979a).

If this interpretation were correct, it would be difficult to explain the persistence of business groups in advanced capitalist economies such as those of Japan, Korea and Western Europe. One position that attempts to address this contradiction is that such groups are 'vestigial' and will therefore soon fade. This position is approximated by Chandler (1982), who argues that 'only the formation of a central administrative or corporate office can permit the [business] group as a whole to become more than the sum of its parts' (p. 4), so that business groups, if they are to become efficient, must eventually move toward the multidivisional form. Thus, the 'most important single event in the history of an industrial group is when those who guide its destinies shift from attempting to achieve market control through contractual cooperation to achieve it through administrative efficiency' (Chandler,

[11] Strachan's 1976 book was submitted in an earlier draft as a 1973 DBA thesis at Harvard Business School.

1982, p. 23) (i.e. merger into a single, consolidated firm). But this prediction has become less tenable with the staying power of business groups, which show no signs of the amalgamation Chandler projects.[12]

An alternative argument, consistent with the New Institutional Economics, is that one should expect to see such groups arise in situations where they provide some type of economic advantage. Caves' (1989) general summary of this literature is that business groups 'apparently represent responses to transaction costs and agency problems' (p. 1230). Thus, Encaoua and Jacquemin (1982) suggest that the existence of the 319 French industrial groups they study should be interpreted as the Chandlerian outcome of a 'search for an efficient organizational adaptation' to characteristics of particular industries (p. 32). They conclude that these groups, though consisting of legally independent firms, are really approximations of the American multidivisional form, with some 'peculiarities due mainly to national characteristics inherited from history' (p. 32).

Goto recognizes the importance of business groups in 'highly industrialized countries like Sweden, West Germany, France and Japan' (Goto, 1982, p. 53). He discusses how firms may reduce the costs of the transactions they must accomplish, suggesting that, by forming or joining a business group, a firm

> can economize on the transaction costs that it would have incurred . . .
> through the market, and at the same time, it can avoid the scale diseconomies or control loss which would have occurred if it had expanded internally
> and performed that transaction within the firm. If the net benefit of forming
> or joining a group exceeds that of implementing transactions within the
> firm or through the market, the firm has the incentive to form or to join
> a group (Goto, 1982, p. 61).

In particular, he believes that firms may 'secure intermediate goods with lower cost and less uncertainty by joining or forming groups rather than by procuring them through the market or integrating vertically' (Goto, 1982, p. 63), and that this explains the predominance of business groups in Japan following World War II (pp. 64–69).

It is not accidental that this type of functionalist interpretation has been developed especially for the context of Japan, whose economy has generally been perceived by Western observers as extremely successful and efficient.[13] This success has spurred rethinking by both economists and popular writers

---

[12] In a later article, Chandler suggests that 'the Japanese experience illustrates . . . a convergence in the type of enterprise and system of capitalism used by all advanced industrial economies for the production and distribution of goods' (Chandler 1992, p. 156). But few detailed studies of Japanese industrial organization would appear to support such a claim (e.g. Gerlach, 1992).

[13] For an overview of efficiency explanations of Japanese enterprise groups, see Gerlach (1992, 11 ff.).

about the possibility that the traditional model of Western capitalism—
independent firms operating across a market interface—may be less efficient
than cooperative capitalism as exemplified by the Japanese. Ironically, an
older convergence theory stipulating that modernization meant approximat-
ing the Western model has begun to give way to a reversed convergence
argument in which Asian models are seen as the measure of modernity and
efficiency.[14]

However, as argued above, the relation between cooperative capitalism,
business groups and economic efficiency is far more complex than these
simple accounts suggest, and as the study of business groups in broadly
unsuccessful economies advances, it will become harder (though it is never
impossible) to sustain optimistic functionalist accounts.

5. *Business Groups: the Empirical Patterns*

Business groups come in a wide variety of types, so much so that a more
refined analysis may ultimately conclude that it is too crude to lump them
all into a single analytic category. This is done here as a first cut into the
little-analyzed immense middle ground between individual firms and the
macroeconomic and macropolitical environment.

Initially, primary dimensions along which business groups vary are identified. Then some guesses will be ventured about how these dimensions relate
to one another and to a more general theoretical framework.

Axes of Solidarity for Business Groups

What distinguishes business groups from collections of firms united by, for
example, common financial origins, as in American conglomerates, is the
existence of social solidarity and social structure among component firms. It
is thus important to examine to what extent such axes of solidarity as region,
political party, ethnicity, kinship and religion are clearly identifiable.

Leff suggests that members of business groups are generally 'linked by
relations of interpersonal trust, on the basis of a similar personal, ethnic or
communal background' (Leff, 1978, p. 663). Arguments about the role of
family in economic life have progressed from the mid-century 'modernization
theory' view that the economy could not grow until kinship was separated
from economic activity to a recognition that families bring advantages to
firms that make them more viable under some circumstances (e.g. Ben-
Porath, 1980). Because the comparative advantage of families in economic

---

[14] For a scholarly account of reversed-convergence ideas in the area of labor relations and worker
commitment to firms, see Lincoln and Kalleberg (1990), and the review of this book (Granovetter, 1990).

life rests on strong trust, however, and because it was assumed that this trust did not guarantee technical or managerial expertise and sharply limited the size of viable firms, this vote of confidence in the role of families in the economy was limited.

Yet, it is 'not hard to find exceptions to the generalization that family firms are limited in scale and tend to be impermanent' (Wong, 1985, p. 62). In many settings, large groups are thoroughly dominated by one or two families. Zeitlin and Ratcliff (1988) coined the concept of the 'kinecon' in Chile to designate a 'complex social unit in which economic interests and kinship bonds are inextricably intertwined': these are effective kinship groups whose combined holdings add up to control of top corporations. In the Korean *chaebol*, families manage as well as own. Steers *et al.* (1989) indicate that in the top twenty *chaebol*, 31% of the executive officers are family members, and that core managerial positions in 'nearly all the companies belonged to family members' (pp. 37–38). It is often asserted that in large companies or groups, the family is bound to lose control as there are just so many members to go around; but this underestimates how effective families can be at placing their members strategically. In one *chaebol*, Lucky-Goldstar, 'the absolute number of family members per company may be small but the power of these members is quite strong' (Steers *et al.*, 1989, p. 38).

Alfred Chandler, among others, has argued that keeping family members in key managerial positions is counterproductive, as expanding firms, especially in technologically complex capital-intensive industries, must have professional management to coordinate economies of scale and scope (Chandler, 1977, 1990). But this assumes that families cannot produce technically sophisticated management. Kim (1991) observes that while the 'share of professional managers in the *chaebol* has increased in recent years, the more important trend is the professionalization of family members. The sons and sons-in-law of the *chaebol* owners are educated as professional managers; often they are sent to the United States to earn MBA's from prominent business schools' (pp. 276–277; see Kiong (1991, p. 189) for a similar observation on Chinese business groups in Singapore).

Where business people are an ethnic minority, this is often a source of solidarity within business groups, supplementing that of pure kinship, since it binds the members of the central family to other key employees. For Chinese in Thailand (Phipatseritham and Yoshihara, 1983), Palestinians in Honduras (Gonzalez, 1992), Lithuanians in Brazil (Evans, 1979, p. 108), Pakistanis in Manchester (Werbner, 1984) or Indians in East Africa (Marris and Somerset, 1971), ethnicity provides an axis of differentiation along which members can build trust.

Region and ethnicity may intersect, to create geographically bounded solidarities of the kind referred to as 'ethnic enclaves', such as Cubans in Miami (Portes and Manning, 1986). Some groups, such as those linking small apparel firms in Italy, are quite localized, so that geographic contiguity and the resulting networks of personal contact help to integrate the units. Ties of formal organization or political party may serve equally well; all that is needed is some cognitive marker around which actors may construct trust relations at higher intensity than with those outside the category.

A significant axis of solidarity is foreign status in countries where this involves being the carrier of significant capital flows from abroad. This can be illustrated, for example, by the pattern that Evans (1979) calls 'dependent development'. In Brazil, nearly all the major business groups formed after World War II were foreign (Evans, 1979, p. 110). Because Brazilian-based groups remain strong in finance and in their links to the state, foreign-based groups 'with partners embedded in the local social structure have a special competitive advantage over those which lack such partners' (Evans, 1979, p. 162). In a non-colonial context, where access to local resources and political favors is crucial, this division of labor cements what Evans calls the 'triple alliance' among Brazil's government, local elites and foreign capital; it also produces a model of the economy more complex than early versions of 'dependency theory', in which foreign domination was complete and unchallenged. Evans suggests that the pattern of 'dependent development' is especially pertinent for Brazil, Mexico, Argentina, Venezuela, Colombia, Philippines and India (Evans, 1979, p. 295).

In a purely functional sense it matters little what principle of solidarity binds a business group so long as it enables mutual trust to proceed and the group to persist. But to analyze the future course of events for particular business groups, one must know what glue holds it together, in order to guess what events and trends will act as solvents. Thus, business groups bound by ethnicity, especially if immigrant ethnicity, are always vulnerable to periods of jingoistic enthusiasm and corresponding demands that the economy be returned to control of indigenous actors; in such cases, we may expect to see a trend toward alliance of groups to powerful factions in the government or military (as for Chinese groups in Thailand (see Skinner, 1957, pp. 349–350 and 360–362) or Indonesia (see Coppel, 1983; Robison, 1986)). Those bound by foreign capital are affected by trade balances, international currency movements and the growth of protectionism. Regionally based groups may rise or fall in their influence as their region is more or less central in the national government. And this is true *a fortiori* for groups based on political party.

In part because of these vulnerabilities, leading actors in business groups normally try to avoid relying on a single axis of solidarity. One of the reasons Indian business houses (the local term for groups) have been so persistently powerful in the economy is precisely their multiple bases of solidarity; Encarnation (1989) notes that in 'each of these houses, strong social ties of family, caste, religion, language, ethnicity and region reinforced financial and organizational linkages among affiliated enterprises' (p. 45). In addition to seeking more such axes, it is common for these actors to try to formalize relations that have been supported mainly by informal sanctions; this may be the origin of some holding companies, as in Nicaragua (Strachan, 1976, pp. 10, 17), and a reason for the persistence of India's 'managing agency' system.

Another mechanism for binding firms together, which may be found in conjunction with any or all of the above, is the interlocking directorate, in which group companies have common members on their boards of directors who may help coordinate group activities. Of all the types of solidarity described, interlocking directorates have been the subject of the largest literature (e.g. Mintz and Schwartz, 1985; Stokman *et al.*, 1985; Scott, 1987). Much of this literature is quantitatively sophisticated and indicates patterns of considerable interest. But in part because there is so little hard information on exactly what corporate directors do, the exact role of interlocks remains in dispute. Strachan warns against taking interlocks as a fundamental definitional feature of business groups, noting that 'membership on the board of directors is far from synonymous with inclusion in the group', and that even a firm ban on interlocks 'would not destroy nor even seriously impair the important group relations and patterns' (Strachan, 1976 p. 18).

Ownership Relations

There is immense variation in the organization of firm ownership in business groups. By hypothesis, all groups consist of firms that have independent legal existence. But in some groups, every firm is owned directly or indirectly, in the sense of a controlling interest being held by a single individual or family, or a set of related families.[15] This is typical of South Korean *chaebol* such as Hyundai, where twenty of the twenty-four component firms are at least half-owned by the founder, Chung Ju-Yung, and his family, or indirectly through other companies that they control (Steers *et al.*, 1989,

[15] This is already less precise than it sounds, since the phrase 'controlling interest' has itself no legal standing, and there can be serious differences among analysts as to what proportion of stock must be held before control is assured. This is the issue that has for so long divided American analysts into 'managerialists', who argue that stock is so widely dispersed that managers control most large firms, and 'elite' theorists, who assert that although leading families may control only 2–5% of stock, this is typically the largest block and therefore can be used to exercise control (e.g. Zeitlin, 1974).

p. 37). This centralized ownership may be associated with highly recogniz-
able groups such as Hyundai, Lucky-Goldstar, Samsung and Daewoo in
Korea, but also with larger numbers of smaller groups such as the 319
French groups studied by Encaoua and Jacquemin (1982) which had much
lower public profiles and no presence in official statistical accounts. Common
ownership therefore does not necessarily provide legal identity to the business group, though it links the firms in a strong indirect manner.

Ownership may be held directly by stockholders, or indirectly through
holding stock of or otherwise controlling companies that hold the stock of
other companies. Such 'holding companies' may be formed for this express
purpose, in which case they are typically not operating companies at all, or
they may be operating companies in their own right that have the additional
function of holding stock.

In the United States the holding company was specifically sanctioned by
state laws, beginning with New Jersey in 1889 (see Chandler, 1977 p. 319;
Fligstein, 1990 p. 58). Before 1889 a special act of a state legislature was
necessary any time a company wanted to hold the property of another company. Although it is well known that holding companies have been quite important in the electric utility industry, and that certain families historically
made use of holding companies to generate control over multiple corporations (e.g. the du Pont and Rockefeller families (see Scherer and Ross, 1990,
p. 66), there has been little systematic attention to the subject. The general
comment of Scherer and Ross (1990) on the significance of group control of
industry through complexes of formal and informal ties—that 'our ignorance
on this subject is great, and so we have only weak insight into the magnitude
of the consequences' (p. 68)—applies especially well to the significance of
holding companies and other forms of indirect control.

Their significance in other countries is clearer though still poorly documented. Mexican business groups, for example, are organized via holding
companies (Camp, 1989, pp. 174–192). It is not unusual for cross-
stockholding arrangements to become extremely complex, involving whole
series of nominee and trustee companies supported by dense networks of
interlocking directorships, as for Chinese business groups in Singapore
(Kiong, 1991, pp. 188–189).

Zeitlin and Ratcliff's detailed analysis of Chile in the 1960s suggests that
extremely complex pyramiding of ownership through operational and non-
operational holding companies, some headquartered in foreign countries,
made it appear that Chilean firms were management-dominated when in fact
a cohesive oligarchy of wealthy industrialists and landholders, allied with
leading political figures, effectively controlled the core of the economy. They
suggest that the 'framework of the single corporation has to be broken out

of in an effort to identify interconnections between it and other corporations, and through them to identify specific individuals, families or other cohesive groups that might exert control' (Zeitlin and Ratcliff 1988, p. 45). Using Berle and Means' original criteria for management control, they found that fifteen of the largest thirty-seven industrial corporations in Chile were in this category, but that in fact, fourteen of these were 'really controlled by minority ownership interests, generally by one or more interrelated families and their associates' (p. 45), what they call the kinecon—a set of 'primary, secondary and other relatives among the officers, directors and principal shareowners whose combined individual and indirect (institutional) shareholdings constitute the dominant proprietary interest in the corporation' (Zeitlin and Ratcliff, 1988 p. 55). They argue that without the detailed information on kinship links that they collected, it would be impossible to understand the actual, as opposed to the nominal, control situations for these companies.

An interesting variant on these themes is a holdover from British colonialism, the 'managing agency system' which dominated Indian business groups until abolished by the government in 1969 (Encarnation, 1989 p. 45). In this system, each participating firm signed 'a management contract with a managing agency which runs the companies' (Strachan, 1976, p. 40).[16] This is quite different from the 'central office' of Chandler's ideal-type multi-divisional form, in that the agency is under contract to manage independent companies; it is also different in principle from a holding company which holds the stock of group firms. Encarnation indicates, however, that in practice, 'equity ownership among companies became linked, and sophisticated systems of interlocking directorates maintained operational control over a large number of companies' (Encarnation, 1989, p. 45).

At the other extreme, many groups have no ownership links. Typical of this situation are the networks of small to very small textile firms that have evolved elaborate systems of cooperation and division of labor in the so-called 'Third Italy' (e.g. Lazerson, 1988). There appears to be a correlation between the size of firms in business groups and their ownership relations, since firms too small to be organized as joint-stock companies, usually single proprietorships, are more likely to be organized as coalitions of the owners, without any interest in making complex ownership arrangements across firm lines.

An intermediate case in which stockholding is mostly confined within business groups but is comparatively symmetrical, so that ownership is dispersed rather than concentrated, is the Japanese pattern in which no new firm is founded to hold stock but, rather, members of a group hold one

---

[16] Strachan's survey of the organization of Indian business houses relies heavily on the work of Hazari (1966) and Kothari (1967).

another's stock. Gerlach points out that such 'crossholdings' do not serve narrow economic rationality; rather, their purpose is, in the phrase of Japanese businessmen, to 'keep each other warm': 'Share crossholdings among group companies create a structure of mutually signified relationships, as well as serve as a means of protecting managers from hostile outsiders' (Gerlach, 1992, pp. 76–77) since the large blocks of shares mutually held are rarely traded and are thus are more difficult to manipulate for the purpose of takeovers and buyouts, as in American financial markets.

Authority Structure

Another fundamental way business groups vary is in the extent to which they are organized by hierarchical authority. As a first approximation we may divide business groups into those that are strongly coordinated in this way and those that are composed more of equal partners. Korean *chaebol* are a clear hierarchical case, which Biggart describes as an example of 'institutionalized patrimonialism'. For each such group, one family owns all the firms and rules autocratically; Biggart indicates that 'consensus is neither sought nor desired' (Biggart, 1991, p. 2). Steers *et al.* (1989, p. 47) indicate that 'Korean CEO's are seldom challenged, however politely; their decisions are absolute'. There is little in the way of lifetime employment (compared to Japan), and employees may well be fired arbitrarily upon an assessment that they have not met desired goals (Biggart, 1991, p. 34). Each *chaebol* was built by an entrepreneur who came to regard it as his own sphere of authority. There is some variation in the degree of professional management, but typically the chairman appoints sons, brothers and sons-in-law to top positions in the firms. Perhaps on account of this strongly authoritarian pattern, rivalries among *chaebol* are 'deep and even acrimonious . . . The familism of modern South Korea often entwines with regionalism and clan rivalries between the *chaebol*; indeed, it is difficult to separate rivalries on these two dimensions because each clan is associated with a region, and within a region, with a town or city' (Biggart, 1991, pp. 2, 28). The competition is so bitter that members of one group will not buy from the other, even if it is the cheapest source, and an American firm that does business with one will not be able to do so with its rivals (Biggart, 1991, p. 30). Group feeling is so intense that one of the two major auto makers 'does not allow anyone driving the other's car to enter its parking lot' (Amsden, 1989, p. 130).

In other countries the components of business groups are on much more equal footing. In Japan, firms within a group, though legally independent, are coordinated in a variety of ways, such as mutual stockholding, President's councils—in which firms' leaders meet periodically—trading companies which serve an explicit coordination role especially for but not limited to primary goods (cf. Yoshino and Lifson, 1986), and financial organizations, mainly banks, which serve as financial anchors especially within the inter-market groups. Orrù *et al.* (1991) suggest that while 'there are clearly more important and more influential firms within enterprise groups, the decision-making unit is the group, and command is exercised not by fiat but by consensus. Decisions are made considering what is best for the collectivity, not simply for individual firms, however powerful' (p. 387).[17]

In groups of firms coordinated by holding companies, the extent of central control exerted has historically been extremely variable. Such control can be very tightly held by a dominant family or two, as with the early twentieth century *zaibatsu*. But holding companies may also serve to organize a formal federation of firms, typically in a single industry, that stops well short of full integration. Chandler offers the example of the British holding company Imperial Tobacco, formed at the turn of the twentieth century, and which was Britain's largest industrial enterprise by the late 1940s. It began as a federation of sixteen firms whose structure was, according to one executive, 'not unlike that of the Thirteen States of America, who, when the Federal Constitution was first adopted, gave the central government as little author-ity as possible and retained as much as they could in their own hands' (Chandler, 1990, p. 247). This federative quality remained in place until the 1960s, with each firm doing its own advertising and competing with one another 'for market share decorously through the years' (Chandler, 1990, p. 248). Chandler suggests that such arrangements, typical in this period, were intended to preserve the personal management of British firms by the families of their original owners, against the possibility of (what he considers the more efficient form of) fully integrated firms run by professional managers trained in engineering or business.

The literature on 'flexible specialization', in its special concern with the evolution away from dominant large firms in an industrial sector to networks of small producers, also is highly oriented to the issue of power among related firms. Many proponents of this industrial path are committed to the proposition that the egalitarian association of large numbers of small pro-ducers is inherently more democratic and desirable than the control by large firms in a corporatist model of economic and political governance.

---

[17] Such a sweeping generalization naturally must be treated with caution. It applies more readily to the large, bank-centered intermarket groups than to the vertical organized, single-industry *keiretsu*, and better to some such groups than others. It is usually thought, for example, that the relatively new (late nineteenth century origin) Mitsubishi group is much more hierarchically organized than the much older Mitsui group (dating to 1615), known for its 'individualism' (see Gerlach, 1992, pp. 87–88).

The horizontal/vertical dimension refers to governance within a business group. The case of Japan already indicates that this dimension need not characterize all the business groups in a country, as both horizontally and vertically oriented groups may coexist. In this respect, the overall picture of business groups within a country shows itself as a special case of all social structures and institutional spheres, since it is a standard element of institutional analysis to sort out the distribution of horizontal and vertical relationships. An interesting subsidiary question then arises: to what extent does one find that the existing set of business groups is mutually exclusive as opposed to overlapping in membership? In Japan, for example, there are firms that participate in more than one group, and some are simultaneously in horizontal and vertical groups. Overlap among groups would be quite uncommon in Korea and relatively less common in most Latin American countries. The extent and nature of overlap is important in business networks as in any other networks, and bears heavily on the extent to which cooperation can be produced over large sectors of the economy without the intervention of government. Causal direction is not asserted here; cooperation is both cause and effect of overlap. This may help explain why, in matters of industrial policy, the Japanese government, though highly active, plays more of an advisory role than the Korean government, which guides the economy more firmly.

This dimension of authority relations is related to the origins of business groups. In his history of American management, Alfred Chandler has commented that the 'modern industrial enterprise followed two different paths to [large] size. Some small single-unit firms moved directly into building their own national and global marketing networks and extensive purchasing organizations and obtaining their own sources of raw materials and transportation facilities. For others, mergers came first. A number of small, single-unit family or individually owned firms merged to form a large national enterprise' (Chandler, 1977, p. 286).

A similar distinction can be made concerning the origins of business groups. At one end of the spectrum are groups that originated in a single firm which grew powerful by setting up, investing in or making arrangements with other firms legally unaffiliated but informally connected to them. In such cases it is clear which person or family is the founder of the business group (which then often—though not always—bears the family name). A case in point is the Mitsubishi group in Japan, originating in a shipping company founded in 1873 by the entrepreneur Iwasaki Yataro. Once established as the dominant force in Japanese shipping, Mitsubishi made substantial investments in mining, electrical engineering, dairy farms, real estate and banking, becoming by World War I one of the two largest *zaibatsu* (Wray, 1984).

By contrast, some business groups are founded over a period of time as the outcome of alliances among a set of leading families, each seeking to extend the reach of its investments and activities. Many Latin American groups seem to have originated in this way, though the few existing historical accounts are sketchy. Strachan recounts the origins of the powerful Banco Nicaraguense group in the early 1950s:

> 'pluralistic composition was a deliberate objective . . . an effort was made to bring into the promoting group wealthy businessmen from the different geographical areas of Nicaragua, from different sectors of the economy, from different political factions, and from different families. To avoid the disproportionate influence within the group of any one faction, the promoters agreed to adopt a policy of limiting the ownership interest of any single person or family to no more than 10 percent' (Strachan, 1976, pp. 15–16).

This process may have been unusually self-conscious, and alliances that form business groups might be more typically spread over time, with groups growing by accretion.

In general, groups originating from a single focal firm are likely to be more vertically oriented, at least at the outset, whereas those formed from a coalition of roughly equal parties will have a much more horizontal character. Whether groups maintain their original configuration of vertical and horizontal ties depends on how this configuration meshes with the rest of their institutional environments over long periods of time, and so must be considered problematic and thus deserving of closer investigation.

Business Groups and Moral Economy

Another important dimension of how business groups function can be called the extent of 'moral economy', a concept first developed by the English historian E. P. Thompson, in a landmark 1971 paper, 'The Moral Economy of the English Crowd in the Eighteenth Century'. Thompson describes the collective action of eighteenth century villagers to affect the price of grain. Though growers or marketers might rationally seek the best possible price, local populations took violent exception to this search if it resulted in a high price in bad times, or in sending grain or bread outside the area to maximize profit.

Thompson shows that violent corrective action was common, and emphasizes that it was orderly and organized rather than spasmodic or non-rational. He asserts that such action was animated not merely by hunger or desperation, but also by a conception of what minimal moral standards must be met by local economic processes; this he called the 'moral economy' of the crowd—their conception that it was 'unnatural' 'that any man should profit from the necessities of others and . . . that in time of dearth, prices of "necessities" should remain at a customary level, even though there might be less all around' (Thompson, 1971, p. 132).

Thompson notes that violence was

> triggered off by soaring prices, by malpractices among dealers, or by hunger. But these grievances operated within a popular consensus as to what were legitimate and what were illegitimate practices in marketing, milling, baking, etc. This in its turn was grounded upon a consistent traditional view of social norms and obligations, of the proper economic functions of several parties within the community, which, taken together, can be said to constitute the moral economy of the poor. An outrage to these moral assumptions, quite as much as actual deprivation, was the usual occasion for direct action (Thompson, 1971, pp. 78–79).

Whether, when and to what extent economic action is the subject of general social agreements about what moral standards it must meet has come to be known as the problem of 'moral economy'. Although even the briefest reflection confirms that modern economic transactions are bounded by normative restrictions (it is virtually never permitted to sell babies, bodily organs or political favors, and only sometimes blood (see Titmuss, 1971; Walzer, 1983)), the debate over moral economy has been conducted in an acrimonious way, with one side insisting on the wide importance of the concept and the other on its unimportance (see, for example, the sharply contrasting views of Scott (1976) and Popkin (1979) on the moral economy or lack thereof of Southeast Asian peasants during the twentieth century).

For business groups, moral economy can be taken as a variable, asking to what extent a group's operations presuppose a moral community in which trustworthy behavior can be expected, normative standards understood and opportunism foregone. For example cartels, an organizational form that is highly vulnerable to cheating on the part of even a few members, and where comprehensive monitoring is normally too expensive to pay off, are unlikely to succeed unless their members partake of some moral community. This is contrary to the usual analysis based entirely on economic or legal incentives.

Chandler, for example, argues that cartels failed in the United States because they could not be legally enforced, and indeed became largely illegal with the Sherman Act of 1890 and subsequent judicial interpretations. But his own account reports the failure of most cartels well before the Sherman Act, a main cause being the presence of renegade speculators like Jay Gould, who were outside the social and moral community formed by other cartel members, and therefore felt free to abrogate pooling and other agreements. Cartel failure forced business to a larger scale of integration than would have been necessary had these agreements been maintained (Chandler, 1977, Chs 4–5). Similarly, it was a Silesian prince whose actions sank the Rhine-

Westphalian Pig-Iron cartel in 1908, perhaps because he was not socially accountable to elites in a different region (Maschke, 1969, pp. 236, 245). Some German cartels, on the other hand, survived even in the face of economic disincentives (Peters, 1989). I suggest that the key here is to understand how social structure facilitated a moral community in one situation but not the other, an issue that goes beyond material incentives and requires a distinctly sociological analysis.

More generally, among business groups the world over, there are clear distinctions in the extent to which members see themselves as a part of a moral economy. The Korean *chaebol*, for example, give the impression that action is not oriented to any set of normative standards or mutual obligation, but rather to profit maximization by the exercise of relatively unopposed power from the top. It does not follow that hierarchically organized groups never partake of moral economy. Indeed, much of the development of the idea has stressed *noblesse oblige*—the obligations attached to a powerful position in many social systems, including but hardly limited to feudalism (cf. Scott, 1976). This appears to be characteristic of Japanese vertical business groups, about which Orrù *et al.* comment that 'domination is not embedded in or legitimized by the right to command. Rather, control is most of all . . . a matter of adhesion to one's own duties as prescribed by role positions. No single firm, however powerful, is exempt from duties; top financial institutions and industrial firms are bound by role expectations as much as the smallest subcontracting firm in the organizational hierarchy' (Orrù *et al.*, 1989, p. 565). Smitka (1991) especially stresses the economic importance of trust in subcontracting by large automotive firms in Japan. For Nicaragua, Strachan indicates that many of his interviewees 'signalled "loyalty and trust" as the main characteristics of a group . . . This group characteristic of mutual trust helps distinguish business groups from other associations, such as the Nicaraguan Chambers of Commerce and Industry' (Strachan, 1976, p. 16).

The concept of moral economy presents troublesome measurement difficulties, but most observers agree that its elements are extremely important for group functioning. Strachan (1976) comments, for example, that mutual trust is 'an essential ingredient if the group is to achieve the close coordination of economic activity which results in a meaningful concentration of economic power' (p. 16). It is especially hard to separate out the idea of moral economy from behavioral indicators consistent with a purely economic-incentive-driven account. Most economic theories of trust and solidarity argue that people act in a trustworthy way, or object to the action of others, when this is in their economic self-interest. Concerns about how a bad reputation may affect future business, for example, may go far toward insuring action that meets moral standards, but is not actually motivated by adherence to those standards. Where economic action attributed to shared normative beliefs is also consistent with the economic self-interest of actors, even in the presence of expressions of beliefs in the norms, rational choice theorists and economists believe that it is more parsimonious to omit actors' ideas about proper action as a causal variable, on the grounds that the behavior would have occurred in any case.[18] We have little way of partitioning the variance between the causal efficacy of ideas and of interests in situations where they overlap, but there are circumstances where the existence of a moral economy should make a difference—where actors should behave in ways that could not be predicted by knowledge of their economic and material incentives alone, if they in fact share beliefs about the proper conduct of economic affairs. The showing that this does in fact occur would be strong evidence for the value of this concept, and would help us see where it has its main significance.

Finance, Capital and the Role of Banks in Business Groups

Previous sections addressed the internal structure of business groups. We need also to know a great deal about how such groups operate in their economic environment. In this section I discuss how business groups relate to the mobilization of capital, and in the next, where they stand in relation to the state.

Economists' interpretations of business groups, as indicated earlier, often cast them as functional substitutes for capital markets. While this view is too narrow in general, many well-defined business groups do have the acquisition, distribution and investment of capital as one of their main activities. In the 'natural history' of business groups, those that begin with no affiliation to financial institutions usually form or acquire a bank early on, in order to assist in accumulating capital for group members from a wide variety of outside sources (Leff, 1978, p. 664).

In a study of banks in early American history, for example, Lamoreaux (1986) notes that since the 1600s, 'New England merchants had operated through complex kinship-based financial alliances. It was inevitable that, with the multiplication of bank charters in the early nineteenth century, these alliances would seek to further their own interests through banks.

---

[18] Of course it is problematic whether one should accept the pursuit of self-interest as some sort of fundamental null hypothesis, which is the claim that implicitly underlies the assumption of parsimony here. For other analysts it would be equally plausible that people are unlikely in general to pursue self-interest and that the null hypothesis should be the pursuit of shared normative principles. Since this paper is not a general treatise on social theory, this fundamental disagreement is merely noted.

Major kinship groups . . . each controlled several banks in their respective cities' (p. 652). The original organization of business groups by kinship had the disadvantage that 'sources of capital accumulation were restricted mainly to members of the kinship group, making it difficult to raise the sums necessary for financing large-scale industrial enterprises . . . Banks tapped the savings of the surrounding communities and thereby expanded the capital resources available to the groups' (p. 653). In early nineteenth century New England, then, banks 'did not operate primarily as public-service institutions. Their main purpose was to serve as the financial arms of the extended kinship groups that dominated the economy' (p. 659).

Lamoreaux (1986) highlights the role of banks in allowing business groups to overcome the limitations inherent in kinship-based firms:

> Without banks, kinship groups would have been forced to depend largely on their own resources to finance investment. This . . . would have re-stricted ventures of any size and importance to the most well-endowed groups. The multiplication of banks in the first half of the nineteenth century enabled families lacking adequate resources of their own to compete in the industrial arena, which in turn gave the economy its particular vitality (p. 666; see Lamoreaux (1994) for a more detailed account of 'insider lending' and its economic context).

This analysis illuminates why most business groups internalize banking functions early in their history.

Even in the mid-twentieth century, when American business groups were harder to identify clearly than in many countries, banks and insurance companies remained quite central. Mintz and Schwartz (1985, p. 150) found that of the twenty American corporations with the most director interlocks in 1962, seventeen were financials.[19] Banks are especially central in interlock networks of regional firms. The 'dense interchanges [of directors] among regional companies . . . reflect long-term business relationships among local elites, one expression of which is board interlocks . . . Every serious study of a major metropolitan area has discovered tight interlock networks with banks as the central nodes' (Mintz and Schwartz, 1985, pp. 195, 196). It is interesting that whereas in many countries, business groups cut across regions, the most clearcut American cases seem to be mainly regionally defined. This may result in part from the size of the USA and the sheer number of substantial cities, each with its own regional identity, at least as

[19] The long-running debate on how influential financial institutions are in domination of the economy is not covered here. An account of this literature is given in Mintz and Schwartz (1985), Ch. 2). For the argument that 'a handful of immense banks, concentrating within their coffers the bulk of the assets and deposits of the entire banking system and providing much of the loans and credits for industry, are the decisive units in the circulation of capital in contemporary capitalist economies', see Soref and Zeitlin (1987).

much as from the alleged individualism of national character and restraints of anti-trust legislation. One would expect less pressure for regionalization of business in a small homogeneous country like Japan (though Korean groups do draw on strong regional loyalties). Much more attention is needed to the role of space in structuring business relations, and the mechanisms by which this structuring occurs. (For an interesting American example, see Saxenian (1994).)

Business Groups and the State

Because business groups are more powerful than single firms and can translate their oligopoly power into political leverage (cf. Leff, 1979b), the relation between such groups and the state must be considered. This relation is not only of concern in understanding problems of power and public policy, however, but is often central in sorting out why business groups exhibit the form, characteristics and behavior that they do, as these are often produced in response to interaction with government.

There is no theoretical reason why business groups might not evolve largely independent of state influence, or at least with an identity quite distinct from and at times in conflict with that of political elites, as has sometimes occurred in Mexico (Camp, 1989). On the other hand it is common for states to be so enmeshed in the world of business groups that key actors within the state themselves form their own firms and business groups, which function by and largely similarly to others, though of course with much better political connections, as for the Somoza group in pre-Sandinista Nicaragua (Strachan, 1976, Ch. 2) and the groups dominated by the Suharto family in Indonesia (Robison, 1986, Ch. 10). Groups may also be dominated by fractions of the state-apparatus, like the military-owned business groups of Indonesia (Robison, 1986, Ch. 8).

The general orientation of the state toward economic development and business may shape the structure of business groups. In the United States even the somewhat inconsistent enforcement of antitrust laws has discouraged routinized cooperation among firms (Fligstein, 1990) On the other hand an attitude of general encouragement and coordination by the Japanese state has facilitated its extensive systems of cooperation.

Evans suggests arranging states on a continuum from 'predatory' to 'developmental', the former being mainly concerned to extract resources from the economy for its own purposes and the latter committed to supporting economic development. A fully predatory state such as Zaire, described as 'klepto-patrimonial' by Evans (1989, p. 576), is unlikely to permit any serious economic development, as it undercuts the possibility of systematic capital accumulation. States with strong patrimonial overtones but with less single-minded devotion to extraction, however, may foster weak but non-negligible business groups. This appears to fit the situation of Indonesia during Sukarno's rule, from 1949 to 1965. During this period, business groups were organized around state-granted monopolies embodied in exclusive import licenses, foreign-exchange credits, government contracts and state-bank credit. (White (1974) gives a similar account of the origins of business groups in Pakistan.) What distinguished this situation from one of pure rent-seeking on the part of business from public funds was the active participation of government and military officials and party officers in setting up business groups of their own—what Robison calls 'politico-economic empires'—to take advantage of their obvious ability to secure government favors. The weakness of non-political groups in such a setting lies in their inability to subsist without government support, and, indeed, after the fall of Sukarno and other patrons, 'many of the most prominent indigenous business groups also collapsed' (Robison, 1986, p. 91).

Korea under Syngman Rhee, from 1948 to 1960, was similar in that a few favored business leaders and groups received enormous benefits from the government, derived especially from foreign aid. Many received substantial 'loans' on which they paid neither interest nor principal (Amsden, 1989, p. 39). The state was a relatively weak partner in these arrangements, and although economic growth was strong for a time, by the end of the 1950s the economy was deeply depressed (Amsden, 1989, p. 40).

One outcome of patrimonial states with largesse to bestow seems to be that business groups emerge that are substantial and centralized, in order to take systematic advantage of the situation, which is more difficult for smaller firms or groups. Robison (1986, p. 267) suggests that in Indonesia, the persistent need to gain protection from generals has pushed business groups in the direction of becoming large conglomerates 'clustered around centres of politico-bureaucratic power'. This was especially important for the Chinese owned groups under Suharto which had special need of political protection on account of being always subject to popular discontent based on resentment of an ethnic minority dominating the economy.

In Korea, when Syngman Rhee was overthrown in 1961 by General Park Chung Hee, one of the government's first official actions was to arrest the now-millionaire businessmen who had profited so extravagantly under Rhee and threaten them with expropriation of their assets. Having placed them in this desperate situation, Park then pardoned them on the condition that they participate in a major push toward economic development. Favoring long-range planning and large enterprises, Park, from his position of strength, presided over the expansion of the *chaebol* that now dominate the economy. Thus, weak and dependent business interests, brought to their knees by the fall of their previous patron, had little choice but to follow the policies prescribed by the military regime, which provided most of the funding but, unlike the earlier period, demanded strong economic performance (Jones and Sakong, 1980). This is another case where many of the groups' characteristics—large size, diversification, especially into heavy industry, and highly centralized leadership—were either mandated by the state or were necessary in order to cope with its demands.

Orrù (1993) suggests that after World War II, the French government embarked on a similar program to that of General Park, to 'nurture the growth of large, internationally-competitive conglomerates' (p. 9). As a result, 'family-owned business networks and densely networked public and private holding companies are the dominant organizational forms in the French economy' (p. 15), which historically had been dominated by small-to medium-sized firms and moderate-sized holding companies.[20]

6. *Discussion*

Empirical correlations among the six dimensions I have discussed, along which business groups vary, are surprisingly weak. We might expect centralized ownership of group firms to predict a clear vertical authority structure, but in fact this depends upon the historical context in which the ownership was established. For the Korean *chaebol*, the vesting of large sums by government in single entrepreneurs to control numerous firms indeed facilitated an authoritarian structure. But for many British groups of the early-to mid-twentieth century, like British Tobacco, which controlled the stock of sixteen firms, centralized ownership by the holding company reflected an agreement to concentrate some functions while preserving maximum independence for the families controlling component firms (Chandler, 1990, pp. 247–248).

Strong moral economy in a business group may typically derive from a substantial level of internal solidarity and cohesion that must include strong horizontal ties and may or may not be accompanied by strong vertical coordination; existing studies barely scratch the surface of this difficult question. Most business groups do display some level of moral economy, however, and it may well be that the inability to generate such a normative structure will leave its mark mainly in the absence of business groups where one might otherwise expect them. In much of Southeast Asia, for example,

---

[20] But Adams argues that the policy of supporting large, integrated firms lost popularity by the late 1970s, on account of concerns about rigidity 'at a time when adaptability was considered essential' (Adams, 1989, p. 54).

this may explain why leading business groups tend to be Chinese rather than indigenous, since overseas Chinese social organization has the cohesion that escapes local business (cf. Geertz, 1963; Robison, 1986; Kiong, 1991; Granovetter, 1992). As Robison (1986) notes for Indonesia, this pattern has the important political consequence that the most powerful business interests, who in other settings might become the core of a politically autonomous middle class, are fundamentally dependent on the government for protection against recurrent xenophobia, and thus unable to unite with indigenous business which sees them as ethnic competitors.

The role of the state is important in shaping ownership, authority structure and relation of groups to financial institutions. States may play especially strong coordinating roles where business groups are largely in competition with or simply separated from one another, so that there is little opportunity for any sense of the national interest to emerge *vis-à-vis* that of particular groups. Korea is a type-case of such strong coordination, and it may be, correspondingly, that the relatively lower level of direction provided by government in Japan has to do with the greater ability of Japanese groups to link up with one another, and negotiate common problems, than those in Korea.

There is no guarantee, outside optimistic functionalist accounts, that the 'correct' level of coordination will be supplied by either government or business groups, but where this does occur we may expect to see better economic outcomes. I have already suggested that selection bias has confused us into thinking that interfirm cooperation within East Asian business groups leads automatically to economic success; in world-historical perspective, such cooperation is common, economic success is not. We thus require a theoretical argument that addresses not only the internal characteristics of business groups but also how these mesh with their institutional context, and that attempts to specify what institutional combinations work best.

When states and business groups can provide a degree of coordination that balances private, sectoral and national interests, aggregate economic performance as well as distributional equity may be achieved. But for this statement to rise above tautology will require considerable theoretical development. One promising direction is suggested by Evans (1989), who argues that for a state apparatus to be effective in forwarding economic development, it must be internally coherent and strong, but also well connected into, but not captive of, the economic sphere. Encarnation notes that although Indian business houses are in many ways similar to Korean *chaebol*, and have achieved similar success in dislodging multinational firms from their country's markets, the far greater autonomy of the Korean than the Indian government *vis-à-vis* such groups allowed it to insist on strong economic performance in export markets, leading to a growing divergence in economic performance between the two countries (Encarnation, 1989, pp. 204–225). Ironically, from the point of view of free-market ideology, the argument is that business groups produce efficient outcomes only when exposed to the rigors of free-market competition, which all avoid unless forced into it by a powerful and autonomous state. The free market then appears as an unnatural social and political construction.

Exactly how autonomous states are in relation to business interests, and from what this autonomy derives, deserves much more attention. Depending on the country, fuller analysis of such arguments may also require an understanding of the position of and relation to business and government of other interest groups such as labor, agrarian elites and foreign firms and investors. It is far beyond the scope of this paper to develop the required arguments in detail. But only by so doing will we clearly connect business groups to important economic and political outcomes. A clear account of such outcomes requires a far better understanding of business groups and their institutional context than we have thus far attained.

References

Adams, W. (1989), *Restructuring the French Economy: Government and the Rise of Market Competition since World War II*. The Brookings Institution: Washington, DC.

Amsden, A. (1989), *Asia's Next Giant: South Korea and Late Industrialization*. Oxford University Press: New York.

Baumol, W. (1968), 'Entrepreneurship in Economic Theory,' *American Economic Review (Papers and Proceedings of the 80th Annual Meeting)*, 58(May), 64–71.

Ben-Porath, Y. (1980), 'The F. Connection: Families, Friends and Firms in the Organization of Exchange,' *Population and Development Review*, 6 (1), 1–30.

Biggart, N. (1991), 'Institutionalized Patrimonialism in Korean Business,' in C. Calhoun (ed.), *Comparative Social Research, Vol. 12 Business Institutions*. JAI Press.

Blaug, M. (1986), *Economic History and the History of Economics*. New York University Press: New York.

Camp, R. A. (1989), *Entrepreneurs and Politics in Twentieth-Century Mexico*. Oxford University Press: New York.

Caves, R. E. (1989), 'International Differences in Industrial Organization,' in R. Schmalensee and R. Willig (eds), *Handbook of Industrial Organization*, Vol II. North Holland: Amsterdam, 1226–1249.

Chandler, A. D. (1962), *Strategy and Structure: Chapters in the History of the Industrial Enterprise*. MIT Press: Cambridge, MA.

Chandler, A. D. (1977), *The Visible Hand: The Managerial Revolution in American Business*. Harvard University Press: Cambridge, MA.

Chandler, A. D. (1982), 'The M-Form: Industrial Groups, American Style,' *European Economic Review*, 19, 3–23.

Chandler, A. D. (1990), *Scale and Scope: The Dynamics of Industrial Capitalism*. Harvard University Press: Cambridge, MA.

Chandler, A. D. (1992), 'The Emergence of Managerial Capitalism, in M. Granovetter and R. Swedberg (eds), *The Sociology of Economic Life*. Westview Press: Boulder, CO, 131–158.

Coase, R. (1937), 'The Nature of the Firm,' *Economica*, 4, 386–405.

Coase, R. (1993), 'The Institutional Structure of Production,' Nobel Prize Lecture delivered to the Royal Swedish Academy of Sciences, Stockholm, December 9, 1991. Reprinted in O. E. Williamson and S. G. Winter (1993), *The Nature of the Firm*. Oxford University Press: New York.

Coppel, C. A. (1983), *Indonesian Chinese In Crisis*. Oxford University Press: Kuala Lumpur.

Davis, G. F., K. Diekmann and C. Tinsley (1944), 'The Decline and Fall of the Conglomerate Firm in the 1980's: a study in the De-Institutionalization of an Organizational Form,' *American Sociological Review*, 59 (August), 547–570.

DiMaggio, P. and W. Powell (1983), 'The Iron Cage Revisited: Institutional Isomorphism and Collective Rationality in Organizational Fields,' *American Sociological Review*, 48, 147–160.

Elbaum, B. and W. Lazonick (eds) (1986), *The Decline of the British Economy*. Oxford University Press: New York.

Encaoua, D. and A. Jacquemin (1982), 'Organizational Efficiency and Monopoly Power. The Case of French Industrial Groups,' *European Economic Review*, 19, 25–51.

Encarnation, D. (1989), *Dislodging Multinationals: India's Strategy in Comparative Perspective*. Cornell University Press: Ithaca, NY.

Evans, P. (1979), *Dependent Development: The Alliance of Multinational, State, and Local Capital in Brazil*. Princeton University Press: Princeton, NJ.

Evans, P. (1989), 'Predatory, Developmental and Other Apparatuses: a Comparative Political Economy Perspective on the Third World State,' *Sociological Forum*, 4 (4), 561–87.

Fligstein, N. (1990), *The Transformation of Corporate Control*. Harvard University Press: Cambridge, MA.

Geertz, C. (1963), *Peddlers and Princes*. University of Chicago Press: Chicago, IL.

Gerlach, M. (1992), *The Alliance Structure of Japanese Business*. University of California Press: Berkeley, CA.

Gonzalez, N. (1992), *Dollar, Dove and Eagle: Palestinians in Diaspora—The Honduran Case*. University of Michigan Press: Ann Arbor, MI.

Goto, A. (1982), 'Business Groups in a Market Economy,' *European Economic Review*, 19, 53–70.

Granovetter, M. (1984), 'Small is Bountiful: Labor Markets and Establishment Size,' *American Sociological Review*, 49, 323–334.

Granovetter, M. (1985), 'Economic Action and Social Structure: The Problem of Embeddedness,' *American Journal of Sociology*, 91(3), 481–510.

Granovetter, M. (1990), 'Convergence Stood on its Head: a New Look at Japanese and American Work Organization' (Review of Lincoln and Kalleberg's *Culture, Control and Commitment*), *Contemporary Sociology*, 19 (6), 789–791.

Granovetter, M. (1992), 'Economic Institutions as Social Constructions: a Framework for Analysis,' *Acta Sociologica*, 35 (March), 3–11.

Hannah, L. (1983), *The Rise of the Corporate Economy*, 2nd edn. Methuen: London.

Hazari, R. K. (1966), *The Structure of the Corporate Private Sector: a Study of Concentration*. Asia Publishing House: London.

Herrigel, G. (1993), 'Large Firms, Small Firms and the Governance of Flexible Specialization: Baden Wuerttemberg and the Socialization of Risk,' in B. Kogut (ed.), *Country Competitiveness: Technology and the Organizing of Work*. Oxford University Press: New York.

Jones, L. P. and I. Sakong (1980), *Government, Business and Entrepreneurship in Economic Development: The Korean Case*. Harvard University Press: Cambridge, MA.

Kim, E. M. (1991), 'The Industrial Organization and Growth of the Korean *Chaebol*: Integrating Development and Organizational Theories,' in Gary Hamilton (ed.), *Business Networks and Economic Development in East and Southeast Asia*. Centre of Asian Studies, University of Hong Kong, 272–299.

Kiong, T. C. (1991), 'Centripetal Authority, Differentiated Networks: the Social Organization of Chinese Firms in Singapore,' in G. Hamilton (ed.), *Business Networks and Economic Development in East and Southeast Asia*. Centre of Asian Studies, University of Hong Kong, 176–200.

Kothari, M. L. (1967), *Industrial Combinations: a Study of Managerial Integration in India Industries.* Chaitanya Publishing House: Allahabad.

Lamoreaux, N. (1986), 'Banks, Kinship and Economic Development: the New England Case,' *Journal of Economic History*, 46 (3), 647–667.

Lamoreaux, N. (1994), *Insider Lending: Banks, Personal Connections and Economic Development in Industrial New England.* Cambridge University Press: New York.

Landes, D. (1965) [1951], 'French Business and the Businessman: a Social and Cultural Analysis,' in H. Aitken (ed.), *Explorations in Enterprise.* Harvard University Press: Cambridge, MA, 184–200.

Lazerson, M. (1988), 'Organizational Growth of Small Firms: an Outcome of Markets and Hierarchies?' *American Sociological Review*, 53, 330–342.

Leff, N. (1976), 'Capital Markets in the Less Developed Countries: the Group Principle,' in R. McKinnon (ed.), *Money and Finance in Economic Growth and Development.* Marcel Dekker: New York, 97–122.

Leff, N. (1978), 'Industrial Organization and Entrepreneurship in the Developing Countries: the Economic Groups,' *Economic Development and Cultural Change*, 26 (July), 661–675.

Leff, N. (1979a), 'Entrepreneurship and Economic Development: the Problem Revisited,' *Journal of Economic Literature*, 17 (March), 46–64.

Leff, N. (1979b), ' "Monopoly Capitalism" and Public Policy in Developing Countries,' *Kyklos*, 32 (Fasc. 4), 718–738.

Levy-Leboyer, M. (1976), 'Innovation and Business Strategies in Nineteenth- and Twentieth-Century France,' in E. C. Carter, R. Forster and J. Moody (eds), *Enterprise and Entrepreneurs in Nineteenth and Twentieth Century France.* The Johns Hopkins University Press: Baltimore, MD, 87–135.

Lincoln, J. and A. Kalleberg (1990), *Culture, Control and Commitment: a Study of Work Organization and Work Attitudes in the United States and Japan.* Cambridge University Press: New York.

Lovins, A. (1977), *Soft Energy Paths.* Ballinger: Cambridge, MA.

Marris, P. and A. Somerset (1971), *The African Businessman: a Study of Entrepreneurship and Development in Kenya.* Routledge & Kegan Paul: London.

Maschke, E. (1969), 'Outline of the History of German Cartels from 1873 to 1914,' in F. Crouzet *et al.* (eds), *Essays in European Economic History.* New York, 226–258.

McCloskey, D. (1981), *Enterprise and Trade in Victorian Britain.* George Allen & Unwin: London.

Meyer, J. and B. Rowan (1977), 'Institutionalized Organizations: Formal Structure as Myth and Ceremony,' *American Journal of Sociology*, 83, 340–363.

Mintz, B. and M. Schwartz (1985), *The Power Structure of American Business.* University of Chicago Press: Chicago, IL.

Nye, J. V. (1987), 'Firm Size and Economic Backwardness: a New Look at the French Industrialization Debate,' *Journal of Economic History*, 47 (3), 649–667.

Olson, M. (1982), *The Rise and Decline of Nations. Economic Growth, Stagflation, and Social Rigidities.* Yale University Press: New Haven.

Orrù, M. (1993), 'Dirigiste Capitalism in France and South Korea,' unpublished manuscript, Department of Sociology, University of South Florida, Tampa, FL.

Orrù, M., G. Hamilton and M. Suzuki (1989), 'Patterns of Inter-Firm Control in Japanese Business' *Organization Studies*, 10 (4), 549–574.

Orrù, M., N. Biggart and G. Hamilton (1991), 'Organizational Isomorphism in East Asia,' in W. Powell and P. DiMaggio (eds), *The New Institutionalism in Organizational Analysis.* University of Chicago Press: Chicago, IL, 361–389.

Peters, L. (1989), 'Managing Competition in German Coal: 1893–1913,' *Journal of Economic History*, 49 (2), 419–433.

Pfeffer, J. and G. Salancik (1978), *The External Control of Organizations: A Resource Dependence Perspective.* Harper & Row: New York.

Phipatseritham, K. and K. Yoshihara (1983), *Business Groups in Thailand.* Research Notes and Discussions Paper No. 41, Institute of Southeast Asian Studies, Singapore.

Piore, M. and C. Sabel (1984), *The Second Industrial Divide: Possibilities for Prosperity*. Basic Books: New York.

Popkin, S. (1979), *The Rational Peasant*. University of California Press: Berkeley, CA.

Portes, A. and R. D. Manning (1986), 'The Immigrant Enclave: Theory and Empirical Examples,' in S. Olzak and J. Nagel (eds), *Competitive Ethnic Relations*. Academic Press: Orlando, FL.

Reddy, W. (1984), *The Rise of Market Culture: The Textile Trade and French Society, 1750–1900*. Cambridge University Press: Cambridge.

Robison, R. (1986), *Indonesia: The Rise of Capital*. Allen & Unwin: Sydney.

Sabel, C. and J. Zeitlin (1992), 'Stories, Strategies, Structures: Rethinking Historical Alternatives to Mass Production,' in C. Sabel and J. Zeitlin (eds), *Worlds of Possibility: Flexibility and Mass Production in Western Industrialization*.

Sanders, E. (1986), 'Industrial Concentration, Sectional Competition and Antitrust Politics in America: 1880–1980,' in K. Oren and S. Skowronek (eds), *Studies in American Political Development*, Vol. 1. Yale University Press: New Haven, CT, 142–213.

Saxenian, A. (1994), *Regional Advantage: Culture and Competition in Silicon Valley and Route 128*. Harvard University Press: Cambridge, MA.

Scherer, F. M. and D. Ross (1990), *Industrial Market Structure and Economic Performance*, 3rd edn. Houghton Mifflin Company: Boston, MA.

Schumacher, E. V. F. (1973), *Small is Beautiful: Economics as If People Mattered*. Harper & Row: New York.

Schumpeter, J. (1979) [1926], *The Theory of Economic Development*, 2nd edn. Transaction Press: New Brunswick, NJ.

Scott, J. (1976), *The Moral Economy of the Peasant*. Yale University Press: New Haven, CT.

Scott, J. (1987), 'Intercorporate Structures in Western Europe: a Comparative Historical Analysis,' in M. Mizruchi and M. Schwartz (eds), *Intercorporate Relations: The Structural Analysis of Business*. Cambridge University Press: New York, 208–232.

Skinner, G. W. (1957), *Chinese Society in Thailand: An Analytical History*. Cornell University Press: Ithaca, New York.

Smitka, M. J. (1991), *Competitive Ties: Subcontracting in the Japanese Automotive Industry*. Columbia University Press: New York.

Soref, M. and M. Zeitlin (1987), 'Finance Capital and the Internal Structure of the Capitalist Class in the United States,' in M. Mizruchi and M. Schwartz (eds), *Intercorporate Relations: The Structural Analysis of Business*. Cambridge University Press: New York, 56–84.

Steers, R. M., K. S. Yoo and G. Ungson (1989), *The Chaebol: Korea's New Industrial Might*. Harper & Row (Ballinger): New York.

Stinchcombe, A. (1990), *Information and Organizations*. University of California Press: Berkeley, CA.

Stokman, F., R. Ziegler and J. Scott (eds) (1985), *Networks of Corporate Power: An Analysis of Ten Countries*. Polity Press: Cambridge.

Strachan, H. (1976) *Family and Other Business Groups in Economic Development: The Case of Nicaragua*. Praeger: New York.

Thompson, E. P. (1971), 'The Moral Economy of the English Crowd in the Eighteenth Century,' *Past and Present*, 50 (February), 76–136.

Titmuss, R. (1971), *The Gift Relationship: From Human Blood to Social Policy*. George Allen & Unwin: London.

Vonk, T. (1992), 'Perspectives on Restructuring: A Comparison of Mechanisms Across Solid and Troubled Organizations,' unpublished manuscript, Kellogg Graduate School of Management, Northwestern University.

Walzer, M. (1983), *Spheres of Justice: A Defense of Pluralism and Equality*. Basic Books: New York.

Werbner, P. (1984), 'Business on Trust: Pakistani Entrepreneurship in the Manchester Garment Trade,' in R. Ward and R. Jenkins (eds), *Ethnic Communities in Business: Strategies for Economic Survival*. Cambridge University Press: Cambridge, 166–188.

Varieties of Hierarchies and Markets: an Introduction

GARY G. HAMILTON[a] AND ROBERT C. FEENSTRA[b]

([a]Department of Sociology, University of Washington, Seattle, WA 98195 and
[b]Department of Economics, University of California, Davis, CA, USA)

The paper presents both a theoretical and an empirical argument that the concept of hierarchy needs to be reconceptualized. In our theoretical discussion we develop a synthesis between Coase's and Williamson's conception of a market/hierarchy dichotomy and Weber's distinction between economic power and authority. We hold that the authoritative aspects of hierarchies, especially within networks of firms, have independent effects on the formation of market economies. We empirically demonstrate the relevance of this reconceptualization in an analysis of the economies of South Korea and Taiwan. With these cases, we show that two different types of authoritative interfirm networks, one vertically and the other horizontally arranged, substantially shape the performance of these economies.

1. Varieties of Markets and Hierarchies

Institutional economics and economic sociology have developed rapidly and in tandem in recent years. Both subfields have moved from positions of peripheral to positions of central concern in their respective disciplines. In the development of both subfields, no distinction has been more formative than that between 'market' and 'hierarchy', between the 'invisible hand' of market forces and the 'visible hand' of authoritative organizations. In most of the literature this distinction is formulated as a continuum connecting polar opposites, with markets at one end and hierarchies at the other. Economists and sociologists enter the discussion about these concepts from opposite poles, with each trying to make their pole of orientation representative of the entire continuum. Economists argue that rational maximizing logics carry over into non-market situations, and sociologists argue that non-market social relations permeate all situations, including markets. Turning on alternative visions of societal order, this debate is less about the distinction between markets and hierarchies than about which interpretation of the world is correct. Because rational calculation and social relationships always co-exist, this debate, though interesting and sometimes fruitful, is unending. More perniciously, however, the rigid adherence to one interpretation over the other undermines the integrity of making the distinction between markets and hierarchies in the first place. As Williamson (1991, p. 271) quipped in a paraphrase of Clausewitz's aphorism, hierarchies are 'a continuation of market relations by other means'.

In this paper we want to reformulate the markets-versus-hierarchies debate by reconceptualizing the notion of hierarchy in line with what Coase (1937, pp. 403–404) regarded as the 'essential' feature of economic organizations: their authoritative structure. Economic organizations ('firms' in Coase's classic article, but viewed more broadly here as economic organizations) are, above all, authoritative organizations that structure relationships according to established rules of conduct and allow, in the context of such organizations, owners and managers of resources to decide how to participate effectively in the marketplace. In most of the recent literature, hierarchy is treated very narrowly, as a 'governance structure' that is internal to the firm but that derives wholly from external market conditions. The narrowness of this characterization of hierarchy, however, produces many ambiguities that limit the clarity and precision of economic and sociological analyses, particularly those having a comparative or a historical focus. One such ambiguity is the necessity to propose omnibus 'hybrid', intermediate or network types of economic organization to analyze those many economic situations that are characterized by neither markets or firms (Thorelli, 1986; Powell, 1990; Williamson, 1991).

In order to clarify the distinction between markets and hierarchies, we will supplement Coase's original distinction and subsequent writings on economic organization, particularly those by Williamson (1975, 1985, 1991), with the nearly identical distinction that Weber (1978, pp. 941–948) made over seventy years ago between economic power and 'authoritative' power. Weber, a legal and economic historian who was highly suspicious of the speculative sociology of his time and who 'avoided the concept of society' in his own work (Schluchter, 1989, pp. 3–4), developed a sophisticated typology of authority structures specifically for the purpose of demonstrating the interrelationship between what we would today call markets and hierarchies.

Using reformulated concepts of markets and hierarchies, we will make three theoretical points. First, markets and hierarchies are not opposites and, therefore, should not be seen as being located at opposite ends of a continuum. Rather, they should be seen, conceptually, as mutually creating and mutually reinforcing aspects of any economic system. Markets and hierarchies exist in a dynamic, creative tension with each other. To conceptualize them as opposites obscures their mutuality. Second, distinct and different market and hierarchy configurations exist empirically and vary historically and geographically. To conceptualize these in an initial way we discuss vertically and horizontally structured network hierarchies and their market affinities. Third, we will illustrate the utility of our approach with an analysis of two very different economic systems: the capitalist economies of Taiwan and South Korea.

2. *The Background to 'Markets and Hierarchies'*

The market/hierarchy distinction has had several independent origins but, in the current revival of interest in economic organization, writers universally trace the present version to Coase (1937). In a sweeping theoretical manner, Coase (1937, p. 390) asked the question of why firms emerge in market economies. Neoclassical theorists suggest that the price mechanism, a function of supply and demand, 'organizes' the economy. Firms, in theory, are merely production units that result from demand for a product and from the economies of scale needed to produce that product efficiently. Coase observed, however, that in the real world firms were quite variable, and often function in a way that supersedes the price mechanism. Firms vertically integrate their production, thereby bypassing price-fixing markets for many inputs and for many steps leading to the finished product. Therefore, he asks why firms exist in market economies. He (1937, p. 390) answers that there 'is a cost of using the price mechanism', a transaction cost that occurs as a result of needing to negotiate exchanges, of ensuring satisfactory compliance with the terms of the negotiations and of the necessity of marketing the finished goods. Firms can potentially avoid some of these costs by 'forming an organization and allowing some authority (an 'entrepreneur') to direct the resources'. In Coase's vision (1937, pp. 403–405), therefore, the crucial aspect of the firm is the authoritative ability of 'some authority' to direct resources efficiently in the production or marketing of goods.

Coase's definition of the firm makes it a two-sided concept. On the one side is the authoritative ability to direct resources effectively. On the other side this ability to direct resources effectively presupposes that whoever is in charge has the legitimate (e.g. legal) authority to do so. In his original article, Coase (1937, p. 430) is quite clear on this point.[1] He states that the

[1] In his recent comments (1991, pp. 64–65) on his 1937 paper, Coase seems to back off from his emphasis on the authoritative relationship within the firm: 'I consider that one of the main weaknesses of my article stems from the use of the employer–employee relationship as the archetype of the firm'. However, he wants to expand the basis of the relationship by clarifying what, in Weberian sociology,

defining quality of the firm is the specific content of the 'relationship' between the 'master and servant' or 'employer and employee'. The subordinate 'must be under the duty of rendering personal services to the master or to others on behalf of the master, otherwise the contract is a contract for the sale of goods or the like', and the 'master must have the right to control the servant's work, either personally or by another servant or agent'.

Both sides of Coase's definition of the firm are essential in making the firm analytically distinct from the market. In the marketplace, decision-making presumes calculations based on information about prices. In firms, decision-making has more latitude because it presumes the ability of the decision-makers, based on an established structure of power and obedience, to direct resources authoritatively to their best advantage. In both markets and firms, of course, decision-makers would pursue and, theoretically at least, attempt to maximize their own interests, however they define them, but the contexts of making decisions substantially differ, markets having price and firms having authority over others as the calculative backdrop.

Coase's original distinction between markets and firms has served as the foundation for a huge and still expanding literature on economic organization.[2] Much of the literature (e.g. Putterman, 1986; Holmstrom and Tirole, 1989; Williamson and Winter, 1991) focuses on debate about the nature of the firm. The most influential interpretations, including agency theories, moral hazard theories, incomplete contracting theories and transaction costs theories, all tend to treat the size and structure of economic organizations (i.e. the firm) as being contingent on external market conditions. Transaction cost theories, especially the version developed by Williamson, is arguably the most influential interpretation and the one on which we will focus. In fact, it was Williamson (1975) who popularized 'hierarchy' as a generic term for the firm.

Hierarchy, however, has a specific meaning in Williamson's transaction cost theory that problematizes only half of Coase's original distinction (Dow, 1987). To Williamson, hierarchy is a governance structure that arises in order for firms, as transactional units, to gain greater efficiency in the

---

would be called the 'basis of legitimacy', which in the case of the modern firm is its contractual and legalistic character. Coase explains, 'As a result of the emphasis of the employer–employee relationship, the contracts that enable the organizers of the firm to direct the use of capital (equipment or money) by acquiring, leasing, or borrowing it were not examined, perhaps because, fifty years ago, I did not know enough to be able to handle these problems'. In making this qualification, however, Coase seems to be embracing Cheung's (1983) interpretation of the firm as the 'nexus of all contracts'. Although this qualification accords with a Weberian reinterpretation, its consequence has been to divert attention away from domination within economic organization to extensive debates on the character of and differences among contracts within and between firms.

[2] The extent of this literature and its contents are well represented in Schmalensee and Willig (1989).

marketplace.[3] Hierarchy is effective centralized decision-making relative to an external market[4] and not authoritative control within the organization. Williamson is very clear on this point, because he views his version of transaction cost theory as being directly challenged by a group of scholars whom he labels the 'Radical Economists'. The Radicals (Stone, 1974; Marglin, 1974; Edwards, 1979; Bowles, 1985) argue that firm organization is a system of control to extract labor from workers, a system that is necessarily exploitative whether or not it is efficient. Williamson (1985, p. 210) replies to their arguments by asserting that 'hierarchy serves to economize on transaction costs'. Hierarchy cannot, however, be equated with power and authority per se, because power is 'so poorly defined that power can be and is invoked to explain virtually anything' (Williamson, 1985, p. 238).

Because power is, to Williamson, an undefined concept, he has left the authoritative side of hierarchy analytically undeveloped.[5] A brief look at the debate between Williamson and the Radicals suggests the reasons for this. Each side in the debate is looking at different phenomena but using the same terminology to describe what they see. The Marxist economists look at the rise and character of the capitalist economy as a whole. They approach this topic from a structural point of view. Looking out at the economic landscape of Western capitalism, they see the central importance of large, vertically integrated firms, containing large numbers of laborers grouped together for the purpose of mass production. With this sight in view, they ask what holds this economic structure together and what makes it different than the preceding traditional structures? They answer that it is power, the power of capitalists to direct labor and the derivative power of a state that establishes legal and political institutions that legitimizes the centralized decision-making of the capitalist class.

Along with most transaction cost theorists, Williamson is examining a different economic terrain. Williamson sees transactions as the basic units of observation. He looks at the level of transactions to understand how one set of exchanges differs from another set. In an exercise in theoretical induction (i.e. theory from the bottom up), he generates categories of transactional differences, classifications of governance structures and micro-economic explanations to account for the resulting array. The nature of transactions tends to constitute the independent variables and the nature of

[3] 'By governance structure, I refer to the institutional setting within which the execution of transactions is accomplished and their integrity is decided' (Williamson, 1986, p. 155).

[4] 'When the responsibility for effecting adaptations is concentrated on one or a few agents, hierarchy is relatively great. Where instead adaptations are taken by individual agents or are subject to collective approval, hierarchy is slight' (Williamson, 1985, p. 221).

[5] Williamson (1991) has recently acknowledged this fact when he 'dimensionalizes' governance by adding the 'hybrid' type of governance structure between the market and hierarchy extremes.

firms the dependent variables. From this perspective, power is an amorphous concept, a result rather than a cause of structure, and is, more or less, a background factor consistently present throughout the field of observation. To explain the classificatory differences that he observes, such as why some firms in some industrial sectors tend to be more vertically integrated than others, something more than just power must be evoked. According to Williamson, the differences emerge as a result of the exigencies encountered in doing business in competitive economies. Different types of business have different transactional requirements that lead, in turn, to a specific range of organizational decisions about how to handle them, such as how to obtain standard but specialized inputs for manufacturing a product. When the process of exchange grows too difficult, too expensive or too unpredictable, for whatever reasons, firms must decide whether or not to expand their boundaries to organize authoritatively those areas once managed through exchanges based on price. Hierarchies, maintains Williamson, grow and change in response to the dynamics of transactions, not in response to the dynamics of power.

Many scholars have criticized the thesis that hierarchy is an outcome of efficiency. Some (Perrow, 1981, 1990; Fligstein, 1985, 1990, 1991; Roy, 1990) attack the thesis empirically, by arguing that efficiency was not the cause for the waves of vertical integration that occurred in the USA and Europe from the 1890s on.[6] Instead, capitalist greed, politicians' connections, legal justifications and simple imitation serve as more reasonable explanations for vertical integration than considerations about efficiency. Others (Granovetter, 1985; Dow, 1987; Perrow, 1990) attack the thesis more theoretically, suggesting that hierarchy provides new sources of opportunity rather than only efficiency, that markets are more structured and hierarchies less authoritative than the distinction would suggest, and that making an outcome (greater efficiency) the cause of a prior condition (hierarchy) is overly functionalist and tautological.

For sociologists the most important critique of Williamson's transaction cost theory comes from Granovetter (1985). Granovetter (1985, p. 501) directly criticizes the market/hierarchy distinction by arguing that 'social relations between firms are more important, and authority within firms less so, in bringing order to economic life, than is supposed in the markets and hierarchies line of thought'. Accepting Williamson's equation of hierarchy with firm, Granovetter maintains that systems of interfirm relations, based on some form of power, are important determinants of market structure.

[6] We should note that, for these scholars, Chandler's *The Visible Hand* (1977) is the first target of criticism, with Williamson coming second.

However, he does not provide a way to conceptualize these interfirm power relationships.

Most of these criticisms do not really engage Williamson's transaction cost theory on its own terms, as a way theoretically to understand the organizational outcomes of firm-level decision-making in a competitive environment. Some of the critics would like to dismiss the entire relevance of a transactional level of analysis, preferring instead a more top-down structuralist perspective. Others would substitute other factors, such as social relationships, for transaction costs and make these decisive for inter-firm relations. We believe, however, that, in the study of economic organization, a transactional level is necessary, because it represents a level of analysis in which economic action can be conceptualized in subjectively meaningful terms.[7] However, without an adequate conceptualization of authority underpinning the concept of hierarchy, the subjective aspect of control within an economic organization is played down in preference to a subjective recognition of external market conditions. With such an emphasis, hierarchy becomes a derivative concept, a tautological outcome of external market conditions, an outcome of market efficiency. In this role, hierarchy is always a dependent rather than an independent variable, a consequence rather than an independent cause, of market conditions. It is the duality of market and hierarchy, a duality between price and the entrepreneur as independent but interrelated modes for organizing market activities, that serves· as the basis for Coase's original conceptualization, and without the duality, the conceptualization is strictly a one-handed approach to economic analysis.

3. *Rethinking the Market/Hierarchy Distinction: the Problem of Boundaries*

Putterman (1986, p. 15) has identified two key steps that need to be taken in order to make the market/hierarchy distinction more useful. Firms and markets, he writes, are 'woven, together, into the cloth that is the economy as a whole. The task of analyzing the economic nature of firms ultimately must include both an understanding of the forces shaping the boundary between firms and markets . . . and a sense of the way in which firm and market fit together in the larger system'. The need to define the boundaries lines is logically the first step. This requirement is satisfied, analytically at least, by defining the reach of authority, for it is authority that determines the extent of economic organization, the limits of authoritative economic action.

---

[7] This level of analysis allows what Weber calls a *Verstehen* interpretation of action, action conceived in terms of the subjective meaning intended by the actors.

In his development of Coase's market and hierarchy distinction, Williamson, following Coase's lead, makes two assumptions that undermine the independent role of authority relations in economic organizations. First, he equates the entrepreneur's authoritative control over resources with the 'governance structure' internal to a firm. In fact, a large part of the recent literature in institutional economics is an attempt to define the economic nature of the firm, instead of the economic role of authoritative organizations. Williamson equates hierarchy with the firm, the modern corporation in particular, and when he discovers that a significant portion of economic activity is organized outside the firm, he posits an organizational category between firms and markets, the hybrid, in which he deposits everything that does not fit in one of the two extremes (Williamson, 1991).

There is no a priori reason to think, however, that structures of authoritative control are necessarily contained in or are limited to the firm. If the ability to make authoritative decisions regarding economic resources is a defining feature of hierarchy, then theory requires that the boundaries of economic organization be defined empirically, in terms of the structures in which authoritative actions take place, rather than arbitrarily assigning those boundaries to that of the firm.[8] Moreover, as Biggart and Hamilton (1992) have argued, the firm does not have the same empirical and conceptual significance throughout the world but, rather, is a prominent feature of what Davis and North (1971) call an institutional environment—'the social and legal ground rules that establish the basis for production, exchange and distribution'—only in modern Western societies, but not, for instance, in Asian societies.

The second assumption about hierarchy that Williamson makes, again following the lead of Coase, leads to misplaced emphasis on the role of contract and law. In Williamson's view, markets operate through contracts that bind participants in economic exchanges. The legal system provides the rules to the game, but is often inadequate to insure timely, cost-effective compliance with the contracts. Within economic organizations, however, contracts give way to the 'efficacy of administrative controls' (Williamson, 1991, p. 280). As a number of critics (e.g. Granovetter, 1985) have maintained, however, relations within firms are also contractual and legalistic, and compliance is just as much a problem in firms as it is in markets. The nature of the contracts, the application of laws and the maximization of individual interests in the two locations, however, differ substantially. Instead of understanding the differences, Williamson generalizes (and cat-

---

[8] Economists sometimes equate the concept of firm with every level of economic organization that acts authoritatively, whether that is a business group (Leff, 1978), a guild (A. Greif, P. Milgrom and B. Weingart, unpublished manuscript) or the modern corporation.

egorizes) the contractual nature of markets, making them, theoretically, a variable feature of all markets. Although he repeatedly claims that transaction cost theory is necessarily comparative, he fixes the very features that do, in fact, differ in inter-market comparisons.[9] For instance, legalistic and contractual thinking and assumptions of firm-based autonomy characterize a particular system of authority (the 'institutional environment' in North's terms) in which both markets and hierarchies exist in the USA (Biggart and Hamilton, 1992). It is an empirical question whether the same institutional environment also obtains in other locations. Our research on East Asia shows that legalistic and contractual thinking do not form the foundations of these market economies in the same way.

The distinction between markets and hierarchies can be greatly strengthened by supplementing it with Weber's distinction between economic power and authority.[10] Weber made this distinction one of the key dividing lines motivating his analysis in *Economy and Society*, sometimes regarded as his magnum opus. In this work, Weber (1978, pp. 63–211) systematically developed an extended typological analysis of the formal and informal constraints on economic action.[11] A market-versus-authority distinction served as the dividing line in this analysis for precisely the same reason that it did in Coase's article: because it distinguishes calculation based upon market conditions from calculation based upon authority. To interpret rational economic calculations, Weber developed an institutional theory similar in spirit and scope to that developed recently by North (1990). Weber assumed that

[9] Williamson notes frequently that his approach is comparative, but comparative methodology for transaction cost theory means the generation of typologies and classifications of differences in transactions and in governance structures. It implies cross-market or even cross-societal comparisons.

[10] Although rarely used by either the new institutional economists or the new economic sociologists, Weber's writings on the economy played a formidable role in the thinking of the earlier generation of institutional economists, notably Knight, who translated Weber's *General Economic History* of 1923 in 1961, and Schumpeter, briefly a colleague of Weber, who 'was greatly influenced by Max Weber's attempt to create a new and broad type of transdisciplinary economies, call *Sozialokonomik* or "social economics"' (Swedberg, 1991, p. 2). Among sociologists, of course, Weber is regarded as a founder of economic sociology (Swedberg, *et al.* 1990), but his contribution is often restricted to his controversial thesis about the Protestant origins of capitalism and to his formulation of bureaucracy as an ideal-type. Despite his relative neglect in both economics and sociology, Weber's writings comprise a highly sophisticated institutional theory of economic activity. Weber's major contribution to institutional economics comes in the decade after he wrote the book on the Protestant ethic, between 1908 and 1920, when he undertook the task of editing and himself writing large portions of a handbook that he entitled the 'Outline of Social Economics'. With this handbook, Weber aimed to correct the theoretical excesses of neoclassical economists in his own day by spelling out the relationships between the economy and socially organized groups. As time went on, Weber's contribution grew as other scholars failed to provide manuscripts of sufficient quality. In the end, Weber himself wrote the main section, which he provisionally titled 'The Economy and the Societal Orders and Powers'. Dying of pneumonia in 1920 before he had the opportunity to prepare the final manuscript for publication, Weber left several versions that were subsequently complied, edited and published posthumously as *Economy and Society*. See Schluchter's definitive account (1989) of the development of this book.

[11] This typological analysis formed a conceptual framework that allowed Weber to develop, in a series of studies on world civilizations, an explanation for the rise of Western capitalism.

participants in market economies reach decisions based on rational means–end calculations of interests. These calculations occur in institutionalized contexts, where only a range of specific options and an array of specific economic organizations are present. In such contexts, economic calculations are conditioned by the fact that economic actions are 'carried' by an existing set of 'economic organizations' (i.e. corporations, cartels and business groups) and are channelled by an existing set of 'economically regulative organizations', a category including everything from 'medieval village associations' to 'the modern state' (Weber, 1978, p. 74). Developmental economic changes over time tend to move economies towards greater means–end systematization. In Weber's terminology, the economy becomes increasingly rationalized, in terms of both the exchange processes and the institutions (including the state) that support them. One of the key features of this economic rationalization is the 'power' of economic actors to control and dispose of economic resources, which implies a system of property relations. [12]

Extrapolating from Weber's discussion of economic action, one can easily see that Weber's analysis could go in the direction pioneered by Williamson. Weber is clear that in any given institutional environment, economic organizations attempt to dictate the terms of exchange, and those in charge of these organizations, if they have the ability, will quickly alter their organizational structures to achieve greater market power. Weber's notion of economic power and Williamson's concept of efficiency are very similar in this regard: the hierarchies that are efficient to Williamson become recognized as economically powerful by other actors who calculate their personal interests in exchanging with them. To Weber, increasing the market power of a firm through vertical integration ('hierarchy' in Williamson's terms) is a rational response to external market conditions. [13]

Weber, however, makes an additional crucial distinction that Williamson

---

[12] In the most modern era, said Weber (1978, p. 67), 'a modern market economy essentially consists in a complete network of exchange contracts, that is, in deliberate planned acquisitions of powers of control and disposal'.

[13] For Weber, a 'typical measure of rational economic action' is similar to what Williamson regards as the calculative motive for vertical integration:

> The systematic procurement through production or transportation of such utilities for which all the necessary means of production are controlled by the actor himself. Where action is rational, this type of action will take place so far as, according to the actor's estimate, the urgency of his demand for the expected result of the action exceeds the necessary expenditure, which may consist in (a) the irksomeness of the requisite labor services, and (b) the other potential uses to which the requisite goods could be put; including, that is, the utility of the potential alternative products and their uses. This is 'production' in the broader sense, which includes transportation (Weber, 1978, p. 71).

does not make: hierarchy in relation to a market is not the same thing as hierarchy inside an organization.

> [I]n addition to numerous other types, there are two diametrically contrast-ing types of domination, viz., domination by virtue of a constellation of interests (in particular, by virtue of a position of monopoly), and domina-tion by virtue of authority, i.e., power to command and duty to obey . . . In its purest form, the first is based upon influence derived exclusively from the possession of goods or marketable skills guaranteed in some way and acting upon the conduct of those dominated, who remain, however, formally free and are motivated simply by the pursuit of their own interests. The latter kind of domination rests upon alleged absolute duty to obey, regard-less of personal motives or interests (Weber, 1978, p. 943).

He illustrates this distinction between the two types of domination with an example of two inter-firm networks:

> [W]e shall not speak of formal domination if a monopolistic position permits a person to exert economic power, that is, to dictate the terms of exchange to contractual partners. Taken by itself, this does not constitute authority any more than any other kind of influence which is derived from some kind of superiority, as by virtue of erotic attractiveness, skill in sport or in discussion. Even if a big bank is in a position to force other banks into a cartel arrangement, this will not alone be sufficient to justify calling it an authority. But if there is an immediate relation of command and obedience such that the management of the first bank can give orders to the others with the claim that they shall, and the probability that they will, be obeyed regardless of particular content, and if their carrying out is supervised, it is another matter. Naturally, here as everywhere the transitions are gradual (Weber, 1978, p. 214).

In these two examples of inter-firm networks, the distinction between power in the market and power in an economic organization rests only on a small difference in the nature of the relationship among the banks, but this difference, according to Weber, is all important. In the first example, the hierarchy is established among independent economic organizations, with the relations among banks being determined by independent calcula-tions of interest. In the second example, however, the hierarchy is internal to the economic organization and rests on the presumed right of command and the presumed duty to obey. The structure of the first networked hierarchy grows out of market conditions, but the structure of the second hierarchy, although perhaps influenced by the market, is determined by the substantive content of authority relationships.

Weber took such care in making this distinction because it served as a dividing point in his analysis: he certainly acknowledged that economic organizations were shaped internally by external economic processes, but they were also and more significantly influenced by the character of authority embodied in the organizations themselves. The calculative logic internal to authoritative organizations turns on the 'principles' used to legitimize the exercise of control within the organization. The internal structures of authoritative organizations, therefore, necessarily articulate the basis of their legitimacy. Weber recognized that even normal routines of action within the organization would reflect specific norms of authority. He illustrated this theoretical conclusion with an extended historically detailed discussion of the three 'pure types' of domination and the characteristic structural arrangements that grow from the organizational logic of each type: legal–rational domination giving rise to variations of bureaucratic organizations; traditional domination giving rise to variations of patrimonial organizations; and charismatic domination giving rise to variations of organizations based on discipleship (Weber, 1978, pp. 212–301, 941–1211).

In *Economy and Society* Weber discussed authoritative organizations at such length because he concluded that authoritative organizations influenced the structure of the economy more than the economy influenced the organizations. [14] This assessment was based on a wide-ranging historical and comparative analysis. The profit-oriented corporation, the legal system upon which it is derived and the market system in which it is located are all part of a distinctly modern developmental process that originated only in the West. [15] Other types of economic organizations existing historically and comparatively also have a great impact on economic endeavors and can also be rational and efficient, given their historical context. In fact, Weber was by no means certain, and expressed profound reservations, that these Western patterns would prevail in the long run despite the process of bureaucratic and economic rationalization.

In summary, Weber's particular perspective on economic organizations provides three very useful additions to Coase's and Williamson's market/hierarchy distinction. First, by defining hierarchy both in terms of authority and economically 'effective' action, the boundaries of economic organization are determined by the reach of authoritative power and are not arbitrarily equated with the firm. With the reformulated definition of hierarchy, the boundaries of economic organizations expand to match the extent of the authority relationship. To the extent that a network of people or firms are linked together by the exercise of binding norms, then that network func-

---

[14] Weber argued that, once the capitalist process began, market processes would further systematize economic organizations: 'All material means become fixed or working capital; all workers become "hands". As a result of the transformation of enterprises into associations of stock holders, the manager himself becomes expropriated and assumes the formal status of an "official" ' (Weber, 1978, p. 148).

[15] For an extended discussion of Weber's analysis of modern capitalism, see Collins (1980), Schluchter (1989) and Hamilton (1994).

tions as an economic organization. To the extent that networks of people or firms are linked together only by their individual economic interests, then that network does not constitute an organization in its own right. The key point in this definition is participants' subjective recognition that they are bound to the authoritative norms of the organization, that they are not formally free to act in other ways and that there is a coercive means to enforce the normative rules.[16] With this distinction, most intermediate types, hybrids and network organizations (Thorelli, 1986; Powell, 1990; Williamson, 1991) would become either market-oriented voluntarist networks or authoritatively grounded networks that are economically active.

Second, no longer attached to historically specific terms (e.g. the firm, laws, exchange contracting), the new concept of hierarchy as economic organization facilitates comparative analyses on the exact nature of the interaction between markets and hierarchies. This, of course, is Putterman's second point of correction: both markets and hierarchies constitute the larger economic system. One must understand how they function together to analyze the larger whole. Weber's key addition to this view is that the structure and array of economic organizations in a given economy create parameters for economic performance. Economic activities in the market-place, in turn, feed back on the structure, substantiating essential roles and systematizing those roles to achieve greater efficiency relative to the goals being sought. In this sense, markets and hierarchies are mutually creating and mutually reinforcing.

Third, the revised distinction provides a way to add Granovetter's embed-dedness perspective (1985) to transaction cost theory without relinquishing the theoretical claims of either approach. Inter-firm networks that rest on strongly normative social bonds are better understood as economic organizations in their own right instead of a residual or intermediate category. Embedded networks become units of economic action rather than the firms that constitute them. What Redding (1991) observed about Chinese inter-firm networks is true of all such embedded networks: the network linkages are stronger than the firms that make up the networks. Firms come and go, but the networks persist over time.

4. *Two Types of Network Hierarchies*

In this section we want to examine these three additions more systematically by analyzing two types of networked economic organizations and their modes

---

[16] In real life, of course, participants often do both at once. They often recognize that they are bound by organizational authority and act in a self-interested way in violation of the organizational norms. Also, in real life, the boundaries of who should obey, of when obedience is required and what the content of compliance should be is highly ambiguous.

of incorporation into economic activities. Network hierarchies obviously differ in how they link people together. With some oversimplification, some types of social networks link people in vertically arranged configurations. For instance, patronage systems in Hispanic societies tended historically to arrange people of power and wealth at the top of the hierarchy, and people of lesser wealth and power were connected to those at the top through some form of clientage, as represented by the *ladifundia* system of allocating rights to land. Other types of social networks, however, are much less hierarchical, and instead horizontally link people who are held to be normatively equivalent.

As we discussed, one of the main factors influencing economic organization is the nature of authority relations linking people together. Verticality tends to build on inequalities in power. Such inequalities can occur in the most diverse historical settings, ranging from bureaucratically defined chains of command common in modern organizations to clearly defined rankings of dependent status positions in patrimonial groups. Horizontal ties, however, tend to develop where relative (but not absolute) equality is normative. Colleagueship among faculty members of the same department or the same college and cooperation among members of a football or baseball team are examples of settings in which the participants may have very different functional roles and levels of income but still be accorded formal equality within an organized setting.[17] It is important to stress that the sociological content of either the vertical or the horizontal bonds differs greatly from context to context, and that these differences will certainly influence the resulting network configurations. However, despite differences in the sociological content, the vertical or horizontal dimensions greatly influence how authoritatively structured networks can be adapted to organizing economic endeavors and how economies, in turn, adapt to them.

One of the clearest illustrations of these differences is Geertz (1963). In this study, Geertz examines economic development in two Indonesian cities. In one of the cities, in Java, the economy is primarily a 'bazaar economy' dominated by Islamic and Chinese merchants, the peddlers. As he describes it, merchant households are typically coterminous with the firm, and these family firms are very small. The interlinkages among firms, however, are horizontal chains through which capital and commodities flow easily. The networks are characterized by their commercialism, by equality among participants and by their loosely coupled character, which in turn creates a 'hyperflexible marketing system' (Geertz 1963, p. 69).[18]

[17] See Hamilton (1978, 1985) for discussions of several types of economic action arising from particular groups in which the participants formally regard themselves as equals.

[18] We should note that Geertz does not explicitly identify the horizontal networks that are present in this case and in the case of other overseas Chinese traders in Southeast Asia. What Geertz observes are individuated households, with each actor making independent economic decisions, a condition that

In the other city, in Bali, the economy was organized through aristocratic households, the princes. The elites used their long-standing authority over more lowly ranked households to organize interhousehold networks for the purpose of commodity production. These princes overlapped authority derived from the traditional social structure with the pursuit of modern economic goals. Differentially ranked households provided the nuclei for vertically integrated economic networks producing such commodities as textiles and tires. Geertz noted that 'in organizational terms there is little doubt that the firms [organized by the princes] are much more impressive that those [organized by the peddlers]', and are capable of 'bringing together hundreds of villages in a common effort' (Geerts 1963, p. 121).

Using this illustration as a starting point, we want to offer a hypothesis, an organizational 'rule of thumb'. The ways an economic organization can be made cohesive, that is, the way it can be grounded in authoritative norms, creates a finite range of possibilities for organizing economic action. When adapted to economic purposes, vertically cohesive groups have an affinity for establishing vertically integrated systems of commodity production, systems whose organization expands along links in commodity chains. Horizontal ties, when adapted directly to economic purposes, do not lead to vertical integration but, rather, are segmental and lead to what we will call 'market integration.'[19]

Vertically Controlled Networks

Vertically arranged hierarchies occur in the most economically diverse settings. In precapitalist societies, economies often developed into what Weber (1978) called *oikos* or manorial economies. *Oikos* economies rest on the economic activities of elites, who authoritatively and patrimonially organize subordinate groups—serfs, slaves and other forms of bound labor—into cohesive economic organizations. Although often agrarian-based, *oikos*

---

indicates, to him (1963, p. 47), an absence of organization. What he describes, however, is a highly organized system of horizontal networking in which 'traders . . . treat each other in precisely formulated and technically restricted terms' (Geertz, 1963, p. 46). 'A trader contracting even a fairly petty agreement will look for others to go in with him, and, in fact, there is widely felt normative obligation on the part of traders to allow other people to cut into a good thing . . . The individual trader, unless he is very small indeed, is the center of a series of rapidly forming and dissolving one-deal, compositely organized trading coalitions' (Geertz 1963, p. 40). Made up of repeat players, these coalitions are the short-term manifestations of the perduring horizontal networks that make up this economy.

[19] For the purposes of this paper, organizations supporting market integration, the opposite of vertical integration, correspond to what Geertz calls 'interstitial' groups that intersect commodities chains. These groupings form an interface between sets of economic actors, such as buyers and sellers, producers and merchandisers in those situations where an organization forms a condition in which each link in a commodity chain is independently constituted and controlled, and forms a distinct transaction with its own costs and efficiencies.

economies can also be urban and oriented toward handicraft production (Weber, 1978, pp. 381–383). The elites or their agents are the economic decision-makers and, as Weber argues, these decision-makers normally sought 'want satisfaction' and not profits or efficiency. In some settings, however, such as in 17th and 18th century England or in the plantation economies of the Americas and Asia in the same period, *oikos* economies could become intensely market-oriented and could produce goods efficiently relative to the market conditions of the time. [20] In all of these cases, the economic organizations, the manors or the plantations, were not firms in a conventional sense. They encompassed many diverse households of unrelated people and placed them under the centralized direction of people in positions of recognized authority.

Authoritatively controlled vertical networks remain important forms of economic organizations in modern capitalist societies as well. Geertz's example of princely households from Indonesia's developing economy might be considered a pre-modern example, except for the fact that such elite households in Indonesia and elsewhere have continued to grow and to flourish in a fully capitalist era (e.g. Robison, 1986). In many parts of the world, such elite households have organized extensive networks of legally independent firms that are known in the literature (Leff, 1977, 1978; Hamilton *et al.*, 1990; Granovetter, 1994) as 'business groups'. Such business groups normally share some form of common ownership. Systems of ownership and control vary, however. The most common system of control is family ownership of at least the top tier of firms. Family members typically exercise their control through a central holding company or family foundation that owns all or a substantial portion of the firms in the group. In addition, many of these business groups intermix modern professional management with systems of control that manipulate ethnicity, status and other features common to patrimonial economies. Variations of such family-owned, vertically integrated business groups are found in India (Encarnation, 1989), Latin America (Strachan, 1976; Aubey, 1979; Ostiguy, 1990; *America Economia*, 1991) and, to a lesser degree, in such countries in Western Europe as France and England (Encaoua and Jacquemin, 1982). The South Korean *chaebol*, which we will describe below, is also an example of this type of vertical network.

---

[20] Weber's evaluation of the *oikos* is worth quoting in this context: '[The oikos] is not simply any large household or one which produces on its own various products, agricultural or industrial; rather, it is the authoritarian household of a prince, manorial lord or patrician. Its dominant motive is not capitalistic acquisition but the lord's organized want satisfaction in kind. For this purpose, he may resort to any means, including large-scale trade. Decisive for him is the utilization of property, not capital investment. The essence of the oikos is organized want satisfaction, even if market-oriented enterprises are attached to it. Of course, there is a scale of imperceptible transitions between the two modes of economic orientation, and often also a more or less rapid transformation from one into the other (Weber, 1978, p. 381).

Japanese business groups, the *keiretsu*, represent another type of vertically controlled hierarchical networks (Futatsugi, 1986; Hamilton *et al.*, 1989; Orrù *et al.*, 1989; Fruin, 1992; Gerlach, 1992). In these networks, the large firms at the top of the hierarchy are mutually owned through overlapping shareholding. Corporate control and economic decision-making, however, is not centralized as it is in most family-owned business groups but, rather, is somewhat decentralized and tends to be coterminous with production sequences (i.e. commodity chains) leading to the production of a common group of products (Aoki, 1988, 1990). These very large corporatized and mutually owned networks dominate the markets for intermediate inputs, labor intensive operations and services. These networks therefore have positions of considerable economic power *vis-à-vis* the thousands of small and medium-sized firms that supply goods and service to them on a long-term non-contractual basis under conditions generally favorable to the *keiretsu* firms. As Orrù (1993) has shown, a similar hierarchical network structure has also developed in the German economy.

In both the family- and corporate-controlled networks, the business strategies of the group have an affinity for vertical integration in the production of commodities and the delivery of goods and services. These economic organizations build upon systems of authority that facilitate the formation of very large, authoritatively controlled groups. The possibilities for creating vertically controlled networks precede their formation and, at least in an economy influenced by capitalism, such possibilities create an affinity for vertical integration in relation to commodity production.[21]

Horizontally Controlled Networks

Horizontally arranged network hierarchies also occur in the most diverse historical locations, but differ in most economic respects from vertical ones. In precapitalist periods, horizontal networks were primarily organized linkages joining independent, economically engaged households into functionally diverse but organizationally encompassed economic endeavors. The best examples of such economic organizations are guilds, *landmanschaften* or *huiguan*, and other types of trade and merchant associations. As Greif *et al.* (1994) argue in the case of medieval guilds in Europe, the guild was the main organizational unit of medieval commerce, the 'nexus of contracts', rather than the households of individual merchants and artisans. The same conclusion also applies to late imperial China, where the *huiguan* and artisan

---

[21] The USA is an exception to this pattern because vertical integration primarily occurred within the boundaries of a legally defined firm instead of occurring within a network of firms. See Biggart and Hamilton (1992) and Hamilton and Sutton (1989) for a discussion of the exceptional nature of the USA.

associations were the organizational focus of all trade and handicraft production (Rowe, 1984; Hamilton, 1985). As a rule, these associations were organized as 'collegial bodies' (Weber, 1978, pp. 271–282), emphasizing the equivalence among members, usually by identifying a common identity. They were usually brotherhoods of fellow-townsmen, fellow-regionals or fellow-ethnics. These associations, when formalized, as were the European guilds and the Chinese *huiguan*, typically had two foci of control (Hamilton, 1985). First, the associational rules aimed at defining the terms of doing business and the quality of the products and services. Second, the associations regulated entry into the associations themselves. These associations endeavored to monopolize their economic sphere and punished those who violated either set of rules.

In the case of some religious and ethnic groups whose members specialized in long distance trade or became non-local merchants in many locales, horizontal networks worked more informally in the sense that the network had no geographical location, no visible building—not even a meeting site. Though more informal, the networks still operated as authoritative economic organizations in the sense that the behavioral expectations rested on sanctionable social rules.[22] Among Jewish and Chinese merchants, business dealings implied a commonality, such as kinship ties or common origins or a common middleman, that preceded transactions and gave the transactions a predictive normative structure that was not intrinsic in the transactions themselves. Violations of the normative expectations could also be sanctioned by expulsion, shunning and others means familiar in close-knit groups for dealing with non-compliance. Such groups handled trade relationships at great distances and in conditions of considerable uncertainty with relative ease.

In capitalistic societies, horizontally arranged networks continue to be a source of important economic organizations. Stock markets and commodities exchanges are modern counterparts to the medieval guilds and other forms of market organization. They represent organizationally encompassed firms, the brokerage houses with seats on the exchange, that work under a common set of rules defining the terms of trade and the conditions of entry (Abolafia, 1984). Even though they differ by size, wealth and functional specialization, the brokerage houses are equivalent in formal terms, each occupying a seat and each possessing rights and duties that ensue from that fact. Actions violating the common rules can be and are punished by the group itself, in addition to any other punishment that might result from legal action in a civil or criminal court.

---

[22] There are many examples of informal, short-term financial associations that are organized on this basis. The rotating credit associations common throughout many parts of the world is one example. Another example is the *compagnia* from medieval Italy (Lopez and Raymond, 1955, pp. 185–187).

Another particularly important variation of horizontal networks in capitalist societies is found in the household-based economies established by such groups as the overseas Chinese—the Chinese living outside the People's Republic of China. In the next section we will discuss one such economy, the Taiwanese economy.

Horizontally networked economic organizations interact with market forces in very different ways than do vertical networks. Horizontal networks are segmented into conceptually equivalent units that all act according to the same *organizational* rules. These rules may be defined in many ways, in terms of ritual decorum, ethnic pride or bureaucratic professionalism. Internally, because the equivalent units act similarly in conformity to known rules, they are highly predictable. Moreover, they are inherently anti-monopolistic. Even though the organizations themselves may monopolize their spheres of economic activity (e.g. the commodity exchange for silver), organizational rules forbid monopolization of that activity by anyone internal to the groups (e.g. a specific brokerage house) (Abolafia and Kilduff, 1988). Associational rules do not facilitate individual strategies leading to vertical and horizontal integration, in part because transaction rules are defined collectively and in part because monopolistic strategies threaten the groups themselves. Because of their organizational characteristics, these organizations and groups occupy economic niches intersecting commodity chains. They have an affinity for being market intermediaries instead of market producers. Guilds and stock markets act as organizational interfaces between buyers and sellers. Long distance merchant groups played much the same role. In capitalist Taiwan, as we will show below, horizontally arranged networks of family firms, wedged in a global economy between big buyers and retail sellers, also play functionally similar roles, although under very different conditions of production and distribution.

To illustrate more precisely the relation between these two types of networked hierarchies and their associated market economies, we will summarize the paired comparisons that we have made between the industrial structures of Taiwan and South Korea.

5. *Business Groups in South Korea and Taiwan*

South Korea and Taiwan are two rapidly industrializing economies; they are located in the same part of the world, about two hours' flight time from each other; they have developed in roughly the same years at roughly the same rapid rates; they have had similar historical influences, both having been socially and culturally dominated first by China and then, in the colonial period, by Japan; and both have used similar economic policies to develop, first supporting a strategy of import substitution and then adopting an aggressive strategy of export-led industrialization. Moreover, in both locations, most private firms, even those making up the largest business groups, are family-owned and controlled, and, significantly, in both locations, family authority and practices draw on Confucian ideology to sustain the patterns of relationships within and among families. In all these background variables—economic, social and cultural—Taiwan and South Korea are as nearly the same as could be imagined between any two countries in the world today. Yet the economies of these two countries are organized in radically different ways, Korea through vertically controlled networks and Taiwan through horizontally controlled networks. We first will outline the economic differences and then account for these differences in terms of the underlying networked hierarchies.

The economies of both countries are structured through networks of legally independent family-controlled firms.[23] Korean business groups, called *chaebol* (or money cliques), play prominent and decisive roles in organizing systems of commodity production and distribution in the total economy. The *chaebol* networks encompass the organization of commodity chains. By contrast, the Taiwanese business groups, sometimes called *guanxichiye* (related enterprises), do not encompass commodity chains; they have niche roles in the economy and are primarily suppliers of intermediate products and services sold domestically in an economy that is predominantly export-oriented. Table 1 gives a comparison of the top business groups in both countries. As is apparent, Korean business groups on balance are much larger than their Taiwanese counterparts. Table 2 describes the shares by industrial sector of the largest business groups in Korea and Taiwan quantitatively. It is clear as well that Korean business groups account for much larger proportions of the total output in the economy than do those in Taiwan. Even so, the Taiwanese business groups are still substantial.

Vertically Arranged Business Networks in Korea

To what degree do the *chaebol* networks represent vertically integrated networks, 'one setism', as such networks are known in the literature on

[23] All the researchers who have studied ownership patterns among large firms in Taiwan (Mark, 1972; Greenhalgh, 1988; Hamilton and Biggart, 1988) have emphasized the importance of family (*jia*) ownership and family control. An analysis of the 1983 and 1986 data on Taiwan business groups, as well as interviews with core people in some of the business groups, substantiates this finding. Majority ownership and control of business group firms are in the hands of core family members and heads of households. Our colleagues in Taiwan who are also working on this project have determined, on a group-by-group basis, that 84 of the top 97 business groups in 1983 can be strictly classified as family-owned business groups (Peng, 1989, p. 277). Of these 23 are primarily owned by a single head of household; the remaining 61 have multiple family members classified among the core people in the group, and most of those family members (54 out of the 61) are of three types: fathers and sons, brothers, and brothers and their sons (Peng, 1989, p. 278).

TABLE 1. East Asian Business Group Comparative Statistics (Expressed in US$)[a]

	Total sales (US$ million)	Total assets (US$ million)	Total no. of firms	No. of firms/BG (by internal)	Total no. of workers	No. of workers/BG (by internal)	No of workers/ firm (by internal)
South Korea (1983)							
Top 5 *chaebol*	35 360	24 872	123	25	322 876	64 575	2625
Top 10 *chaebol*	47 317	33 772	202	16	425 872	20 599	1304
Top 20 *chaebol*	58 187	44 078	328	13	550 458	12 457	989
Top 30 *chaebol*	64 509	49 611	412	8	688 385	13 793	1641
Top 50 *chaebol*	70 772	56 391	552	7	798 976	5530	780
Taiwan (1983)[c]							
Top 5 BGs	5084	5547	90	18	85 719	17 144	952
Top 10 BGs	7488	9660	180	18	164 129	15 682	871
Top 20 BGs	10 444	13 744	283	10	220 413	5628	546
Top 30 BGs	12 084	16 002	375	9	251 616	3120	339
Top 50 BGs	14 027	17 902	494	6	289 787	1908	321
Top 96 BGs	15 842	19 763	743	5	330 098	876	162

[a] Exchange rate per US$: Japan, 233 Yen; Korea, 772 Won; Taiwan, 40 NT$.

[b] *Source:* Ibo Hankook (1985), *Pal Ship O nyndo bankook ui 50 dae jae bul* [*The 50 top 'chaebol' Korea*]. Seoul, Korea.

[c] *Source:* Zhonghua Zhengxinso (China Credit Information Service) (1985), *Taiwan diqu jituan qiye yanjiu* [*Business Groups in Taiwan*]. Zhonghua Zhengxinso: Taipei.

TABLE 2. Business Group Shares in the Manufacturing Sectors of the Economies of South Korea (1989) and Taiwan (1988)

Manufacturing sector[a]	South Korean BG%[b]	Taiwan BG%[c]
Food products	34.79	13.60
Beverage	31.87	00.22
Textiles	46.73	42.26
Garments and apparel	1.17	06.40
Leather products	4.63	00.00
Lumber and wood products	11.21	05.20
Pulp and paper products	13.54	22.24
Printing and publishing	7.16	00.40
Chemical materials and plastics	38.62	15.80
Chemical products	6.18	04.54
Petroleum and coal products	91.20	00.00
Rubber products (not footwear)	29.05	12.80
Non-metallic mineral products	26.72	25.90
Basic metals	36.93	04.00
Metal products	19.05	17.10
Machinery	21.14	18.50
Electrical and electronic products	63.14	11.65
Shipbuilding and repairing	74.16	02.40
Transportation equipment	50.39	28.70
Precision machinery	13.95	00.20
Miscellaneous industrial products	02.43	06.14

[a] Classification based on *The Report on Industrial and Commercial Census, Taiwan-Fukien Area, the Republic of China*. Directorate-General of Budget, Accounting and Statistic, Executive Yuan (with minor modifications).
[b] 1989 Business Groups data are based on Korea Investors Service (1990) and *1990 Annual Report of Korean Companies*, KPC.
[c] Data are based on Zhonghua Zhengxinso (China Credit Information Service) (1990), *Taiwan diqu jituan quive yanjiu [Business Groups in Taiwan]*. Zhonghua Zhengxinso: Taipei.

Japanese business groups (Gerlach, 1992, p. 85)? We can measure this quite precisely. The degree of vertical integration within the networked group can be conceptualized as the degree to which firms within the group supply the demand for intermediate inputs and essential services necessary to produce and distribute a finished commodity. The more vertically integrated the inter-firm networks, the more likely it is that the firms in the group will transact their business with other firms in the same group. We can therefore conceptualize 'one setism' as the internalization of transactions within a business group.

To measure the rate of internalization for the South Korean case, we use self-reported accounting data that were compiled for Korean Investors Service (Lim *et al.*, 1993).[24] These data contain, among other things, the inter-firm

[24] Our source for these data is Korea Investors Service (1990). These data have been recompiled in a database, Business Networks in Korea, 1989 (Lim *et al.*, 1993).

TABLE 3. Internal Transactions for Korean Business Groups (With Trading Companies Excluded)

Degree of internal transaction
  Measured relative to total sales of the business groups   21.98%
  Measured relative to total input demand (as weighted average)   17.53%

Correlation
(A) Internal transaction as proportion of each business group's total sales

	Year.1	Year.S	Sales fig.	Asset	No. of Co.
In.trans	−0.0513	0.0169	0.4051	0.3571	0.2977

(B) Internal transaction as proportion of each business group's total input

	Year.1	Year.S	Sales fig.	Asset	No. of Co.
Int.trans	−0.352	0.0349	0.3961	0.3512	0.2962

Int.trans, degree of internal transaction of each business group (%) being measured in two different ways; Year.1, number of year of establishment of each group's first company; Year.S, number of year of establishment of each group's biggest company (in terms of sales figure); Sales fig., total sales figure of each business group; Asset, total asset of each business group; No. of Co., total number of companies in each business group.
Source: Korea Investors Service (1990); *1990 Annual Report of Korean Companies*. KPC; *Yearbook on the Korean Economy and Business 1991/1992*. Business Korea.

transactions for all the firms within each *chaebol*. These data are presented in Appendix 1. In Table 3 the degree of internalization for the top 43 *chaebol* is summarized as the ratio of internal sales of firms in a group to total demand for intermediate inputs.[25] The average rate of internalization for the 43 *chaebol* is a little over 17%. This figure represents the amount of the total demand for intermediate inputs that is supplied by firms within the business groups.

Table 3 also shows that the degree of internalization is correlated with the total size of the *chaebol*. The larger the *chaebol* in total sales and assets, the higher the rate of internalization becomes.

How high is this rate of internalization? One can think of a network of firms in which there are no internal sales at all; each firm produces products and sells to firms outside the group. The degree of internalization for such

[25] The total demand figure is reached by subtracting value added for each group (i.e. labor costs plus profits) from the total sales of the group. The remainder approximates the amount of purchases made by firms in a *chaebol* in order to produce final products. The calculations at every level have been adjusted to eliminate any double counting of purchases and sales of the trading companies within the *chaebol*. All of the largest *chaebol* have trading companies. Unlike their Japanese counterparts, the *sogo shosha*, the *chaebol* trading companies primarily distribute group products, usually in foreign markets. In the data on inter-firm transactions, *chaebol* trading companies are usually among the main buyers of goods sold by other firms in the *chaebol*, and they are the main seller of products in a final form. In order not to double count a purchase and a sale of the same goods within the *chaebol* network, we decided to eliminate all possibility of double counting by subtracting the internal purchases but not the sales of *chaebol* trading companies. This precaution lowers the rate of internalization, sometimes substantially.

a group would be zero. At the other extreme would be a situation in which a group of firms buys no intermediate goods from any outside source—no electricity, no gas, no raw products of any kind—sells 100% of their intermediate products to other firms in the group and at the end of the day produces a final commodity that is sold outside the group. The degree of internalization in this group would be 100%, but in today's manufacturing economy such a group is clearly impossible.

In comparative terms, the 17% figure represents a substantial degree of internalization. First of all, this figure does not measure the vertical integration that occurs within firms, only between firms, and we know that the largest firms in the largest *chaebol* are themselves highly vertically integrated (Amsden, 1989). The 17% figure therefore is in addition to such vertical integration as occurs at the firm level. Recognizing this fact, one can compare the Korean rate to the rate of internal transfers within US corporations that have accounting procedures based on multiple internal profit centers. In a survey of 237 US corporations engaging in pricing internal transfers, Vancil (1978, p. 176; also cited by Eccles, 1985, pp. 106–113) showed that over 77% of these corporations had 15% or less of their total cost (or total sales) for intermediate inputs satisfied by divisions within their own corporations. Within Japanese automobile manufacturing groups, J. H. Dyer (unpublished manuscript) cites MITI statistics showing that 31% of the costs of the products sold are manufactured internally by firms within the group, as compared with 45% of the cost for the more vertically integrated US automobile manufacturing firms. Considering just the inter-firm transactions of the Hyundai group, Korea's top automobile manufacturer, these figures fall between the Japanese and the US case. However, if both intra- and inter-firm sources of vertical integration were included, the Hyundai group would likely be even more vertically integrated than the US automobile makers are. For business groups in Japan as a whole, Gerlach (1992, pp. 143–149) reports that the rate of internal transactions within the inter-market groups has been variously calculated to be around 10% or less.

Based on these rather inexact comparisons, it would appear that Korean *chaebol* networks would rank very highly among the world's most vertically integrated economies. Additional evidence for this impression comes from our comparisons of the Korean and Taiwanese imports into the USA (Feenstra *et al.*, 1983). Data from the US Customs show that Korean imports are predominantly high volumes of a limited number of finished consumer products. The *chaebol* networks tend to make automobiles, VCRs, television sets and computers rather than only the component parts for these products. The firms in the *chaebol* are the principal upstream suppliers for the big downstream *chaebol* assembly firms. For instance, we have been told in interviews that in Samsung electronics, most of the main component parts for the consumer electronics division are manufactured and assembled in the same compound by Samsung firms. Our statistical data correspond to what we were told: for Samsung, nearly 25% of all intermediate demands are filled by Samsung firms—almost 32% if we count the contribution of the Samsung trading company.

Horizontally Arranged Business Networks in Taiwan

In contrast with the *chaebol*'s vertical networks, Taiwan business networks are highly segmented in distinct economic niches and show little evidence of vertical integration even within those niches. Our measurement of the rate of internalization for Taiwan's largest business groups is an estimation.[26] The estimate, based on sales figures for member groups, reveals much lower levels of internalization. The estimates we arrive at for each business group are presented in Appendix 2. As shown in Table 4, when adjusted for value added, the average of these estimates for the top 96 business groups is only a little over 4%.

Our calculations suggest that only six of the 96 business groups had a rate of internalization of 17% or above, which was the average rate for the top 50 Korean *chaebol*. Moreover, unlike the Korean case, there was no correlation between size, as measured in assets or sales, and the rate of internalization. Nor was the rate correlated with the age or the number of firms in the business groups.[27] Figure 1 displays the comparison of business group internalization between Korea and Taiwan.

The low rank of internalization matches other data from Taiwan showing that neither state enterprises nor large business groups are vertically integrated producers of finished products.[28] State-owned enterprises primarily supply infrastructure and basic initial goods and services, such as electricity,

---

[26] Although we have reported accounting data on the sales and assets for the firms in Taiwan's 100 largest business groups, as well as whether or not firms in a business group make transactions with each other, we do not have exact figures on the amount of those transactions. The source for our Taiwan business group data is the 1990 Zhonghua Zhengsinso (China Credit Information Service), *Business Groups in Taiwan*. From this and from official government statistics, we have compiled a database to estimate the internalization rate for the business groups in Taiwan (Chung *et al.*, 1993). Lacking the precise data on inter-firm transactions within business groups, we have estimated the amount of internal transactions by using the 'input–output tables' published by the Taiwan government. The input–output tables come from comprehensive government-run surveys on the state of the economy. A part of the survey compiles the transaction levels between economic sectors. For our estimate, we categorized each firm in a business group into the sector of their business. Then we used the general rate of transaction among sectors in the economy to estimate the amount of transactions among firms in business groups.

[27] The only correlation we could discover was with the sector of business. Business groups specializing in textiles showed marginally higher rates of internalization than did other groups.

[28] These data are discussed at greater length in G. G. Hamilton, N. W. Biggart and M. Orrù (unpublished manuscript).

TABLE 4. Internal Transactions for Taiwanese Business Groups

Degree of internal transaction
   Measured relative to total sales of the business groups   2.05%
   Measured relative to total input demand (as weighted average)   4.41%

Correlation
Internal transaction as proportion of each business group's total sales

	Year.1	Year.S	Sales fig.	Asset	No. of Co.
In.trans	0.0345	−0.0561	−0.0777	−0.0726	−0.0268

Internal transaction as proportion of each business group's total input

	Year.1	Year.S	Sales fig.	Asset	No. of Co.
Int.trans	−0.129	−0.0915	−0.0452	−0.049	−0.0531

Int.trans, degree of internal transaction of each business group (%) being measured in two different ways; Year.1, number of year of establishment of each group's first company; Year.S, number of year of establishment of each group's biggest company (in terms of sales figure); Sales fig., total sales figure of each business group; Asset, total asset of each business group; No. of Co., total number of companies in each business group.

Source: All calculations are based on 1988 data reported by Zhonghua Zhengxinso (China Credit Information Service), (1990), *Taiwan diqu jituan qiye yanjiu [Business Groups in Taiwan]*, 1990/1991 ed. *Taipei. Zhonghua Zengxinso*: Out of the 100 biggest business groups recorded, four have been deleted in this study because of some analytical problems.

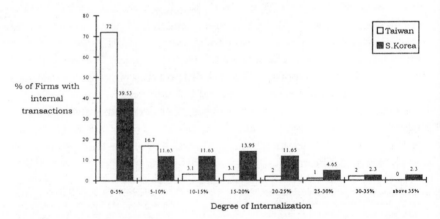

FIGURE 1. Rates of internalization for Taiwanese and South Korean business groups.

gasoline and steel. They sell to all firms, regardless of size. The largest business groups predominantly produce intermediate products and sell their products to all firms, regardless of size. Table 2 shows this tendency in comparison with Korean business groups. Whereas the *chaebol* command a large share of the manufacturing sectors having final export products as well as the basic upstream sectors required to produce those products, Taiwanese business groups have significant shares only in intermediate product categories: textiles, but not garments; chemical materials, but not plastic products. Even in automobile production (Taiwan has 27 automobile manufacturing firms, all for domestic sales), the largest business groups only have a 28% share of the automobile manufacturing market, as compared with the *chaebol*'s near-100% domination in this sector. Simply examining the business sectors of the firms in the largest ten business groups in Taiwan reveals that only one of them—Tatung, a conglomerate producing electrical appliances and electronics goods—engages in sizable exports of finished products, and even Tatung specializes in producing component parts for the export market (G. G. Hamilton, N. W. Biggart and M. Orrù, unpublished manuscript). The rest of the top ten business groups specialize in separate service or upstream manufacturing niches. For instance, Formosa Plastics, by far the largest business group in Taiwan, primarily supplies plastic material to domestic manufacturers who, in turn, make plastic products for the export market. Our estimate shows that the rate of internalization (the demand for inputs that are supplied by member firms) among the 18 firms in the Formosa Plastic group is considerably less than 1%.

In light of these figures, it is important to remember that Taiwan is aggressively export-oriented. Taiwan's manufactured exports as the percentage of total GNP is 51%, as compared with South Korea's 37.5% and Japan's 16.4%. The government statistics show that 65% of these exports are produced by firms having less than 300 employees, a percentage that has been steadily increasing for last two decades. Moreover, if we examine these exports we see that the products differ substantially from products produced by Korean *chaebol*. Our analysis of Taiwanese exports into the USA shows conclusively that, in comparison with Korea, a country twice its size, Taiwan exports a much wider variety of products in all industrial categories except one, transportation equipment (Feenstra *et al.*, 1993). Specializing in a high volume of a few 'big ticket' consumer items, Korea exceeds Taiwan only in certain categories of high value final goods. In all other categories, Taiwan beats Korea.

It is obvious that production of exports is not handled through vertical integration. In Taiwan, small and medium-sized firms use the intermediate goods and services supplied by larger Taiwanese and foreign firms to manufacture the products that Taiwan exports.[29] Unlike in Japan and Korea, large firms and large networks of large firms do not organize the production of small firms by creating a demand structure for intermediate goods and services. In Taiwan the reverse is true. Every level of the economy, from upstream producers to downstream manufacturers, is segmented and driven

---

[29] This is the reason that Taiwan runs such a huge trade deficit with Japan.

by downstream demand. Looking at the distribution of firm size, one must conclude that the small firm tail wags the entire economy.

The networks that form in this economy are not, typically, vertical networks that link upstream and downstream firms. Instead, our research shows that two types of networks are common. One is an ownership network of family enterprises. As we have shown from the internalization measures, the embedded networks of the largest Chinese family-owned business groups are not vertically integrated, but, rather, are highly diversified conglomerates. Our analysis of the development strategy of these business groups over time reveals that their typical mode of development is to intensify production in a core area in order to satisfy existing and future demand for the product or service and then, using the profits from the core business, to diversify into unrelated areas, often into real estate or financial services (G. G. Hamilton, N. W. Biggart and M. Orrù, unpublished manuscript). In short, in Taiwan, embedded networks of family ownership and commodity chains are not coterminous.

The second type of networks are production networks. These networks, sometimes called 'satellite assembly systems', consist of independently owned small, medium-sized and some large firms joined together to manufacture products for the export market. These assembly systems typically work with local and foreign buyers, who supply the specifications for the products needed. Network organizers put together the needed firms to manufacture the product in the amount required.

What makes these production networks so successful rests on two features: first, Taiwan's production networks represent the production end of a global commercial network. As Gereffi (1993) shows, the rise of Taiwan economy corresponds to the rise of the mass-marketing retail revolution which has been orchestrated by 'big buyers', such as the Gap, Reebok, the Price Club, Walmart and other mass merchandisers that never owned or stopped owning their own factories in preference for global sourcing. These supply-on-demand production networks occupy a niche between global buyers and mass merchandisers. They are more commercial than industrial. Second, the networks are so successful because they organizationally encompassed household-based production systems that run according to the rules of Chinese society, as we will explain below.

In summary, conceptualizing production and distribution networks as a commodity chain, we can say that in South Korea the large *chaebol* are the main organizing nodes in the economy's system of production and distribution. These are 'producer-driven' networks (G. Gereffi and G. G. Hamilton, unpublished manuscript) and are structured so that the larger firms in the network create the demand for the smaller firms outside the networks.

Through research and development, advertising and aggressive merchandising by their own trading companies, these large firms also promote, if not create, final consumer demand for their products as well. In this sense, efficient production in these networks is based on achieving economies of scope and scale, a sort of 'network-based Fordism'. In economic terms, these are 'demand-creating' networks.

By contrast, in Taiwan the large firms and large business groups are not organizing nodes in commodity chains. Big businesses are upstream suppliers of intermediate goods and services, responding to the demands generated by manufacturing networks of the small and medium-sized firms which, in turn, respond to the demands of buyers external to the producing networks. Gereffi (1993) calls this type of networks 'buyer driven'. Production in these networks relies on external markets. The responsiveness to buyers makes Taiwan's small-firm economy highly integrated in the global economy. These networks, therefore, can be termed 'demand-responsive'.

6. *Embedded Networks Hierarchies*

What factors account for the huge differences in the industrial structures of these two countries? As we noted previously, the two countries share many similar features. Most observers, so bent on explaining the success of Asian economies in general, have in fact missed the major differences in industrial structure and economic performance between them.[30] In suggesting an explanation for these differences in general terms, most analysts would be inclined to look for some peculiar difference in the timing of industrialization or in the action of the state. Such differences can certainly be located, but are these differences that explain the difference? We do not believe the differences can be explained idiosyncratically as a set of events or a group of persons that created a path-dependent trajectory, in part because of the general patterns of organizational isomorphism within each economy (Orrù *et al.*, 1991). The few transaction cost theorists (Levy, 1988, 1991) who have examined the differences in the economies have concluded that transaction costs are lower in Taiwan than in Korea, and therefore the Korean economy is more vertically integrated. But for the explanations, the end result is projected backwards in time and makes the cause of the imputed outcome. In other words, transaction costs are as much a consequence of hierarchies as a cause of them.

It is our hypothesis that the differences in industrial structure can best be accounted for by differences in the network hierarchies between the two

[30] For one of the best exceptions to this general pattern of reporting, see Scitovsky (1985).

locations that stem, in turn, from differences in social structures growing out of the transmission and control of family property. In South Korea, the kinship system supports a clearly demarcated, hierarchically ranked class structure in which core segments of lineages acquire elite rankings and privileges. These are the 'great families' (*dajia*). As Biggart (1990) describes, this pattern harkens back to the social structure of the Yi dynasty (1392–1910), when the rural-based ruling class, the *yangbang*, consisted of privileged clans that competed for control of society. The lineage was centrally controlled by the eldest son of the dominant segment of the lineage. The clan head inherited from his father all the communal clan landholdings and his own dominant share (about 60%) of the father's private estate, with the younger sons dividing up the rest. This system preserved the aristocratic clan as the principal unit of political and economic action.

These inheritance practices are still in force, and a highly privileged, lineage-based class hierarchy was reinstituted after the Korean War, especially after the Park Chung Hee coup in 1961, as a direct consequence of Korea's industrial policy (Kim, 1991, 1994). At that time, Park tried to stimulate the economy aggressively by selecting certain successful and politicallly trustworthy businessmen to create large, family-owned business groups similar to the *zaibatsu* in pre-war Japan. Precedents for Park's action were there in Korea's history. Park acted on an affinity for elites (i.e. deference patterns and class expectations) that existed in Korean society; it was a logical and rational choice and, in retrospect, it is clear that this choice led to a reincorporation of patrimonialism in the management of Korea *chaebol* (Biggart, 1990).

In Taiwan, however, the Confucian family was situated in a very different social order. In China's early dynastic period, roughly from 221 BC until the end of the Sung period in 1280 AD, Chinese social structure also rested on privileged lineage groups. Especially in the middle period, during the Sui (589–618) and Tang (618–907) dynasties, the great families controlled the countryside, and vied with the emperor's family for aristocratic prestige. After the Mongol victory in 1280, however, the corporate, aristocratic lineages gave way to a segmented patrilineal kinship system in which households, not lineages, were the key building blocks in rural society (Twitchett, 1959, pp. 131–133; Hamilton, 1991). Internal segments would cut across class lines. Unlike in Korea (and in the early Chinese dynasties), where the eldest son inherited the lion's share of the estate and all the lineage's communal holdings, in late imperial China the Chinese practiced partible inheritance, in which all sons equally split the father's estate. Also, communal lands of lineages tended to be very small. This set of practices preserved the household and made it the key unit of action, rather than the lineage itself. Lineage became a ritual community, as opposed to a key unit of action. Over time, partible inheritance and associated practices of lineages segmentation led to an economy that mirrored the society. Land holdings were divided into small plots and were dispersed in space. Large landowners did not have contiguous holdings. Instead of managing their agricultural resources, they rented their land to tenants, who fully appropriated usage rights to the top soil.

Taiwan was largely settled during the Qing dynasty (1644–1911) with migrants from Fukien province. The landholding patterns were based on a Southern Chinese model of strong segmented patrilineages, with some households in a lineage having substantial holdings and others in the same lineage being landless or becoming tenants tilling their kinsmen's land. This pattern of landowning continued largely in place even after the Japanese takeover of Taiwan in 1895, a concession from the Sino-Japanese War. However, in the 1950s, after Chiang Kai Skek and his Kuomintang forces had taken control of Taiwan, the Kuomintang instituted a comprehensive land reform that distributed the land in small plots to the people who tilled the soil. A similar reform occurred in Korea, but unlike in Korea, in Taiwan the government did not at the same time attempt to create an industrial structure based on elite holdings. Instead, the Taiwan government tried to stimulate the private sector of the economy by nourishing Chinese family economic practices, a solution that favored the reinstitutionalization of a household-based economy that became filled, in time, with commercially oriented industrialists.

A number of analysts (Hwang, 1987; King, 1991; Hamilton, 1991, 1992, 1995; Fei, 1992) have described the Chinese economic practices and have argued that Chinese patrilineal kinship patterns produce strong pressures on Chinese to develop enduring working relations with equally ranked people outside of their immediate kinship group. These horizontal ties become the chief vehicle for individuals to marshall resources, including economic resources, for the purposes of household and personal advancement. The strength of these horizontal ties further undermines the influence of the lineage group over its members and enforces the norms that favor the household (*jia*) to be the central nodes in extensively organized horizontal networks.

In summary, although based on similar kinship principles, the Korean and the Chinese kinship systems operate in very different ways.[31] In South Korea, kinship norms can be used coercively to incorporate people and

---

[31] Transaction cost theories might be tempted at this point, and profitably so, to argue that the analytic way to explain the differential outcomes is to apply transaction cost theory to the family structures themselves. For a transaction cost approach to family and households, see Pollak (1985).

groups beyond the household, creating the cohesion necessary to form and maintain large groups. To the extent that these relational norms are used as models for managing extra-kin groups, the organizations formed are, by definition, patrimonial.[32] And in this sense, the Korean *chaebol* are patrimonial. In the Chinese society of Taiwan, kinship norms do not apply to people beyond the household but rigidly apply to members of the household. Outside the household, reciprocal norms based on some form of commonality (*guanxi*) tie people together authoritatively in horizontal networks (King, 1991; Fei, 1992). Large, far flung but narrowly cohesive networks result, but these lack the coerciveness of authority possessed by groups organized through patrimonial and bureaucratic means. In both cases an affinity for economic action is present, but these affinities push people to go in very different directions when they organize efficiently to achieve 'rational' economic goals.

7. Conclusion

Williamson (1991) writes that vertical integration is a 'paradigm problem' for transaction cost theory. We have argued in this paper, however, that hierarchy needs to be a two-sided concept, one that deals with more than simply organizational efficiency in the economy. Although one side of the definition should stress the organization's effective integration in a market economy, the other should stress the authoritative structure of the organization and its basis of legitimacy. When conceptualized in this way, hierarchy becomes a way to organize groups that cohere on the basis of subjectively held and coercively enforced rules of conduct. Depending on the internal structure of such authority, economically active groups have a prior affinity for size and scope. As pre-existing groups interact within a market environment, they create, based on their repertoire for action, their own sources of transactional efficiency. Out of this interaction between market and hierarchy comes an industrial structure, a line-up of economic organizations that operative effectively in the marketplace.

Applying this reasoning to the East Asian cases, we would argue as follows: the current shapes of the market structures of Taiwan and South Korea have been greatly influenced by several decades of success in the global economy. The early and continuing success of these two economies in larger economic arenas has had substantial impact on the development of their

[32] The distinction between patrimonialism and patriarchalism is crucial in this comparison. Weber (1978, pp. 1006–1069) defined patriarchalism as the authority of the master over his household, and patrimonialism as the extension of patriarchal principles beyond the household. In the latter case, patrimonial authority within groups is created through the manipulation of relationships so that the loyalty and dependence of household members is approximated in individuals outside the household.

economic structures. The early decisions, however, based on social structural affinities have led not only to a path of development, but also to an organizational environment that feeds back on itself (path-dependence), creating an economic system that has an internal dynamic and institutionalized rules of the game. It is the organizational dynamic, rather than specific features of embeddedness, that produces and sustains market structures. Embedded structural features provide direction to trajectories of economic development, but structure should not be confused with economic development itself. For an analysis of the dynamic interaction between markets and hierarchy, we feel that transaction cost theory has many contributions to make, but a theory of transactions is not, at the same time, a theory of hierarchies.

Acknowledgements

The authors gratefully acknowledge the research assistance of Wai-keung Chung and Eun Mie Lim, and the support of the Ford Foundation for this research project. We also wish to thank Richard Swedberg for his comments on an earlier draft.

References

Abolafia, M. Y. (1984), 'Structured Anarchy: Formal Organization in the Commodity Futures Markets', in P. Adler and P. Adler (eds), *The Social Dynamics of Financial Markets*, JAI Press: Greenwich, CT, pp. 129–150.

Abolafia, M. Y. and M. Kilduff (1988), 'Enacting Market Crisis: The Social Construction of a Speculative Bubble', *Administrative Science Quarterly*, 33, 126–142.

America Economia (1991), 'The Economic Groups', December, Special Issue, pp. 48–53.

Amsden, A. H. (1989), *Asia's Next Giant: South Korea and Late Industrialization*. Oxford University Press: New York.

Aoki, M. (ed.) (1984), *The Economic Analysis of the Japanese Firm*. North-Holland: Amsterdam.

Aoki, M. (1988), *Information, Incentive, and Bargaining in the Japanese Economy*. Cambridge University Press: Cambridge.

Aoki, M. (1990), '*Toward an Economic Model of the Japanese Firm*', *Journal of Economic Literature*, 28 (March), 1–27.

Aubey, R. (1979), 'Capital Mobilization and the Patterns of Business Ownership and Control in Latin America: The Case of Mexico', in S. Greenfield, A. Strockon and R. Aubey (eds), *Entrepreneurs in Cultural Context*, University of New Mexico Press: Albuquerque, NM, pp. 225–242.

Ben-Porath, Y. (1980), 'The F-Connection: Families, Friends and Firms in the Organization of Exchange', *Population and Development Review*, 6, 1–30.

Biggart, N. W. (1990), 'Institutionalized Patrimonialism in Korean Business', *Comparative Social Research*, 12, 113–133.

Biggart, N. W. and G. G. Hamilton (1992), 'On the Limits of a Firm-based Theory to Explain Business Networks: The Western Bias of Neoclassical Economics', in N. Nohria and R. G. Eccles (eds). *Networks and Organizations: Structure, Form and Action*, Harvard Business School Press: Boston, MA, pp. 471–490.

Bowles, S. (1985), 'The Production Process in a Competitive Economy: Walrasian, Neo-Hobbesian, and Marxian Models', *The American Economic Review*, 75, 16–36.

Chandler, A. D. (1977), *The Visible Hand: The Managerial Revolution in American Business*. Harvard University Press: Cambridge, MA.

Cheung, S. N. S. (1983), 'The Contractual Nature of the Firm', *Journal of Law and Economics*, 26, 1–21.

Chung, W. K., R. C. Feenstra and G. G. Hamilton (1993), 'Business Networks in Taiwan, 1989: A Database', East Asian Business and Development Program, Institute of Governmental Affairs, University of California, Davis, CA.

Coase, R. 1937, 'The Nature of the Firm', *Economica*, 4, 386–405.

Coase, R. (1991), 'The Nature of the Firm: Influence', in O. E. Williamson and S. G. Winter (eds). *The Nature of the Firm: Origins, Evolution, and Development*, Oxford University Press: New York, 61–74.

Collins, R. (1980), 'Weber's Last Theory of Capitalism: A Systematization', *American Sociological Review*, 45, 925–942.

Davis, L. E. and D. C. North (1971), *Institutional Change and American Economic Growth*. Cambridge University Press: Cambridge.

Dow, G. K. (1987), 'The Function of Authority in Transaction Cost Economics,' *Journal of Economic Behavior and Organization*, 8, 13–38.

Eccles, R. G. (1985), *The Transfer Pricing Problem: A Theory for Practice*. Lexington Books: Lexington, MA.

Edwards, R. (1979), *Contested Terrain: The Transformation of the Workplace in the Twentieth Century*. Basic Books: New York.

Encaoua, D. and A. Jacquemin. (1982), 'Organizational Efficiency and Monopoly Power, The Case of French Industrial Groups', *European Economic Review*, 19, 25–51.

Encarnation, D. J. (1989), *Dislodging Multinationals: India's Strategy in Comparative Perspective*. Cornell University Press: Ithaca, NY.

Feenstra, R. C., Yang and G. G. Hamilton (1993), 'Market Structure and International Trade: Business Groups in East Asia', Working Paper in the Research Program in East Asian Business and Development Working Paper Series.

Fei, X. (1992), *From the Soil: The Foundations of Chinese Society*. Trans., Introduction, and Epilogue by G. G. Hamilton and W. Zheng. University of California Press: Berkeley. CA.

Fligstein, N. (1985), 'The Spread of the Multidivisional Form among Large Firms, 1919–1979', *American Sociological Review*, 50, 377–391.

Fligstein, N. (1990), *The Transformation of Corporate Control*. Harvard University Press: Cambridge, MA.

Fligstein, N. (1991), 'The Structural Transformation of American Industry: An Institutional Account of the Causes of Diversification in the Largest Firms, 1919–1979', in W. Powell and P. DiMaggio (eds), *The New Institutionalism in Organizational Analysis*. Chicago University Press: Chicago, IL, pp. 311–336.

Fruin, W. M. (1992), *The Japanese Enterprise System: Competitive Strategies and Cooperative Structures*. Clarendon Press: Oxford.

Futatsugi, Y. (1986), *Japanese Enterprise Groups*. School of Business, Kobe University: Kobe.

Geertz, C. (1963), *Peddlers and Princes: Social Development and Economic Change in Two Indonesian Towns*. University of Chicago Press: Chicago, IL.

Gereffi, G. (1993), 'The Organization of Buyer-Driven Global Commodity Chains: How US Retail Networks Shape Overseas Production', in G. Gereffi and M. Korzeniewicz (eds), *Commodity Chains and Global Capitalism*. Greenwood Press: Westport, CT, pp. 95–122.

Gerlach, M. (1992), *Alliance Capitalism: The Strategic Organization of Japanese Business*. University of California Press: Berkeley, CA.

Granovetter, M. (1973), 'The Strength of Weak Ties'. *American Journal of Sociology*, 91, 481–510.

Granovetter, M. (1985). 'Economic Action and Social Structure: The Problem of Embeddedness'. *American Journal of Sociology*, 91, 481–510.

Granovetter, M. (1994), 'Business Groups', in N. Smelser and R. Swedberg (eds), *Handbook of Economic Sociology*. Princeton University Press: Princeton, NJ, pp. 453–475.

Greenhalgh, S. (1988), 'Families and Networks in Taiwan's Economic Development', in E. A. Winckler and S. Greenhalgh (eds), *Contending Approaches to the Political Economy of Taiwan*. M. E. Sharpe: Armonk, NY, pp. 224–248.

Greif, A., P. Milgrom and B. Weingast (1994), 'Coordination, Commitment, and Enforcement: The Case of the Merchant Guild', *Journal of Political Economy*, 102, 732–745.

Hamilton, G. G. (1985) 'Why No Capitalism in China', *Journal of Developing Societies*, 2, 187–211.

Hamilton, G. G. (1991), 'The Organizational Foundations of Western and Chinese Commerce: A Historical and Comparative Analysis', in G. G. Hamilton (ed.), *Business Networks and Economic Development in East and Southeast Asia*. Centre of Asian Studies, University of Hong Kong: Hong Kong, pp. 48–65.

Hamilton, G. G. (1995), 'Overseas Chinese Capitalism', in Tu Wei-ming (ed.), *The Confucian Dimensions of Industrial East Asia*. Harvard University Press: Cambridge, MA, in press.

Hamilton, G. G. and N. W. Biggart (1988), 'Market, Culture, and Authority: A Comparative Analysis of Management and Organization in the Far East', *American Journal of Sociology*, 94, (Supplement), S52–S94.

Hamilton, G. G. and J. Sutton (1989), 'The Problem of Control in the Weak State: Domination in the U.S., 1880–1920', *Theory and Society*, 18, (January), 1–46.

Hamilton, G. G., W. Zeile and W.-J. Kim (1989), 'The Network Structures of East Asian Economies', in S. Clegg and G. Redding (eds), *Capitalism in Contrasting Cultures*. Walter de Gruyter: Berlin, pp. 105–129.

Holmstrom, B. R. and J. Tirole (1989) 'The Theory of the Firm', in R. Schmalensee and R. D. Willig (eds), *Handbook of Industrial Organization*, Volume One. North-Holland: Amsterdam, pp. 61–133.

Hirsch, P., S. Michaels and R. Friedman (1990), 'Clean Models Vs Dirty Hands: Why Economics Is Different from Sociology', in S. Zukin and P. DiMaggio (eds), *Structures of Capital: The Social Organizations of the Economy*. Cambridge University Press: Cambridge, pp. 39–56.

Hwang, (1987), 'Face and Favor: The Chinese Power Game', *American Journal of Sociology*, 92, 944–974.

Jorgensen, J. J., T. Hafsi and M. N. Kiggundu (1986), 'Towards a Market Imperfections Theory of Organizational Structure in Developing Countries', *Journal of Management Studies*, 24, 419–442.

Kim, E. M. (1991), 'The Industrial Organization and Growth of the Korean Chaebol: Integrating Development and Organizational Theories', in G. G. Hamilton (ed.), *Business Networks and Economic Development in East and Southeast Asia*. Centre of Asian Studies, University of Hong Kong: Hong Kong, pp. 272–299.

Kim, E. M. (1994), *Big Business, Strong State: Collusion and Conflict in Korean Development*. University of California Press: Berkeley, CA.

King, A. Y. (1991), 'Kuan-hsi and Network Building: A Sociological Interpretation', *Daedalus*, 120, 63–84.

Korea Investors Service (1990), *Chaebol Boon Suk Bo Go Seo* (1990 Chaebol Analysis Report). Seoul.

Leff, N. (1977), 'Capital Markets in the Less Developed Countries: The Group Principle', in R. I. McKinnon (ed.), *Money and Finance in Economic Growth and Development: Essays in Honor of Edward S. Shaw*. Dekker: New York, pp. 97–122.

Leff, N. (1978), 'Industrial Organization and Entrepreneurship in the developing Countries: The Economic Groups', *Economic Development and Cultural Change*, 26, 661–675.

Levy, B. (1988), 'Korean and Taiwanese Firms as International Competitors: The Challenges Ahead', *Columbia Journal of World Business*, (Spring), 43–51.

Levy, B. (1991), 'Transactions Costs, the Size of Firms, and Industrial Policy: Lessons from a Comparative Case Study of the Footwear Industry in Korea and Taiwan', *Journal of Development Economics*, 34, 151–178.

Lim, E. M., R. C. Feenstra and G. G. Hamilton (1993), 'Business Networks in Korea, 1989: A Database', East Asian Business and Development Program, Institute of Governmental Affairs, University of California, Davis, CA.

Lopez, R. S. and I. W. Raymond (1995), *Medieval Trade in the Mediterranean World*. Columbia University Press: New York.

Marglin, S. A. (1974), 'What Do Bosses Do? The Origins and Functions of Hierarchy in Capitalist Production', *Review of Radical Political Economy*, 6, 33–60.

Mark, L. L. (1972), *Taiwanese Lineage Enterprises: A Study of Familial Entrepreneurship*, Unpublished Dissertation, University of California, Berkeley, CA.

North, D. C. (1990), *Institutions, Institutional Change and Economic Performance*. Cambridge University Press: Cambridge.

North, D. C. and R. P. Thomas, (1973), *The Rise of the Western World: A New Economic History*. Cambridge University Press: Cambridge.

Orrù, M. (1993), 'Institutional Cooperation in Japanese and German Capitalism', in S.-E. Sjostrand (ed.), *Institutional Change: Theory and Empirical Findings*. M. E. Sharpe: Armonk, NY, pp. 171–198.

Orrù, M., G. G. Hamilton and M. Suzuki (1989) 'Patterns of Inter-Firm Control in Japanese Business', *Organization Studies*, 10, 549–574.

Orrù, M., G. G. Hamilton and N. Biggart (1991), 'Organizational Isomorphism in East Asia: Broadening the New Insitutionalism', in W. W. Powell and P. J. DiMaggio (eds), *The New Institutionalism in Organizational Analysis*. University of Chicago Press: Chicago, IL, pp. 361–389.

Ostiguy, P. (1990), *Los "Capitanes de la industria." Gràndes empresarios, politica y economia en la Argentina de los anos 80*. Editorial Legasa: Buenos Aires.

Peng, H. (1989), '*Taiwan qiue yezhu de 'guanxi' jiqi zhuanbian, yige shehuixue de fenxi*' (Relationships among Taiwan business owners and their changes: A sociological analysis), unpublished dissertation, Tunghai University.

Perrow, C. (1981), 'Markets, Hierarchies and Hegemony', in A. Van de Ven and W. Joyce (eds), *Perspectives on Organizational Design and Behavior*. Wiley: New York, pp. 371–386.

Perrow, C. (1990), 'Economic Theories of Organization', in S. Zukin and P. DiMaggio (eds), *Structures of Capital: The Social Organization of the Economy*. Cambridge University Press: Cambridge, pp. 121–152.

Pollak, R. A. (1985), 'A Transaction Cost Approach to Families and Households', *Journal of Economic Literature*, 23, 581–608.

Powell, W. (1990), 'Neither Market nor Hierarchy: Network Forms of Organization', in B. Staw and L. L. Cumming (eds), *Research in Organization Behavior*. JAI Press: Greenwich, CT, pp. 295–336.

Putterman, L. (ed.) (1986), *The Economic Nature of the Firm: A Reader*. Cambridge University Press: Cambridge.

Redding, G. (1991), 'Weak Organizations and Strong Linkages: Managerial Ideology and Chinese Family Business Networks', *Business Networks and Economic Development in East and Southeast Asia*, in G. G. Hamilton (ed.), Hong Kong: Centre of Asian Studies, University of Hong Kong, pp. 30–47.

Robison, R. (1986), *Indonesia, The Rise of Capital*. Allen and Unwin: Sydney.

Rowe, W. T. (1984), *Hankow: Commerce and Society in a Chinese City, 1796–1889*. Stanford University Press: Stanford, CA.

Roy, W. G. (1990), 'Functional, and Historical Logics in Explaining the Rist of the American Industrial Corporation', *Comparative Social Research*, 12, 19–44.

Scherer, R. M. and D. Ross, (1990), *Industrial Market Structure and Economic Performance*, 3rd edn. Houghton Mifflin Company: Boston, MA.

Schluchter, W. (1981), *The Rise of Western Rationalism: Max Weber's Developmental History*. University of California Press: Berkeley, CA.

Schluchter, W. (1989), *Rationalism, Religion, and Domination*. Trans. Neil Solomon. University of California Press: Berkeley, CA.

Schmalensee, R. and R. D. Willig (eds) (1989), *Handbook of Industrial Organization*. North-Holland: Amsterdam.

Scitovsky, T. (1985), 'Economic Development in Taiwan and South Korea: 1965–81', *Food Research Institute Studies*, 19, 215–264.

Stichcombe, A. (1990), *Information and Organizations*. University of California Press: Berkeley, CA.

Stigler, G. J. (1968), *The Organization of Industry*. The University of Chicago Press: Chicago, IL.

Stone, K. (1974), 'The Origins of Job Structures in the Steel Industry', *Review of Radical Political Economic*, 6, 61–97.

Strachan, H. (1976), *Family and Other Business Groups in Economic Development: The Case of Nicaragua*. Praeger: New York.

Swedberg, R. (1991), *Schumpeter, A Biography*. Princeton University Press: Princeton, NJ.

Swedberg, R., U. Himmelstrand and G. Brulin (1990), 'The Paradigm of Economic Sociology', in S. Zukin and P. DiMaggio (eds), *Structures of Capital: The Social Organization of the Economy*. Cambridge University Press: Cambridge, pp. 57–86.

Thorelli, H. B. (1986), 'Networks: Between Markets and Hierarchies', *Strategic Management Journal*, 7, 37–51.

Twitchett, D. (1959), 'The Fan Clan's Charitable Estate, 1050–1760', in D. S. Nivison and A. F. Wright (eds), *Confucianism in Action*. Stanford University Press: Stanford, CA, pp. 97–133.

Vancil, R. F. (1978), *Decentralization: Managerial Ambiguity by Design*. Dow Jones-Irwin: Homewood, IL.

Weber, M. [1921–22] (1978), *Economy and Society*. Trans. and ed. G. Roth and C. Wittich. University of California Press: Berkeley, CA.

Weber, M. [1923] (1961), *General Economic History*. Trans. F. Knight. Collier: New York.

Williamson, O. E. (1975), *Markets and Hierarchies: Analysis and Antitrust Implications*. Free Press: New York.

Williamson, O. E. (1985), *The Economic Institutions of Capitalism*. Free Press: New York.

Williamson, O. E. (1991), 'Comparative Economic Organization: The Analysis of Discrete Structural Alternatives', *Administrative Science Quarterly*, 36, 269–296.

Williamson, O. E. (1986), 'Vertical Integration and Related Veriations on a Transaction–Cost Economics Theme', in J. E. Stiglitz and G. F. Mathewson (eds), *New Developments in the Analysis of Market Structure*. Cambridge, MA: The MIT Press, pp. 149–176.

Williamson, O. E. (1992), 'Calculativeness, Trust, and Economic Organization', Organizational Behavior and Industrial Relations Working Paper OBIR-59.

Williamson O. E. and S. G. Winter (1991), *The Nature of the Firm: Origins, Evolution, and Development*. Oxford University Press: New York.

Wong, S. (1985), 'The Chinese Family Firm: A Model, *British Journal of Sociology*, 36, 58–72.

APPENDIX 1. Rate of Internalization in Korean Business Groups[a]

Group[b]	Number of companies	Rate of internal transactions (%)[c]
1. Hyundai	30	25.83
2. Samsung	37	24.24
3. Lucky-Goldstar	46	20.18
4. Sunkyong	16	19.63
5. Daewoo	25	13.11
6. Ssangyong	15	16.55
7. Korea Explosives	19	6.48
8. Han Jin	11	3.72
9. Hyosung	20	3.74
10. Daelim	12	5.29
11. Doosan	18	15.69
12. Lotte	23	12.20
13. Kolon	14	5.08
14. Han Yang	4	1.60
15. Kumho	8	.66
16. Sammi	5	33.94
17. Dongbu	8	21.15
18. Kia	10	21.06
19. Dong Ah Construction	12	1.84
20. Donkuk Steel Mill	10	4.51
21. Miwon	13	8.10
22. Hanil	12	11.57
23. Tong Yang	5	16.74
24. Taihan Electric Wire	3	4.04
25. Donkuk Corporation	7	1.43
26. Samyang	5	2.12
27. Kangwon Industries	12	39.58
28. Byucksan	18	.95
29. Hanbo	3	2.66
30. Daesung Industries	8	2.45
31. Jinro	10	3.60
32. Tongil	10	6.51
33. Oriental Chemical Ind.	9	13.03
34. Poongsan	6	4.42
35. Kohap	6	17.20
36. Life Construction	4	2.53
37. Kuk Dong Construction	4	.32
38. Kukdong Oil	3	21.64
39. Halla	7	15.02
40. Woosung Construction	6	2.85
41. Anam Industrial	5	14.08%
42. Kyesung Paper	5	26.62%
43. You One Construction	2	0.00%

[a] *Source*: Korea Investors Service Inc. (1990); *1990 Annual Report of Korean Companies*. KPC; *Yearbook on the Korean Economy and Business 1991/1992*. Business Korea.
[b] Ranked by total sales.
[c] Ratio of internal sales/intermediate inpute.

APPENDIX 2. Rate of Internalization in Taiwanese Business Groups[a]

Group[b]	Number of companies	Rate of internal transactions (%)[c]
1. Formosa Plastics	11	0.27
2. Hua Lon	8	0.42
3. Lin Yuan	5	0.0075
4. Shin Kong	18	0.63
5. Far Eastern	14	2.50
6. China Trust	15	8.50
7. Tatung	5	1.68
8. Yue Loong	11	32.50
9. President	13	2.40
10. Wei-Chuan Ho-Tai	20	1.00
11. National Electric	13	0.0005
12. Chi Mei	7	2.33
13. Tuntex	14	1.26
14. Pacific Wire & Cable	12	0.43
15. Teco Electric	8	2.98
16. Tainan Spinning	17	0.57
17. Sam Shin Trading	7	0.00
18. China General Plastics	7	0.50
19. Chung Shing	9	6.26
20. Yuen Foong	7	3.30
21. Acer	4	0.011
22. Sampo	6	5.41
23. China Rebar	–	–
24. Taiwan Cement	8	1.22
25. Yeu Tyan Machinery	7	0.37
26. Cheng Loong	6	24.26
27. San Fu Motors	5	1.77
28. Chun Yuan	5	0.24
29. Chang Chun	5	0.82
30. Sun Moon Star	11	7.47
31. Foremost	8	1.22
32. Yieh Loong	4	8.47
33. Lien Hwa Industry	6	0.00
34. Chen Zhen	–	–
35. Hsiu Chu Trucking	8	0.22
36. Walsin Lihwa	7	0.00
37. Shung Ye Trading	5	4.84
38. Shin Lee	9	0.27
39. Shih Lin Paper	4	8.47
40. Kuo Chan	7	0.37
41. Prince Motors	6	2.95
42. Taiwan Glass	9	0.00
43. Mercuries & Associates	2	0.00
44. Nam Chow Chemical	9	0.27
45. Lien-I Textiles	6	15.03
46. Ve Wang	3	0.20
47. Hwa Eng. Wire & Cable	4	11.73

APPENDIX 2. Continued

Group[b]	Number of companies	Rate of internal transactions (%)[c]
48. Tah Tong Textile	13	8.47
49. Ve Dan	7	3.40
50. Pou Chen	3	0.26
51. Lily Textile	5	6.06
52. Great Wall	–	–
53. Fwu Sow Grain Products	6	3.27
54. Tah Hsin	6	0.00
55. Ocean Plastics	3	0.00
56. Ta Ya Electric Wire	3	7.55
57. Tung Ho Steel	3	9.11
58. Microtek	–	–
59. Formosan	2	0.00
60. Tai Roun	7	1.47
61. International Auto	3	2.58
62. Chu Che	3	5.93
63. Kung Hsue She Co	3	0.00
64. Lee Tah	3	0.00
65. Associated	11	0.00
66. Far East Machinery	4	0.00
67. Ho Cheng	7	4.19
68. Tung-Kuang	5	8.07
69. Southeast Cement	5	12.30
70. Pievue	4	0.00
71. U-lead	3	0.00
72. Kwong Fong	4	0.41
73. Chun Yu Works	5	6.40
74. Ever Fortune	3	0.00
75. UB	6	0.00
76. Tai Hwa	4	3.34
77. Rexon Industry	8	7.95
78. Lien Fu	5	2.64
79. Hui Shung	8	1.00
80. Sino-Japan	5	1.01
81. San Yu	3	0.98
82. Chih Lien Industry	7	17.00
83. China Chemical	5	6.40
84. Ability	7	1.95
85. Fu Tai Umbrella	6	6.95
86. Nice	3	0.00
87. Fu I Industrial	6	14.67
88. Victor	6	0.00
89. Kaisers Plastic	6	0.19
90. Sun Wu	4	15.50
91. Tong Hsing	4	0.00
92. Fong Kuo	3	0.54
93. Cosmos	7	0.00
94. Typhone	4	2.49
95. Ye Shan Mu	5	0.00

APPENDIX 2. Continued

Group[b]	Number of companies	Rate of internal transactions (%)[c]
96. Trans-world	3	0.29
97. OEMEC	3	0.00
98. Cheng Hong	7	0.00004
99. Chin Ho Fa Steel & Iron	4	9.36
100. Tai Hsin	4	0.00

[a] *Source*: Data of Taiwanese business groups are based on Zhonghua Zhengxinso (China Credit Information Service) (1990), *Taiwan diqu jituan qiye yanjiu* [*Business Groups in Taiwan*], 1990/1991 edn. Zhonghua Zhengxinso: Taipei. Out of the 100 biggest business groups recorded, four have been deleted in this study because of some analytical problems.

[b] The ranking is based on the size of the business groups' total sales. Zhonghua Zhengxinso (China Credit Information Service) (1990), *Taiwan diqu jituan qiye yanhiu* [*Business Groups in Taiwan*], 1990/1991 edn. Zhonghua Zhengxinson: Taipei, 2.

[c] The proportion of total estimated demand (input) of the business group which is internal transaction. It is interpreted as the proportion of demand (input) which is satisfied by the companies within the group.

Information, Knowledge, Vision and Theories of the Firm*

M ARTIN F RANSMAN

(Institute for Japanese-European Technology Studies, University of Edinburgh, 25 Buccleuch Place, Edinburgh EH8 9LN, UK)

Economists have, of course, always recognized the dominant role that increasing knowledge plays in economic processes but have, for the most part, found the whole subject of knowledge too slippery too handle . . . (p. 77).

A 'firm' is by no means an unambiguous clear-cut entity; it is not an observable object physically separable from other objects, and it is difficult to define except with reference to what it does or what is done within it. Hence each analyst is free to choose any characteristics of firms that he is interested in, to define firms in terms of those characteristics, and to proceed thereafter to call the construction so defined a 'firm'. Herein lies a potential source of confusion . . . (p. 10).

> Edith Penrose, *The Theory of the Growth of the Firm*, 1959

Where is the wisdom we have lost in knowledge?
Where is the knowledge we have lost in information?

> T. S. Eliot, 'Choruses from "The Rock" '

1. Purposes

This paper has the following purposes. The first purpose is to demonstrate that many of the best-known approaches to the firm in economics have in common a starting-point which sees the firm as a response to information-related problems. The second purpose is to review critically some of these approaches on the basis of the internal structure of their arguments. The

* The author would like to thank the following who gave comments on an earlier, longer version of the present paper: Alfred Chandler, Edith Penrose, Brian Loasby, Richard Nelson, David Teece and Oliver Williamson. They are, however, not responsible for the contents of the present paper.

third purpose is to analyze some of the limitations of the 'information-related paradigm' in the light of the distinction which it is argued must be drawn between 'information' and 'knowledge'. Finally, the last purpose is to propose some additional approaches to the firm which merit further exploration.

2. *Introduction*

The Firm as a Response to Information-related Problems

Information may be defined as data relating to states of the world and the state-contingent consequences that follow from events in the world that are either naturally or socially caused. The total set of data is closed in that there is a closed set of states and consequences.

Several well-known approaches to the firm begin (implicitly) with this definition of information, plus the assumption that information is unevenly distributed among agents (that is, that there is asymmetric information). For example, as is shown in this paper, Alchian and Demsetz's (1972) theory of the firm as joint team production, and Jensen and Meckling's (1976) theory of the firm as a nexus of contracts between principals and agents, are derived directly from this definition and assumption. Coase's approach to the firm, it is shown, is also essentially an approach based on information-related problems.

Williamson, however, challenges the view that asymmetric information *per se* presents problems. If people were honest they could be asked to 'tell the truth, the whole truth, and nothing but the truth'; and they would. In this way asymmetric information could become symmetrical. The problem is that people may become opportunistic. According to Williamson it is, therefore, opportunism rather than asymmetric information *per se* that presents problems. However, as argued later, asymmetric information is a necessary condition for opportunism: if information were symmetrically distributed, opportunism could not arise.

A further information-related problem which is given a central role in Williamson's approach is that of bounded rationality. In the present paper this important concept is traced back to the original writings of Herbert Simon. For Simon, both human beings and their organizations are essentially information processors. It is this which links humans to computers and creates the basis for artificial intelligence, a field to which Simon has made important contributions.

It is shown later that according to a strict interpretation of Simon's most frequently quoted definition of bounded rationality, the problem arises where the quantity of relevant information is great relative to the ability of humans to deal with information (an ability, Simon stresses, which is not only physical, but is also psychologically and organizationally caused). Since humans often cannot deal with the entire set of relevant information, they have no alternative but to deal with only a subset. In this sense their decisions are 'bounded', based on the processing of only a subset of all the relevant information. (How 'rational' their decisions are is a question taken up in the later discussion on Simon.)

All the above-mentioned writers are united in their approach to the firm, and the economics of organization more generally, by their concern with individual and organizational responses to information-related problems.

The Firm as a Repository of Knowledge

In the present paper a second approach to the firm is identified, namely an approach which sees the firm as a repository of knowledge. There is, however, a common starting-point between the second approach and the concerns of some in the first approach, namely the problem of bounded rationality. According to Nelson and Winter the routinization of activities in the firm is largely a response to the quantity (including complexity) of information. However, although routines may be a response to information-related problems, attention in the Nelson and Winter approach to the firm shifts to the routines themselves. It is in its routines that a firm's organizational knowledge is stored. This is the source of differences among firms. It is difference or variety which, together with a selection mechanism, drives the evolutionary process. At the same time it is the firm's routines which give Nelson and Winter a way of modeling the joint determination of the different behavior patterns of different firms and market outcomes.

Although their particular purposes differ to some extent, it is shown that there is an important similarity between Nelson and Winter's approach and those of Penrose, Chandler, and Teece. For all of them the focus is on the firm as a repository of specific knowledge (including organizational and technological competence).

Information and Knowledge

In all the above writings there is implicitly a 'tight coupling' between the concepts of 'information' and 'knowledge'. In view of this tight coupling none of the writers has felt it necessary to distinguish clearly between the two concepts. Following the philosopher Dretske (1982), the tight coupling may be expressed in the following way: information is a commodity that is capable of yielding knowledge; and knowledge is identified with information-produced (or sustained) belief. As this formulation makes clear, the line of causation is from information to knowledge. Knowledge is processed information.

There are, however, two major problems with this tight coupling of information and knowledge, both of which have important implications for the theory of the firm. The first is that under some circumstances a 'wedge' may be driven between information and knowledge with the result that they may become loosely coupled, or even uncoupled. Secondly, while information is a closed set, knowledge is essentially open (an insight that I owe to Brian Loasby). Following from the latter point, the process of knowledge-creation, a process central to all firms, cannot be analyzed entirely in terms of the 'information-processing paradigm'. Both these problems require some elaboration.

To pursue the first problem, under conditions of incomplete information it will, by definition, be impossible to generate unambiguous knowledge from the information set used by the agent. Under such conditions the agent may derive alternative, even contradictory, 'knowledge' from the information set. Furthermore, different agents may derive different, even contradictory, 'knowledge' from the same set of information. Under these conditions a situation arises which may be referred to as one of 'interpretive ambiguity'. It is intuitively obvious that situations of interpretive ambiguity will often arise. Under these conditions knowledge can only be coupled loosely to information and in the extreme case knowledge may become completely uncoupled.

(Uncertainty is a special case of incomplete information. Under conditions of uncertainty, information cannot be derived regarding future states and state-contingent consequences, including probabilistically-generated information. Under these conditions interpretive ambiguity will always exist.)

In the presence of interpretive ambiguity, the beliefs which comprise knowledge are not unambiguously sustained by the agent's information set. To go one step further, it may happen under these conditions that the agent's beliefs, which are relatively autonomous from the subjective information set, provide the basis for interpreting this set of information as well as new information. Under these circumstances the line of causation between information and knowledge will be reversed compared to the tight coupling case. Knowledge (belief) will be used to interpret the incomplete information (which cannot 'interpret itself' through the generation of unambiguous knowledge).

The second problem referred to above is somewhat different. Here the concern is not with the relationship between information and knowledge, as in the first problem, but with the different nature of information and knowledge. Information, as defined earlier, refers to data regarding states of the world and state-contingent consequences. Information refers inherently to a closed set of data. However, knowledge is essentially open-ended.

Knowledge is always in a process of becoming, extending beyond itself. The firm's knowledge, therefore, (that is the knowledge of its decision makers including the knowledge of those who create the firm's knowledge) must be conceived of as being open-ended.

Implications for the Theory of the Firm

What are the implications for the theory of the firm of the present discussion of information and knowledge? In general, it is necessary to go beyond the 'information processing paradigm' in order to develop a more robust theory and understanding of the firm, while incorporating the important insights that this paradigm has provided. This requires two related conceptual advances.

First, knowledge (equated with belief) must be 'freed' from total dependence on processed information. While processed information may be an important input into the knowledge-creation process, the creation of knowledge involves more than the processing of information. In order to analyze the process of knowledge creation, a process central to most large firms, it is necessary to go beyond an analysis of information processing and treat knowledge in its own terms.

In the concluding section of this paper the new concept of 'vision' is developed for this purpose. While vision, which is based on a structure of beliefs, is influenced by processed information, it also embodies insight, creativity and misconception. These are determinants of belief which, while drawing on processed information, go beyond it. The concept of vision is illustrated through a study of what is referred to as the 'IBM paradox'. Here the paradox is examined whereby IBM, the information processing company *par excellence*, clung until 1991 to the mistaken belief in the ability of the mainframe computer to sustain its profitability, size and growth. This belief was contradicted by information which IBM had processed regarding the increasing performance—cost ratio of the microprocessor which resulted in the undermining of the mainframe.

Secondly, and closely following on the first point, a more sophisticated conceptualization of the knowledge-creation process within firms must be developed. While this will require an understanding of the role of information processing, the conceptualization must go further to treat knowledge in its own terms as an open-ended process.

3. *The Firm as Response to Information-related Problems*

The authors included in the first approach to the firm have in common their view of the firm as a response to information-related problems. These include Alchian and Demsetz, Coase, Jensen and Meckling, Simon and Williamson.

Asymmetrical Information

In elaborating on the information-related problems that are referred to by these authors we may begin with a few simplifying assumptions. Let it therefore be assumed that all possible states of affairs and state-contingent consequences relevant to a decision are common knowledge. Accordingly, there is a closed set of possibilities. Furthermore, let it be assumed that the state of affairs which actually pertains is unknown to one or more of the interactors. Under these conditions there is asymmetrical information, that is some have information about the prevailing state of affairs that others do not have.

These conditions are sufficient, for both Alchian and Demsetz (1972) and Jensen and Meckling (1976), to explain the existence of the firm. But what, according to these authors, is a firm and what do firms do?

The firm as joint team production. For Alchian and Demsetz (1972) the firm is a specific form of organizing cooperative productive activity, which they refer to as team production. The essential feature of team production is that it involves cooperation between the team members who together produce a joint output. However, the contribution to join output made by each team member is not completely transparent. This creates the possibility of shirking. (Alchian and Demsetz actually go further than this and talk of an incentive to shirk.) To put it slightly differently, there is an asymmetrical distribution of information among the members of the team which prevents them all from knowing the precise contribution that has been made by each of them. Under these conditions it is not possible to fine-tune the alignment of contribution and reward, leading to the possibility of efficiency losses.

Furthermore, it is the information asymmetry and the resulting inability to align contributions and rewards that produces a need to monitor and control the activities or output of the team members. But who is to perform the monitoring and control function, and how is the monitor and controller to be monitored and controlled?

Alchian and Demsetz's answer to this question is that the team members have an incentive to consent to, and contractually-speaking in effect to appoint, a monitor and controller. This incentive arises from the greater productivity, the fruits of which will be enjoyed by all team members, that will follow from the reduction in shirking as a result of the advent of monitoring and controlling, (More specifically, it is assumed that the benefit of monitoring and controlling, following from the greater productivity will exceed the cost of this activity.)

From the present discussion it is clear that Alchian and Demsetz's (1972) purpose is to examine the organizational implications of joint team production which takes place under conditions of asymmetrical information. This is apparent in the title of their paper, 'Production, Information Costs, and Economic Organization'. This purpose leads them on to their answer to the twin questions, what is a firm and what do firms do?: '. . . the firm is the particular policing device utilized when joint team production is present' (p. 121). More generally, 'The problem of economic organization [is] the economical means of metering productivity and rewards' (p. 113).

This view of what a firm is leads Alchian and Demsetz to dispute Coase's argument (that will be taken up again later) that the distinguishing feature of the firm is the allocation of resources by direction rather than by the price mechanism. As they put it:

> It is common to see the firm characterized by the power to settle issues by fiat, by authority, or by disciplinary action superior to that available in the conventional market. This is delusion. The firm does not own all its inputs. It has no power of fiat, no authority, no disciplinary action any different in the slightest degree from ordinary market contracting . . . What then is the content of the presumed power to manage and assign workers to various tasks? . . . To speak of managing, directing, or assigning workers to various tasks is a deceptive way of noting that the employer continually is involved in renegotiation of contracts on terms that must be acceptable to both parties. Telling an employee to type this letter rather than to file that document is like my telling a grocer to sell me this brand of tuna rather than that brand of bread. I have no contract to continue to purchase from the grocer and neither the employer nor the employee is bound by any contractual obligations to continue their relationship. Long-term contracts between employer and employee are not the essence of the organization we call a firm (p. 112).

The firm as a nexus of contracts between principals and agents. In approaching the firm, Jensen and Meckling's (1976) main purpose is to explore the significance of contracting relationships and of agency costs within these relationships. It is this purpose which leads them on to their answer to the two questions, what is a firm and what do firms do?, an answer that is significantly different from that proposed by Alchian and Demsetz (1972). According to Jensen and Meckling:

> Contractual relations are the essence of the firm, not only with employees but with suppliers, customers, creditors, etc. The problem of agency costs

and monitoring exists for all of these contracts, independent of whether there is joint production in their [Alchian and Demsetz's] sense; i.e., joint production can explain only a small fraction of the behavior of individuals associated with a firm' (p. 215).

Jensen and Meckling define the agency relationship as 'a contract under which one or more persons (the principal(s)) engage another person (the agent) to perform some service on their behalf which involves delegating some decision making authority to the agent' (p. 212). Agency costs arise from the fact that 'If both parties to the relationship are utility maximizers . . . the agent will not always act in the best interests of the principal' (p. 212). Both principal and agent will normally attempt to accommodate such agency costs although they will be unable to eliminate them:

> The *principal* can limit divergences from his interest by establishing appropriate incentives for the agent and by incurring monitoring costs designed to limit the aberrant activities of the agent. In addition in some situations it will pay the *agent* to expend resources (bonding costs) to guarantee that the principal will be compensated if he does take such actions. However, it is generally impossible for the principal or the agent at zero cost to ensure that the agent will make optimal decisions from the principal's viewpoint (p. 212).

What, therefore, is a firm? According to Jensen and Meckling, a firm is 'the nexus of a set of contracting relationships among individual's' (p. 215). They continue, 'it makes little or no sense to try to distinguish those [contractual relationships] which are "inside" the firm (or any other organization) from those . . . that are "outside" of it. There is in a very real sense only a multitude of complex relationships (i.e., contracts between the legal fiction (the firm) and the owners of labor, material and capital inputs and the consumers of output)' (p 215). In Jensen and Meckling's view, therefore, the firm is a form of market.

In commenting on Jensen and Meckling's view of the firm it must be noted that the problem of agency, which as we have seen is central to their view, is largely reducible to the problem of information asymmetry and the cost which arises in attempting to cope with the consequences of such asymmetry. If the principal possessed (and processed) the same information set as the agent, the 'agency problem' would be transformed since the principal would know if the agent's actions were inconsistent with his/her interests, even though he/she (the principal) would still have to decide how best to act in the light of this knowledge.

Ronald Coase and why firms exist. As Ronald Coase (1988) explains regarding his writings in the 1930s on the firm, 'my purpose . . . was to explain why there are firms' (p. 38). It was this purpose that led him to focus on two puzzles.

The first puzzle that Coase defined and began to tackle in the early 1930s was the following: if specialization is efficient, why does integration, a move away from specialization, frequently take place? As early as 1932 Coase had defined integration as 'The bringing together under one control of different functions' (Coase, 1988, p. 19). This puzzle was closely related to a second puzzle that Coase posed in his famous 1937 article, 'The Nature of the Firm': 'In view of the fact that, while economists treat the price mechanism as a co-ordinating instrument, they also admit the co-ordinating function of the "entrepreneur", it is surely important to enquire why co-ordination is the work of the price mechanism in one case and of the entrepreneur in another' (p. 20).

It was these puzzles that led Coase to ask the question: why do firms exist? In order to deal with this question, however, Coase needed to deal with a logically prior question: what is a firm? Only by having a conception of what a firm is could he begin to explore why it existed.

Coase's answer to the question 'What is a firm?' emerges in his conceptualization of an economy without any firms. In such an economy, Coase (1988) later explained, 'All transactions are carried out as a result of contracts between factors, with the services to be provided to each other specified in the contract and without any direction involved . . . In such a system, the allocation of resources would respond directly to the structure of prices . . .' (p. 38).

While in the economy without firms economic activity is coordinated by contracts, within the firm it is coordinated by direction. Accordingly, the answer to the question 'What is a firm?' is: a firm is a form of coordination of economic activity by direction rather than by contract (although this did not rule out the possibility of some contracting within the firm). For Coase, therefore, a sharp boundary can be drawn between the firm and the market, unlike both Alchian and Demsetz (1972) and Jensen and Meckling (1976) for whom contracting is the main characteristic of the firm's activities.

With this conceptualization of the firm in mind, Coase in his 1937 article went on to explain why firms exist: 'The main reason why it is profitable to establish a firm would seem to be that there is a cost of using the price mechanism' (p. 38). In 1988 Coase summarized the main idea in his earlier contribution: 'The key idea in "The Nature of the Firm" [is] the comparison of the costs of coordinating the activities of factors of production within the firm with the costs of bringing about the same result by market transactions or by means of operations undertaken within some other firm' (p. 38). Firms, therefore, exist where the costs of coordinating economic activities through the market exceed the costs of coordinating them within the firm. (In passing, it is worth noting Coase's insistence in the last quotation on a three-way comparison of coordination costs: within the market, within the firm and within some other firm.)

What are the costs of using the price mechanism which Coase identified? Reference is made here to three of the costs analyzed by Coase (1937). First, 'The most obvious cost of "organizing" production through the price mechanism is that of discovering what the relevant prices are' (p. 38). Second, 'The costs of negotiating and concluding a separate contract for each exchange transaction which takes place on a market must also be taken into account' (pp. 38–39). Coase recognized that long-term contracting might reduce some of the costs of concluding several shorter-term contracts. But 'owing to the difficulty of forecasting, the longer the period of the contract is for the supply of the commodity or service, the less possible and, indeed, the less desirable it is for the person purchasing to specify what the other contracting party is expected to do' (pp. 39–40).

Third, at the time that he wrote 'The Nature of the Firm', Coase was also aware of the problem now referred to as 'asset specificity'. In 1932 Coase discussed the following example of asset specificity in a letter to his colleague and friend, Fowler: 'Suppose the production of a particular product requires a large capital equipment which is, however, specialized insofar that it can only be used for the particular product concerned or can only be readapted at great cost. Then the firm producing such a product for one consumer finds itself faced with one great risk—that the consumer may transfer his demand elsewhere or that he may exercise his monopoly power to force down the price—the machinery has no supply price' (Coase, 1988, p. 13).

What bearing does asymmetric information have on Coase's approach to the firm? As we saw earlier, asymmetric information was central to the approaches of Alchian and Demsetz (1972) and Jensen and Meckling (1976).

Asymmetric information may significantly increase the costs of using the price mechanism. This is clear in the case of Coase's second cost, namely the cost of negotiating and concluding contracts. In the case of long-term contracts, however, in addition to possible problems arising from the asymmetrical distribution of information regarding the states of affairs which currently pertain, there is a further problem. This is the problem of knowing what future states may pertain, or as Coase put it, the 'difficulty of forecasting'.

Similarly, asymmetric information may increase Coase's first cost, namely the cost of 'discovering what the relevant prices are'. In the case of Coase's third cost, asset specificity, the problem may arise from the difficulty of foreseeing how the purchaser might in the future change his mind regarding his demand for the output from the assets or the price he is willing to pay

Again, as in the case of long-term contracting, this is a problem of forecasting future states.

It may be concluded, therefore, that the availability and cost of information is a major determinant, from Coase's point of view, of the existence of firms.

Opportunism

The problem of asset specificity raises a further difficulty, namely the possibility of opportunistic behavior. The owner of transaction-specific assets, in addition to confronting the possibility that the purchaser may change his/her mind, may also have to deal with the possibility that he/she will behave opportunistically (for example, with malintent, encouraging the seller to invest in specific assets only to exploit the seller's unavoidable commitment to the transaction later). Oliver Williamson's development of the implications of opportunism adds a new dimension to the problems of information and contracting which have been discussed so far in this paper.

Indeed, contrary to what has been argued thus far, Williamson suggests that asymmetrical information does not provide an independent explanation for the existence and activities of the firm. Instead he proposes that opportunism is one of the key explanatory factors. The reason is simply that asymmetrical information is only a problem in the presence (or possible presence) of opportunism. Absent opportunism, Williamson argues, and the problems associated with asymmetrical information disappear. This follows since if there is no opportunism the principal or other team members can simply ask the agent or remaining team member to 'tell the truth, the whole truth, and nothing but the truth', to which they will get a truthful answer.

In this way, relevant information which may have been asymmetrically distributed in the first place can be made symmetrical. In other words, a further assumption has in fact been implicitly present in the discussion so far, namely the possibility of opportunism. When this assumption is made explicit, however, asymmetrical information disappears as a separate category explaining the existence and activities of the firm.

(In passing, it is worth noting that Williamson here implicitly assumes that the costs of asking that the truth be told, and getting an answer, are negligible. If these costs were not negligible then the request to tell the truth would only be worth making if the value of the answer at least compensated for the costs incurred. But if there is asymmetrical information to begin with, the requester may not be able to assess the value of the information he is requesting. The requester will then be unable to make a rational decision regarding whether or not to request the information. The only way he or she could make a rational decision would be to know the value of the information in advance of incurring the cost of obtaining it. But then the requester would have obtained the information without having paid for it and without having compensated the person from whom the information has been requested for the costs of providing the information. Under these conditions asymmetrical information would present problems even in the absence of opportunism.)

But, to return to the discussion, what is opportunism and where does it come from? Williamson defines opportunism as self-seeking with guile and argues that it is one of two key 'behavioral assumptions' characterizing 'human nature' (Williamson, 1987, p. 44). (Williamson's other behavioral assumption is bounded rationality which is brought into the present discussion later.) These two behavioral assumptions are crucial because of the impact that they have on the cost of making transactions, and for Williamson 'the transaction is the basic unit of analysis' (p. 18). As will become apparent later, it is Williamson's focus on the transaction as the basic unit of analysis which leads on to his conception of what a firm is and what it does.

To take the present discussion of opportunism further, two points are worth noting. The first is that Coase explicitly considered the possibility of opportunism, or 'fraud' as he put it, in his discussion of the 'risk' facing the holder of specific assets. Around 1934 Coase addressed the question of the role of fraud in contracting. In this connection he referred to Marshall's observation that 'Money is more portable than a good reputation', which might provide an incentive for fraud. However, Coase 'concluded that the avoidance of fraud was not an important factor in promoting integration' of coordinated activities within the firm (Coase, 1988, p. 31).

The second point is that, despite the centrality of the concept of opportunism in his approach to transactions in general and the firm in particular, Williamson's work begs the question regarding whether opportunism is a cause, as he generally argues, or a consequence of organization.

On the one hand, Williamson insists that opportunism is an essential part of 'human nature', and it is for this reason that he incorporates it as a 'behavioral assumption' in his conceptual framework: 'Transaction cost economics characterizes human nature as we know it by reference to bounded rationality and opportunism' (Williamson, 1987, p. 44).

On the other hand, Williamson notes that:

> Both institutional and personal trust relations evolve. Thus the individuals who are responsible for adapting the interfaces have a personal as well as an organizational stake in what transpires. Where personal integrity is believed to be operative, individuals located at the interfaces may refuse to be part of opportunistic efforts to take advantage of (rely on) the letter of the contract when the spirit of the exchange is being emasculated. Such refusals

can serve as a check upon organizational proclivities to behave opportunistically. Other things being equal, idiosyncratic exchange relations that feature personal trust will survive greater stress and will display greater adaptability (Williamson, 1987, pp. 62–63).

In a footnote, Williamson, referring to Dore's 1983 article on 'Goodwill and the Spirit of Market Capitalism', notes that 'Ronald Dore's assessment of Japanese contracting practices also suggests that personal integrity matters' (p. 63).

However, Williamson cannot have it both ways, at least if he is to provide a consistent explanation of forms of organization. In a causal explanation the cause must precede the effect. In the main thrust of Williamson's argument the cause (opportunism, an inherent part of human nature) precedes the effect (forms of organization designed to safeguard against opportunism). But elsewhere he reverses the argument: the cause becomes forms of organization which precede (and produce) the effect, personal integrity and trust, thus contradicting the previous argument that opportunism is part of human nature. However, opportunism must be either a cause or a consequence of organization or, if in some cases it is the one and in other cases the other, a careful account is required of the reasons for the difference. This presents a significant theoretical dilemma for Williamson's theoretical schema which, as we have seen, is largely based on deduction from the twin behavioral assumptions of bounded rationality and opportunism.

This brings us to Williamson's second characteristic of 'human nature', namely bounded rationality.

Bounded Rationality

According to Williamson (1990), bounded rationality is the most important assumption on which the theory of contracting is based: 'Although frequently unexpressed, bounded rationality has become the operative behavioral assumption out of which the economics of contracting increasingly works' (p. 11).

But what, precisely, is bounded rationality? To answer this question it is necessary to turn to Herbert Simon.

Herbert Simon and bounded rationality. Herbert Simon's purpose is to provide an intentional explanation for the existence and activities of organizations in general and the firm in particular.[1] According to this

---

[1] Simon's intentional explanation of the existence, activities and organization of the firm is to be contrasted with causal and functional explanations. See Elster's (1983) useful discussion of the distinction between these different types of explanation.

explanation, human action is oriented to the achievement of purposes or objectives. Human beings intend to act 'rationally' in the sense that they attempt to achieve their objectives to the greatest extent that they feel is possible under the circumstances as they see them.

However, it is in attempting to act rationally that human beings inevitably run into information-related problems. These problems arise because rational action in this sense requires information regarding both the alternative courses of action that are available to the actor, and the consequences of these actions. In some cases, but not necessarily all, the quantity of information required to make a rational decision is great relative to the ability of the individual to acquire, store, process and recall that information.

These cases refer to what Simon calls bounded rationality, which he defines in the following way: 'the capacity of the human mind for formulating and solving complex problems is very small compared with the size of the problems whose solution is required for objectively rational behavior in the real world—or even for a reasonable approximation to such objective rationality' (Simon, 1957, p. 198). Accordingly, under conditions of bounded rationality, 'human behavior is *intendedly* rational, but only *limitedly* so' (Simon, 1961, p. xxiv).

But why is the capacity of the human mind 'very small' relative to the capacity that would be necessary for objectively rational behavior? Simon makes it clear that the limitations of the human mind are not only or primarily physiological in nature, but are also psychological, social and organizational:

> Administrative man is limited also by constraints that are part of his own psychological make-up—limited by the number of persons with whom he can communicate, the amount of information he can acquire and retain, and so forth. The fact that these limits are not physiological and fixed, but are instead largely determined by social and even organizational forces, creates problems of theory construction of great subtlety; and the fact that the possibilities of modifying and relaxing these limits may themselves become objects of rational calculation compounds the difficulties.[2]

Simon goes on to explain the existence of organizations (and also their activities) in terms of bounded rationality. This provides, in the case of the firm as a special kind of organization, Simon's answer to the two questions, 'What is a firm? What do firms do?' In short, firms provide a way for people,

---

[2] Simon (1957, p. 199). Williamson in *Markets and Hierarchies* (1975) is therefore incorrect when he states that bounded rationality 'refers to neurophysiological limits on the one hand and language limits on the other' (p. 9). The present quotation from Simon comes four paragraphs after the one where Simon provides his definition of bounded rationality which was cited above, a definition which Williamson quotes on page 9.

through cooperation, to pool the 'very small' capacities of their individual minds, their bounded rationalities, and in this way to achieve collectively what they cannot achieve individually. Simon notes, however, that collective achievements are dependent on the ability of the group to agree on goals, to communicate and to cooperate:

> It is only because individual human beings are limited in knowledge, foresight, skill, and time that organizations are useful instruments for the achievement of human purpose; and it is only because organized groups of human beings are limited in ability to agree on goals, to communicate, and to cooperate that organizing becomes for them a 'problem' (Simon, 1957, p. 199).

But how 'rational' is the behavior that Simon analyzes? In answering this question it is worth noting that bounded rational behavior is even more limitedly rational than Simon suggests, or his followers imply.[3] This conclusion, as will now be demonstrated, follows logically from Simon's own analysis.

To begin with, bounded rational behavior can be rational only with respect to given objectives. These objectives and their choice lie outside the rationality process, even if individuals are consistent regarding the objectives they have chosen. Accordingly, the objectives themselves cannot be assumed to be rational.

Secondly, it may be deduced that it is impossible to choose rationally the information set on which a decision or choice is made. At any point in time the boundedly rational individual has the choice whether or not to expand the information set at his/her disposal by acquiring and processing additional information. There is, however, a cost to the individual of so doing, at least in terms of the time taken to acquire and process information and the opportunity cost of that time.

How can a rational decision be made regarding whether or not to seek more information? In line with Simon's analysis, this decision can only be made on the basis of a calculation of the consequences of seeking or not seeking more information. However, since the individual does not yet possess the additional information, he/she will not be able to assess the consequences of having that information. He/she is therefore unable to calculate whether the benefit of having the additional information is sufficiently

---

[3] Williamson (1990) argues that 'Although it is sometimes believed that Simon's notion of bounded rationality is alien to the rationality tradition of economics, Simon actually enlarges rather than reduces the scope for rationality analysis' (p. 11). Similarly, Jensen and Meckling (1976) state that 'Unfortunately, Simon's work has often been misinterpreted as a denial of maximizing behavior, and misused, especially in the marketing and behavioral science literature. His later use of the term "satisficing" . . . has undoubtedly contributed to this confusion because it suggests rejection of maximizing behavior rather than maximizing subject to costs of information and decision-making' (Putterman, 1986, p. 211).

great to compensate for the associated costs. The only way of making the choice is to possess the information already, in which case the costs have been incurred in advance of an assessment of the benefits. In this case the decision to acquire the information could not have been rational. It is therefore possible that, *ex post*, the decision to acquire the information may turn out to be irrational.

Neither can a rational decision be salvaged by bringing expectations into the argument, that is by arguing that the rational decision regarding whether or not to seek more information will be made on the basis of the consequences that are expected. Since, *ex hypothesi*, the individual does not yet possess the information, there is no rational way of formulating expectations regarding the consequences of having the information. A rational decision, in the sense of a decision which enables the greatest achievement of the individual's objectives subject to the costs of information and decision making—to use Jensen and Meckling's words (cf. footnote 3)—therefore cannot be made. It is not possible, accordingly, to make a rational decision regarding whether or not to acquire more information. Bounded rationality, therefore, can only be rational with respect to a given and closed set of information.

Furthermore, there is no guarantee that under the conditions of bounded rationality postulated by Simon a decision will be 'intersubjectively rational', in the sense that two individuals will agree that the decision is rational. Indeed, the logic of Simon's own argument suggests that it is unlikely that a decision will be intersubjectively rational.

For Simon the essential assumption is that people are information-processing organisms. But what is the 'information' that they process, how do they acquire it, and how do they process it?

In answering these questions Simon makes it clear that it is necessary to distinguish the 'objective' information which exists 'out there' in the individual's environment from the information which 'enters' his or her faculties and is processed by them. The information which first enters an individual's faculties is selected from the total set of objective information. This selection process follows from the individual's 'perception' and 'attention': 'Every human organism lives in an environment that generates millions of bits of new information each second, but the bottleneck of the perceptual apparatus certainly does not admit more than 1,000 bits per second, and probably much less' (Simon, 1959, p. 273).

This perceptual bottleneck, however, cannot be thought of as a 'filter', but rather involves 'attention' which serves as an inclusion/exclusion mechanism. The selection from objective information based on perception and attention means that the information that first 'enters' the individual's faculties is not necessarily 'representative' of the objective information which is 'out there'.

It is for this reason that Simon objects to the notion of the individual 'filtering' objective information:

> Perception is sometimes referred to as a 'filter'. This term is as misleading as 'approximation', and for the same reason: it implies that what comes through into the nervous system is really quite a bit like what is 'out there'. In fact, the filtering is not merely a passive selection of some part of a presented whole, but an active process involving attention to a very small part of the whole and exclusion, from the outset, of almost all that is not within the scope of attention (Simon, 1959, pp. 272–273).

After the information, selected by the individual's perception and attention, first 'enters' the individual's faculties, it is subjected to what we may refer to as a secondary selection process. This secondary selection process results from the problem-solving strategy which the individual has chosen. Accordingly, a subset of information will be selected, contingent on the problem-solving strategy which has been chosen, from the set of information which first enters the individual's faculties:

> . . . there are hosts of inferences that *might* be drawn from the information stored in the brain that are not in fact drawn. The consequences implied by information in the memory become known only through active information-processing, and hence through active selection of particular problem-solving paths from the myriad that might have been followed (Simon, 1959, pp. 272–273).

The information that the individual eventually ends up processing, therefore, has gone through this double selection process. We may refer to this information as subjective information.

March and Simon (1958) acknowledge that both rounds of selection, involving perception and attention in the first round and choice of problem-solving path in the second, are influenced by psychological, sociological and organizational determinants:

> The theory of rational choice put forth here incorporates two fundamental characteristics: (1) choice is always exercised with respect to a limited, approximate, simplified 'model' of the real situation ... We call the chooser's model his 'definition of the situation'. (2) The elements of the definition of the situation are not 'given'—that is, we do not take these as data of our theory—but are themselves the outcome of psychological and sociological processes, including the chooser's own activities and the activities of others in his environment (March and Simon, 1958, p. 12).

Because of the importance of what we have referred to here as subjective information, Simon argues that a theory of rational behavior must also pay attention to the procedures that individuals use to choose their actions. This he calls 'procedural rationality':

> . . . a theory of rational behavior must be quite as much concerned with the characteristics of the rational actors—the means they use to cope with uncertainty and cognitive complexity—as with the characteristics of the objective environment in which they make their decisions. In such a world, we must give an account not only of *substantive rationality*—the extent to which appropriate courses of action are chosen—but also *procedural rationality*—the effectiveness, in light of human cognitive powers and limitations, of the *procedures* used to choose actions (Simon, 1978, pp. 8–9).

Returning to intersubjective rationality, it is clear from the present discussion that there is no inherent reason why different individuals in the same objective situation should end up with the same simplified 'model' of this situation, that is with the same 'definition of the situation'. Indeed, through his discussion of the importance of psychological factors, such as perception and attention, and social and organizational factors, Simon implies it is unlikely that different individuals will end up with the same definition of the situation.

To the extent that their definitions of the situation differ, however, different individuals may disagree in any objective situation regarding what constitutes a rational decision. 'Rationality' is therefore dependent on the individual making the judgment. The possibility of different individuals arriving at different conclusions regarding what is a rational decision raises problems for explanations of firm behavior based on rational calculation. A case in point, as we shall see later, is explanations based on transaction costs.

Similar objections confront 'intertemporal rationality', namely decisions that are assumed to remain rational over time. The reason is simply that perception, attention and the other determinants of the decision maker's definition of the situation are a function of time and are therefore likely to change over time. With a changing definition of the situation over time it is possible that a decision judged to be rational at time t will seem to be irrational at $t + 1$. By limiting rationality to a point-in-time judgment, however, further problems are posed for explanations couched in terms of rationality, since what is judged rational today may be judged irrational tomorrow.

[Intersubjective rationality may in fact be more common than is acknowledged in the present discussion based on Simon. While the unlikelihood of intersubjective rationality follows logically from Simon's focus on the decision-making individual as the appropriate unit of analysis, it may be that judgments regarding rationality are more of a social process, discussed, negotiated and agreed between individuals. From the social point of view, decisions within organizations may be seen to be made socially, rather than individually, within the context of the processes of interpersonal dynamics, power relationships, etc. that exist within the organization.

However, while Simon acknowledges that social determinants and the functioning of organizations influence factors such as perception and attention and therefore the decision maker's definition of the situation, his focus remains at the individual rather than the social level. From the social point of view, it might be that 'intraorganizational rationality', involving shared judgments regarding what is rational within an organization, is more likely than 'interorganizational rationality', that is shared judgments across different organizations.

This, however, necessitates an explanation of the social processes which are responsible for the emergence of a social consensus regarding rationality and, on occasion, the emergence of social conflict. Such an examination requires the investigation of factors that go beyond Simon's writings.]

Simon's chess example. What Simon means by bounded rationality is made clearer by the example of chess to which he frequently refers. Indeed, according to Simon *et al.* (1992), 'Chess has become for cognitive science research [which for Simon includes both economics and artificial intelligence] what the Drosophila, fruit fly, is for research in genetics. We need standard organisms so that we can accumulate knowledge. That's my excuse for talking so much about chess' (p. 29).

At this point let us return to the simplifying assumptions that were made at the beginning of section 3. There it was assumed, firstly, that all possible states of affairs and state-contingent consequences relevant to a decision are common knowledge. There is, therefore, a closed set of possibilities. Secondly, it was assumed that the state of affairs which actually pertains is unknown to one or more of the interactors. It will be recalled that in analyzing the implications of these assumptions the discussion went on to consider asymmetrical information and opportunism.

In the case of chess, however, only the first of these assumptions is necessary. A knowledge of the characteristics of the chess board and of the rules of the game provides knowledge of all possible states of affairs (configurations of chess pieces on the board) and state-contingent consequences (*if* a piece moves here, *then* . . .).

What is the problem posed by chess that makes it suitable, according to Simon, as an 'ideal type' in cognitive science research? In the case of chess the significance of the information that is provided in the game is clear-cut and unambiguous (a point to which we shall later return). An opponent's move provides information regarding the new state of affairs which now pertains, information that is shared (once the move is made) with the other player.

This indicates the set of options that now remain open (and also those that are foreclosed) to both players.

It is worth stressing that the problem which chess presents to the other player has nothing to do with information asymmetry (as least once the move is made). Both players then have the same set of information regarding the state of affairs which pertains. The difficulty, rather, arises from the lack of cognitive competence on the part of both players to compute, within the time allowed, all the possible moves that may be made, all the possible counter-moves, all the possible counter-counter-moves, etc. In other words, the problem arises from the quantity of information relative to the ability of the player to process it. The problem, therefore, is one of bounded rationality. Under these circumstances the player resorts to strategies or heuristics.

Bounded rationality, principals and agents and joint team production. How does bounded rationality relate to our earlier discussions of the principal–agent and joint team production problems? The point to make here is that the latter two cases do not necessarily involve bounded rationality (although it is possible that bounded rationality could be a further complicating factor). In the principal–agent and joint team production cases the problem arises from the asymmetrical distribution of information plus, following Williamson, possibly the potential for opportunism. The great quantity of information relative to the ability of the individual to process this information, that is bounded rationality as strictly defined by Simon, is not necessarily a problem.

It is therefore possible to take issue with Williamson (1990) who, as quoted earlier, has suggested that 'bounded rationality has become the operative behavioral assumption out of which the economics of contracting increasingly works' (p. 11).

The firm as organizational innovation for economizing on bounded rationality and opportunism. Having provided a critical analysis of the concept of bounded rationality, Williamson's approach to the firm will now be considered in more detail.

Williamson's purpose is largely to examine the implications of transaction costs which he carefully distinguishes from production costs. As he defines it, 'Transaction cost economics characterizes human nature as we know it by reference to bounded rationality and opportunism' (Williamson, 1987, p. 44).

It is Williamson's concern with transaction costs that shapes his approach to the firm. According to Williamson, therefore, 'the modern corporation is mainly to be understood as the product of a series of organizational innovations that have had the purpose and effect of economizing on transaction costs' (ibid. p. 273).

It is the attempt to economize on transaction costs which leads people to devise and select structures which appropriately govern the costs of transaction, that is governance structures. As Williamson puts it, 'Transaction cost economics is principally concerned . . . with the economizing consequences of assigning transactions to governance structures in a discriminating way' (ibid. p. 46). Accordingly, 'the firm is (for many purposes at least) more usefully regarded as a governance structure' (ibid. p. 13).

Based on this kind of reasoning, Williamson derives the 'organizational imperative that emerges in such circumstances . . . . : Organize transactions so as to economize on bounded rationality while simultaneously safeguarding them against the hazards of opportunism' (ibid. p. 32, emphasis removed).

But what, precisely, does Williamson mean by 'economizing' and how consistent is this with other concepts which he employs? Williamson (1990) has recently stated that 'The new theories of the firm to which I refer [that is, the so-called New Institutional Economics which includes his own work] were initially regarded as rivals to the neoclassical theory. Increasingly, however, they are coming to be treated as complements' (p. 23). It is largely as a result of the common ground provided by 'economizing' that this has been possible.

Williamson makes it clear that there is a close link between his concept of economizing and Simon's concept of bounded rationality. According to Williamson, in both concepts a 'semistrong form of rationality' is posited. In both concepts people intend to act rationally (intend to economize) but because of the very small capacity of the human mind (to use Simon's words) are able to do so only to a limited extent. As Williamson (1987) puts it: 'Transaction cost economics acknowledges that rationality is bounded and maintains that both parts of the definition should be respected. An economizing orientation is elicited by the intended rationality part of the definition, while the study of institutions is encouraged by conceding that cognitive competence is limited' (p. 45).

As we have seen, Williamson's 'organizational imperative' is to economize on bounded rationality while safeguarding against opportunism. But when is the point reached where bounded rationality has been 'economized' and where opportunism has been 'safeguarded'? More specifically, from an *ex ante* point of view, how does the actor know that bounded rationality has been economized?

Following Simon's own logic underlying his concept of bounded rationality, a logic clearly spelled out earlier in this paper, it can be argued that there is little reason for the actor to be sure that 'economization' has been achieved, or for other actors to agree that this is the case. This conclusion follows from the complexity of the context that is likely to surround any attempt to economize on bounded rationality and safeguard against opportunism, including the unknowns and uncertainties involved.

Under these circumstances it is possible that the actor's 'definition of the situation', to use Simon's phrase, will differ in significant respects firstly from the 'objective situation', and secondly from the way in which other actors have defined 'the situation'. In other words, under these circumstances economizing itself is subjective and intersubjective rationality and intertemporal rationality (in the senses defined earlier in the discussion on Simon) may not exist.

If this is accepted, however, the exhortation to economize on bounded rationality and safeguard against opportunism must be understood in a very different way from that implied by Williamson. In short, the notion of economizing will have to be watered down considerably: do what you think will have the effect of economizing on bounded rationality and safeguarding against opportunism. To the extent that this amended version of economizing is accepted, however, the common ground with neoclassical economics is largely undermined.

4. *The Firm as a Repository of Knowledge*

The hallmark of the second approach to the firm identified in this paper is that the firm is seen, not only as a response to information-related difficulties as in the first approach, but also as a repository of knowledge. In this section the work of five sets of authors will be examined: Nelson and Winter, Penrose, Chandler, Marshall and Teece.

The Firm as Part of the Evolutionary Process of Economic Change

The discussion of bounded rationality in section 3 of this paper provides a direct link to the work of Nelson and Winter. Before this link can be explored further, however, it is necessary to examine their overall purpose since, as we shall see, it is this purpose which structures their approach to the firm.

Richard Nelson has clearly outlined the purpose which underlies Nelson and Winter (1982), *An Evolutionary Theory of Economic Change*:

> The theory of the firm in conventional microeconomics (and conventional macroeconomics) was developed as part of a theoretical structure whose central concern was to explain prices and quantities through the employ-

ment of the constructs of demand and supply curves . . . Our central
interests, at least in our book [i.e. Nelson and Winter (1982)], were with
economic growth fuelled by technical advance. So also, of course, are
neoclassical growth theorists. Given their view of growth, the latter could
work with 'a theory of the firm' essentially of the sort employed in conventional demand curve, supply curve, analysis. Given our view of technical
advance, and of economic growth driven by changes in technology, Winter
and I could not live with that kind of theory of the firm. We had to develop
a theory of the firm in which 'firm differences matter'.[4]

As this quotation makes clear, Nelson and Winter's 'theory of the firm', at
least that theory of the firm explicit and implicit in their 1982 book, did not
emerge from an attempt to understand the firm *per se*, but rather emerged in
response to the need for a conceptual tool that would enable them to analyze
the relationship between technical change and economic growth. The conceptual tool that they developed for this purpose, their 'theory of the firm',
accordingly differed in significant respects from those developed by others in
response to different purposes. For this reason Nelson and Winter's (1982)
approach is to be distinguished from that, for example, of the behavioral
writers such as Simon, Cyert and March:

> We diverge from the behavioral theorists in our interest in building an
> explicit theory of industrial behavior, as contrasted with individual firm
> behavior. This means on the one hand that our characterizations of indi-
> vidual firms are much simpler and more stylized than those employed by
> the behavioral theorists, and on the other hand that our models contain a
> considerable amount of apparatus linking together the behavior of collections
> of firms. Perhaps in the future it will become possible to build and compre-
> hend models of industry evolution that are based on detailed and realistic
> models of individual firm behavior. If so, our work will at that point
> reconverge with the behavioralist tradition (Nelson and Winter, 1982,
> p. 36).

But, to suit their purpose, how do Nelson and Winter develop a theory of
the firm in which 'firm differences matter'?

Bounded rationality and routines. The starting-point for Nelson and
Winter's theory of the firm is the same information-excessive world (excessive
relative to the ability of individuals to process that information) with which
Simon begins. How do individuals, and the organizations within which they
work, deal with this world?

In answer to this question Nelson and Winter draw directly on the ideas of

---

[4] Personal communication from Richard Nelson, August 17, 1992.

March and Simon (1958) in which the importance of routinized behavior is analyzed:

> Activity (individual or organizational) can usually be traced back to an environmental stimulus of some sort, e.g., a customer order or a fire gong . . . The responses to stimuli are of various kinds. At one extreme, a stimulus evokes a response—sometimes very elaborate—that has been developed and learned at some previous time as an appropriate response for a stimulus of this class. This is the 'routinized' end of the continuum, where a stimulus calls forth a performance program almost instantaneously (p. 139).

As Nelson and Winter (1982) put it:

> Man's rationality is 'bounded': real-life decision problems are too complex to comprehend and therefore firms cannot maximize over the set of all conceivable alternatives. Relatively simple decision rules and procedures [i.e. routines] are used to guide action; because of the bounded rationality problem, these rules and procedures cannot be too complicated (p. 35).

Routines, therefore, refer to the 'regular and predictable' aspects of firm behavior (ibid. p. 14). To explain the behavior of the firm is to explain its routines: 'the behavior of firms can be explained by the routines that they employ . . . Modeling the firm means modeling the routines and how they change over time' (ibid. p. 128).

In short, it is the firm's routines which render predictable and 'modelable' the response of the firm to its changing environment. 'The overall picture of an organization in routine operation can now be drawn. A flow of messages comes into the organization from the external environment and from clocks and calendars. The organization members receiving these messages interpret them as calling for the performance of routines from their repertoires . . . the performance of routines by each organization member generates a stream of messages to others', etc. (ibid. p. 103).

(In passing, it is worth noting that Nelson and Winter's emphasis on routines is in line with Simon's insistence (discussed above) on the importance of procedural rationality in addition to substantive rationality. This concern with procedural rationality, however, is not shared by Williamson in his approach to transaction cost economics).[5]

---

[5] As Williamson (1987) puts it:

> Economizing on bounded rationality takes two forms. One concerns decision processes, and the other involves governance structures. The use of heuristic problem-solving . . . is a decision process response. Transaction cost economics is principally concerned, however, with the economizing consequence of assigning transactions to governance structures in a discriminating way. Confronted with the realities of bounded rationality, the costs of planning, adapting, and monitoring transactions need expressly to be considered. Which governance structures are more efficacious for which type of transaction? *Ceteris paribus,*

Routines and the firm as repository of knowledge. It is clear from the discussion so far that Nelson and Winter see routinized behavior as both an individual and organizational response to complexity and uncertainty under conditions of bounded rationality. To this extent their routine-based theory of the firm shares with the other theories discussed in section 3 a view of the firm as a response to information-related difficulties.

However, in elaborating on the importance of routines, Nelson and Winter go beyond an approach which sees the firm primarily as a *response* to information-related problems. More specifically, the firm for Nelson and Winter itself becomes a *repository* of knowledge. And it is as a repository of knowledge, contingent on the firm's past history, that one firm differs from another. The focus accordingly shifts to the firm and the *knowledge* on which it is based. In turn this raises new questions that were not central in the theories examined in section 3. This is evident in the following quotations from Winter (1988) which give his answer to the questions, 'What is a firm? What do firms do?':

> Fundamentally, business firms are organizations that know how to do things. Firms are repositories of productive knowledge. In fact . . . a particular firm at a particular time is a repository for a quite specific range of productive knowledge, a range that often involves idiosyncratic features that distinguish it even from superficially similar firms in the same line(s) of business (p. 175).

However:

> it is necessary to unpack the metaphorical statement that 'organizations know how to do things' into an account of the processes by which productive knowledge is preserved in an organization while individual members come and go (ibid. p. 176).

It is in its routines that an organization stores its knowledge: 'where and what is the memory of an organization? We propose that the routinization of activity in an organization constitutes the most important form of storage of

modes that make large demands against cognitive competence are relatively disfavored' (ibid. p. 46).

Williamson's de-emphasis of 'decision process responses' to bounded rationality, like heuristic problem solving, marks a significant point of departure between transaction cost economics and evolutionary economics of the kind proposed by Nelson and Winter which is based strongly on decision process responses such as routinized behavior. In this respect Williamson also deviates from Simon who, as was shown earlier, insists that in a world of uncertainty and cognitive complexity—which is also Williamson's world—'we must give an account not only of *substantive rationality*—the extent to which appropriate courses of action are chosen—but also *procedural rationality*—the effectiveness, in light of human cognitive powers and limitations, of the *procedures* used to choose actions' (Simon, 1978, pp. 8–9).

the organization's specific operational knowledge' (Nelson and Winter, 1982, p. 99).

As is clear from these quotations, the routine has a multipurpose use in Nelson and Winter's theory of the firm. Firstly, it allows the firm to cope with complexity and uncertainty under the constraint of bounded rationality. At the same time, by linking bounded rationality and routines, Nelson and Winter are able to provide a realistic basis to their approach to the firm. This basis is superior to that of conventional economics with its demanding assumptions regarding the possession and cost of information.

Secondly, routinized behavior allows Nelson and Winter to develop a theory in which firms differ, and in which the differences matter. This follows since there is no reason why different firms, even those in the same industry confronting similar complex and uncertain circumstances, should devise the same or even similar routines. Thirdly, routines provide a way of storing an organization's accumulated knowledge.

Fourthly, routinized behavior provides a mechanism which allows Nelson and Winter to link, in both directions, market changes and firm responses. In this way they are able also to link technical changes and economic growth. Fifthly, routines, the source of a firm's distinctiveness, are also the source of its competitiveness.

The firm in the evolutionary process. How does Nelson and Winter's routine-based theory allow them to analyze the evolutionary process of economic change which embodies the relationship between technical change and economic growth?

Nelson and Winter (1982) make it clear that there are three key concepts in their theory of evolutionary change: routine, search and selection (p. 400). The following is a summary of their understanding of the evolutionary process:

> The core concern of evolutionary theory is with the dynamic process by which firm behavior patterns and market outcomes are jointly determined over time. The typical logic of these evolutionary processes is as follows. At each point of time, the current operating characteristics [i.e. routines] of firms, and the magnitudes of their capital stocks and other state variables, determine input and output levels. Together with market supply and demand conditions that are exogenous to the firms in question, these firm decisions determine market prices of inputs and outputs. The profitability of each individual firm is thus determined. Profitability operates, through firm investment rules, as one major determinant of rates of expansion and contraction of individual firms. With firm sizes thus altered, the same operating characteristics would yield different input and output levels, hence different prices and profitability signals, and so on (ibid. p. 19).

Nelson and Winter continue:

> By this selection process, clearly, aggregate input and output and price levels for the industry would undergo dynamic change even if individual firm operating characteristics were constant. But operating characteristics, too, are subject to change, through the workings of the search rules of firms. Search and selection are simultaneous, interacting aspects of the evolutionary process: the same prices that provide selection feedback also influence the directions of search. Through the joint action of search and selection, the firms evolve over time, with the condition of the industry in each period bearing the seeds of its condition in the following period (ibid. p. 19).

Search. Just as in the case of routines, Nelson and Winter draw on March and Simon (1958) for the idea of search. As the latter express it:

> At the other extreme [of the continuum beginning with routinized responses], a stimulus evokes a larger or smaller amount of problem-solving activity directed toward finding performance activities with which to complete the response. Such activity is distinguished by the fact that it can be dispensed with once the performance program has been learned. Problem-solving activities can generally be identified by the extent to which they involve *search*: search aimed at discovering alternatives of action or consequences of action. 'Discovering' alternatives may involve inventing and elaborating whole performance programs where these are not already available in the problem solver's repertory (pp. 139–140).

For Nelson and Winter (1982), the main features of search 'are irreversibility (what is found is found), its contingent character and dependency on what is "out there" to be found, and its fundamental uncertainty' (p. 247). Like routines, however, search according to Nelson and Winter is a rule-based activity.

In the case of R&D, for example, the 'decision maker is viewed as having a set of decision-rules . . . these rules determine the direction of "search" . . . and may be termed a "search strategy". A strategy may be keyed to such variables as the size of the firm, its profitability, what competitors are doing, assessment of the payoff of R&D in general and of particular classes of projects in particular, evaluation of the ease or difficulty of achieving certain kinds of technological advances, and the particular complex of skills and experience that the firm possesses' (ibid. p. 249).

It is search which generates the *variety* which is, together with selection, the basis of evolutionary change. 'Our concept of search obviously is the counterpart of that of mutation in biological evolutionary theory. And our treatment of search as partly determined by the routines of the firm parallels the treatment in biological theory of mutation as being determined in part by the genetic makeup of the organism' (ibid. p. 18).

Selection environment.   The third key concept is that of the 'selection environment' of an organization which 'is the ensemble of considerations which affect its well-being and hence the extent to which it expands or contracts' (ibid. p. 401).

However, it is important to realize that from an evolutionary perspective it is not the fate of individual firms that is of interest. 'Differential growth [of firms] plays much the same role in our theory as in biological theory; in particular, it is important to remember that it is ultimately the fates of populations or genotypes (routines) that are the focus of concern, not the fates of individuals (firms)' (ibid. p. 401).

Routines, rules and decision making within the firm.   The present discussion of Nelson and Winter (1982) has stressed that their 'theory of the firm' emerged from the need for a conceptual tool which would allow them to examine the co-relationship between the firm and market outcomes, and between technical change and economic growth. However, a conceptual tool fashioned for one purpose may not be well adapted for another. It is therefore necessary to ask how relevant their 'theory of the firm' is as a theory of the firm, that is as a conceptual tool for understanding the firm, even though it is acknowledged that this was not their purpose.

In answering this question it is clear that Nelson and Winter's (1982) approach to the firm has several particularly attractive features. Its grounding in an acceptance of complexity, uncertainty, and limited cognitive competence gives it a reality basis that, all other things equal, puts it ahead of theories which assume, explicitly or implicitly, that decision makers know most of what there is to know and can acquire information at relatively little cost. It is these assumptions that usually underlie the conventional approach to the firm and the use of a production function. Similarly, the weight given to routines, including search as a routinized activity, and rule-driven behavior is justified by the increasing amount of evidence which shows these to be important in both firms and organizations more generally (such as bureaucracies).

But, as an approach to the firm, an approach which in Nelson and Winter's own words is a 'simple and stylized' characterization of individual firms, it is clear that there are important shortcomings. In this sense their conceptual tool, honed for one purpose, imposes significant costs when used for another purpose.

The main shortcoming stems from the need in Nelson and Winter's models for a mechanism that will allow them to co-relate changes in the market with firms' responses. This mechanism is provided, of course, by the firms' routines which mediate the interaction between market and firm, thus providing a deterministic outcome which in turn generates the model's results. While this mechanism may be appropriate for Nelson and Winter's purpose, as part of an attempt to understand the firm it has the cost of forcing the firm into a deterministic straitjacket, governed wholly by routine and rule. The point, however, is not that human beings never make or obey routines and rules; only that they may unpredictably change them. And this, surely, should be a feature of any attempt to theorize the firm *per se*.

Following the same line of reasoning, it is worth commenting on the divergence between the approach to the firm taken in the more discursive parts of the book as well as in some of Nelson and Winter's other writings, and that taken in the formal sections. More specifically, the mechanistic nature of the firm's response to its environment through its routinized and search behavior appears to be at variance with the conception of human (and firm) action and knowledge given elsewhere in the same book. This is evident, for example, in the authors' discussion of firm strategy:

> the economic world is far too complicated for a firm to understand perfectly; therefore the attempts of firms to do well must be understood as being conditioned by their subjective models or interpretations of economic reality. These interpretations tend to be associated with strategies that firms consciously devise to guide their actions. Such strategies differ from firm to firm, in part because of different interpretations of economic opportunities and constraints and in part because different firms are good at different things (Nelson and Winter, 1982, p. 37).

Presumably, different subjective interpretations may also lead different individuals in the same firm to different conclusions regarding strategy, or the same individual to different conclusions at different points in time. To view the firm wholly in terms of routine- and rule-driven activities is to suppress an essential aspect of the way decisions are made under conditions of complexity, uncertainty regarding the future and significant information costs.

Nelson and Winter (1977) are surely nearer the mark when they state that 'Because of the uncertainty involved, different people, and different organizations, will disagree as to where to place their R&D chips, and on when to make their bets. Some will be proved right and some wrong. Explicit recognition of uncertainty is important . . .' (p. 47). While the routine-based approach does not assume certainty, it does not deal adequately with the way in which uncertainty is confronted in decision making in the firm. The very nature of routine abstracts from this process. The contrast with the notion of 'vision' discussed later in this paper is worth noting.

Explaining the Growth of the Firm

Unlike any of the other writers discussed so far, the purpose of the next two authors, Edith Penrose and Alfred Chandler, is to explain the growth of the firm. More specifically, Penrose's purpose is to develop a theory of the growth of the firm, while Chandler's is to explain both the origin and the growth of the large, multiproduct and multidivisional firms which currently dominate both national economies and the international economy.

But what, for Penrose and Chandler, is a firm, and what do firms do? While the answer given by both writers to the first question is fundamentally the same, their answer to the second question is significantly different.

For Penrose (1959), the business firm is 'both an administrative organization and a collection of productive resources', both human and material (p. 31). However, echoing a distinction that others have drawn,[6] Penrose is adamant that 'it is never *resources* themselves that are the "inputs" in the production process, but only the *services* that the resources can render' (p. 25). These services are also a function of the experience and knowledge that have been accumulated within the firm. Services, according to Penrose, are to a significant extent firm-specific and therefore 'it is largely in this distinction [between resources and services] that we find the source of uniqueness of each individual firm' (p. 25).

From Chandler's perspective the modern business firm may be seen as a collection of 'dynamic organizational capabilities' which are the source of the firm's competitiveness. Like Penrose's services, Chandler's organizational capabilities are accumulated in the course of carrying out the firm's activities, and 'depend on knowledge, skill, experience, and teamwork—on the organized human capabilities essential to exploit the potential of technological processes' (Chandler, 1990a, p. 24).

It is in their view of what firms do, however, that a significant difference becomes apparent between Penrose's and Chandler's analysis of the firm. For Penrose (1959) 'the primary economic function of an industrial firm is to make use of productive resources for the purpose of supplying goods and services to the economy *in accordance with plans developed and put into effect within the firm*' (p. 15, emphasis added). The emphasis on the process of 'planning' within the firm in Penrose's conceptualization of what firms do

---

[6] Penrose's distinction between resources and services is similar to Marx's distinction between 'labor power', the commodity or resource which is bought on the market, and 'labor' which refers to the services which are extracted from the laborer. For Marx it is this inevitable distinction which requires that forms of organization and control be developed within the firm to ensure that labor services will be satisfactorily obtained from the labor power that has been bought. Ironically, Marx's viewpoint is not too distant from Alchian and Demsetz's (1972) concern with the possibility of shirking in team production. This is ironic since Alchian and Demsetz, contra Marx, were also concerned to stress the symmetry in the relationship between employer and employee.

requires Penrose, as we shall see, to explore a number of difficult issues relating to information and knowledge. These are issues which Chandler, with a different view of what firms do, does not delve into.

What, then, in Chandler's view do firms do? For Chandler, firms and their managers are engaged in the pursuit of the 'dynamic logic of growth and competition' (Chandler, 1990b, p. 133). This logic involves managers, within their hierarchically structured organizations, using their dynamic organizational capabilities (and in the process accumulating further capabilities) in order to reap competitive advantages from three primary sources: economies of scale, economies of scope, and reduced transaction costs between the operating units of the firm.

The firm as an information processor versus the firm as an image creator. How does Penrose theorize the planning process in firms, a process which is a central determinant of the growth of firms? More specifically, how do the firm's planners come to grips with the problems of information and knowledge which are inherent in any planning process?

In answering the latter question first, it is illuminating to compare Penrose's approach with that of Simon which has already been examined. For Simon the firm is essentially a form of organization for the effective processing of information. Simon's view of the firm follows directly from his view of human beings. In an article significantly titled, 'Information Processing in Computer and Man', Simon (1964) argues that 'the thinking human being is also an information processor' (p. 76) and that we can 'explain human thinking in terms of the organization of information processes'.[7]

In contrast to Simon, Penrose makes it clear that she sees the firm's planners as 'image creators' rather than as 'information processors'. In other words, rather than beginning with the objective environment of the firm, and the information that this environment generates—in the form, for example, of market prices, market demands, the activities of competitors etc.—Penrose starts with the mental world of the planners who are situated within the context of their own firm and its specific productive services. These planners have to do at least two closely related things. First, they need to appraise the productive services at their disposal—their strengths and weaknesses, the uses to which they can and cannot be put etc. Secondly, the planners must appraise the environment within which they find themselves. What are the opportunities and constraints that this environment presents?

In Penrose's (1959) words, 'the environment [of the firm] is treated . . . as an "image" in the entrepreneur's mind of the possibilities and restrictions

---

[7] This article, originally published in 1964, is contained in Simon (1992).

with which he is confronted, for it is, after all, such an "image" which in fact determines a man's behaviour' (p. 5).

But where do the planners' 'images' come from, if not from the processing of external information? Penrose makes it clear that in her view these images emerge from the experience and knowledge that is generated *within the firm*. According to Penrose:

> I have placed emphasis on the significance of the resources with which a firm works and on the development of the experience and knowledge of a firm's personnel because these are the factors that will to a large extent determine the response of the firm to changes in the external world *and also determine what it 'sees' in the external world* (Penrose, 1959, pp. 79–80, emphasis added).

Later Penrose elaborates:

> for an analysis of the growth of firms it is appropriate to start from an analysis of the firm rather than the environment and then proceed to a discussion of the effect of certain types of environmental conditions. If we can discover what determines entrepreneurial ideas about what the firm can and cannot do, that is what determines the nature and extent of the 'subjective' productive opportunity of the firm, we can at least know where to look if we want to explain or predict the actions of particular firms (ibid. p. 42).

This way of dealing with the information and knowledge problems facing the firm leads on to what is probably Penrose's most important contribution to the theory of the firm, namely her concept of 'productive opportunity', which is a key determinant of the growth of the firm:

> The productive activities of . . . a firm are governed by what we shall call its 'productive opportunity', which comprises all of the productive possibilities that its 'entrepreneurs' see and can take advantage of. A theory of the growth of firms is essentially an examination of the changing productive opportunity of firms; in order to find a limit to the growth, or a restriction on the rate of growth, the productive opportunity of a firm must be shown to be limited in any period. It is clear that this opportunity will be restricted to the extent to which a firm does not see opportunities for expansion, is unwilling to act upon them, or is unable to respond to them (op. cit., pp. 31–32).

The origin and growth of the large modern firm. The large modern firms which came to dominate the world economy first emerged in the 1880s in a number of industrial sectors. Why did this enterprise appear when it did?

Chandler's explanation rests on a chain of interlinked events. The first link in the chain was a cluster of interrelated innovations that together constituted a revolution in the field of transport and communications. These included the railroad and telegraph, steamship and cable. The significance of these innovations was that they facilitated a substantial increase in both volume and speed of output. This meant that for the first time, the enterprise could increase dramatically in size. At the same time this increased the ability of these firms to realize the 'dynamic logic of growth and competition' based on the economies of scale, scope and transaction costs.

The potential for realizing these economies, however, was not divided equally among all sectors. Accordingly, Chandler (1990a) notes, 'In 1973, 289 (72.0%) of the 401 [of the world's largest industrial enterprises] were clustered in food, chemicals, petroleum, primary metals, and the three machinery groups—nonelectrical and electrical machinery and transportation equipment' (p. 20).

The 'logic' of economies of scale, scope and transaction costs, however, was achieved neither automatically nor effortlessly. Rather, the realization of the logic required, as a necessary precondition, the acquisition of dynamic organizational capabilities. In turn, these capabilities required investment, more specifically 'three pronged investment in production, distribution, and management'.

Once in existence, however, how did the modern industrial enterprise grow? According to Chandler:

> The first entrepreneurs to create such enterprises acquired powerful competitive advantages. Their industries quickly became oligopolistic . . . These firms, along with the few challengers that subsequently entered the industry, no longer competed primarily on the basis of price. Instead they competed for market share and profits through functional and strategic effectiveness. They did so *functionally* by improving their product, their processes of production, their marketing, their purchasing, and their labor relations, and *strategically* by moving into growing markets more rapidly, and out of declining ones more quickly and effectively than did their competitors' (Chandler, 1990a, p. 8).

Chandler continues:

> . . . rivalry for market share and profits honed the enterprise's functional and strategic capabilities. These organizational capabilities, in turn, provided an internal dynamic for the continuing growth of the enterprise. In particular, they stimulated its owners and managers to expand into more distant markets in their own country and then to become multinational by moving abroad. They also encouraged the firm to diversify by developing products competitive in markets other than the original one and so to become a multiproduct enterprise . . . Salaried managers, not owners, came to make the decisions about current operating activities and long-term growth and investment (ibid. pp. 8–9).

Bounded rationality, images, organizational capabilities and the growth of the firm. It is worth noting that the problems arising from bounded rationality are not dealt with explicitly in the writings of Penrose and Chandler. Penrose's company entrepreneurs are primarily preoccupied with the resources and services of their own company and it is these services and resources which shape what they see, and how they interpret what they see. Their problem, therefore, is not the Simonian bounded rationality problem of being condemned to attempt to make rational decisions by trying to take account of all the relevant information 'out there', while being unable to process it all. Rather, Penrose's entrepreneurs are led from 'in here'. It is their resources and competences which they can and do know; bounded rationality does not prevent them from knowing them. And it is these resources and competences which determine what they do (and should do, if they are to take advantage of the competence-led opportunities which they face).

Chandler's managers are also 'driven' by the capabilities they have accumulated in the past. However, unlike Penrose's, they also confront the problem of trying to grasp the 'logic' of capitalist industrialization based on economies of scale, scope and transaction costs, and pursuing this logic once they have grasped it.

For Chandler, therefore, the managers of large firms are not so much *ex ante* appraisers of the world as followers of the logic of industrial capitalism. As a result, they are not bedeviled by the problem of attempting to know in a world of complexity, uncertainty, and costly information. Chandler's account of the origin and growth of the firm, in marked contrast to Simon and Penrose, is therefore an *ex post* account, that is an *ex post* explanation of why the firms originated when and where they did, why they grew as they did, etc. In this account, however, the problem of knowing in a complex, uncertain and information costly world is absent, is abstracted from.

Corporate capabilities and the question of strategy. The discussion of Chandler's work, specifically the strategic implications of his analysis of the origins and growth of large industrial companies, raises by implication the minor role that has been allocated to the analysis of corporate strategy in the rest of the literature examined so far in this survey. This minor role is exemplified, for example, in Williamson's 'organizational imperative': 'economize on bounded rationality while safeguarding against opportunism'. This imperative, clearly, does not enable the analyst of the firm to address many of the wider strategic issues confronted by firms.

Furthermore, it is probably fair to say that it is the absence of an applicable approach to corporate strategy in the economics literature on the firm, more than any other issue, which distinguishes the work of economists in this field from that of 'business analysts' (and has the unfortunate consequence of inhibiting intellectual communication between them).[8]

The question of strategy, however, is central in Teece *et al.* (1990). This work is referred to here primarily because it stems from the 'firm as repository of knowledge' approach.

In Teece *et al.* (1990) a 'dynamic capabilities approach' is proposed. This approach, as Teece *et al.* acknowledge, is best seen as an extension of the ideas developed by Penrose. As in Penrose, the firm is seen as a collection of capabilities which embody its knowledge. Following Penrose, causation runs from capabilities to strategy. While the firm's capabilities are the effect of learning, technological opportunities and the selection process, at any point in time these capabilities are not only inherited from the past, they are also constrained by the past. In Teece's words, capabilities are 'sticky' in the sense that they cannot easily, quickly and at low cost be acquired or passed on. Certainly, there is no well-oiled market in capabilities. It is this key fact of life, present also in Penrose, from which the rest of the Teece *et al.* argument follows.

Since capabilities are sticky, they present the firm with its most important opportunity, the chance to become and remain competitive through its distinctiveness. Other potential competitors, constrained by their own capabilities, are not readily able to acquire a successful firm's distinctive capabilities. From this follows Teece's *et al.* definition of 'the concept of core or distinctive competence': 'A core competence is a set of differentiated skills, complementary assets, and routines that provide the basis for a firm's competitive capacities and sustainable advantage in a particular business' (p. 28).

The analysis of strategy follows logically from the analysis of capability or competence. Capability affects strategy in both a positive and a negative way. In a negative way, a firm's capability constrains the strategic possibilities which are open to it. As Teece *et al.* put it:

> Because of imperfect factor markets, or more precisely the non-tradeability of 'soft' assets like values, culture, and organizational experience, these capabilities generally cannot be acquired; they must be built. This sometimes takes years—possibly decades. The capabilities approach accordingly sees definite limits on strategic options at least in the short run. Competitive success occurs in part because of policies pursued and experience obtained in earlier periods (pp. 30–31).

[8] Increasing concern is being expressed regarding the opportunities that are being lost as a result of the absence of intellectual interaction between economists and 'business analysts' working on the firm. See, for example, Kay (1991) and, in a more satirical vein, *The Economist* (December 21, 1991–January 3, 1992).

However, in a positive way, a firm can devise successful strategies by making use of its distinctive capabilities in order to earn an economic rent. On this basis, Teece *et al.*, following Penrose directly, develop the following strategic imperative:

> the process of strategic formulation proceeds as follows: (1) identify your firm's unique resources; (2) decide on which markets those resources can earn the highest rents; and (3) decide whether the rents from those assets are most effectively utilized by (a) integrating into related market(s), (b) selling the relevant intermediate output to related firms, or (c) selling the assets themselves to a firm in a related business (p. 16).

Routines, resources and services, and strategic capabilities. At the beginning of this section we saw that in Nelson and Winter (1982) the routines of the firm serve the function of enabling the firm to deal with bounded rationality while at the same time acting as the firm's 'memory', as the place where its knowledge is stored. In this way the firm is both a response to information-related problems (specifically, bounded rationality) and a repository of knowledge. In Penrose, Chandler, and Teece *et al.*, however, the firm is seen exclusively as a repository of knowledge and Nelson and Winter's concern with bounded rationality is left in the background.

Conceiving of the firm in terms of knowledge is by no means new. Indeed, according to Alfred Marshall (1969), 'Capital consists in a great part of knowledge and organisation . . . Knowledge is our most powerful engine of production; it enables us to subdue Nature and force her to satisfy our wants. Organisation aids knowledge' (p. 115).[9] However, by viewing the firm as a repository of firm-specific knowledge—embodied in the firm's routines, services and strategic capabilities—an approach to the firm is taken which differs significantly both from the approach in orthodox economics and that taken in the 'firm as response to information-related problems' approach discussed in section 3 of this paper.

As repositories of firm-specific knowledge, firms by definition differ from one another. Furthermore, firms are significantly constrained in what they know and what they can do. Moreover, it is their firm-specific capabilities which play a particularly important role in their competitiveness, and therefore in the process of competition more generally. Finally, the 'firm as repository of knowledge' approach leads logically on, as we have seen, to a detailed analysis of corporate strategy. By facilitating an analysis of corporate strategy, this approach also provides a spin-off benefit by creating an intellec-

---

[9] It is worth noting in passing, however, that Marshall's observation on the relationship between knowledge and organization has not yet received the attention it deserves from economists.

tual bridge to some of the work being done by business analysts of the firm. [10]

5. The IBM Paradox

In this section some of the implications of 'the IBM story' will be examined for the theories of the firm discussed in this paper. Particular attention will be paid to what will be called the 'IBM paradox'.

The Information Processing Paradigm

It is clear from the approaches to the firm examined critically in this paper that what may be referred to as an 'information processing paradigm' has exerted a significant conceptual influence. According to this paradigm the firm is seen as a form of organization whose primary task is to acquire and process information, making decisions on the basis of the information so processed. The main characteristic of many of the theories of the firm examined here has been the identification of specific information-related problems, followed by an analysis of the way in which these problems are dealt with by the firm.

This line has also been followed by some of the proponents of what has been called the 'firm as repository of knowledge approach'. This is particularly clear in the case of Nelson and Winter whose concept of routine, as we have seen, is derived directly from information-related difficulties, although in the writings of Penrose, Chandler and Teece *et al.* there is less emphasis on information processing and more on the firm-specific competences that are accumulated.

As pointed out in the introduction to this paper, one of the most important features of the information processing paradigm is the 'tight coupling' that it implies between 'information' and 'knowledge'. In short, 'information' is implicitly defined as a commodity that is capable of yielding knowledge; while 'knowledge' is implicitly conceptualized as belief which is sustained by information. Accordingly, 'knowledge' is equated with processed information: the firm knows what it knows because of the information it has acquired and processed.

---

[10] Examples of work being done by business analysts of the firm—where an intellectual bridge may be built connecting what has been referred to here as the 'firm as repository of knowledge' approach—include Prahalad and Hamel (1990) and Stalk *et al.* (1992) whose articles appear in the *Harvard Business Review*. For both Prahalad and Hamel (1990) and Stalk *et al.* (1992) the concept of competences or capabilities is central in deriving appropriate strategy for the firm. The main difference between them is that while the former define 'competences' largely in terms of technology and products, the latter insist that 'capabilities' must refer to the entire value chain, thus including marketing, distribution, and consumer satisfaction.

The IBM Story

The IBM story should be of great interest to analysts of the firm. Not only is it the story of the unexpected downfall of a great company which was almost universally admired by analysts (corporate, financial and academic), the significance of its demise has resulted in an unusual amount and quality of information about what happened inside the company.

There are many lessons from the IBM story which have implications for the theories of the firm which have been examined in this paper. These include, for example, the shortcomings of the M-form (multidivisional form) of organization. According to Williamson, the evolution of the M-form is to be explained in terms of its efficiency in the processing of information which results in the economization of bounded rationality at the same time as safeguarding against opportunism.

The IBM story, however, suggests that while the M-form might have provided information processing benefits, its main shortcoming lay in the conflicts that it generated between the contradictory interests of the different divisions. In the end it was the interests of the mainframe division which triumphed. These interests, however, became reactionary after the failure of the Future Systems project in the 1970s designed to produce a great leap forward in computer systems. The political interdependence of the divisions under the hegemony of the mainframe division resulted in IBM's failure to take full advantage even of many of the breakthrough products and technologies which it had been the first to invent, such as the personal computer and RISC (reduced instruction set) microprocessor.

In order to deal with these problems (which had little to do with information processing *per se*) IBM, in December 1991, followed the example which AT&T had set in 1988. In so doing, IBM transformed its M-form of organization into what may be called an S-form, a segmented form of organization based on 13 relatively autonomous business and geographic units with significantly reduced powers for its headquarters. At the same time this radical reorganization assigned a significantly enhanced role to internal market mechanisms in order to coordinate and control the activities of these units. This reversed significantly the tendency that Coase and Williamson had seen for activities to be increasingly integrated under the hierarchical control of the modern corporation. The S-form firm itself (as opposed to the networks of firms which surround it) is simultaneously both market and hierarchy, in a way the M-form firm never was. For an elaboration on the transition from the M-form to the S-form in AT&T, IBM and NEC, see Fransman (1994a).

The IBM Paradox

Another lesson for the theory of the firm emerges from what will be called the 'IBM paradox'. This refers to the paradox arising from IBM, the information processing company *par exellence*, clinging until at least 1991[11] to a mistaken belief in the ability of the mainframe computer to sustain its profitability, growth and size, *despite the information which it possessed (and processed) contradicting this belief*. The paradox, furthermore, extends beyond IBM itself to all those analysts in financial, academic and other institutions who were free to arrive at their own independent assessment of the information relating to the company, but who chose to interpret it in a similar way to IBM's leaders (as is evident from IBM's share price movement up to the early 1990s).

IBM's belief in the mainframe emerges clearly from the now-famous public forecast which it made in 1984 of revenue of $100 billion by 1990 and $185 billion by 1994. This compares with actual revenue of $69 billion in 1990, $64.77 billion in 1991, and $64.52 billion in 1992.

Was IBM's belief in the mainframe the result of the company's processing of information, as a tight coupling of information and knowledge/belief suggests? To answer this question let us examine some information which IBM undoubtedly possessed and had processed.

Increasing performance of microprocessors.   The first microprocessor ('computer on a chip'), the Intel 4004, was produced by Intel (now the world's largest semiconductor company) in 1971. As early as 1964 Gordon Moore, Chairman and co-founder of Intel, had noted that with the development of the planar transistor in 1959 the number of elements in advanced integrated circuits had been doubling each year. This observation led him to formulate the well-known Moore's Law, which states that the complexity of integrated circuits would double each year. Figure 1 shows the evolution of Intel's microprocessors in accordance with Moore's Law. In terms of MIPS (millions of instructions per second), the standard measure of microprocessor performance, over the 20 years that elapsed between the original Intel 4004 and the 80486 microprocessors, performance increased almost 280 times. By 1984, therefore, when IBM made its $100 billion revenue forecast, the evolutionary trend toward increasing microprocessor power was already very well established.

---

[11] The present author's interviews at IBM's headquarters at Armonk, New York in early 1993 indicate that it was only in 1991 that IBM's leaders amended their belief in the mainframe.

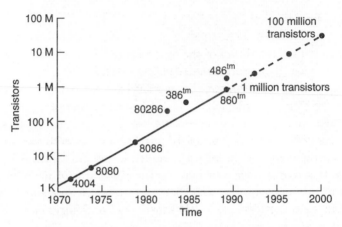

FIGURE 1. Evolution of Moore's Law for Intel microprocessors. Source: Molina, 1992

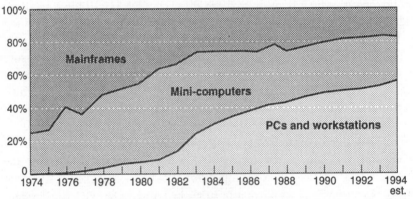

FIGURE 2. European computer market share (by product category). Source: Datastream and OTR Pedder

Increasing substitution of smaller computers for mainframes. One of the main implications of increasing microprocessor power was that smaller computers became increasingly powerful as well as cheap (in terms of cost of information unit processed). This meant that smaller computers, particularly personal computers and workstations, began increasingly to be substituted for mainframes, often in distributed networks. By 1984 the trend for PCs and workstations to win a larger share of the computer market was also well established. In Figure 2, for example, data is presented on this trend for the European computer market, one of IBM's most important. By 1984 PCs and workstations made up more than 30% of the market.

IBM's beliefs regarding smaller computers. Furthermore, the information regarding the increasing power of microprocessors and the move toward 'downsizing' had been processed by IBM as early as the mid-1970s and the implications distilled. This is evident in the commitment that Frank Cary, who became IBM's chief executive officer in 1972, made to personal computers. Cary had led IBM into minicomputers in the late 1960s and was convinced that the greatest growth in the computer industry would come from the smaller end. Indeed, in the 1960s IBM built the SCAMP, probably the world's first personal computer, and followed this with the 5100 in the mid-1970s even though it made little progress in commercializing them (Ferguson and Morris, 1993).

In the light of evidence such as this it is a puzzle that IBM's leaders continued to believe until as late as 1991 in the ability of the mainframe to sustain its growth, profitability and size. As expressed in one of the best of the current accounts of IBM's demise, 'it is more surprising that IBM's top management missed the straws swirling in the wind in the 1970s and 1980s that computing was undergoing fundamental change, that the 360/370 [IBM's major mainframe systems introduced in 1964 and 1970 respectively] —indeed, the whole mainframe principle—was heading for a dead end' (Ferguson and Morris, 1993, p. 16). Closer to the concerns of the present paper, *The Economist* (1993) noted that 'Mr Akers [who became Chairman of IBM in 1985 and resigned in 1993] and his colleagues had access to more information about the industry than any of their rivals . . . [However,] their flood of information did them little good'.

IBM, Information and Knowledge

It is clear from the evidence presented here that during the 1980s there was a growing disjuncture in IBM between information that the company had processed (regarding the increasing performance–cost ratio of microprocessors and substitutability of smaller computers and mainframes) and the company's knowledge-belief (in the ability of the mainframe to sustain its profitability, growth and size). It is possible, however, that in the early 1980s the information was still incomplete in the sense that ambiguity still surrounded the available information regarding the extent of the 'downsizing' that would occur. Under these conditions of 'interpretive ambiguity' it may still have been reasonable to interpret this information as suggesting that substitution would only take place at the fringes of the mainframe market, leaving largely intact IBM's market growth and profit margins on mainframes.

But as the decade progressed, IBM's belief in the mainframe remained unaltered while the information became less and less ambiguous. By 1991, however, under the weight not only of complete information but also of the feedback provided from IBM's selection environment in the form of falling revenues and profit margins on mainframes, the belief finally cracked. (It is worth noting, incidentally, that the disjuncture between information and belief had nothing to do with bounded rationality as strictly defined by Simon. That is, the problem was not the quantity of information relative to the company's ability to acquire and process information; the problem followed rather from the way in which the leaders of the company chose to interpret the information available in the light of their belief in the mainframe.)

Two questions are raised by the IBM paradox. The first (and for present purposes less important) question is the following: what caused this belief in IBM and how was it sustained in the face of growing information to the contrary? The second, more important, question is: what are the implications for the theory of the firm?

Although this is not the place for an exhaustive enquiry into the first question (and it may be that the evidence necessary to answer it is not yet available), the following three elements appear to be important parts of the answer. The first element was IBM's historical and spectacular experience of success with mainframes, particularly Systems 360 and 370 on which many of the company's leaders in the 1980s cut their teeth. This experience colored the beliefs of the leaders. Secondly, the failure of the Future Systems project in the mid-1970s, which was intended to displace current computers with a quantum jump in computer technologies, was a blow to the confidence and morale of IBM's leaders. This resulted in a regressive and defensive tendency to cling to past beliefs.

The third element in the wake of the failed Future Systems project was the fear of encouraging products and technologies that might undermine what was believed to be the company's lifeblood—System 370 and its various incarnations. This further reinforced the hegemony of the mainframe division and its beliefs at the expense of the other divisions producing smaller computers and technologies (such as RISC microprocessors) which it was feared might eat into the revenue from mainframes.

It is a fitting conclusion to this discussion of the IBM paradox to lament with T. S. Eliot (1963), 'Where is the wisdom we have lost in knowledge? Where is the knowledge we have lost in information?', a lament that is all the more pertinent in the so-called 'information age'.

6. Implications for the Theory of the Firm

The Concept of Vision

The IBM paradox is a particularly dramatic example of a disjuncture between information and knowledge. However, interpretive ambiguity (which occurs whenever there is incomplete information, driving a 'wedge' between information and knowledge) and the tenacity of beliefs are sufficiently frequent occurrences to merit inclusion in the theory of the firm. How can this be done?

The way forward, it is proposed, is to distinguish 'information' from 'knowledge'. Information is defined, as above, as data relating to states of the world and the state-contingent consequences that follow from events in the world. Knowledge, on the other hand, is defined as belief. While belief is influenced by information processed by the believer, belief is not necessarily wholly determined by processed information. In the formation of belief, accordingly, there is room for insight, creativity and misconception. Furthermore, while information is a closed set, knowledge is essentially open-ended. Information and knowledge as thus defined, therefore, are loosely coupled.

The 'vision' of a firm is defined as the dominant set of beliefs in the firm regarding the firm's internal and external circumstances, the shape of things to come in the future and, in the light of these factors, the way the firm should 'play its cards'. Since vision depends on the particular construction of particular beliefs, vision is by definition always bounded. 'Bounded vision' and the possibility of 'vision failure' are, therefore, logical implications of this conception of vision. The concept of vision is further elaborated upon in the context of the evolution of firms, technologies and national innovation systems in Fransman (1994b).

Routine, Competence and Knowledge-creation

In the concept of vision, knowledge is treated on its own terms, as an open-ended process, and not merely as processed information. While the concept of vision relates primarily to the way in which the firm appraises its circumstances and decides on the actions it should take, it is suggested that the conception of knowledge which underlies the notion of vision should also be extended to the analysis of the firm's knowledge base.

While we agree with Marshall that 'Knowledge is our most powerful engine of production', and while it is acknowledged that this idea is embodied in the concepts of 'routine' and 'competence' examined earlier in this paper, it is necessary to go beyond these *ex post* concepts to an analysis of the knowledge-creation process itself within the firm. This also requires treating knowledge on its own terms, as an open-ended process. This involves, *inter alia*, the integration of knowledge fragmented in various parts of the firm (confronting within the context of the firm Hayek's problem of utilizing knowledge not known to anyone in its entirety); mobilizing and combining tacit and explicit knowledge; understanding the learning process in all its manifestations; and understanding the process of creativity involved in all innovative activity, including research. These, however, are complex issues that cannot be analysed here.

7. *Conclusion*

As Penrose notes in the quotation reproduced at the beginning of this paper, knowledge is such a difficult concept with the result that most economists have found it 'too slippery to handle'. The recognition, however, of the 'dominant role that increasing knowledge plays in economic processes' leaves us with little option but to take this concept fully on board in the attempt to produce a more robust theory of the firm.

References

Alchian, A. and H. Demsetz (1972), 'Production Information Costs, and Economic Organization,' *The American Economic Review*, 62, 777–795.

Chandler, A. D. (1990a), *Scale and Scope. The Dynamics of Industrial Capitalism*. The Belknap Press of Harvard University: Cambridge, MA.

Chandler, A. D. (1990b), 'The Enduring Logic of Industrial Success,' *Harvard Business Review* (March–April), 132–140.

Coase, R. H. (1937), 'The Nature of the Firm,' *Economica N.S.*, 4, 386–405.

Coase, R. H. (1988), 'The Nature of the Firm: Origin,' *Journal of Law, Economics, and Organization*, 4, (1), Spring, 3–47.

Dore, R. P. (1983), 'Goodwill and the Spirit of Market Capitalism,' *The British Journal of Sociology*, **XXXIV** (4), 459–482.

Eliot, T. S. (1963), 'Choruses from "The Rock",' *Collected Poems, 1909–1962*. Faber and Faber: London, 161.

Elster, J. (1983), *Explaining Technical Change: Studies in Rationality and Social Change*. Cambridge University Press: Cambridge.

Ferguson, C. H. and C. R. Morris (1993), *Computer Wars. How the West Can Win in a Post-IBM World*. Times Books: New York.

Fransman, M. (1994), 'Different Folks, Different Strokes—How IBM, AT&T and NEC Segment to compete,' *Business Strategy Review*, 5, 1–20.

Fransman, M. (1994), *NTT and the Evolution of Japanese Information and Communication Industry*.

Jensen, M. and W. Meckling (1976), 'Theory of the Firm: Managerial Behavior, Agency Costs, and Ownership Structure,' *The Journal of Financial Economics*, 3, 305–60.

Kay, J. (1991), 'Economics and Business,' *Economic Journal*, (January).

March, J. G. and H. A. Simon (1958), *Organizations*. Wiley: New York.

Marshall, A. (1969), *Principles of Economics*. Macmillan: London.

Molina, A. H. (1992), 'Current Trends, Issues and Strategies in the Development of the Microprocessor Industry,' Programme On Information and Communication Technologies (PICT), Working Paper No. 42, University of Edinburgh.

Nelson, R. R. and S. G. Winter (1977), 'In Search of a Useful Theory of Innovation,' *Research Policy*, 6, 36–76.

Nelson, R. R. and S. G. Winter (1982), _An Evolutionary Theory of Economic Change_. The Belknap Press of Harvard University Press: Cambridge, MA.

Penrose, E. T. (1959), _The Theory of the Growth of the Firm_. Basil Blackwell: Oxford.

Prahalad, C. K. and G. Hamel (1990), 'The Core Competence of the Corporation', _Harvard Business Review_ (May–June), 78–91.

Putterman, L. (ed.) (1986), _The Economic Nature of the Firm. A Reader_. Cambridge University Press: Cambridge.

Simon, H. A. (1957), _Models of Man_. John Wiley & Sons: New York.

Simon, H. A. (1959), 'Theories of Decision Making in Economics and Behavioral Science,' _American Economic Review_, 49 (June), 253–283.

Simon, H. A. (1961), _Administrative Behavior_. 2nd edition, Macmillan: New York, xxiv.

Simon, H. A. (1964), 'Information Processing in Computer and Man,' in H. A. Simon _et al._ (1992), _Economics, Bounded Rationality and the Cognitive Revolution_. Edward Elgar: Aldershot.

Simon, H. A. (1978), 'Rationality as Process and as Product of Thought,' _American Economic Review_, 68 (May), 1–16.

Simon, H. A., M. Egidi, R. Marris and R. Viale (1992), _Economics, Bounded Rationality and the Cognitive Revolution_. Edward Elgar: Aldershot.

Stalk, G., P. Evans and L. E. Shulman (1992), 'Competing on Capabilities: The New Role of Corporate Strategy,' _Harvard Business Review_ (March–April), 57–69.

Teece, D. J., G. Pisano and A. Shuen (1990), 'Firm Capabilities, Resources and the Concept of Strategy,' CCC Working Paper No. 90–8.

The Economist (1991/1992), 'An Economist Takes Tea with a Management Guru,' _The Economist_, December 21, 1991–January 3, 1992, 107–109.

The Economist (1993), January 16–22, 24.

Williamson, O. E. (1975), _Markets and Hierarchies: Analysis and Antitrust Implications. A Study in the Economics of Internal Organization_. The Free Press: New York.

Williamson, O. E. (1987), _The Economic Institutions of Capitalism_. The Free Press: New York.

Williamson, O. E. (1990), 'The Firm as a Nexus of Treaties: An Introduction,' in M. Aoki, B. Gustafson and O. E. Williamson (eds) (1990), _The Firm as a Nexus of Treaties_. Sage: London, 1–25.

Winter, S. G. (1988), 'On Coase, Competence and the Corporation,' _Journal of Law, Economics and Organization_, 4 (1), Spring, 163–180.

The Dynamic Capabilities of Firms: an Introduction

DAVID TEECE AND GARY PISANO*

(Institute of Management, Innovation and Organization, 554 Barrows Hall, University of California, Berkeley CA 94720 and *Graduate School of Business, Harvard University, Morgan Hall, Room T97, Soldiers Field, Boston, MA 02163, USA)

An expanded paradigm is needed to explain how competitive advantage is gained and held. Firms resorting to 'resource-based strategy' attempt to accumulate valuable technology assets and employ an aggressive intellectual property stance. However, winners in the global marketplace have been firms demonstrating timely responsiveness and rapid and flexible product innovation, along with the management capability to effectively coordinate and redeploy internal and external competences. This source of competitive advantage, 'dynamic capabilities', emphasizes two aspects. First, it refers to the shifting character of the environment; second, it emphasizes the key role of strategic management in appropriately adapting, integrating, and re-configuring internal and external organizational skills, resources, and functional competences toward changing environment.[5] Only recently have researchers begun to focus on the specifics of developing firm-specific capabilities and the manner in which competences are renewed to respond to shifts in the business environment. The dynamic capabilities approach provides a coherent framework to integrate existing conceptual and empirical knowledge, and facilitate prescription. This paper argues that the competitive advantage of firms stems from dynamic capabilities rooted in high performance routines operating inside the firm, embedded in the firm's processes, and conditioned by its history. It offers dynamic capabilities as an emerging paradigm of the modern business firm that draws on multiple disciplines and advances, with the help of industry studies in the USA and elsewhere.

1. Introduction

The global competitive battles in high technology industries such as semi-conductors, information services, and software have demonstrated the need for an expanded paradigm to understand how competitive advantage is gained and held. Well-known companies like IBM, Texas Instruments, Phillips, and others appear to have followed a 'resource-based strategy' of accumulating valuable technology assets, often guarded by an aggressive intellectual property stance. However, this strategy is often not enough to support a significant competitive advantage. Winners in the global market-place have been firms that can demonstrate timely responsiveness and rapid and flexible product innovation, coupled with the management capability to effectively coordinate and redeploy internal and external competences. Not surprisingly, industry observers have remarked that companies can accumulate a large stock of valuable technology assets and still not have many useful capabilities.

We refer to this source of competitive advantage as 'dynamic capabilities' to emphasize two key aspects which were not the main focus of attention in previous strategy perspectives. The term 'dynamic' refers to the shifting character of the environment; certain strategic responses are required when time-to-market and timing is critical, the pace of innovation is accelerating, and the nature of future competition and markets is difficult to determine. The term 'capabilities' emphasizes the key role of strategic management in appropriately adapting, integrating, and re-configuring internal and external organizational skills, resources, and functional competences toward changing environment.

The notion that competitive advantage requires both the exploitation of existing internal and external firm-specific capabilities and of developing new ones is partially developed in Penrose (1959), Teece (1982), and Wernerfelt (1984). However, only recently have researchers begun to focus on the specifics of how some organizations first develop firm-specific capabilities and how they renew competences to respond to shifts in the business environment.[1] These issues are intimately tied to the firm's business processes, market positions, and expansion paths. Several writers have recently offered insights and evidence on how firms can develop their capability to adapt and even capitalize on rapidly changing environments.[2] The dynamic capabilities approach provides a coherent framework which can both integrate existing conceptual and empirical knowledge, and facilitate prescription. In doing so, it builds upon the theoretical foundations provided by Schumpeter (1934), Penrose (1959), Williamson (1975, 1985), Barney (1986), Nelson and Winter (1982), Teece (1988), and Teece *et al.* (1994).

---

[1] See, for example, Iansiti and Clark (1994), and Henderson (1994).
[2] See Hayes *et al.* (1988), Prahalad and Hamel (1990), Dierickx and Cool (1989), Chandler (1990), and Teece (1993).

2. Toward a Dynamic Capabilities Framework

Markets and Strategic Capabilities

Different approaches to strategy view sources of wealth creation and the essence of the strategic problem faced by firms differently. The competitive forces framework sees the strategic problem in terms of market entry, entry deterrence, and positioning; game-theoretic models view the strategic problem as one of interaction between rivals with certain expectations about how each other will behave;[3] resource-based perspectives have focused on the exploitation of firm-specific assets. Each approach asks different, often complementary, questions. A key step in building a conceptual framework related to dynamic capabilities is to identify the foundations upon which distinctive and difficult-to-replicate advantages can be built.

A useful way to vector in on the strategic elements of the business enterprise is to first identify what is not strategic. To be strategic, a capability must be honed to a user need (so that there are customers), unique (so that the products/services produced can be priced without too much regard to competition), and difficult to replicate (so that profits will not be competed away). Accordingly, any assets or entity which is homogeneous and can be bought and sold at an established price cannot be all that strategic (Barney, 1986). What is it, then, about firms which undergirds competitive advantage?

To answer this, one must first make some fundamental distinctions between markets and internal organization (firms). The essence of the firm, as Coase (1937) pointed out, is that it displaces market organization. It does so in the main because inside the firms one can organize certain types of economic activity in ways one cannot using markets. This is not only because of transaction costs, as Williamson (1975, 1985) has emphasized, but also because there are many types of arrangements where injecting high powered (market-like) incentives might well be quite destructive of the cooperative activity and learning. Indeed, the essence of internal organization is that it is a domain of unleveraged or low-powered incentives. By unleveraged we mean that rewards are determined at the group or organization level, not primarily at the individual level, in an effort to encourage team behavior, not individual behavior, in order to accomplish certain tasks well. Inside an organization, exchange cannot take place in the same manner that it can outside an organization, not just because it might be destructive to provide high powered individual incentives, but because it is difficult if not impos-

---

[3] In sequential move games, each player looks ahead and anticipates his rivals' future responses in order to reason back and decide action, i.e. look forward, reason backward.

sible to tightly calibrate individual contributions to a joint effort. Hence, contrary to Arrow's (1969) view of firms as quasi markets, and the task of management to inject markets into firms, we recognize the inherent limits and possible counterproductive results of attempting to fashion firms into clusters of internal markets. In particular, learning and internal technology transfer may well be jeopardized.

Indeed, what is distinctive about firms is that they are domains for organizing activity in a non-market-like fashion. Accordingly, as we discuss what is distinctive about firms, we stress competences/capabilities which are ways of organizing and getting things done which cannot be accomplished by using the price system to coordinate activity. The very essence of capabilities/competences is that they cannot be readily assembled through markets (Teece, 1982, 1986a; Kogut and Zander, 1992). If the ability to assemble competences using markets is what is meant by the firm as a nexus of contracts (Fama, 1980), then we unequivocally state that the firm about which we theorize cannot be usefully modeled as a nexus of contracts. By contract we are referring to a transaction undergirded by a legal agreement, or some other arrangement which clearly spells out rights, rewards, and responsibilities. Moreover, the firm as a nexus of contracts suggests a series of bilateral contracts orchestrated by a coordinator, where our view of the firm is that the organization takes place in a more multilateral fashion, with patterns of behavior and learning being orchestrated in a much more decentralized fashion.

The key point, however, is that the properties of internal organization cannot be replicated by a portfolio of business units amalgamated through formal contracts, as the distinctive elements of internal organization simply cannot be replicated in the market.[4] That is, entrepreneurial activity cannot lead to the immediate replication of unique organization skills through simply entering a market and piecing the parts together overnight. Replication takes time, and the replication of best practice may be illusive. Indeed, firm capabilities need to be understood not in terms of balance sheet items, but mainly in terms of the organizational structures and managerial processes which support productive activity. By construction, the firm's balance sheet contains items that can be valued, at least at original market prices (cost). It is necessarily the case, therefore, that the balance sheet is a poor shadow of a firm's distinctive competence.[5] That which is distinctive

---

[4] As we note in Teece *et al.* (1994), the conglomerate offers few, if any, efficiencies because there is little provided by the conglomerate form that shareholders cannot obtain for themselves simply by holding a diversified portfolio of stocks.

[5] Owners' equity may reflect, in part, certain historic capabilities. Recently, some scholars have begun to attempt to measure organizational capability using financial statement data. See Baldwin and Clark (1991) and Lev and Sougiannis (1992).

cannot be bought and sold short of buying the firm itself, or one or more of its subunits.

There are many dimensions to the business firm that must be understood if one is to grasp firm-level distinctive competences/capabilities. In this paper we merely identify several classes of factors that will help determine a firm's dynamic capabilities. We organize these into three categories: processes, positions, and paths.

Processes, Positions, and Paths

We advance the argument that the strategic dimensions of the firm are its managerial and organizational processes, its present position, and the paths available to it. By managerial and organizational processes we refer to the way things are done in the firm, or what might be referred to as its 'routines', or patterns of current practice and learning. By position we refer to its current endowment of technology and intellectual property, as well as its customer base and upstream relations with suppliers.[6] By paths we refer to the strategic alternatives available to the firm, and the attractiveness of the opportunities which lie ahead. Our focus throughout is on asset structures for which no ready market exists, as these are the only assets of strategic interest. A final section focuses on replication and imitation, as it is these phenomena which determine how readily a competence or capability can be cloned by competitors, and therefore the durability of its advantage.

The firm's processes and positions collectively encompass its capabilities or competences. A hierarchy of competences/capabilities ought be recognized, as some competences may be on the factory floor, some in the R&D labs, some in the executive suites, and some in the way everything is integrated. A difficult-to-replicate or difficult-to-imitate competence/capability can be considered a distinctive competence. As indicated, the key feature of distinctive competences and capabilities is that there is not a market for them, except possibly through the market for business units[7] or corporate control. Hence competences and capabilities are intriguing assets as they typically must be built because they cannot be bought. Dynamic capabilities are the subset of the competences/capabilities which allow the firm to create new products and processes, and respond to changing market circumstances.

---

[6] We also recognize its strategic alliances with competitors.
[7] Such competences may unravel if the subunit is separated from the parent.

Organizational and Managerial Processes

Integration. While the price system supposedly coordinates the economy, managers coordinate or integrate activity inside the firm. How efficiently and effectively internal coordination or integration is achieved is very important (Aoki, 1990).[8] Likewise for external coordination.[9] Increasingly, strategic advantage requires the integration of external activities and technologies. The growing literature on strategic alliances, the virtual corporation, and buyer–supplier relations and technology collaboration evidences the importance of external integration and sourcing.

There is some field-based empirical research that provides support for the notion that the way production is organized by management inside the firm is the source of differences in firms' competence in various domains. For example, Garvin's (1988) study of eighteen room air conditioning plants reveals that quality performance was not related to either capital investment or the degree of automation of the facilities. Instead, quality performance was driven by special organizational routines. These included routines for gathering and processing information, for linking customer experiences with engineering design choices, and for coordinating factories and component suppliers.[10] The work of Clark and Fujimoto (1991) on project development in the automobile industry also illustrates the role played by coordinative routines. Their study reveals a significant degree of variation in how different firms coordinate the various activities required to bring a new model from concept to market. These differences in coordinative routines and capabilities seem to have a significant impact on such performance variables as development cost, development lead times, and quality. Furthermore, they tended to find significant firm-level differences in coordination routines and these differences seem to have persisted for a long time. This suggests that routines related to coordination are firm-specific in nature.

Also, the notion that competence/capability is embedded in distinct ways of coordinating and combining helps to explain how and why change can have devastating impacts on incumbent firms' abilities to compete in a market. Henderson and Clark (1990), for example, have shown that

[8] Indeed, Ronald Coase, author of the pathbreaking 1937 article 'The Nature of the Firm', which focused on the costs of organizational coordination inside the firm as compared to across the market, half a century later has identified as critical the understanding of 'why the costs of organizing particular activities differ among firms' (Coase, 1988; p. 47). We argue that a firm's distinctive ability needs to be understood as a reflection of distinctive organizational or coordinative capabilities. This form of integration (i.e. inside business units) is different from the integration between business units; they could be viable on a stand-alone basis (external integration). For a useful taxonomy, see Iansiti and Clark, *op. cit.* (1994).

[9] Amy Shuen (1994) examines the gains and hazards of the technology make-versus-buy decision and supplier co-development.

[10] Garvin (1994) provides a typology of organizational processes.

incumbents in the photolithographic equipment industry were devastated by innovations that had major impacts on the configuration of systems. They attributed these difficulties to the fact that systems-level or 'architectural' innovations often require new routines to integrate and coordinate engineering tasks. These findings and others suggest that productive systems display high interdependency, and that it may not be possible to change one level without changing others. This appears to be true with respect to the 'lean production' model (Womack *et al.*) which has now transformed the Taylor or Ford model of manufacturing organization in the automobile industry.[11] Lean production requires distinctive shop floor practices and processes as well as distinctive higher order managerial processes. Put differently, organizational processes often display high levels of coherence, and when they do, replication may be difficult because it requires systemic changes throughout the organization and also among interorganizational linkages which might be very hard to effectuate. Put differently, partial imitation or replication of a successful model may yield zero benefits.

The notion that there is a certain rationality or coherence to processes and systems is not quite the same concept as corporate culture, as we understand

---

[11] Fujimoto (1994, pp. 18–20) describes key elements as they existed in the Japanese auto industry as follows: "The typical volume production system of effective Japanese makers of the 1980s (e.g. Toyota) consists of various intertwined elements that might lead to competitive advantages. Just-in-Time (JIT), Jidoka (automatic defect detection and machine stop), Total Quality Control (TQC), and continuous improvement (Kaizen) are often pointed out as its core subsystems. The elements of such a system include inventory reduction mechanisms by Kanban system; levelization of production volume and product mix (heijunka); reduction of 'muda' (non-value adding activities), 'mura' (uneven pace of production) and muri (excessive workload); production plans based on dealers' order volume (genyo seisan); reduction of die set-up time and lot size in stamping operation; mixed model assembly; piece by piece transfer of parts between machines (ikko-nagashi), flexible task assignment for volume changes and productivity improvement (shojinka); multi-task job assignment along the process flow (takotei-mochi); U-shape machine layout that facilitates flexible and multiple task assignment, on-the-spot inspection by direct workers (tsukurikomi); fool-proof prevention of defects (poka-yoke); real-time feedback of production troubles (andon); assembly line stop cord; emphasis on cleanliness, order, and discipline on the shop floor (5-S); frequent revision of standard operating procedures by supervisors; quality control circles; standardized tools for quality improvement (e.g. 7 tools for QC, QC story); worker involvement in preventive maintenance (Total Productive Maintenance); low cost automation or semi-automation with just-enough functions); reduction of process steps for saving of tools and dies, and so on. The human-resource management factors that back up the above elements include stable employment of core workers (with temporary workers in the periphery); long-term training of multi-skilled (multi-task) workers; wage system based in part on skill accumulation; internal promotion to shop floor supervisors; cooperative relationships with labor unions; inclusion of production supervisors in union members; generally egalitarian policies for corporate welfare, communication and worker motivation. Parts procurement policies are also pointed out often as a source of the competitive advantage; relatively high ratio of parts out-sourcing; multi-layer hierarchy of suppliers; long-term relations with suppliers; relatively small number of technologically capable suppliers at the first tier; subassembly functions of the first-tier parts makers; detail-engineering capability of the first tier makers (design-in, back box parts); competition based on long-term capability of design and improvements rather than bidding; pressures for continuous reduction of parts price; elimination of incoming parts inspection; plant inspection and technical assistance by auto makers, and so on."

the latter. Corporate culture refers to the values and beliefs that employees hold; culture can be a *de facto* governance system as it mediates the behavior of individuals and economizes on more formal administrative methods. Rationality or coherence notions are more akin to the Nelson and Winter (1982) notion of organizational routines. However, the routines concept is a little too amorphous to properly capture the congruence amongst processes and between processes and incentives that we have in mind. Consider a professional service organization like an accounting firm. If it is to have relatively high-powered incentives that reward individual performance, then it must build organizational processes that channel individual behavior; if it has weak or low-powered incentives, it must find symbolic ways to recognize the high performers, and it must use alternative methods to build effort and enthusiasm. What one may think of as styles of organization in fact contain necessary, not discretionary, elements to achieve performance. Recognizing the congruences and complementarities among processes, and between processes and incentives, is critical to the understanding of organizational capabilities. In particular, they can help us explain why architectural and radical innovations are so often introduced into an industry by new entrants. The incumbents develop distinctive organizational processes that cannot support the new technology, despite certain overt similarities between the old and the new. The frequent failure of incumbents to introduce new technologies can thus be seen as a consequence of the mismatch that may exist between the set of organizational processes needed to support the conventional product/service and the requirements of the new. Radical organizational re-engineering will usually be required to support the new product, which may well do better embedded in a separate subsidiary where a new set of coherent organizational processes can be fashioned. [12]

Learning.   Perhaps even more important than integration is learning. Learning is a process by which repetition and experimentation enable tasks to be performed better and more quickly and new production opportunities to be identified. [13] In the context of the firm, if not more generally, learning has several key characteristics. First, learning involves organizational as well as individual skills. [14] While individual skills are of relevance, their value depends upon their employment, in particular organizational settings. Learning processes are intrinsically social and collective and occur not only through the imitation and emulation of individuals, as with teacher–student or master–apprentice, but also because of joint contributions to the under-

---

[12] See Abernathy and Clark (1985).
[13] For a useful review and contribution, see Levitt and March (1988).
[14] See Mahoney (1994).

standing of complex problems. Learning requires common codes of communication and coordinated search procedures. Second, the organizational knowledge generated by such activity resides in new patterns of activity, in 'routines', or a new logic of organization. As indicated earlier, routines are patterns of interactions that represent successful solutions to particular problems. These patterns of interaction are resident in group behavior, though certain subroutines may be resident in individual behavior. The concept of dynamic capabilities as a coordinative management process opens the door to the potential for interorganizational learning. Researchers (Doz and Shuen, 1989; Mody, 1990) have pointed out that collaborations and partnerships can be vehicles for new organizational learning, helping firms to recognize dysfunctional routines, and preventing strategic blindspots.

Reconfiguration and Transformation. In rapidly changing environments, there is obviously value in the ability to sense the need to reconfigure the firm's asset structure, and to accomplish the necessary internal and external transformation (Amit and Schoemaker, 1992; Langlois, 1994). This requires constant surveillance of markets and technologies and the willingness to adopt best practice. In this regard, benchmarking is of considerable value as an organized process for accomplishing such ends (Camp, 1989). In dynamic environments, narcissistic organizations are likely to be impaired. The capacity to reconfigure and transform is itself a learned organizational skill. The more frequently practiced, the more easily accomplished.

Change is costly and so firms must develop processes to minimize low payoff change. The ability to calibrate the requirements for change and to effectuate the necessary adjustments would appear to depend on the ability to scan the environment, to evaluate markets and competitors, and to quickly accomplish reconfiguration and transformation ahead of competition. Decentralization and local autonomy assists these processes. Firms that have honed these capabilities are sometimes referred to as 'high flex'.

Positions. The strategic posture of a firm is determined not only by its learning processes and by the coherence of its internal and external processes and incentives, but also by its location at any point in time with respect to its business assets. By business assets we do not mean its plant and equipment unless they are specialized; rather we mean its difficult-to-trade knowledge assets and assets complementary to them, as well as its reputational and relational assets. These will determine its market share and profitability at any point in time.

Technological Assets. While there is an emerging market for know-how

(Teece, 1981), much technology does not enter it. This is either because the firm is unwilling to sell it[15] or because of difficulties in transacting in the market for know-how (Teece, 1980). A firm's technological assets may or may not be protected by the standard instruments of intellectual property law. Either way, the ownership protection and utilization of technological assets are clearly key differentiators among firms. Likewise for complementary assets.

Complementary Assets.   Technological innovations require the use of certain related assets to produce and deliver new products and services. Prior commercialization activities require and enable firms to build such complementarities (Teece, 1986b). Such capabilities and assets, while necessary for the firm's established activities, may have other uses as well. Such assets typically lie downstream. New products and processes can either enhance or destroy the value of such assets (Tushman *et al.*, 1986). Thus the development of computers enhanced the value of IBM's direct sales force in office products, while disc brakes rendered useless much of the auto industries' investment in drum brakes.

Financial Assets.   In the short run, a firm's cash position and degree of leverage may have strategic implications. While there is nothing more fungible than cash, it cannot always be raised from external markets without the dissemination of considerable information to potential investors. Accordingly, what a firm can do in short order is often a function of its balance sheet. In the longer run, that ought not to be so, as cash flow ought to be more determinative.

Locational Assets.   Geography matters too. Uniqueness in certain businesses can stem from locational assets which are non-tradable (e.g. positioning of a refinery in a certain geographic market). While real estate markets are well developed, land use and environmental restrictions often make locational assets non-tradable, and hence may be the source of difficult-to-replicate advantages which manifest themselves in lower transport costs, superior convenience, and the like.

Paths

Path Dependencies.   Where a firm can go is a function of its current position and the paths ahead. It is of course also shaped by the path behind. In standard economics textbooks, firms have an infinite range of technologies

---

[15] Managers often evoke the 'crown jewels' metaphor. That is, if the technology is released, the kingdom will be lost.

from which they can choose and markets they can occupy. Changes in product or factor prices will be responded to instantaneously, with technologies moving in and out according to value maximization criteria. Only in the short run are irreversibilities recognized. Fixed costs — such as equipment and overheads — cause firms to price below fully amortized costs but never constrain future investment choices. 'Bygones are bygones.' Path dependencies are simply not recognized.

The notion of path dependencies recognizes that 'history matters'. Bygones are rarely bygones, despite the predictions of rational actor theory. Thus a firm's previous investments and its repertoire of routines (its 'history') constrains its future behavior. Leonard-Barton (1992) notes that an organization's core capabilities can just as easily create 'core rigidities'. This follows because learning tends to be local. That is, opportunities for learning will be 'close in' to previous activities and thus will be transaction and production specific (Teece, 1988). This is because learning is often a process of trial, feedback, and evaluation. If too many parameters are changed simultaneously, the ability of firms to conduct meaningful natural quasi experiments is attenuated. If many aspects of a firm's learning environment change simultaneously, the ability to ascertain cause–effect relationships is confounded because cognitive structures will not be formed and rates of learning diminish as a result. One implication is that many investments are much longer term than is commonly thought.

Technological Opportunities. The concept of path dependencies can be given forward meaning through the consideration of an industry's technological opportunities. It is well recognized that how far and how fast a particular area of industrial activity can proceed is in part due to the technological opportunities that lie before it. Such opportunities are usually a lagged function of foment and diversity in basic science, and the rapidity with which new scientific breakthroughs are being made.

However, technological opportunities may not be completely exogenous to industry, not only because some firms have the capacity to engage in or at least support basic research, but also because technological opportunities are often fed by innovative activity itself. Moreover, the recognition of such opportunities are affected by the organizational structures that link the institutions engaging in basic research (primarily the university) to the business enterprise. Hence, the existence of technological opportunities can be quite firm specific.

Important for our purposes is the rate and direction in which relevant scientific frontiers are being rolled back. Firms engaging in R&D may find the path dead ahead closed off, though breakthroughs in related areas may be sufficiently close to be attractive. Likewise, if the path dead ahead is extremely attractive, there may be no incentive for firms to shift the allocation of resources away from traditional pursuits. The depth and width of technological opportunities in the neighborhood of a firm's prior research activities thus are likely to impact a firm's options with respect to both the amount and level of R&D activity that it can justify. In addition, a firm's past experience conditions the alternatives management is able to perceive. Thus, not only do firms in the same industry face 'menus' with different costs associated with particular technological choices, they also are looking at menus containing different choices.[16]

Assessment.   The assessment of a firm's strategic capability at any point in time is presented here as a function of the firm's processes, positions, and paths. What it can do and where it can go is thus heavily constrained by the typography of its processes, positions, and paths. Each component of this capability framework needs to be analyzed in a strategic audit.

We submit that if one can identify each of these components and understand their interrelationships, one can at least predict the performance of the firm under various assumptions about changes in the external environment. One can also evaluate the richness of the menu of new opportunities from which the firm may select, and its likely performance in a changing environment.

The parameters we have identified for determining performance are radically different from those in the standard textbook theory of the firm, and in the competitive forces and strategic conflict approach to strategy.[17] Moreover, the agency theoretic view of the firm as a nexus of contracts would put no weight on processes, positions, and paths. While agency approaches to the firm may recognize that opportunism and shirking may limit what a firm can do, they do not recognize the opportunities and constraints imposed by processes, positions, and paths. Moreover, the firm in our conceptualization is much more than the sum of its parts — or a team tied together by contracts.[18] Indeed, to some extent individuals can be moved in and out of organizations and, so long as the internal processes and structures remain in place, performance will not be necessarily impaired. A shift in the environment is a far more serious threat to the firm than is the loss of key individuals, as individuals can be replaced more readily than organizations can be transformed. Furthermore, the dynamic capabilities view of the firm

---

[16] This is a critical element in Nelson and Winter's (1982) view of firms and technical change.

[17] In both the firm is still largely a black box. Certainly, little or no attention is given to processes, positions, and paths.

[18] See Alchian and Demsetz (1972).

would suggest that the behavior and performance of particular firms may be quite hard to replicate, even if its coherence and rationality are observable. This matter and related issues involving replication and imitation are taken up in the section that follows.

Replicability and Imitatability of Organizational Processes and Positions

Thus far, we have argued that the capabilities of a firm rest on processes, positions, and paths. However, distinctive organizational capabilities can provide competitive advantage and generate rents if they are based on a collection of routines, skills, and complementary assets that are difficult to imitate.[19] A particular set of routines can lose their value if they support a competence which no longer matters in the marketplace, or if they can be readily replicated or emulated by competitors. Imitation occurs when firms discover and simply copy a firm's organizational routines and procedures. Emulation occurs when firms discover alternative ways of achieving the same functionality. There is ample evidence that a given type of competence (e.g. quality) can be supported by different routines and combinations of skills. For example, the Garvin (1988) and Clark and Fujimoto (1991) studies both indicate that there was no one 'formula' for achieving either high quality or high product development performance.

Replication.   Replication involves transferring or redeploying competences from one economic setting to another. Since productive knowledge is embodied, this cannot be accomplished by simply transmitting information. Only in those instances where all relevant knowledge is fully codified and understood can replication be collapsed into a simple problem of information transfer. Too often, the contextual dependence of original performance is poorly appreciated, so unless firms have replicated their systems of productive knowledge on many prior occasions, the act of replication is likely to be difficult (Teece, 1976). Indeed, replication and transfer are often impossible absent the transfer of people, though this can be minimized if investments are made to convert tacit knowledge to codified knowledge. Often, however, this is simply not possible.

In short, organizational capabilities, and the routines upon which they rest, are normally rather difficult to replicate.[20] Even understanding what

---

[19] See Dierickx and Cool (1989) for a discussion of the characteristics of assets which make them a source of rents.

[20] See Gabriel Szulanski's (1993) discussion of the intra-firm transfer of best practice. He quotes a senior vice-president of Xerox as saying 'you can see a high performance factory or office, but it just doesn't spread. I don't know why.' Szulanski also discusses the role of benchmarking in facilitating the transfer of best practice.

all the relevant routines are that support a particular competence may not be transparent. Indeed, Lippman and Rumelt (1992) have argued that some sources of competitive advantage are so complex that the firm itself, let alone its competitors, does not understand them.[21] As Nelson and Winter (1982) and Teece (1982) have explained, many organizational routines are quite tacit in nature. Imitation can also be hindered by the fact that few routines are 'stand-alone'; coherence may require that a change in one set of routines in one part of the firm (e.g. production) requires changes in some other part (e.g. R&D).

Some routines and competences seem to be attributable to local or regional forces that shape firms' capabilities at early stages in their lives. Porter (1990), for example, shows that differences in local product markets, local factor markets, and institutions play an important role in shaping competitive capabilities. Differences also exist within populations of firms from the same country. Various studies of the automobile industry, for example, show that not all Japanese automobile companies are top performers in terms of quality, productivity, or product development (see, for example, Clark and Fujimoto, 1991). The role of firm-specific history has been highlighted as a critical factor explaining such firm-level (as opposed to regional- or national-level) differences (Nelson and Winter, 1982). Replication in a different context may thus be rather difficult.

At least two types of strategic value flow from replication. One is the ability to support geographic and product line expansion. To the extent that the capabilities in question are relevant to customer needs elsewhere, replication can confer value.[22] Another is that the ability to replicate also indicates that the firm has the foundations in place for learning and improvement. Empirical evidence supports the notion that the understanding of processes, both in production and in management, is the key to process improvement (Hayes *et al.*, 1988). In short, an organization cannot improve that which it does not understand. Deep process understanding is often required to accomplish codification. Indeed, if knowledge is highly tacit, it indicates that underlying structures are not well understood, which limits learning because scientific and engineering principles cannot be as systematically applied. Instead, learning is confined to proceeding through trial and error, and the leverage that might otherwise come from the application of scientific theory is denied.

---

[21] If so, it is our belief that the firm's advantage is likely to fade, as luck does run out.

[22] Needless to say, there are many examples of firms replicating their capabilities inappropriately by applying extant routines to circumstances where they may not be applicable, e.g. Nestlé's transfer of developed country marketing methods for infant formula to the third world (Hartley, 1989). A key strategic need is for firms to screen capabilities for their applicability to new environments.

Imitation. Imitation is simply replication performed by a competitor. If self-replication is difficult, imitation is likely to be even harder. In competitive markets, it is the ease of imitation that determines the sustainability of competitive advantage. Easy imitation implies the rapid dissipation of rents.

Factors that make replication difficult also make imitation difficult. Thus, the more tacit the firm's productive knowledge, the harder it is to replicate by the firm itself or its competitors. When the tacit component is high, imitation may well be impossible, absent the hiring away of key individuals and the transfer of key organizational processes.

However, another set of barriers impedes imitation of certain capabilities in advanced industrial countries. This is the system of intellectual property rights, such as patents, trade secrets, and trademarks, and even trade dress.[23] Intellectual property protection is of increasing importance in the USA, as since 1982 the legal system has adopted a more pro-patent posture. Similar trends are evident outside the USA. Besides the patent system, several other factors cause there to be a difference between replication costs and imitation costs. The observability of the technology of the organization is one such important factor. Whereas vistas into product technology can be obtained through strategies such as reverse engineering, this is not the case for process technology, as a firm need not expose its process technology to the outside in order to benefit from it.[24] Firms with product technology, on the other hand, confront the unfortunate circumstances that they must expose what they have got in order to profit from the technology. Secrets are thus more protectable if there is no need to expose them in contexts where competitors can learn about them.

One should not, however, overestimate the overall importance of intellectual property protection; yet it presents a formidable imitation barrier in certain particular contexts. Intellectual property protection is not uniform across products, processes, and technologies, and is best thought of as an island in a sea of open competition. If one is not able to place the fruits of one's investment, ingenuity, or creativity on one or more of the islands, then one indeed is at sea.

We use the term 'appropriability regimes' to describe the ease of imitation. Appropriability is a function both of the ease of replication and the efficacy of intellectual property rights as a barrier to imitation. Appropriability is

---

[23] Trade dress refers to the 'look and feel' of a retail establishment, e.g. the distinctive marketing and presentation style of The Nature Company.

[24] An interesting but important exception to this can be found in second sourcing. In the microprocessor business, until the introduction of the 386 chip, Intel and most other merchant semi producers were encouraged by large customers like IBM to provide second sources, i.e. to license and share their proprietary process technology with competitors like AMD and NEC. The microprocessor developers did so to assure customers that they had sufficient manufacturing capability to meet demand at all times.

		INHERENT REPLICABILITY	
		EASY	HARD
INTELLECTUAL PROPERTY RIGHTS	LOOSE	**WEAK**	**MODERATE**
	TIGHT	**MODERATE**	**STRONG**

FIGURE 1.   Appropriability regimes.

strong when a technology is both inherently difficult to replicate and the intellectual property system provides legal barriers to imitation. When it is inherently easy to replicate and intellectual property protection is either unavailable or ineffectual, then appropriability is weak. Intermediate conditions also exist (see Figure 1).

Strategic Issues from a Dynamic Capabilities Perspective

The dynamic capabilities approach views competition in Schumpeterian terms. This means, at one level, that firms compete on the basis of product design, product quality, process efficiency, and other attributes. However, in a Schumpeterian world, firms are constantly seeking to create 'new combinations', and rivals are continuously attempting to improve their competences or to imitate the competence of their most qualified competitors. Rivalry to develop new competences or to improve existing ones is critical in a Schumpeterian world. Such processes drive creative destruction. Differences in firms' capabilities to improve their distinctive competences or to develop new distinctive domains of competence play a critical role in shaping long-term competitive outcomes.

The strategic problem facing an innovating firm in a world of Schumpeterian competition is to decide upon and develop difficult-to-imitate processes and paths most likely to support valuable products and services. Thus, as argued by Dierickx and Cool (1989), choices about how much to spend (invest) on different possible areas are central to the firm's strategy. However, choices about domains of competence are influenced by past choices. At any given point in time, firms must follow a certain trajectory or path of competence development. This path not only defines what choices are open to the firm today, but it also puts boundaries around what its repertoire is likely to be in the future. Thus, firms, at various points in time, make *long-term, quasi-irreversible* commitments to certain domains of competence. Deciding, under significant uncertainty about future states of the world, which long-term paths to commit to and when to change paths is the central strategic problem confronting the firm.[25]

3. *Conclusion*

We posit that the competitive advantage of firms stems from dynamic capabilities rooted in high performance routines operating inside the firm, embedded in the firm's processes, and conditioned by its history. Because of imperfect factor markets, or more precisely the non-tradability of 'soft' assets like values, culture, and organizational experience, these capabilities generally cannot be bought; they must be built. This may take years — possibly decades. In some cases, as when the competence is protected by patents, imitation by a competitor is illegal as a means to access the technology. The capabilities approach accordingly sees definite limits on strategic options, at least in the short run. Competitive success occurs in part because of processes and structures already established and experience obtained in earlier periods.

The notion that competitive success arises from the continuous development, exploitation, and protection of firm-specific assets, while not the dominant view in industrial organization, nevertheless has a long tradition going back at least to Schumpeter. Schumpeter, in his *Theory of Economic Development* (1934), saw economic development as consisting of a process where entrepreneurs dipped into a stream of technical opportunities ostensibly made for reasons independent of particular markets and brought those innovations to market. The successful innovator achieved a monopoly in a particular market through bringing to market something which was quite unique, only to have that monopoly successfully whittled away by the entry (swarming) of imitators. The dynamic capabilities approach is a descendant of the Schumpeterian. However, it emphasizes organizational processes inside the firm more than Schumpeter ever did; and it is not just a positive theory of industrial change. It can also offer prescription because of its firm-level orientation, and it looks inside firms to help explain market processes.

Because it is hard to transform organizational processes, the dynamic capabilities approach sees value augmenting strategic change as being diffi-

---

[25] In this regard, the work of Ghemawat (1991) is highly germane to the dynamic capabilities approach to strategy.

cult and costly. Moreover, it can generally occur only incrementally. Because capabilities cannot easily be bought and must be built,[26] opportunities for growth from diversification are thus likely to be limited, lying 'close in' to the firm's existing lines of product (Rumelt, 1974; Teece *et al.*, 1994). In attempting to explicate competitive advantage, the dynamic capabilities approach places emphasis on the firm's internal processes, assets and market positions, the path along which it has traveled, and the paths that lie ahead. The framework also explicitly takes into account replicability and imitatability.

We offer dynamic capabilities as an emerging paradigm of the modern business firm. It is an eclectic paradigm drawing from multiple disciplines, and advancing with the help of industry studies in the USA and elsewhere. There are, of course, a wide variety of theories of the firm, each sometimes highlighting a different aspect.[27] It appears that the dynamic capabilities approach is seeking attention by promising to explain matters such as the limits of diversification, the feasibility of 'converting' firms from military to civilian purposes, the adaptability of some firms and the intransigence of others, etc. Perhaps a decade from now we will be able to assess whether the promise has been honored, and whether as a consequence the fields of industrial organization and business strategy can help us solidly come to grips with the challenges of our times.

Acknowledgements

We would like to thank Amy Shuen for useful comments. This introduction draws from D. J. Teece, G. Pisano, and A. Shuen, 'Dynamic Capabilities and Strategic Management,' CCC Working Paper #94–9, University of California, Berkeley (August, 1994).

References

Abernathy, W. J. and K. Clark (1985), 'Innovation: Mapping the Winds of Creative Destruction,' *Research Policy*, 14, 3–22.

Alchian, A. A. and H. Demsetz, (1972), 'Production, Information Costs, and Economic Organization,' *American Economic Review*, 62, 777–795.

Amit, R. and P. Schoemaker (1992), 'Strategic Assets and Organizational Rent,' Working Paper, University of British Columbia, Canada, August 7.

Aoki, M. (1990), 'The Participatory Generation of Information Rents and the Theory of the Firm,' in M. Aoki *et al.* (eds), *The Firm as a Nexus of Treaties*, Sage: London.

---

[26] Robert Hayes (1985) has noted that American companies tend to favor 'strategic leaps', while, in contrast, Japanese and German companies tend to favor incremental, but rapid, improvements. If this is correct, it seems to indicate that the Japanese and German managers more fully recognize the validity of the dynamic capabilities framework than do their American counterparts.

[27] Thus transaction cost economics highlights boundaries, agency theory highlights incentives and control, and the production function highlights the role of fixed factors.

Arrow, K. (1969), 'The Organization of Economic Activity: Issues Pertinent to the Choice of Market vs. Nonmarket Allocation,' in *The Analysis and Evaluation of Public Expenditures: The PPB System*, 1, US Joint Economic Committee, 91st Session. US Government Printing Office: Washington, DC; 59–73.

Baldwin, C. and K. Clark (1991), 'Capabilities and Capital Investment: New Perspectives on Capital Budgeting,' Harvard Business School Working Paper 92–004.

Barney, J. B. (1986), 'Strategic Factor Markets: Expectations, Luck, and Business Strategy,' *Management Science*, 32, 1231–1241.

Camp, R. (1989), *Benchmarking: The Search for Industry Best Practice That Lead to Superior Performance*. Quality Resources: White Plain, NY.

Chandler, A. D., Jr (1990), *Scale and Scope: The Dynamics of Industrial Competition*. Harvard University Press: Cambridge, MA.

Clark, K. and T. Fujimoto (1991), *Product Development Performance: Strategy, Organization and Management in the World Auto Industries*. Harvard Business School Press: Cambridge MA.

Coase, R. (1937), 'The Nature of the Firm,' *Economica*.

Coase, R. (1988), 'Lecture on the Nature of the Firm, III,' *Journal of Law, Economics and Organization*, 4, 33–47.

Dierickx, I. and K. Cool (1989), 'Asset Stock Accumulation and Sustainability of Competitive Advantage,' *Management Science*, 35, 1504–1511.

Doz, Y. and A. Shuen (1990), 'From Intent to Outcome: A Process Framework for Partnerships,' INSEAD Working Paper.

Fama, E. F. (1980), 'Agency Problems and the Theory of the Firm,' *Journal of Political Economy*, 88, 288–307.

Fujimoto, T. (1994), 'Reinterpreting the Resource-Capability View of the Firm: A Case of the Development-Production Systems of the Japanese Automakers.' Draft working paper, Faculty of Economics, University of Tokyo (May).

Garvin, D. (1988), *Managing Quality*. The Free Press: New York.

Garvin, D. (1994), 'The Processes of Organization and Management,' Harvard Business School Working Paper #94-084.

Ghemawat, P. (1991), *Commitment: The Dynamics of Strategy*. The Free Press: New York.

Hartley, R. F. (1989), *Marketing Mistakes*. John Wiley: New York.

Hayes, R. (1985), 'Strategic Planning: Forward in Reverse,' *Harvard Business Review* (November–December); 111–119.

Hayes, R., S. Wheelwright and K. Clark (1988), *Dynamic Manufacturing: Creating the Learning Organization*. The Free Press: New York.

Henderson, R. M. (1995), 'The Evolution of Integrative Capability: Innovation in Cardiovascular Drug Discovery,' *Industrial and Corporate Change*, 3, 607–630.

Henderson, R. M. and K. B. Clark (1990), 'Architectural Innovation: The Reconfiguration of Existing Product Technologies and the Failure of Established Firms,' *Administrative Science Quarterly*, 35, 9–30.

Iansiti, M. and K. B. Clark (1995), 'Integration and Dynamic Capability: Evidence from Product Development in Automobiles and Mainframe Computers,' *Industrial and Corporate Change*, 3, 557–605.

Kogut, I. and U. Zander (1992), 'Knowledge of the Firm, Combinative Capabilities, and the Replication of Technology,' *Organizational Science*.

Langlois, R. (1994), 'Cognition and Capabilities: Opportunities Seized and Missed in the History of the Computer Industry,' Working Paper, University of Connecticut. Presented at the conference on Technological Oversights and Foresights, Stern School of Business, New York University, March 11–12, 1994.

Leonard-Barton, D. (1992), 'Core Capabilities and Core Rigidities: A Paradox in Managing New Product Development,' *Strategic Management Journal*, 13, 111–125.

Lev, B. and T. Sougiannis (1992), 'The Capitalization, Amortization and Value-Relevance of R&D,' Unpublished manuscript, University of California, Berkeley, and University of Illinois, Urbana-Champaign (November).

Levitt, B. and J. March (1988), 'Organizational Learning,' *Annual Review of Sociology*, 14, 319–340.

Lippman, S. A. and R. P. Rumelt (1992), 'Demand Uncertainty and Investment in Industry-Specific Capital,' *Industrial and Corporate Change*, 1, 235–262.

Mahoney, J. (1994), 'The Management of Resources and the Resources of Management,' *Journal of Business Research*, in press.

Mody, A. (1990), 'Learning through Alliances,' Working Paper, The World Bank, Washington, DC, September 6.

Nelson, R. and S. Winter (1982), *An Evolutionary Theory of Economic Change*. Harvard University Press: Cambridge, MA.

Penrose, E. (1959), *The Theory of the Growth of the Firm*. Basil Blackwell: London.

Porter, M. E. (1990), *The Competitive Advantage of Nations*. The Free Press: New York.

Prahalad, C. K. and G. Hamel (1990), 'The Core Competence of the Corporation,' *Harvard Business Review*, (May–June), 79–91.

Rumelt, R. P. (1974), *Strategy, Structure, and Economic Performance*. Harvard University Press: Cambridge, MA.

Schumpeter, J. A. (1934), *Theory of Economic Development*. Harvard University Press: Cambridge, MA.

Shuen, A. (1994), 'Technology Sourcing and Learning Strategies in the Semiconductor Industry.' Unpublished PhD dissertation, University of California, Berkeley.

Szulanski, G. (1993), 'Intrafirm Transfer of Best Practice, Appropriate Capabilities, Organizational Barriers to Appropriation,' Working Paper, INSEAD (March).

Teece, D. J. (1976), *The Multinational Corporation and the Resource Cost of International Technology Transfer*. Ballinger: Cambridge, MA.

Teece, D. J. (1980), 'Economics of Scope and the Scope of an Enterprise, *Journal of Economic Behavior and Organization*, 1, 223–247.

Teece, D. J. (1982), 'Towards an Economic Theory of the Multiproduct Firm,' *Journal of Economic Behavior and Organization*, 3, 39–63.

Teece, D. J. (1986a), 'Transactions Cost Economics and the Multinational Enterprise,' *Journal of Economic Behavior and Organization*, 7, 21–45.

Teece, D. J. (1986b), 'Profiting from Technological Innovation,' *Research Policy*, 15.

Teece, D. J. (1988), 'Technological Change and the Nature of the Firm,' in G. Dosi *et al.* (eds), *Technical Change and Economic Theory*.

Teece, D. J. (1993), 'The Dynamics of Industrial Capitalism: Perspectives on Alfred Chandler's *Scale and Scope* (1990),' *Journal of Economic Literature*, 31.

Teece, D. J., R. Rumelt, G. Dosi and S. Winter (1994), 'Understanding Corporate Coherence: Theory and Evidence,' *Journal of Economic Behavior and Organization*, 23, 1–30.

Tushman, M. L., W. H. Newman and E. Romanelli (1986), 'Convergence and Upheaval: Managing the Unsteady Pace of Organizational Evolution,' *California Management Review*, 29, 29–44.

Wernerfelt, B. (1984), 'A Resource-Based View of the Firm,' *Strategic Management Journal*, 5, 171–180.

Williamson, O. E. (1975), *Markets and Hierarchies*. The Free Press: New York.

Williamson, O. E. (1985), *The Economic Institutions of Capitalism*. The Free Press: New York.

Womack, J., D. Jones and D. Roos (1991), *The Machine That Changed the World*. Harper-Perennial: New York.

PART B

FROM FIRMS TO INDUSTRIES

Technological Discontinuities, Organizational Capabilities, and Strategic Commitments

RICHARD S. ROSENBLOOM and CLAYTON M.
CHRISTENSEN
(Graduate School of Business Administration, Harvard University, Soldiers Field,
Boston, MA 02163, USA)

Innovations based on radically new technologies are believed to create advantages for entrants over incumbents in the relevant markets. Under what circumstances is this true? To what extent do incumbents' disadvantages stem from their failure to make timely commitments to new capabilities and new strategies as opposed to their inability to implement those commitments effectively? We explore those questions in relation to recent literature in economics and organization theory and introduce the concept of the 'value network'. Historical evidence suggests that entrants find greatest advantage when innovations disrupt established trajectories of technological progress, a circumstance associated with moves to new value networks. The incumbent's disadvantage, hence, seems to be associated with an inability to change strategies, not technologies.

1. Introduction

Most technological change is incremental; that is, each innovation constitutes a relatively small step built on the base of established practice (Nelson and Winter, 1982). Although each step is small, the cumulative economic consequences of incremental change are large (Hollander, 1965). In a variety of industries, leading firms have prospered for extended periods by successfully exploiting a series of incremental technological innovations built on their established organizational and technological capabilities (Chandler, 1992). But, because of its capacity to render those capabilities obsolete, radical change in technology is one of the greatest threats to incumbents whose competitive positions were built in that way.

One of the 'stylized facts' prominent in the literatures of technological innovation is that radically new technologies are often pioneered by firms new to the industries that they ultimately transform. The conventional wisdom holds that the attacker has the advantage in these cases, that is, that even powerful incumbents in established industries are at a disadvantage when new technology emerges. The 'attacker's advantage' is typically seen as deriving from the incumbent's disadvantage. Although large and long-established incumbents are likely to have substantial resources that ought to be advantageous —greater financial strength, broader and deeper technical resources, or significant other intangible assets, such as credibility in the marketplace— in practice they are often apparently outweighed by other forces.

For example, in a recent survey of the emergence of new technologies for financial services, *The Economist* (October 9, 1993, p. 21) asserts that:

> . . . the inherent conservatism of the big financial firms towards new-fangled technology is handing great new opportunities to small entrepreneurial ones that are inventing new systems from scratch. *It was always such.* It was Apple, not IBM, that had faith in the personal computer. . . . *In every industry*, large companies promote safe, predictable bureaucrats [emphasis added].

The same viewpoint pervades an often-cited book on the subject whose theme is conveyed by its subtitle: *The Attacker's Advantage* (Foster, 1986).

In this common view, when new technology powers the Schumpeterian forces of creative destruction, the 'creation' is usually accomplished by invaders—new firms or entrants from other industries—while the 'destruction' is suffered by the incumbents. One of the first systematic academic studies of the phenomenon described a 'typical sequence of events [beginning] with the origination of a technological innovation outside the industry, often pioneered by a new firm'. The authors found that '[d]espite substantial commitments, the traditional firm is usually not successful in building a long-run competitive position in the new technology' (Cooper and Schendel, 1976, p. 61).

Despite the wide currency given these generalizations about what 'usually' happens to established firms in the course of radical technical change, one should be cautious about their validity. Counterexamples are too prominent to be ignored. For example: for at least a quarter of a century, the new market for electronic data processing was dominated by the firms that had previously led in producing electro-mechanical office equipment (Flamm, 1988); Du Pont pioneered in synthetic fibers despite its earlier dominant position in rayon (Hounshell and Smith, 1988); General Electric strengthened its position in medical diagnostic imaging equipment by its innovations in CT and MRI technologies (Morone, 1993).

Research about technological change seems in many ways to be in the pre-paradigmatic stage of knowledge development, in the sense that Thomas Kuhn defined it. Kuhn (1962) noted that in the early stages of research in a given field, the most that scholars typically can do is to report the phenomena they observe, without a unifying theory or framework to help them categorize or make sense of what they see. As a result, this stage of knowledge accumulation is characterized by confusion and contradiction. Theories are put forward, but reports of anomalous phenomena accumulate. This seems to us to be a fair characterization of the present state of scholarship on radical technological innovation. Respected scholars define terms like radical and incremental innovation in completely different ways. And seemingly contradictory phenomena abound, as we have suggested above.

Rather than describing what 'usually' happens, a good theory would help one understand the forces that create the attacker's advantage when it does obtain. One would like to identify the particulars of the 'rule' to which the above cases are 'exceptions'. For example, one would like to discover under what circumstances incumbents will be at a disadvantage when new technologies displace old. And when incumbents are disadvantaged, to what extent does that stem from their failure to make timely commitments to new capabilities and new strategies as opposed to their inability to implement those commitments effectively?

Later in this paper we explore those questions by examining a detailed history of innovations over several generations of products in the computer disk drive industry, as well as considering a range of historical examples from other industries and time periods. But first we turn to a brief review of the way that they have been analyzed by other scholars. Following that, to aid in our analysis we introduce the concept of the 'value network', the system of producers and markets serving the ultimate users of the products or services to which a given innovation contributes. The value network defines the context within which each firm identifies and responds to customers needs, procures inputs, and reacts to competitors.

2. *Radical Innovation and the Attacker's Advantage*

Only relatively recently have studies in economics, organization theory and the management of technology begun to examine the forces underlying the competitive shifts brought about by radical technological innovation. Economic theory points to the importance of the incentives for established producers to make strategic commitments to new capabilities. Organization theorists call attention to the inertias inherent in organizations structured around capabilities geared to the old technology and the difficulties both of anticipating the destruction of the value of those capabilities and of efficiently creating new ones called for in the new technological regime.

As Rebecca Henderson points out, the economic and organization theorists seem to agree that 'established firms are likely to dominate incremental innovation, while entrants are likely to dominate radical innovation' (Henderson, 1993, p. 252).[1] The implications of this conclusion obviously depend on how one identifies a 'radical' innovation. To the economists, a new technology is radical (in their terminology, 'drastic') if it leads to products that dominate and make obsolete the previous products in established markets. A novel technology that merely competes with the older products is not considered 'drastic'. The organizational literature, however, looks to effects within the firm, rather than in the marketplace; 'competence-destroying' innovations are radical and 'favor new entrants at the expense of entrenched defenders' (Tushman and Anderson, 1986, p. 446).[2] In other usage, innovations are considered 'radical' when they draw on new or different science bases or, more generally, when they require the development of qualitatively new technological capabilities within the innovating organization.

Some innovations are radical in every sense. The development of electronic desktop calculators is an example: it rapidly made electromechanical products obsolete and destroyed the value of factories and service organizations that embodied the distinctive capabilities of the established producers, who—in line with both theoretical perspectives—saw their businesses taken away by entrants (Majumdar, 1980). But, in many cases the definitions diverge. For example, when radial tires replaced bias-ply designs the innovation was incremental in the economists' sense, and in the sense that it drew largely on the same technological base as its predecessor, while it called for new and difficult-to-achieve manufacturing capabilities and was thus radical in that respect.

A managerially useful theory ought to be able to identify, *ex ante*, those innovations that will be radical in their consequences. In their later work, Anderson and Tushman (1990) shifted their criterion to focus on discontinuities, which they defined as 'fundamentally different product forms [or ways of making a product] that command a decisive cost, performance, or quality advantage over prior forms.[3] But, while that criterion may suffice for

---

[1] While distinction between radical and incremental innovations has been common for decades in discussions of technical change, the line between them has been drawn in varying ways, and often with a lack of precision. A thoughtful overview of the processes of innovation argues that the terms do not denote distinct categories of innovation but rather represent poles on a continuum (Kline and Rosenberg, 1986).

[2] In a subsequent paper, discussed below, these authors adopt a different definition of 'discontinuities' that is congruent with the economist's sense of what is 'radical' (Anderson and Tushman, 1990).

[3] Anderson and Tushman (1990, p. 606) cite Schumpeter's (1942, p. 84) identification of innovations that 'command a decisive cost or quality advantage and that strike not at the margins of the profits and the outputs of existing firms, but at their foundations and their very lives'.

ex post analysis, it is not very robust when applied *ex ante*. For example, for several of the cases they cite to illustrate such discontinuities, including jet (versus piston) aircraft engines, diesel (versus steam) locomotives, and integrated circuits (versus transistors)—the relative advantage of the new technology was hotly debated at first. While the superiority of the new technologies ultimately proved decisive, it was a decade or more before that was clear. Initially such innovations often create what is merely a different constellation of costs and benefits, in which neither old nor new dominates the other. In many cases, although the new product's performance may be greatly superior, it also is much more expensive—as, for example, when xerography enabled plain-paper dry copying, but required a machine 20 times the cost of predecessors.

In a related recent paper (Christensen and Rosenbloom, forthcoming) we suggested that one should identify radical innovations by a different sort of discontinuity: the emergence of what Giovanni Dosi calls a new 'technological paradigm' (Dosi, 1982). By analogy to Thomas Kuhn's (1962) notion of scientific paradigms, Dosi characterized a 'technological paradigm' as a 'pattern of solution of selected technological problems, based on selected principles derived from natural sciences and on selected material technologies' (p. 152). Dosi distinguished 'normal' modes of technological progress— which propel a product's progress along a defined, established path—from the introduction of new technological paradigms. New paradigms represent discontinuities in trajectories of progress which were defined within earlier paradigms. They tend to redefine the very meaning of 'progress', and point technologists toward new classes of problems as the targets of ensuing 'normal' technology development.

In our earlier paper, we analyzed a detailed history of the disk-drive industry (Christensen, 1992), and concluded that the success or failure of incumbents was independent of the capabilities demanded (or made obsolete) by important innovations, and much more related to whether or not they created opportunities within the established 'value network' served by the innovator. How an innovation is valued in such a network depends on whether the innovation continues or breaks the established trend of technological progress.[4]

We will show below that it is useful to identify as 'radical' any technological innovation that depends for its value on a substantial departure from the path of 'normal' technological progress in the relevant industrial field. In other words, an innovation is radical when it introduces a discontinuity in

---

[4] This argument is extended in a subsequent paper by one of the current authors in which the focus is on 'technology-disrupting' changes and the evidence is drawn from four industries in addition to disk-drives (Christensen and Bower, 1993).

the way that performance is evaluated. Radical innovations disrupt the established trajectories of technical advance; incremental innovations reinforce and extend them.

Which leads to the more fundamental question: why do radical innovations tend to disadvantage incumbents? What mechanisms might explain the observable phenomena? Two contending types of explanation have emerged so far: one emphasizing strategic commitments, the other organizational capabilities. Radical innovations call for significant (and risky) investments as well as the creation of new competences. Do incumbents fall short because of their failure to invest or because of their inability to invest effectively to create requisite new capabilities?[5]

There is no shortage of examples in which incumbents seemed to resist making the investments necessary to creating new capabilities and deploying new technologies in the marketplace. Some ascribe this to bureaucratic rigidities (*The Economist*, 1993), others to management 'myopia' (Foster, 1986). More sophisticated analysis points to other considerations. Recent work in economic theory explores the relative incentives apparent to incumbents and entrants under varying circumstances of technical change. It is clear that there are important asymmetries at work—incumbents, especially those with a dominant market position, have something to lose as well as opportunities to exploit. Economic analysis of patent and R&D 'races' illuminates the circumstances of market structure which favor investment by entrants or incumbents, but so far provides no clear-cut resolution of the basic question.[6] In organizational theory, another line of inquiry suggests that, even when investment in innovation is the profit-maximizing choice, administrative processes can bias strategic choice against investment (Burgelman, 1991).

While readiness to invest is necessary, it is not a sufficient basis for the successful exploitation of radically new technology; the innovator must also succeed in creating a new set of capabilities. The organizational literature suggests that, when an innovation destroys established competences, incumbents are often inhibited in their efforts to create the requisite new ones. To be sure, a substantial literature points to the superior capabilities of large research-based corporations (Freeman, 1982; Mowery and Rosenberg, 1989). But, in a notable number of cases of radical innovation, the failing incumbents have been corporations of just that character. As recent scholarship in

---

[5] As Elizabeth Teisberg has suggested to us, a related set of interesting questions might also be addressed by studies of radical innovation, although they are ignored by the existing literature. Since there are usually multiple incumbent firms affected by a given innovation, as well as multiple contending entrants, what factors influence the relative success of various entrants, and the several incumbents? In other words, one ought to be interested in analysis within the two groups, as well as between them. But pursuit of those issues will have to await further study.

[6] Henderson (1993, p. 250) presents a concise summary and analysis of this work.

organization studies suggests, substantial experience may also create dis-advantages in innovation, as core capabilities harden into 'core rigidities' (Leonard-Barton, 1992).

It is beyond the scope of this paper to evaluate the relative usefulness of the economic and organizational perspectives for explaining the consequences of technological discontinuities. We aim, instead, to suggest a somewhat different perspective, built on analysis of the impact of the innovation on the relevant 'value network'. We will explain the concept and then illustrate its explanatory power, first by describing a series of innovations in the disk drive industry and then by briefly examining a larger number of historical examples from a range of industries.

3. Nested Hierarchies and Value Networks

Scholars seeking to explain the outcomes of major technological changes typically have focused on their consequences within the productive systems within which the technology is deployed or which it will displace. (Abernathy and Utterback, 1978; Tushman and Anderson, 1986). In that genre, for example, analysis of the implications for tire producers of the emergence of radial tires would focus on the tire factory.

We believe that the scope of analysis should also include the 'system-of-use' in which the technology is ultimately employed. The tire, itself the final product of a major industry, is also a component in complex products—automobiles and trucks—which, in turn, function as elements of more complex systems-of-use, such as the freight transport system or the personal mass transportation system. In these terms, a given system-of-use can be viewed as comprising a hierarchically nested set of constituent systems and components.

This is illustrated in Figure 1 by the example of a hypothetical management information system (MIS) for a large organization. The design of the MIS ties together various 'components'—a mainframe computer, peripheral equipment such as line printers, tape and disk drives; software; a large, air-conditioned room with cables running under a raised floor; and a staff of data processing professionals whose training and language are unique. At the next level, the mainframe computer is itself a complex system, comprising components such as a central processing unit, multi-chip packages and circuit boards, RAM circuits, terminals, controllers, disk drives and other peripherals. Telescoping down still further, the disk drive is a system whose components include a motor, actuator, spindle, disks, heads and controller. In turn, the disk itself can be analyzed as a system composed of an aluminum platter, magnetic material, adhesives, abrasives, lubricants and coatings.

Although the goods and services which constitute the system of use

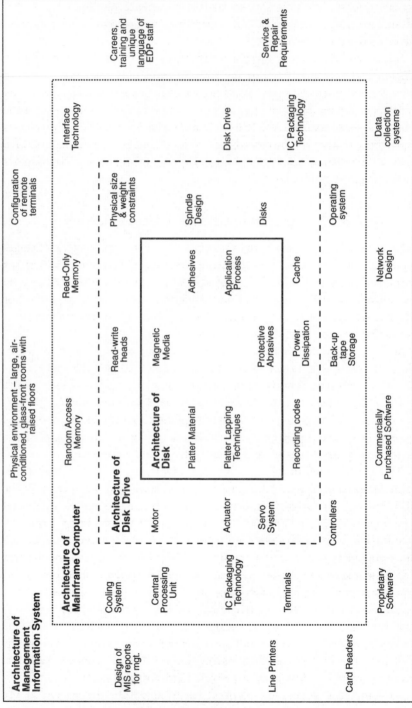

FIGURE 1. A nested, or telescoping system of product architectures.

illustrated in Figure 1 could all be made or provided within a single, extensively integrated corporation such as AT&T or IBM, most of these goods and services are tradable. This means that, while Figure 1 is drawn to describe the hierarchical architecture of the system-of-use and its constituent elements, it also implies the existence of a nested network of producers and markets through which the tradable components at each level are made and sold to integrators at the next higher level in the system. For example, firms which design and assemble disk drives—such as Quantum, Conner Peripherals and Maxtor—procure read-write heads from a group of firms which specialize in the manufacture of those heads, disks from a different set of disk manufacturing firms, and spin motors, actuator motors and cache circuitry from different, unique sets of firms. Firms which design and assemble computers at the next higher level may buy their integrated circuits, terminals, disk drives, IC packaging and power supplies from firms focused on manufacturing and supplying those particular products. We call this nested commercial system a value network. Three illustrative value networks for computing applications are shown in Figure 2. The top network depicts the commercial infrastructure which creates the corporate MIS system-of-use depicted in Figure 1. The middle network depicts a portable personal computing value network, while the bottom one represents a computer automated design/computer automated manufacturing (CAD/CAM) value network. As this suggests, a number of distinct value networks may interact within the same broadly-defined industry.

Two points are most pertinent here. First, the potential value inherent in any new technology is a function of the characteristics of the ultimate systems-of-use in which products or services based on that technology will be employed. For example, a more costly drive technology that increased the product's ruggedness would be more valuable in the network leading to portable personal computing than in others. The metrics by which value is assessed will therefore differ across networks. Specifically, associated with each network is a unique rank ordering of the importance of various performance attributes. Figure 2 depicts the characteristic rank-orderings of important product attributes in the three networks described, as shown at the right of the center column of component boxes. In the top-most value network, performance of disk drives is measured primarily in terms of capacity, speed and reliability. In the portable computing value network depicted beneath it, the more important performance attributes are ruggedness, power consumption and physical size.

Second, the firm contemplating adoption of a new technology may be separated from the final system-of-use by a series of intermediate markets and producers along a specific pathway through the relevant value network. The position of a given established producer within a value network—the pathways

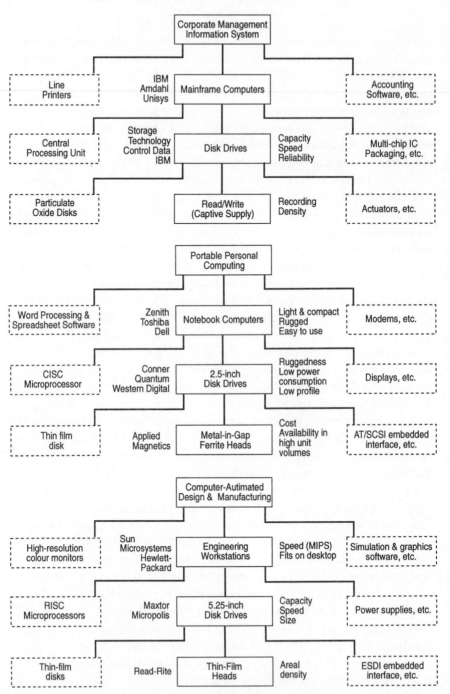

FIGURE 2. Examples of three value networks: a corporate MIS system, portable personal computing and CAD/CAM (dated approximately 1989).

it is supplying through downstream markets and producers to ultimate users, and its upstream supply network—therefore influences and even defines to a considerable degree the nature of the incentives associated with different opportunities for technological innovation which are perceived by the firm's managers.

Both the perceived attractiveness of a technological opportunity and the degree of difficulty a producer will encounter in exploiting it are determined, among other factors, by the firm's position in the relevant value network. As firms gain experience within a given network, they are likely to develop their capabilities, structures and cultures to 'fit' that position better by meeting that network's distinctive requirements. Manufacturing volumes, the slope of ramps to volume production, product development cycle times and organizational consensus about who the customer is and what the customer needs, may differ substantially from one value network to the next. In other words, over time and within an established value network, technologies, markets and organizations co-evolve. As they become increasingly well-adapted to a given environment, and it to them, incumbents may therefore become progressively less well suited to compete in other networks. Their abilities and incentives to create new market applications for their technology— giving rise to new value networks—may atrophy. While successful incumbents will become more cognizant of relevant information pertaining to the networks in which they compete, they may have greater difficulty acquiring and assessing information about others. The longer the firm has been in a given position, and the more successful it has been, the stronger these effects are likely to be. Hence it faces significant barriers to mobility—barriers to those innovations whose intrinsic value is greatest within networks other than those with which it already is engaged.

The key consideration determining the relative advantage of incumbents and attackers, in this view, is whether the performance attributes implicit in the innovation will be valued within networks already served by the incumbent, or whether other networks must be addressed or new ones created in order to realize value for the innovation. To illustrate this proposition we turn to a case study of innovation in the rigid disk drive industry.

4. *Innovation in the Rigid Disk Drive Industry*[7]

Disk drives are magnetic information storage and retrieval devices used with

---

[7] The following section draws on Christensen (1992) and Christensen and Rosenbloom (forthcoming). The database rests on field-based studies of six leading disk drive manufacturers, which historically have accounted for over 70% of industry revenues, and detailed technical specifications of every disk drive model announced in the world between 1975 and 1990. Technical data come from *Disk/Trend Report*, *Electronic Business Magazine*, and manufacturers' product specification sheets.

most types of computers and a range of other products, such as high speed digital reprographic devices and medical imaging equipment. Magnetic recording and storage of digital information was pioneered with the earliest commercial computer systems, which used reels of coated mylar tape. IBM introduced the use of rigid rotating disks in 1956 and flexible ('floppy') disks in 1971. The dominant design for what are now called 'hard' drives was provided by the IBM 'Winchester' project, introduced as the Model 3340 in 1973.

Although IBM and its early rivals in the computer market were vertically integrated, the emergence in the 1970s of smaller, non-integrated computer makers spawned an OEM market for disk drives as well. By 1976 the output of rigid disk drives was valued at about $1 billion, of which captive production accounted for 50% of unit production. The next dozen years brought rapid growth, market turbulence and technology-driven 'creative destruction'. The value of drives produced worldwide rose to more than $13 billion by 1989, with OEM output two-thirds of the total. Of the 17 firms which had populated the industry in 1976—all of which were relatively large, diversified corporations—14 had failed and exited or had been acquired by 1989. During this period an additional 124 firms entered the industry, and 100 of these also failed.

Throughout the period, technological change enabled dramatic improvements in performance at constantly decreasing cost. As sequential waves of innovation swept through the industry, disk diameters shrank from 14 to 2.5 inches while storage capacities continued to climb. The annual increase in capacity per drive sometimes approached 50%. At the same time, the emergence of new applications redefined the parameters along which performance was assessed. For example, size, weight, ruggedness and power consumption were all important attributes of performance in the design used for portable computers. None of these attributes had been critical in the designs used in mainframes or minicomputers.

The industry's first major transition was the switch from removable disk packs to the fixed-disk Winchester design beginning in 1973. This transition is shown in Figure 3, which shows that, as the rate of capacity improvement available in disk pack drives began to level off, the 14-inch Winchester architecture emerged to sustain the historical rate of improvement. The first-movers—IBM, and Control Data in the OEM market—continued to dominate the 14-inch rigid drive market based on this powerful new technology. During the 1970s, the 14-inch disk pack and Winchester drives were sold primarily to mainframe computer manufacturers. Figure 3 shows that the hard disk capacity provided in the median-priced, typically-configured mainframe computer system in 1976 was about 170 Megabytes

(Mb) per computer. the hard disk capacity supplied with the typical main-frame increased at a 15% annual rate over the next 15 years. At the same time, the capacity of the average 14-inch drives introduced for sale each year increased at a faster 22% rate, reaching beyond the mainframe market to the large scientific and supercomputer markets. These trends are shown in Figure 3 by the lines originating at point A. Subsequent innovations reduced disk diameter from 14 to 8, 5.25, 3.5 and then 2.5 inches between 1978 and 1990. Entrant firms pioneered the introduction of, and later dominated the markets for 8-inch, 5.25-inch and 3.5-inch drives. As a consequence, 60% of the producers remaining by 1989 had entered the industry as *de novo* start-ups since 1976. Figure 3 also maps the trajectories of performance improvement demanded in the subsequent applications for increasingly smaller drive designs (the solid lines emanating from points B, C, D and E), as well as the performance made available within each successive design by changes in component technology and refinements in system design (the dotted lines emanating from those same points). The methods used to derive these trajectories are described in Appendix 1.

Between 1978 and 1980, several entrant firms—Shugart Associates, Micropolis, Priam and Quantum—developed new families of 8-inch drives with 10, 20, 30 and 40 Mb capacity. These 8-inch drives were of no interest to mainframe computer manufacturers, who at that time were demanding drives with 300–400 Mb capacity. These entrants therefore sold their small, low-capacity drives into new application—minicomputers. Their customers—Wang, Digital Equipment, Data General, Prime and Hewlett Packard—did not manufacture mainframes: minicomputer users, furthermore, often used software that was substantially different from programs used by mainframe computer users. In other words, 8-inch drives found their way into a differ-ent value network, leading to a different system-of-use. Although the cost per megabyte of capacity of 8-inch drives initially was higher than that of 14-inch products, minicomputer producers and users were willing to pay a premium for other attributes of the 8-inch drive that were important to them—especially its smaller size.

Once the use of 8-inch drives became established, minicomputer users developed an appetite for ever-larger storage capacities, as had happened with mainframe computers. The capacity of the hard disks shipped with median-priced minicomputers increased about 25% per year, but the rapidly-moving technology made it possible to increase the capacity of the newest 8-inch drive designs even more rapidly than that. By the mid-1980s, 8-inch drive makers were able to provide the capacities required for lower-end mainframe computers. By then, unit volumes had grown sufficiently that the cost per megabyte of 8-inch drives had declined below that of

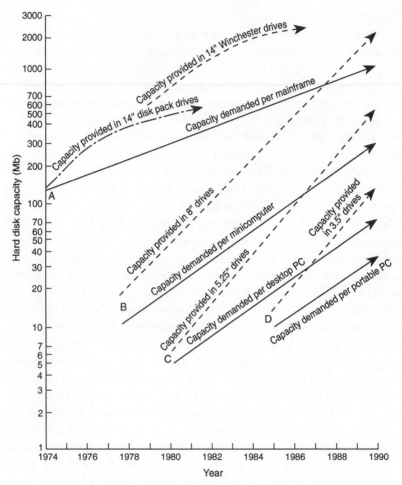

FIGURE 3. A comparison of the trajectories of disk capacity demanded per computer, versus capacity provided in each architecture.

14-inch products. Other advantages of 8-inch drives also became apparent. For example, the same percentage mechanical vibration in an 8-inch drive caused the head to vary its absolute position over the disk much less than it would in a 14-inch product. Within a three to four-year period, therefore, 8-inch drives began to invade an adjacent, established value network, substituting for 14-inch drives in the lower-end mainframe computer market.

When 8-inch products began to penetrate the mainframe computer market, most of the established manufacturers of 14-inch drives began to fail. Two-thirds of these manufacturers never introduced an 8-inch model. The others did so with about a two-year lag behind the 8-inch entrant manufacturers. The failure of the established producers of drives for mainframes cannot be explained by a lack of technological capability; some were able to produce competitive 8-inch products when they chose to do so. Table 1 shows, for example, that the population of 8-inch models introduced by the established firms in 1981 possessed performance attributes which, on average, were nearly identical to the average of those introduced that year by the entrant firms. In addition, the rates of improvement in those attributes were stunningly similar for both established and entrant firms.

In 1980 Seagate Technology (a new firm) introduced the next generation, 5.25-inch drives, with capacities of 5 and 10 Mb. These were of no interest to minicomputer manufacturers, who were demanding drives of 40 and 60 Mb from their suppliers. Seagate—and the other firms that entered with 5.25-inch drives in the 1980–83 period (such as Miniscribe, Computer Memories and International Memories)—had to pioneer new applications for their products—primarily desktop personal computers. As with 8-inch drives, the technology improved at nearly twice the rate demanded in the new market—the capacity of 5.25-inch drives increased about 50% per year between 1980 and 1990. By 1985, 50% of the firms which had produced 8-inch drives had introduced 5.25-inch models, but of those, only Micropolis survived to become a significant manufacturer of 5.25-inch drives, and that was accomplished only with Herculean managerial effort.

Seagate's experience was an archetype of the histories of many of the disk drive industry's leading firms. Its entry strategy employed an innovative design comprising standard, commercially available components. Its appeal was in an emerging value network—desktop computing. Once it was established in that value network, Seagate's engineering effort shifted toward innovations in component technology. As a consequence, it was slow to

TABLE 1. A Comparison of the Average Attributes of the 8-Inch Drives Introduced by Established and Entrant Firms

Attributes	Level of performance (of 1981 products)		Annual rate of performance improvement (1979–1983)	
	Established firms	Entrant firms	Established firms	Entrant firms
Capacity (Mb)	19.2	19.1	61.2%	57.4%
Area density (Mb per in²)	3.213	3.104	35.5%	36.7%
Access time (milliseconds)	46.1	51.6	−8.1%	−9.1%
Price per megabyte	$143.03	$147.73	−58.8%	−61.9%

Source: Analysis of data from *Disk/Trend Report* as reported in Christensen, 1992.

respond when the next generation of designs, 3.5 inch drives, began to emerge. Its behavior was not atypical; by 1988, only 35% of the drive manufacturers that had established themselves making 5.25-inch products for the desktop PC market had introduced 3.5-inch drives. As in earlier transitions, the barrier to development of a competitive 3.5-inch product does not appear to have been a lack of requisite capabilities or failure to recognize new technological possibilities.

Seagate engineers anticipated the emergence of the 3.5-inch design, even though its commercialization was pioneered by a start-up, Conner, in 1987. Two years before Conner Peripherals started shipping its product. Seagate personnel had shown working 3.5-inch prototype drives to customers for evaluation. The initiative for the new drives came from Seagate's engineering organization. Opposition to the program came primarily from the marketing organization and Seagate's executive team, on the grounds that the market wanted higher capacity drives at a lower cost per megabyte, and that 3.5-inch drives could never be built at a lower cost per megabyte than 5.25-inch drives.

The customers to whom the Seagate 3.5-inch drives were shown were firms within the value network already served by Seagate: they were manufacturers of full-sized desktop computer systems. Not surprisingly, they showed little interest in the smaller drive. They were looking for capacities of 40 and 60 megabytes for their next generation machines, while the 3.5-inch design could only provide 20 Mb—and at higher costs. In response to these lukewarm reviews from customers, Seagate's program manager lowered his 3.5-inch sales estimates, and the firm's executives cancelled the 3.5-inch program. Their reasoning was that the markets for 5.25-inch products were larger and that the sales generated by spending the engineering effort on new 5.25-inch products would generate greater revenues for the company than would efforts targeted at new 3.5-inch products.

In retrospect, it appears that Seagate executives read the market—at least their own market—very accurately. Their customers were manufacturers and value-added resellers of relatively large-footprint desktop personal computers such as the IBM XT and AT. With established applications and product architectures of their own, these customers saw no commercial value in the reduced size, weight and power consumption, and the improved ruggedness of 3.5-inch products.

The customers that did see value in the 3.5-inch drives were an emerging group of portable computer makers, including Compaq, Toshiba and Zenith. A group of start-up drive manufacturers, led by Conner Peripherals, led in the sale of 3.5-inch drives to this market. Seagate finally began shipping 3.5-inch drives in early 1988—the same year in which the performance trajectory of 3.5-inch drives intersected the trajectory of capacity demanded in desktop computers (shown in Figure 3). By that time nearly $750 million in 3.5-inch products had been shipped cumulatively in the industry. According to industry observers, as of 1991 almost none of Seagate's 3.5-inch products had been sold to manufacturers of portable/laptop/notebook computers. Seagate's primary customers still were desktop computer manufacturers, and many of its 3.5-inch drives were shipped with frames which permitted them to be mounted in computers which had been designed to accommodate 5.25-inch drives.

As in other data processing subsystems, disk drive technology advanced rapidly through the 1970s and 80s, increasing drive capacity and performance, and reducing size and cost, at rates that would have been astonishing in almost any other industry. One of the primary technical trends behind increasing capacity was the relentless increase in the recording density achieved—a trend which was largely driven by improvements in component technology. The earliest drives could hold only a few kilobytes of data per square inch of drive surface; by 1967 this had risen to 50 kilobytes; within six years, the first Winchester design held 1.7 megabytes per square inch; by 1981 the IBM 3380 boasted a density greater than 12 Mb/sq. in. In 1990, densities of 50 Mb/sq. in. were common, marking a 3000-fold increase in 35 years. As in other applications of magnetic technology (e.g. video recording) greater density led to smaller, less expensive devices. Costs also were driven down by a constellation of incremental improvements in components and materials, by manufacturing experience and by huge increases in scale.

Improvements in component technology and refinements in system design were the primary drivers of continuing performance improvement for disk drives of all sizes. They were the innovations behind each of the dotted-line technological trajectories plotted in Figure 3, and were the means by which firms attentive to customers' demands for improved performance addressed those needs. It is not surprising, therefore, that throughout the history of the industry, the leading innovators in the development and use of component technology were the industry's leading, established firms. Those firms led, not only in undertakings to develop risky, complex and expensive component technologies such as thin film heads and disks, but in literally every component-level innovation. Even in relatively simple but important innovations—such as Run Length Limited (RLL) recording codes (which took the industry from double- to triple density disks), embedded servo systems, zone-specific recording densities and higher RPM motors—established firms were the successful pioneers, while entrant firms were the technology followers.

As shown in Table 2, the converse was true for the series of technological discontinuities introduced by the new design types whose performance

TABLE 2. Number of Entrant versus Established Firms Offering the new Product Designs Creating Technological Discontinuities

		Number of firms offering one or more models of the new product design							
		First year		Second year		Third year		Fourth year	
		No. of firms	(%)	No. of firms	(%)	No. of firms	(%)	No. of firms	(%)
8-*inch drives*	Entrants	1	100	4	67	6	55	8	62
(1978)	Established	0		2	33	5	45	5	38
	Total	1	100	6	100	11	100	13	100
5.25-*inch drives*	Entrants	1	50	8	80	8	50	13	54
(1980)	Established	1	50	2	20	8	50	11	46
	Total	2	100	10	100	16	100	24	100
3.5-*inch drives*	Entrants	1	100	2	67	3	75	4	50
(1983)	Established	0		1	33	1	25	4	50
	Total	1	100	3	100	4	100	8	100

Source: Analysis of data from *Disk/Trend Report* as reported in Christensen, 1992.

trajectories are mapped in Figure 3.[8] In each case, the new, smaller drives were sold to new customers in new applications—in new value networks— and the majority of producers were new entrants. Although incumbents appear to have possessed the technological capabilities required to participate in this series of innovations, they generally failed to do so. Two years after the introduction of the first 8-inch rigid drive, four of the six firms offering the product were entrants newly arrived in the industry. At the end of the second year of the 5.25-inch generation, eight of the 10 producers were entrants. A similar pattern characterized the early population of firms offering 3.5-inch drives.

The history summarized in Figure 3 seems to be a relatively clear empirical example of the emergence of a sequence of what Dosi (1982) calls 'technological paradigms' and their associated new trajectories. Point A, where the Winchester drive began to supplant the disk pack approach, represented a sustaining innovation within an existing paradigm—the Winchester

[8] Although the 2.5-inch drive represented a new engineering architecture, it was developed and deployed within the same value network as the 3.5-inch product. The leading customers were largely the same firms. Toshiba, Zenish, Compaq and Sharp, which were the leading laptop computer manufacturers, became the leading notebook PC makers. Their customers, and the spreadsheet and word processing software they used, were the same. In other words, the system of use was the same; hence, and most importantly; the way disk drive performance was assessed—capacity per cubic inch and per ounce, ruggedness, power consumption, etc., was unchanged.

was faster and had higher capacity and density than the predecessor techno-logy. But at points B, C and D, product performance came to be defined differently; new trajectories were established; and engineers began to focus, within each new paradigm, on new sets of problems. For example power consumption, ruggedness and weight simply were not on the development agendas of any practitioners of the 14 and 8-inch generations, whereas they became the dominating issues on the technology agendas of every firm competing within the 3.5 and 2.5-inch generations. Each of these techno-logical paradigms emerged within a different value network—for mainfra-mes, minicomputers, desktop PCs and portable computers. The forces which defined the trajectories of performance demanded in each value network tended to be at the broader, higher system-of-use levels in each network—the software used, the data processed, the training level of operators, the locations of use, etc.

5. *Conclusions*

This account of the history of disk drive innovation suggests that the degree to which technological discontinuities have radical competitive consequences is related to the extent to which they facilitate success within, or require mobility across value networks. If no mobility or change in strategic direc-tion is required—if the new technology is valuable within a firm's estab-lished value network—the consequences of the innovation are likely to be reinforcing, regardless of its intrinsic technological difficulty or riskiness. If realization of inherent value requires the establishment of new systems of use—served by new value networks—the consequences are likely to be radical—even if the innovation is technologically simple. This may occur because such innovations require far more than technological activity—complementary assets must be created or acquired as new commercial capabili-ties become significant.

In the disk drive story, entrant firms had the advantage in innovations that redefined the level, rate and direction of progress of an established techno-logical trajectory. This was not because of any difficulty or unique skill requirements intrinsic to the new technology, but rather because the new technological paradigm addressed a differently-ordered set of performance parameters valued in a new or different value network. It was difficult in this industry for established firms to marshal resources behind innovations that did not address the needs of known customers. Although the 'attacker's advantage' was associated with technical change, the essence of the advantage seemed to lie in the entrant's greater ability to identify and to make strategic commitments to develop emerging market applications found in new or

TABLE 3.

	Scientific and technological roots compared to those of predecessor business		Value network	
	Similar	Different	Same	New
Entrants were lead innovators and became overall market leaders				
Desktop xerographic copiers	×			×
Electronic calculators		×		×
Hydraulic earth moving equipment		×		×
Minimill steel making	×			×
Portable transitor radios	×			×
Programmable motor controls		×		×
Radial tires in North America	×		×	
RISC microprocessors	×			×
Semiconductor electronics		×		×
Steamships		×		×
Incumbents were the lead innovators but entrants gained market leadership				
Helical scan videotape recorders	×			×
Incumbents were the lead innovators and maintained leadership				
Electronic data processing		×	×	
Float glass		×	×	
Synthetic fibers		×	×	
CT scanning		×	×	
Electronic cash registers		×	×	
Incumbents were the lead innovators but the innovation failed to displace established technology				
Optical data recording		×	×	
Videodisc		×		×
Wankel auto engine	×		×	

different value networks. The issue, at its core, may be the relative abilities of successful incumbent firms to change strategies, not technologies.

Before we can conclude that the obstacle to prosperous firms' ability to promote radical innovations lies more within their strategy-making capacity than in their technological capabilities, the phenomenon needs to be explored systematically among a wider range of historical cases. Table 3 offers a listing of 19 innovations (see Appendix 2) that had the effect of disrupting established trajectories of technical progress in predecessor industries.[9] Table 3 is

[9] It should be noted that these examples, like those cited in the few other pertinent empirical studies of the topic (Cooper and Schendel, 1976; Foster, 1986; Tushman and Anderson, 1986), are limited to cases in North American markets where the principal incumbents were North American firms. Examination of similar cases from Europe and Asia may disclose rather different patterns. We are grateful to Giovanni Dosi for suggesting this point.

organized according to whether incumbents or entrants appear to have been more successful in markets for the new technology.[10] We further classify the innovations according to two criteria: (i) whether or not the innovation required substantial capabilities rooted in science or technology different from those supporting the predecessor business; and (ii) whether or not it was relevant to established value networks. This preliminary analysis seems to support the proposition that competitive outcomes following technological discontinuities are related to differences in the relevant value network and are largely independent of whether or not the innovations required that incumbents develop substantial new capabilities.[11]

We conclude from this preliminary examination that it would be worthwhile to examine a number of these historical cases more closely in a comparative framework. More detailed historical accounts, where available, could be used to examine the explanations given by economic and organization theory for the lags (or failures) of incumbents in making strategic commitments to what proved to be substitute technologies for their core businesses. One could also explore the significance of various organizational capabilities —technological and strategic—as explanations of observed outcomes.

At some point in the development of this field, a useful organizing theory— a Kuhnian paradigm—will gain broad acceptance. That will happen when a given theory enables scholars to identify more precisely and consistently the phenomena they observe, and to show how what previously had seemed to be anomalous, contradictory observations could sensibly be comprehended within the same framework. Kuhn is careful to point out that such paradigms are generally limited in scope. Nor do they resolve every issue in that field of inquiry. Rather, they provide an organizing framework within which subsequent scholars can productively conduct their research, and communicate clearly their findings and questions. We think that at this stage in the study of innovation, a comparative historical analysis to test our framework and others would move the field closer to that goal.

Acknowledgements

Helpful comments on earlier versions of this paper and related work were provided by Fred Carstensen. Rongxin Chen, Giovanni Dosi, Marco Iansiti,

---

[10] It should be emphasized that the classifications in Table 3 in several instances might warrant revision after more detailed historical study.

[11] Another plausible criterion was suggested by Henderson and Clark (1990). They point out that innovations requiring new 'architectures' will require new capabilities, even if the technological foundations of the various components are familiar. Since almost all of the cases in Table 3 involved architectural innovation in the sense they defined it, that distinction does not seem to serve well to discriminate between incumbents and entrants.

Anita McGahan, Elizabeth Teisberg, and members of the Business History Seminar at Harvard Business School. The authors also express their appreciation for funding and other support provided by the Division of Research of the Harvard Business School.

References

Abernathy, W. J. and J. H. Utterback (1978), 'Patterns of Innovation in Technology,' *Technology Review*, **80**, 40–47.

Anderson, P. and M. L. Tushman (1990), 'Technological Discontinuities and Dominant Designs: A Cyclical Model of Technological Change,' *Administrative Science Quarterly*, **35**, 604–33.

Barbour, E. N. (1971), *Pilkington Float Glass (A)*. Case Study 9-672-569, Harvard Business School: Boston, MA.

Boston Consulting Group (1982), 'The Programmable Controls Market,' Unpubl5shed study.

Braun, E. and S. MacDonald (1982), *Revolution in Miniature* (Second Edition). Cambridge University Press: Cambridge.

Burck, C. G. (1972), 'A Car that May Reshape the Industry's Future,' *Fortune*, (July), 74–79.

Burgelman, R. A. (1991), 'Intraorganizational Ecology of Strategy-making and Organizational Adaptation: Theory and Field Research,' *Organizational Science*, **2**, 239–62.

Chandler, A. D. (1992), 'Organizational Capabilities and the Economic History of the Industrial Enterprise,' *Journal of Economic Perspectives*, **6**, 79–100.

Child, J. (1972), 'Organizational Structure, Environment, and Performance: The Role of Strategic Choice,' *Sociology*, **6**, 2–22.

Christensen, C. M. (1992), 'The Innovator's Challenge: Understanding the Influence of Market Environment on Processes of Technology Development in the Rigid Disk Drive Industry,' Doctoral Dissertation, Harvard University Graduate School of Business Administration: Boston, MA.

Christensen, C. M and J. L. Bower (1993), *Catching the Next Wave: Why Good Customers Make It Hard*. Working Paper 94–008, Harvard Business School: Boston, MA.

Christensen, C. M. and R. S. Rosenbloom (forthcoming), 'Explaining the Attacker's Advantage: Technological Paradigms, Organizational Dynamics, and the Value Network', *Research Policy*.

Cobelli, D. H. and W. Rudelius (1987), 'Managing Innovation: Lessons from the Cardiac-Pacing Industry,' in E. B. Roberts (ed.), *Generating Technological Innovation*. Oxford University Press: New York.

Cooper, A. C. and D. Schendel (1976), 'Strategic Responses to Technological Threats,' *Business Horizons*, (February), 61–69.

Dosi, G. (1982), 'Technological Paradigms and Technological Trajectories,' *Research Policy*, **11**, 147–162.

The Economist (1993), 'Frontiers of Finance.' October 9, 1993, 'Special Report.'

Ferguson, C. H. and C. R. Morris (1993), *Computer Wars*. Time Books: New York.

Fishman, K. D. (1981), *The Computer Establishment*. Harper & Row: New York.

Flamm, K. (1988), *Creating the Computer: Government, Industry, and High Technology*. The Brookings Institution: Washington DC.

Foster, R. N. (1986), *Innovation: The Attacker's Advantage*. Summit Books: New York.

Freeman, C. (1982), *The Economics of Industrial Innovation (Second edition)*. MIT Press: Cambridge, MA.

French, M. J. (1991), *The US Tire Industry: A History*. Twayne Publishers: Boston, MA.

Graham, M. B. W. (1986), *RCA and the VideoDisc: The Business of Research*. Cambridge University Press: Cambridge.

Hannan, M. T. and J. Freeman (1989), *Organizational Ecology*. Harvard University Press: Cambridge, MA.

Henderson, R. and K. B. Clark (1990), 'Architectural Innovation: The Reconfiguration of Existing Product Technologies and the Failure of Established Firms,' *Administrative Science Quarterly*, **35**, 9–30.

Henderson, R. (1993), 'Underinvestment and Incompetence as Responses to Radical Innovation: Evidence from the Photolithographic Alignment Equipment Industry,' *RAND Journal of Economics*, 24, 248–270.

Hogan, W. T. (1982), *Minimills and Integrated Mills: A Comparison of Steelmaking in the United States*. Lexington Books: Lexington, MA.

Hollander, S. (1965), *The Sources of Increased Efficiency: A Study of DuPont Rayon Plants*. MIT Press: Cambridge, MA.

Hounshell, D. A. and J. K. Smith Jr (1988), *Science and Corporate Strategy: Du Pont R&D, 1902–1980*. Cambridge University Press: Cambridge.

Jacobson, G. and J. Hillkirk (1986), *Xerox: American Samurai*. Macmillan Publishing Company: New York.

Kline, S. J. and N. Rosenberg (1986), 'An Overview of Innovation,' in R. Landau and N. Rosenberg (eds), *The Positive Sum Strategy*. National Academy Press: Washington, DC.

Kuhn, T. (1962), *The Structure of Scientific Revolutions*. University of Chicago Press: Chicago, IL.

Leonard-Barton, D. (1992), 'Core Capabilities and Core Rigidities: A Paradox in Managing New Product Development,' *Strategic Management Journal*, 13, 111–125.

Majumdar, B. A. (1980), 'Technology Transfers and International Competitiveness: The Case of Electronic Calculators,' *Journal of International Business Studies*, 11, 103–111.

Morone, J. G. (1993), *Winning in High-Tech Markets: The Role of General Management*. Harvard Business School Press: Boston, MA.

Mowery, D. C. and N. Rosenberg (1989), *Technology and the Pursuit of Economic Growth*. Cambridge University Press: Cambridge.

NCR Corporation (1984), *Celebrating the Future: A Centennial History*. NCR Corporation: Dayton, Ohio.

Nelson, R. R. and S. G. Winter (1982), *An Evolutionary Theory of Economic Change*. Harvard University Press: Cambridge, MA.

Rosenbloom, R. S. (1986), *Discerning User Needs for Digital Optical Recording*. Working Paper 87–068, Harvard Business School: Boston MA.

Rosenbloom, R. S. and M. A. Cusumano (1987), 'Technological Pioneering and Competitive Advantage,' *California Management Review*, 29, 51–76.

Schiffer, M. B. (1991), *The Portable Radio in American Life*. The University of Arizona Press: Tucson, AZ.

Stross, R. E. (1993), *Steve Jobs and the NeXT Big Thing*. Atheneum: New York.

Tushman, M. L. and P. Anderson (1986), 'Technological Discontinuities and Organizational Environments,' *Administrative Science Quarterly*, 31, 439–465.

Appendix 1

A Note on the Data and Methods Used to Generate Figure 3

The trajectories mapped in Figure 3 were calculated as follows. Data on the capacity provided with computers was obtained from *Data Sources*, an annual publication which lists the technical specifications of all computer models available from each computer manufacturer. Where particular models were available with different features and configuration, the manufacturer provided *Data Sources* with a 'typical' system configuration, and defined random access memory (RAM) capacity; performance specifications of peripheral equipment (including disk drives); list price; and year of introduction. In instances where a given computer model was offered for sale over a sequence of years, the hard disk capacity provided in the typical configuration typically increased. *Data Sources* divides computers into mainframe, mini-midrange, desktop personal, portable and laptop, and notebook computers. For each class of computers, all models available for sale in each year were ranked by price, and the hard disk capacity provided with the median-priced model identified, for each year. The best-fit line through the resultant time series is plotted as the solid lines in Figure 3. These single solid lines are drawn in Figure 3 for expository simplification, to indicate the trend in typical machines. In reality, of course, there is a wide band around these lines. The frontier of performance—the highest capacity offered with the most expensive computers—was substantially higher than the typical values shown.

The dotted lines in Figure 3 represent the best-fit line through the un-weighted average capacity of all disk drives introduced for sale in each given architecture, for each year. This data was taken from *Disk/Trend Report*. Again, for expository simplification, only this average line is shown. There was a wide band of capacities introduced for sale in each year, so that the frontier, or highest capacity drive introduced in each year was substantially above the average shown. Stated in another way, a distinction must be made between the full range of products available for purchase, and those in typical systems of use. The upper and lower bands around the median and average figures shown in Figure 3 are generally parallel to the lines shown.

Because drives with higher capacities were available in the market than the capacities offered with the median-priced systems, we state in the text that the solid-line trajectories in Figure 3 represent the capacities 'demanded' in each market. In other words, the capacity per machine was not constrained by technological availability. Rather, it represents a choice for hard disk capacity, made by computer users, given the prevailing cost.

Appendix 2

Cases Cited in Table 3

Computerized tomography. The first computerized tomography (CT) scanner was developed by Godfrey Houndsfield, a scientist at Britain's EMI Ltd, a diversified company with strong positions in the audio recording and military electronics markets. Because CT scanners could create clear images of soft internal body tissues, they represented a significant advance in performance over conventional X-ray equipment, which could only provide images of hard internal tissues such as bones. The CT scanner was EMI's first product for the medical imaging market. Its announcement caught the world's four leading makers of X-ray equipment—General Electric, Philips, Siemens and Picker—completely unprepared. Yet within two years, each of these companies had announced CT scanners of their own. By 1976 EMI had withdrawn from the market. General Electric was particularly successful with its CT scanning product line and used the technology to build a world-leading position in medical imaging (Morone, 1993).

Desktop personal photocopiers.   Plain paper photocopiers were commercially pioneered by Xerox. Because of the expense of the machines, Xerox generally sold or leased them to large companies' central photocopying departments, or to independent printing/photocopying shops. Because fast service and equipment utilization was critical in these applications, copier performance was measured in terms of copies per minute. Fast, efficient equipment service was also paramount. Canon entered the photocopier industry by designing 'a totally new copier for people who currently weren't using a copier machine'. Canon executives guessed that in this potential market, speed would not matter nearly so much as physical size (it needed to be as small as a typewriter); its simplicity and reliability (it had to be self-serviceable); and its costs (retail price under $1000). Canon became the leading maker of desktop personal photocopiers, although Xerox subsequently entered the market (Jacobson and Hillkirk, 1986).

Electronic calculators.   In the 1960s, the North American market for electromechanical calculators was shared by five major producers. Electronic calculators made obsolete those producers' existing technological capabilities in mechanical design and machine fabrication and assembly, as well as complementary assets such as dealership service networks. Products based on electronic circuitry were introduced by entrants, using different channels and, initially, meeting different needs. With the introduction of integrated circuitry in the 1970s, electronics dominated and all five of the original oligopoly had lost leadership (Majumdar, 1980).

Electronic cash registers.   National Cash Register (NCR), the dominant worldwide producer of electro-mechanical registers, aggressively developed related electronic products while resisting introduction of electronic registers, even as entrants began to take share away in the late 1960s. Electronics, and complementary developments in computer technology and use, promised to change the function of registers in most stores, transforming them from stand-alone devices to 'point-of-sale terminals' in larger systems. In the late 1960s, entrants—both start-ups and established firms like Singer—began to offer terminals and systems, taking share from NCR. When NCR made the transition to electronics in the 1970s, its great marketing assets quickly propelled it back into leadership and most of the entrants were forced to exit (NCR Corporation, 1984).

Electronic data processing. The first commercial electronic computer (Univac I) was delivered to the Bureau of the Census in 1951 by Remington Rand, an established producer of electro-mechanical data processing equipment. Although scientific and military applications were initially a significant segment of demand, the new computers rapidly began to displace mechanical tabulators in routine applications within offices. By the mid-1950s, IBM— which had dominated the punched-card tabulator business, had taken the lead in the new market. Major electronics companies, like GE, Raytheon and RCA, entered but ultimately failed; office equipment producers NCR and Burroughs survived (Fishman, 1981; Flamm, 1988).

Float glass. For the first half of this century the manufacture of plate glass was an extremely expensive, mechanically difficult process. Thick but uneven plates of glass had to be ground and then polished on production lines that often were a half mile long. Britain's Pilkington Glass, one of the world's largest plate glass manufacturers, was the industry's technology leader, licensing its proprietary equipment to most of the world's leading plate glass makers. In the mid-1950s Pilkington invented a new process in which molten glass from a furnace flowed on to a long, narrow bed of molten tin and emerged, solidified, with two perfect, parallel surfaces, exactly to the thickness required, without grinding. Developing the process required completely different technical skills than Pilkington had ever used, and once perfected, Pilkington's float glass process rendered obsolete all of the company's expertise in mechanical grinding and polishing. Yet, starting in the mid-1960s, the company aggressively switched its own manufacturing capacity over to the float glass process, and then began licensing the process to its competitors. Today, every piece of plate glass manufactured in the world is made under Pilkington license (Barbour, 1971).

Helical scan videotape recorders. The first magnetic videotape recorder, invented and commercialized by Ampex Corporation, used a transverse recording format. Five years later, Ampex introduced machines using helical scanners that were less expensive but of lower quality. N. V. Philips, Sony and other Japanese producers soon followed. The helical machines, unsuitable for broadcasters, nevertheless stimulated emergence of a range of new 'closed-circuit' applications. Sony and Ampex even offered products for home use in 1967. Success in the marketplace proved to require persistence in the development of more advanced design configurations, low-cost, reliable manufacturing capabilities and microelectronic circuitry. By the early 1970s, the firms that had entered the business a decade earlier on the basis of the new technology, dominated the market worldwide (Rosenbloom and Cusumano, 1987).

Hydraulic earth moving equipment. The fundamental technology used in mechanical earthmoving equipment went largely unchanged for 70 years after the first steam shovel was invented in 1848: the machines were powered by steam and actuated by a system of cables, winches, clutches and pulleys. When gasoline engines with sufficient power emerged in the 1920s, and again when viable diesel engines emerged in the late 1940s, the established makers of earthmoving equipment such as Bucyrus Erie aggressively incorporated the new sources of power. This was not the case with hydraulically actuated shovels, however. These were first introduced in 1947 by the J. C. Bamford Company in Britain and by three start-up companies in the US. Even the most powerful early hydraulic shovels were small and weak compared to the huge diesel and cable-powered machines used by most large earthmoving contractors. But their small size, reliability and low cost were viewed as strengths by residential contractors, who generally had not been able to use mechanical earthmoving equipment. Hence, the early hydraulic manufacturers sold their shovels as 'backhoes' to attach on the back of small tractors, so that small contractors could use them to dig narrow, shallow trenches in order to connect homes to water and sewer lines in the streets. Such trenches previously had been dug by hand. By the late 1970s hydraulic backhoes were offered by all leading tractor manufacturers, such as J. I. Case, John Deere and International Harvester. As these companies improved the power and reach of their hydraulic equipment, they began offering larger-capacity hydraulic excavators to large earthmoving contractors as well. By 1975, hydraulic excavators were large and powerful enough to satisfy nearly all earthmoving contractors' needs. The farm equipment manufacturers and a later entrant, Caterpillar, came to dominate this market. Of the 30 or so makers of cable actuated excavators, only one—Koehring—successfully made the transition to hydraulically actuated machinery. A few of the other manufacturers, such as Bucyrus Erie and Marion continue to produce huge cable-actuated draglines for use in strip mining. The others have all exited the business (Christensen and Bower, 1993).

Minimill steel making. Steel minimills employ a very different process architecture than integrated mills: they use only steel scrap as raw material, melt it in electric arc furnaces and then cast and roll it into relatively simple shapes. Minimills generally are built with much lower capital cost per ton of capacity and enjoy lower operating costs compared to integrated steel mills. Because of the inconsistent metallurgical properties of their early products and because of the relatively low capital costs involved, initially the minimills focused on making steel reinforcing bar for concrete—a price-competitive market where quality standards were not stringent. As their capabilities for producing higher-quality steels improved, minimills entered markets for other types of steel bars and angle products; structural steel beams; and most recently, rolled sheet steel. By 1992 the minimills had captured nearly 40% of the US steel market, and had made substantial inroads in European and Asian markets as well. Yet the minimill manufacturers, such as Nucor, Chaparral and North Star, are entrants to the industry: not a single US or European integrated steel maker, and only one Japanese integrated steel maker, has yet built a minimill (Hogan, 1982).

Optical data recording. Optical disk recording, an alternative to magnetic media, although pioneered for entertainment applications was quickly perceived to be applicable for data storage as well. The basic technologies for media on which lasers could record and read back digital data—called WORM, for 'write-once, read many times'—were developed during the 1970s in research laboratories at Philips (where it was created), IBM, Xerox, RCA, Hitachi and others. Optical disks offered greater capacity—up to 1000 times that of removable magnetic disks—at the expense of higher cost and slower data transfer, thus departing from the established trajectories of performance improvement for disk drives. In the early 1980s a number of incumbents in the magnetic disk drive industry—including leaders like Shugart and CDC—and some start-ups began to offer optical drives for evaluation by computer manufacturers. Commercial sales began in the late 1980s but volumes were modest. The first model of the NeXT workstation was marketed with mass storage provided by an optical drive (produced by an entrant—Canon), but other computer manufacturers continued to rely on magnetic hard disks. By the early 1990s, despite the important use of read-only optical recording for audio compact disks and growing use of CD-ROM drives in personal computers, WORM technology had failed to displace magnetic recording for data storage (Rosenbloom, 1986; Stross, 1993).

Portable transistor radios. The world's first transistorized portable radio was marketed in the US in late 1954 under the Regency brand by an entrant, IDEA Corporation, which had been induced to do so by Texas Instruments to create a market for its transistors after major producers like GE and RCA had declined. A host of American imitators soon followed. But the mass market was created by Sony, entering the US market in 1957. Sony used novel distribution channels and offered a superior product using an innovative tuner. Numerous Japanese imitators followed Sony and the Japanese collectively and quickly dominated the new mass market (Schiffer, 1991).

Programmable motor controls.   Motor controls—large switches that start, stop and protect electric motors, were initially electromechanical devices manufactured by firms such as Square D, Cutler Hammer, Westinghouse, General Electric and Allen Bradley. In 1968, solid-state motor controls were introduced by an entrant to the industry, Modicon. Modicon sold its products to sophisticated machine tool users such as Ford, which found they could more flexibly link machines in transfer lines together using the programmable technology, than with 'hard-wired' electro-mechanical relays. By the mid-1980s, most machine tool manufacturers had substituted solid-state programmable controls for electro-mechanical products. In this transition, only one of the electromechanical control manufacturers, Allen Bradley (through its acquisition of a Bunker Ramo division), was able to maintain a strong position in the programmable control world. The others either withdrew from the market or have maintained only marginal positions. Modicon and Texas Instruments joined Allen Bradley as the leading makers of solid-state programmable motor controls (Boston Consulting Group, 1982).

Radial tires in North America.   This innovation was pioneered in Europe by Michelin. Technological novelty lay in the changed configuration of tire plies and the use of steel wire in place of the fabric cords of conventional bias-ply tires. Successful manufacture required new equipment and substantial new 'know-how'. Tire performance, especially durability, was substantially enhanced, but tire cost was doubled. When US producers were slow to adopt radial designs, despite their success in Europe, Michelin used its advantage to gain entry to the North American market. Hence an established producer exploited an 'attacker's advantage' in a regional market (French, 1991).

RISC microprocessors.   Reduced Instruction Set Computing (RISC) represents a very different microprocessor design architecture that enables computers to run up to four times faster than is possible with Complex Instruction Set Computing (CISC) chips. RISC was invented over a decade, beginning in 1968, at IBM. IBM executives recognized the value of RISC, but refused to introduce a line of computers using RISC chips that was incompatible with the software used in its 360/370 line of mainframe computers. The process of trying to adapt RISC to IBM's embedded set of microcode took significant time and seriously compromised the RISC chips' performance. Most members of IBM's RISC team subsequently left the company in frustration. One founded MIPS Computer Systems, which today is the world's independent leading manufacturer of RISC microprocessors. Another left to head up Hewlett Packard's RISC development effort. RISC microprocessors today are used extensively in engineering workstations manufactured by firms such as Sun Microsystems and Hewlett Packard. In the late 1980s, IBM finally began using RISC chips in its highly successful RS6000 line of workstations (Ferguson and Morris, 1993).

Semiconductor electronics.   Commercial production of transistors began in the US in 1951 under license from Bell Telephone Laboratories, the inventor. By 1953 all eight producers of vacuum tubes were in the business, competing with a steadily increasing number of entrants, including start-ups like Transitron and diversifiers like Texas Instruments. Compared to vacuum tubes, transistors represented a radically different constellation of cost and performance characteristics. Many early applications featured uses where tubes were severely inadequate (e.g. hearing aids) or not at all practical (e.g. rocket guidance). The entrants had captured two-thirds of the market by 1957 and all of the old tube producers ultimately failed in the semiconductor industry (Braun and MacDonald, 1982).

Steamships.   Robert Fulton demonstrated his first steamboat on the Hudson River in 1819. In subsequent decades steam power came to be used extensively on inland waterways where sailing ships could not be used reliably. Steam-powered ships were not used in transoceanic commerce because they were vulnerable to breakdown; were more expensive; and were not as fast as sailing ships. The makers of transoceanic sailing ships could not have adopted steam power, in fact, unless they had made the parallel strategic commitment to manufacture very different types of vessels for the very different inland waterway market. Steam-powered ships were developed and refined in the inland waterway market for nearly 70 years before they had the speed and reliability required to compete in oceanic commerce. When the technology reached that point in the 1890s, however, the makers of steam ships displaced the manufacturers of sailing ships with stunning speed; the last sail-powered commercial transoceanic vessel was made in 1907. None of the leading transoceanic sailing ship manufacturers successfully made the transition to manufacturing steam-powered ships (Foster, 1986).

Synthetic fibers.   Nylon, the first true synthetic fiber, was invented by Du Pont and first marketed in 1940 to be knit into women's hosiery. By its second year it captured 30% of that market. Du Pont, building on its leading position as a rayon supplier, went on to develop a wide range of successful applications of nylon, as well as inventing and commercializing a stream of other synthetic fibers. The technology for nylon and its successors was based on pioneering research by Du Pont in polymerization and on outstanding engineering capabilities required to translate laboratory advances to commercial scale. Du Pont's commercial lead was protected by patents (Houndshell and Smith, 1988).

Videodisc. The videodisc pioneers, bringing products to market 1978–81, were RCA, Philips and Matsushita, then the world's largest producers of home entertainment electronics and also pioneers in the development of the rival VCR technology. As the VCR grew to be a mass-market success worldwide, it pre-empted demand. By 1984 the RCA product was withdrawn and soon after the company itself was taken over and broken up. Other disk products languished on the market (Graham, 1986).

Wankel auto engine. The rotary engine, invented in Germany and first commercialized by Toyo Kogyo (Mazda) in Japan in 1967, attracted great attention in the US in the early 1970s. Rotary-powered Mazda cars were imported beginning in 1971 and General Motors tooled up to offer Chevrolet cars with the new engine. Hailed as offering nearly irresistible performance and cost advantages, the rotary engine departed from the trajectory of conventional internal combustion engine technology as it offered the 'only path . . . to simultaneously improve fuel economy, vehicle performance, and emissions' (Burck, 1972). Although development of engine design and manufacturing facilities suitable for low-cost reliable mass production presented formidable engineering challenges, those tasks built on the established technical capabilities of the auto makers and their vendors. By 1972 some analysts were predicting that rotary designs would constitute more than 75% of the engines produced in the US in 1980. But the engineering challenges proved more formidable than anticipated. GM never brought the rotary-powered Chevrolet to market and Mazda had to withdraw its rotary models—an expensive failure that nearly sank Toyo Kogyo.

Organizational Integration and Competitive Advantage: Explaining Strategy and Performance in American Industry

WILLIAM LAZONICK[a] AND JONATHAN WEST[b]

([a]University of Massachusetts Lowell and
[b]Graduate School of Business Administration, Harvard University)

This paper proposes an analytical framework that can comprehend how and to what extent the interaction of institutions, industries, and enterprises has contributed to the decline of US competitiveness. The analytical framework builds on the notion that, ultimately, competitive advantage depends on the strategies and structures of the business enterprises on which Americans rely for most of the nation's productive investments. We argue that, over time, to gain sustained competitive advantage, business enterprises in the USA and elsewhere have had to achieve increasingly higher degrees of 'organizational integration'. We argue that, as a general rule, the USA's prime competitors, and particularly the Japanese, have gained competitive advantage by becoming more organizationally integrated than their American rivals. For some industries, moreover, organizational integration is more important than others; hence the variation in the extent to which certain American industries have been affected by foreign competition. And even within the more vulnerable industries such as electronics and automobiles, some American companies have responded to the competitive challenge more quickly and effectively than others. The organizational integration hypothesis argues that an important determinant of differences among American companies in the same industry in the quickness and effectiveness of their strategic responses — whether they are 'first movers', 'fast movers', 'slower movers', 'no movers', or 'removers' — to competitive challenges is the extent to which these companies are organizationally integrated.

1. The Organizational Integration Hypothesis

In the 1950s and 1960s American industry dominated in global competition.

The USA was the world's productivity leader over a wide range of industries: science-based, research-intensive industries such as chemicals, pharmaceuticals, computers and commercial aircraft; capital-intensive mass-production industries such as steel, automobiles and consumer electronics; relatively labor-intensive manufacturing industries such as textiles; not to mention agriculture and related industries. This industrial pre-eminence gave the United States by far the highest level of per capita income in the world. Although American society has never been a leader in income equality, increasing numbers of Americans were nonetheless sharing in the prosperity of the 'American century'. For those Americans whom economic advance tended to leave behind, the government stood ready to undertake ambitious social programs to help them catch up.

Since the 1960s the experience of American industry has been declining competitiveness on global markets. Manifesting America's economic decline have been slow productivity growth relative to Japan, the newly industrializing countries and many western European nations; declining real incomes of most American wage-earners; and a failure of massive government spending to rectify social and economic ills. The decline of American industrial competitiveness has, however, been uneven across industries. In some industries, such as consumer electronics, this decline has been almost absolute and apparently irreversible. In many other industries, such as commercial aircraft, automobiles, computers and steel, this decline has been relative to the rise of formidable foreign competitors who have been able to encroach on the shares of American enterprises in both US and foreign markets (see Dertouzas *et al.*, 1989).

There now exists a large and growing literature that attempts to analyze and explain American industrial decline, and that seeks to discern whether any forces are at work to reverse the trend. Some of the research focuses on highly aggregated international productivity comparisons (e.g. Baumol *et al.*, 1989). Some research stresses the institutional weaknesses of America's educational and financial systems (e.g. Porter, 1992; Ferleger and Mandle, 1994, Chs 2 and 3). Other research has analyzed productivity differences at the industry level (Dertouzas *et al.*, 1989; Dollar and Wolff, 1993; McKinsey Global Institute, 1993). And other research has analyzed the decline of particular firms (e.g. Graham, 1986; Holland, 1989; Keller, 1993).

What is now required is a common analytical framework that can comprehend how and to what extent the interaction of institutions, industries and enterprises has contributed to the decline of US industrial competitiveness. This paper is a contribution to such a project. The analytical framework that is developed here builds on the notion that, ultimately, competitive advantage depends on the strategies and structures of the business enterprises on which

Americans rely for most of the nation's productive investments. We argue that, over time, to gain sustained competitive advantage, business enterprises in the USA and elsewhere have had to achieve increasingly higher degrees of 'organizational integration'. We argue that, as a general rule, America's prime competitors, and particularly the Japanese, have gained competitive advantage by becoming more organizationally integrated than their American rivals. For some industries, moreover, organizational integration is more important than others; hence the variation in the extent to which certain American industries have been affected by foreign competition. And even within the more vulnerable industries such as electronics and automobiles, some American companies have responded to the competitive challenge more quickly and more effectively than others. The organizational integration hypothesis argues that an important determinant of differences among American companies in the same industry in the quickness and effectiveness of their responses to competitive challenges is the extent to which these companies are organizationally integrated.

What, then, is organizational integration? It is a set of ongoing relationships that socializes participants in a complex division of labor to apply their skills and efforts to the achievement of common goals. The foundation of the socialization process that achieves organizational integration is 'membership': the inclusion of the individual or group into the organization with all the rights and responsibilities that membership entails. In a business organization, a fundamental right of membership is employment security, and a fundamental responsibility is to ensure that the pursuit of one's individual interests are consistent with organizational goals.

It should be emphasized that our use of the term 'organizational integration' focuses on the social process that achieves cooperation among individuals and groups of individuals, whether they are employed by the same firm or different firms. This usage differs from the common notion that terms such as 'vertical integration' or 'horizontal integration' apply only to individuals and groups employed by the same firm. Our conception of organizational integration may include individuals and groups who are employed by legally distinct firms that pursue common goals. Conversely, individuals and groups employed by the same firm may not cooperate to achieve common goals.

For the business enterprise engaged in competition for product markets, organizational integration permits the specialized division of labor to generate higher quality and/or lower cost products than the enterprise had previously been capable of producing. Organizational integration provides the capability to learn as an enterprise and the potential to innovate in market competition.

At the same time, organizational integration is a costly process. To build the relationships among the participants in the specialized division of labor that are the social substance of organizational integration requires substantial commitments of resources over sustained periods of time. The high fixed costs of building these relationships will place the enterprise at a competitive disadvantage until such time that the learning process that these relationships generate yields returns. The prospects of returns, moreover, are always highly uncertain, in part because the expected learning may not occur and in part because even when it does occur this learning may not be sufficient to meet the challenge of more innovative competitors (see Lazonick, 1991, Chs 3 and 6). The building of the relationships that constitute organizational integration must therefore be strategic.

To test the organizational integration hypothesis as an explanation for American decline in global competition, we must first derive from the study of the American economy as a whole a model of organizational integration that represents a norm for American business enterprises in general for the 1960s and 1970s, when the global competitive challenges began to be felt. We must then show how this American norm of organizational integration differs from that of the successful global competitors, and in particular, the Japanese, the competitors who have most successfully challenged the Americans.

Both the Japanese and Americans possessed organizationally integrated managerial structures. Both societies underwent a thoroughgoing managerial revolution during the first half of the twentieth century. But, coming into the second half of the century, organizational integration in Japan differed from organizational integration in the United States along two key dimensions. First, in contrast to American companies, Japanese enterprises included shop-floor workers in the process of planned coordination, investing in their skills and extending to them permanent employment status. Second, also in contrast to American companies, Japanese enterprises developed long-term relations with other firms that supplied them with inputs and distributed their outputs, and that, as with Japanese shop-floor workers, enabled these firms to participate in an organizationally integrated learning process.

The organizational integration hypothesis predicts that the Japanese gained competitive advantage over the Americans in those industries — steel, consumer electronics and automobiles are three striking examples — in which the organizational integration of the managerial structure (including technical specialists) was critical for product innovation but also in which the evolution of process technology made organizational integration of shop-floor workers, suppliers and distributors of central importance for process innovation. In industries in which, from the 1960s, an organizationally integrated managerial structure alone continued to suffice in global competition

—industries such as pharmaceuticals and chemicals—the Americans continued to be leading innovators, and Japanese companies were unable to mount an effective competitive challenge.

The organizational integration hypothesis also predicts that, within industries in which the American model of organizational integration no longer sufficed to generate competitive advantage, those American companies that, for whatever historical reasons, were able to confront the Japanese competitive challenge with a 'Japanese' model of organizational integration responded more quickly and effectively to the Japanese challenge. Similarly, the hypothesis predicts that those American companies that, lacking sufficient organizational integration, had problems responding to Japanese competition but that then integrated shop-floor workers and/or vertically related enterprises into the process of planned coordination were able, as a result, to respond effectively to the Japanese challenge. By the same token, the hypothesis predicts that such companies that failed to alter their organizational structure remained unable to respond effectively to the Japanese challenge.

2. Responses to Competitive Challenges

Central to American industrial dominance in the post-World War II decades were a few hundred industrial corporations that, during the previous decades and often going back to the late nineteenth century, had been in the forefront of technological and organizational innovation. They had been successful in not only dominating American product markets but also, through investments in multinational operations, exporting their organizational and technological capabilities around the world. From the late 1950s, however, as the nations of Western Europe recovered from the devastation of World War II, and as the so-called Japanese 'economic miracle' became a reality, competitive challenges from abroad began to confront these American corporations. The severity of the competitive challenge depended on the industry in which these companies competed. Within particular industries, different companies responded to the competitive challenges in different ways, at different speeds, and with different outcomes.

To explain these differences requires a categorization of the range of possible strategic responses to competitive challenges in terms of qualitative type and speed of response. Qualitatively, strategic responses can be categorized as either innovative or adaptive (Lazonick, 1991, Ch. 3). An innovative strategy entails investments that enhance the productive capability of new combinations of inputs, thus making possible the generation of higher quality, lower cost outputs. Whether any particular innovative strategy succeeds depends on whether the upgrading and recombination of inputs yields sufficient increases in quality and decreases in cost to make the enterprise's products competitive.

In contrast, an adaptive strategy does not attempt to upgrade and recombine the productive capabilities of the enterprise's accumulated assets and purchased inputs. At best, an adaptive strategy merely seeks to add inputs to the production process without transforming their productive capabilities. The stronger the competitive challenge, the greater will be the necessity for an adaptive strategy to cut costs by lowering the returns to productive factors. In its extreme form, the adaptation process can entail disinvestment that, by extracting value today without putting any new value-creating capabilities in its place, reduces the ability of a company to create value tomorrow. Ultimately, when the returns to productive factors cannot be reduced further and the productive assets inherited from the past have been consumed, the adaptive enterprise will no longer be able to compete (see Lazonick, 1991, Ch. 3).

When, as is generally the case, a competitive challenge entails innovation, an innovative response will be required for a company to regain a sustainable competitive advantage. A sustainable competitive advantage is one that does not rely on permanently reducing returns to productive factors or living off a company's existing resources. The timing of an enterprise's strategic response to a competitive challenge is critical because of the need to augment the productive capabilities of the enterprise's resources. The innovation process that is set in motion by an innovative strategy is a developmental process that takes time. In competition with innovative rivals, a delay in introducing an innovative strategy can make it all the more difficult to develop an effective innovative response.

It is useful, therefore, to distinguish the strategic responses of companies according to whether they are (i) innovative or adaptive, and (ii) prompt or delayed. In considering differences among companies in response to competitive challenges, we shall employ five categories of investment strategies: first mover (innovative), fast mover (innovative), slow mover (adaptive, but then innovative), no mover (adaptive) and remover (adaptive).

As a first mover, a company implements an innovative strategy that initiates a competitive challenge to which later movers will have to respond. A prime example, discussed later, is Motorola.

As a fast mover, a company sets in motion an innovative strategy as soon as it experiences an innovative competitive challenge. IBM's responses to a number of computer companies in the early 1960s and to the Apple personal computer around 1980 illustrate a fast mover.

As a slow mover, a company, for a significant period of time, attempts to meet a competitive challenge by using and reproducing its existing organizational structures and technological capabilities, but then, recognizing the sustained innovation inherent in the competitive challenge, shifts course by implementing an innovative investment strategy. The Ford Motor Company, which considerably altered its competitive capabilities in the 1980s after an initial failure to respond to the Japanese challenge in the late 1970s, is a good example of a slow mover.

As a no mover, in contrast, a company seeks to compete without upgrading its capabilities. It cannot or will not embark on an innovative strategy. General Motors in the 1970s and 1980s is a good example of a no mover.

Finally, as a remover, a company, when confronted by a competitive challenge, pursues a strategy of disinvesting from its industry. Many American companies that have been thrown into conglomerate structures have been the focus of the remover strategy. An example is the fate of the machine tool maker, Burgmaster, from the 1960s to the 1980s, when its investment strategy was being set by top management of the Houdaille conglomerate.

Given this spectrum of investment strategies ranging from anticipatory innovation (first movers) to disinvesting adaptation (removers), our analytical task is to explain (i) why the competitive challenges to American industry have been more sustained and effective in some industries rather than others since the 1960s, and (ii) why some American companies within those industries that have been most challenged have made innovative responses more quickly and more effectively than others. Such an analysis is obviously the work of a multiyear, multiperson research project that has yet to be done. Our purposes here are to outline a theoretical framework to guide such a project and to adduce some illustrative case material that suggests that, in using the organizational integration hypothesis for analyzing the dynamic interaction of investment strategy and organizational structure, we are focused on a central determinant of sustained competitive advantage.

3. *The Theory of the Innovative Enterprise*

To generate the higher quality, lower cost products that bring competitive advantage, an innovative enterprise (or enterprise group) must have an organizational structure to implement an innovative strategy to develop and utilize technology. The organizational integration hypothesis focuses on the social structure of the enterprise as a determinant of competitive advantage. To put this organizational structure in place and to sustain the learning process that this organizational structure must generate requires that strategic decision-makers have access to what we call 'financial commitment'.

Financial commitment represents the willingness of those who control financial resources to commit these resources to financing the high fixed costs of developmental investments that, because they entail innovation, promise uncertain returns (see Lazonick, 1992; Lazonick and O'Sullivan, 1995). Financial commitment plays a critical role in the innovation process because those who control money get to choose what type of strategy an enterprise will pursue. An innovative strategy inherently entails fixed costs because investments have to be made in physical and human capital with a time lag before the receipt of returns. These fixed costs are high because of not only the scale of investments but also the developmental period that (by definition) must occur before the investments that entail fixed costs can generate returns.

Those who control financial resources may or may not make strategic decisions that entail innovation—they may or may not act as entrepreneurs. Strategic decision-makers can, and often do, decide not to be innovative but to produce on the basis of resources that already exist within the company or that can be readily purchased on factor markets—what we have labeled an adaptive strategy. A necessary condition for innovation is that those who control financial resources choose innovative investment strategies rather that adaptive investment strategies.

They must, moreover, keep financial resources committed to the innovative strategy until the products and processes are sufficiently developed and utilized so that they generate returns. A failure to generate returns at any point in time may be a manifestation not of a failed strategy but of the need to commit even more financial resources to an ongoing learning process (Lazonick, 1993). To keep money committed to the innovative investment strategy, those who control money must have intimate knowledge of the problems and possibilities of the investment strategy, or entrust their money to strategic managers who have such knowledge.

Given the requisite financial commitment, a managerial organization is required to plan and coordinate the development of the specialized division of labor and the integration of the specialized productive activities required for an innovation to emerge. Competitive advantage requires a learning process that results in the generation over time of higher quality and/or lower cost products. We summarize the general attributes of the learning process as concentrated, continuous, cumulative and collective. Concentrated learning ensures that one focuses on the objects of productive transformation to acquire best-practice skills. Without concentrated learning, bad habits become routine. Continuous learning results in productivity enhancement in particular skills. Without continuous learning, acquired productivity in these skills decline, and the skills themselves atrophy. Cumulative learning permits new skills to build on the foundation of previously acquired skills. Without cumulative learning, previously unknown products and processes cannot be generated. Collective learning enables the planned coordination of specialized divisions of labor to develop complex technology and generate productivity. Without collective learning, specialized individuals cannot enhance their skills through communication with each another. Management's role is to ensure the concentration continuity, cumulativity, and collectivity of the learning process.

For innovation to occur, the combination of financial commitment (strategy) and organizational integration (structure) must result in the development of technology that yields higher quality products and the utilization of technology that yields lower unit costs. The development of technology entails the combination of machines, materials and labor in the learning process. Labor is the most critical input into the innovation process because it is the input that can potentially learn. Because of the concentrated, continuous, cumulative and collective character of the learning process, however, individuals cannot learn just as they please.

Central to the innovative strategy is investment in the capabilities of those people who comprise the specialized division of labor that management must plan and coordinate. Strategic decision-makers do not invest in all of the people whom they employ, but only in those people whom they expect to participate in the collective learning process. Strategic decision-makers do not want to invest in people who will leave the enterprise with their human assets. Nor do they want to invest in people who will use their voice within the enterprise to subvert rather than support the process of innovation.

Machines combine with labor to transform materials into products. Innovation in machinery is both skill-displacing and skill-augmenting. It is skill-displacing because certain productive capabilities that formerly resided in labor can now more effectively be performed by machines. It is skill-augmenting because innovation in machinery requires the application of new knowledge to develop the machinery and utilize it effectively in the production process. Machines can affect the productivity of a given product and the quality of the product produced. There is generally an intricate relation between innovation in materials and innovation in machines. Innovation in machines and materials both in turn depend on the complementary skills of manpower.

Materials are the substances that people as the providers of labor transform into products. As such, materials become embodied in work-in-process — components, parts and intermediate goods. An understanding of the character of these materials in their raw and semi-processed states is critical for the innovation process to take place.

A key innovation may entail the creation of new materials through chemistry or the blend of materials that enter the production process. The quality of materials and semi-processed inventories will affect not only the quality of the product but also the ways in which machines and labor are developed and utilized. In particular, high-throughput production processes require 'high-throughput' materials—that is, materials that do not cause machine stoppages and costly downtime. At the same time, costs are also increased by the wastage of materials because of the application of inadequate skills and inferior machinery in the production process.

Whatever the development of productive resources, an enterprise must have access to markets to utilize these resources. Markets provide the opportunity to generate returns on the investment in innovation. Management's role is not only to ensure the transformation of inputs into outputs but also to ensure that the resultant products are ones that buyers both want and can afford. Identification of markets, actual or potential, that can be served be the enterprise's technological capabilities is critical to the strategic decision-making process, while gaining access to new markets is central to the actual innovation process.

4. *The Japanese Challenge*

From the perspective of the American economy, the most formidable competitive challenges since the 1960s have come from the Japanese. These competitive challenges did not occur in those industries in which it was weakest but in industries devoted to the mass production of consumer durables—specifically, consumer electronics and automobiles—in which the USA led the world. To complement these strategies, the Japanese also developed a steel industry that far surpassed that of the USA in productivity. Initially undertaken as backward linkages from their sustained competitive advantage in consumer durables, the Japanese pursued effective innovative strategies in semiconductors and machine tools that eventually enabled these capital-goods industries to capture large shares of global markets. An understanding of the sources of Japanese competitive advantage requires an analysis of how financial commitment, organizational integration, and the development and utilization of technology differed in Japan and the USA, and why these differences have resulted in marked shifts in competitive advantage.

Financial Commitment

Innovation requires financial commitment so that high fixed-cost investments in physical and human resources can be transformed into high quality, low cost products. In Japan, before World War II, the prime source of financial commitment was the family firm. Continuous innovation came from owner-entrepreneurs who used their profits from one successful investment to fund the next investment. In mining, shipping, shipbuilding and steel, however, the innovative family firm was typically a 'house' of family members—the *zaibatsu*—which delegated operating control, and usually strategic decision-making as well, to professional managers. The *zaibatsu*, or their constituent companies, also provided funds to new ventures with varied success (Morikawa, 1992).

After World War II, under the American occupation, the *zaibatsu* were dissolved and shares dispersed among companies, financial institutions and individuals (Gerlach, 1992; Miyajima, 1994). When the Americans left, a movement began among Japanese enterprises engaged in long-term investment strategies to ensure that ownership stakes in their companies rested in the hands of stable shareholders—generally other companies and banks with whom they had long-term business relations—who would provide financial commitment. These stable shareholders did not, and still do not, sell their shares to public portfolio investors (for example, those who speculate on the Tokyo Stock Exchange). Nor do they demand high dividends. Stable shareholders instead ensure that company earnings remain under the control of the professional managers who run the enterprises, thus creating the financial commitment necessary for continuous innovation. It is through their business relations rather than through their equity stakes that stable shareholders actually share in the gains of innovation.

In the USA, owner-entrepreneurs have played the same role as in Japan in pursuing innovative investment strategies. Contrary to American folklore, new ventures have never been financed by the stock market. Rather, the stock market serves as a means for successful companies—ones that through innovation have transformed themselves from new ventures into going concerns—to permit the owner-entrepreneurs and their backers (venture capitalists) to monetize the productive assets that they have accumulated. This monetization occurs by the transfer of ownership rights from the original owner-entrepreneurs to portfolio investors willing to hold the shares of the companies that the entrepreneurs have built up (the following arguments are based on Lazonick, (1992, 1994) and Lazonick and O'Sullivan, (1995)).

As a result of the creation of a national market in industrial securities around the turn of the century, shares in the major American industrial corporations became widely distributed among wealth-holding households that would not and could not exercise strategic control over the corporations whose shares they now owned. Rather, legal ownership of the company was separated from control over strategic decision-making. The strategic decision-makers were professional managers, many of whom had the interest and ability to use the financial resources of their companies to engage in continuous innovation.

In Japan, strategic decision-making power was often, although not always, delegated to managers in the pre-World War II *zaibatsu*. Under these arrangements, enterprise earnings tended to be plowed back into new investments. Those who controlled money were professional managers who understood the opportunities and requirements of innovative investment strategies. The dissolution of the *zaibatsu* only increased the incentive and ability of top managers in Japan to engage in innovation.

In the USA, by contrast, the widespread distribution of shareholders left professional managers in positions of strategic decision-making power by default rather than design. This separation of ownership from control persisted well into the post-World War II decades. By virtue of professional careers spent primarily climbing up and around the managerial organization, these strategic decision-makers had an intimate knowledge of an enterprise's organization and technology. Possession of this knowledge enabled these top managers to evaluate the prospects for success of innovative investment strategies, while their own individual goals, shaped as they were by their professional careers and membership in the organization, gave them a bias in favor of innovating rather than adapting.

Over the past two decades or so, however, the rise of the institutional portfolio investor in the USA has permitted the concentration of share ownership. These new shareholders have been willing and able to extract earnings from existing industrial corporations, but without ensuring that this money would end up under the control of new organizations that are able and willing to engage in continuous innovation. In many industrial corporations, even when strategic decision-makers are not threatened with a loss of control over the allocation of financial resources, their backgrounds and their own financial portfolios lead them to identify more with immediate financial returns than with the long-term requirements of innovation.

In sum, even though from the late nineteenth century both Japan and the USA experienced a managerial revolution that persists to the present, the systems of corporate governance in the two nations have differed significantly. During the first half of this century, American top managers as strategic decision-makers controlled money and invested in innovation. The fragmentation of shareholders rendered owners impotent in influencing the choice of corporate strategy.

Since the 1950s, Japanese managers as strategic decision-makers have controlled money and have invested in innovation not because owners have been rendered impotent but because ownership is in the hands of business organizations that have a common interest in innovation. This pressure to invest in innovation has been increased by the ability of enterprise unions to ensure that a large proportion of the labor force has permanent employment status, and hence has an interest in the long-term prosperity of the enterprise.

Meanwhile, American managers as strategic decision-makers have progressively lost control over money, and have become less able and willing to invest in innovation. Increasingly, financial interests that seek to extract the returns of past investments—or, as some financial economists put it, to 'disgorge the free cash flow' (Jensen, 1989)—have gained influence and control over corporate strategy. At the same time, the declining power of the organized labor movement in the USA and the erosion of employment security within managerial structures themselves have reduced the number and power of stakeholders in the enterprise who have an interest in an innovative investment strategy or the ability to carry one out. The result has been a mounting tendency in American corporations to choose adaptive strategies that live off resources accumulated in the past rather than invest in innovation for the sake of future prosperity.

Organizational Integration

The shift in strategic decision-making from innovation to adaptation manifests the notion, prevalent in the USA but not in Japan, that the company is run for its owners. Yet, even in the USA during the period when share ownership was effectively separated from strategic control, companies were *de facto*, even if not *de jure*, run for the sake of their organizations—which in the USA meant their managerial structures (or what Galbraith (1967) called the 'technostructure').

Especially where complex technologies were the foundation of a corporation's competitive advantage and market dominance, a company required managerial structures to plan and coordinate the specialized divisions of labor of their enterprises. These highly collectivized managerial structures could engage in continuous and cumulative learning. It was this collective—or organizational—capability embodied in cohesive managerial structures that made the USA a formidable industrial power.

The key to creating these organizational capabilities was the long-term attachment of managerial employees to the enterprise—similar in practice to what the Japanese call 'permanent employment'. American companies recruited graduates of colleges or professional schools to begin their careers as lower level specialists within the managerial structure. Subsequently, management development programs transferred the most promising specialists around the organization and promoted them up the managerial hierarchy. By giving these employees a broader understanding of company operations and by placing them in positions of increasing authority and responsibility, the management development programs gradually transformed a portion of the specialists into generalists who could plan and coordinate the specialized divisions of labor under their control. After two or three decades with the company, a small number of these generalists would reach top management positions where they would assume control over strategic decision-making. This system of career-long employment and advancement not only transformed specialists into generalists but also worked as a powerful motivator for specialists and generalists alike to identify with the goals of the enterprise. Given the separation of ownership from control, it was this integration of highly skilled individuals into the organization as a collectivity that was the essence of the managerial revolution in the USA (Lazonick, 1986).

As both cause and effect of the movement from innovative to adaptive investment strategies in the USA, organizational integration of the managerial structure has been breaking down. At the top, strategic managers, rewarded with exceedingly high pay and valuable stock options, have been under pressure to show high earnings and pay out high dividends in the short run at the expense of long-run investments in innovation. With the turn from innovation to adaptation, strategic managers cease to consider the long-term attachment of skilled personnel to the organizational as a costly-to-replace organizational asset but simply as an immediate expense that drags down earnings. Short-term relations with consultants, contractors and employees become viewed as essential to 'flexibility'. These relations may permit flexibility in maintaining high corporate earnings. They do not, however, provide flexibility for shifting from one innovation to the next as a continuous process.

From this perspective on the rise and decline of US managerial capitalism, the formidable organizational capabilities that the Japanese have put in place reflect a more thoroughgoing elaboration of an earlier US model rather than a wholly new departure in internal organization. The Japanese corporations have elaborated American managerial capitalism of an earlier era into a more collective capitalism by developing long-term relations with employees not only in the managerial structure but also on the shop floor. In terms of mode of payment (salaries and shares in the gains of innovation) and employment conditions (permanent tenure and skill development), male blue-collar workers in major Japanese corporations are in much the same position as managerial employees in both Japanese and American enterprises. Similarly, the long-term relationship between major Japanese corporations and their suppliers and distributors—that is, with vertically related, but legally distinct, firms—is today even stronger than the relationship between American corporations and their managerial employees. Japanese enterprises are more organizationally integrated than American enterprises, and it is this superior organizational integration that is the key to the competitive success of Japanese industry.

Organizationally integrated relations with shop-floor workers and vertically related enterprises permit Japanese managers to plan and coordinate specialized divisions of labor in ways that are unattainable for most American managers, who at best have access to collective capabilities only within the managerial structure. As a result, Japanese managers can contemplate innovative investment strategies that are not realistic options for strategic decision-makers in typical US enterprises even when their managerial organizations are integrated and intact. As an elaboration of the organizational principles of American managerial capitalism, Japanese collective capitalism creates very different possibilities for the development and utilization of productive resources.

The Development and Utilization of Productive Resources

American industry became dominant in the world economy during the era when the separation of ownership from control characterized those corporations engaged in continuous innovation. The American ideology was, and remains, that the managers (in many cases tens of thousands of them) were but the agents of the owners (as 'principals'), and that 'hourly workers' were interchangeable units of a commodity called labor. Consistent with the ideology of the 'hourly worker', the innovative strategies of most major US corporations have entailed massive investments in the capabilities of employees within the managerial structure but do not typically include investing in the skills of shop-floor workers. Because of a historical legacy of conflict with craft labor over the utilization of new technology, American managers became obsessed with taking skills off the shop floor, vesting them instead in managerial (professional, technical and administrative) employees and the machines that these managerial employees designed, installed and repaired (Lazonick, 1990, Chs 7–10).

This investment strategy worked in the first half of this century. In industries based on complex technology, the companies that made the innovative investments in organizational capabilities within the managerial structure gained sustained competitive advantage. Particularly in science-based electrical and chemical industries, critical organizational capabilities resided in the corporate laboratories put in place to engage in continuous innovation. In the 1920s those companies that had emerged as dominant used their sustained competitive advantages to gain the cooperation of non-unionized shop-floor labor by offering them more employment security and higher wages than they could get elsewhere in the economy. During the

Great Depression of the 1930s, the gains of the 1920s were used to keep managerial structures and their capabilities for continuous innovation intact. In the 1940s and 1950s, sustained competitive advantage was used, as in the 1920s, to gain the cooperation of shop-floor workers, but under the changed conditions of institutionalized collective bargaining with the new mass-production unions.

The American investment strategy began to break down when the Japanese built organizational capabilities not only within the managerial structure but also on the shop floor. In a nation that embarked on a mission of industrialization without a legacy of craft skills, Japanese companies never had to confront craft unions over the utilization of new technology. In sharp contrast to American investment strategies that were bent on taking skills off the shop floor, a prime focus of the investment strategies of Japanese companies was to develop skills on the shop floor. For this reason, Japanese companies have always invested in the skills of those blue-collar workers who were committed to the paid labor force (that is, males).

To protect these investments in human assets, Japanese companies have extended to those shop-floor employees in whom they have invested permanent membership in the organization on a par with most managerial employees. In the post-World War II period, the rise of enterprise unions made this permanent membership explicit in the form of the widely recognized, even if non-contractual, practice of permanent employment. The other side of the same collective coin is the subordinate position of ownership rights to membership rights in the Japanese corporation (Dore, 1990, Afterword). The Japanese company is run for its employees, not for its owners, because it is recognized that it is the employees as a collectivity who constitute the unique competitive assets that the company possesses. That these assets include the skills of shop-floor workers has permitted the Japanese to develop and utilize materials and machines in ways that are not compatible with the organizational capabilities of most American companies, even when the capabilities of their managerial structures have remained intact (Lazonick, 1990, Chs 9–10).

From the industrial revolution in the Lowell textile mills and the advent of the 'American system of manufactures' in the Springfield Armory, Americans pioneered mass production methods that embodied the strength and skill requirements of production in machines. The innovations in machinery displaced the skills of craft workers on the shop floor. At the same time, the integrated character of these innovations created demands for engineering skills that could be systematically applied in one factory after another, and for managerial coordination to ensure high rates of utilization of the investments in expensive machines and highly trained personnel.

The American system of mass production evolved over decades not only within industrial sectors but also through the intersectoral transfer of mass-production technologies (Hounshell, 1984; Thomson, 1989). At every stage, the design of machinery reflected the managerial goal of taking skills off the shop floor. At the same time, ever more formidable organizational capabilities were put in place within the managerial structures of the major corporations to develop new technologies and ensure their utilization.

The Japanese confronted these capabilities head on. In the decades after World War I they took on the once-dominant British economy in cotton textiles—an industry in which the UK had continued to dominate global competition before the war (Lazonick and Mass, 1993). In the decades after World War II, they took on the USA not, as we have already mentioned, in those industries in which the Americans were weakest but, on the contrary, in those industries—steel, consumer electronics and automobiles—in which the USA had reigned supreme. Nor was it a 'miracle' that Japan was able to challenge the USA in these industries after World War II. Japan had already accomplished much the same feat in cotton textiles against the British before World War II, and had, in the process, built up technical capabilities that could be transferred to the higher value-added industries.

What had enabled the Japanese to challenge the British so successfully were their investments from the 1870s in engineering skills that could be embodied in new technologies on the shop floor. And what made the Japanese challenge to the USA so successful was the combination of investments in engineering skills (in which the Americans had invested as well) and complementary shop-floor skills. Indeed, it is widely recognized that the ability of engineers to interact with shop-floor workers has been key to Japanese success in introducing and making effective use of flexible manufacturing systems in such industries as automobiles and consumer electronics (Hayes, 1981; Jaikumar, 1986). Such organizational integration of technical skills has also been key to the success of the Japanese in rapid product development (Clark and Fujimoto, 1991). In the USA, the failure to invest in the skills of shop-floor workers and the deeply entrenched segmentation between management (including engineers) and labor have posed formidable constraints on companies in utilizing advanced machine technologies.

The emphasis in the development of US manufacturing methods has been on the attainment of high levels of throughput by integrating the strength and skill requirements of the production process into the capabilities of machines. The high-throughput potential of these machines cannot be realized, however, without materials of sufficient durability and flexibility to undergo processing at high speed without breaking. Hence the need for American mass-producers to integrate the preparation of key materials into the process of planned coordination in order to ensure such consistently high quality.

Typically, American companies have achieved such integration through in-house producers, leaving it to external suppliers to supply materials that can be produced subject to standard specifications and that do not require further transformation by high-throughput machinery. In the preparation of those materials that are integral to high-throughput methods, however, the lack of skills on the American shop-floor makes it difficult to control for quality, and hence large inventories are required to ensure that enough materials of sufficiently high quality are constantly available to avoid disruptions to the flow of work. Any such disruptions are particularly serious in the American context, moreover, because shop-floor workers typically have neither the skills nor the prerogative to determine the source of quality problems.

The absence of inventories in Japanese just-in-time production systems means that defective materials can stop the entire flow of work. Such stoppages are minimized, however, by the production of materials of consistent quality, while stoppages that do occur serve as sources of improved flow over time because the skills of shop-floor workers permit speedy and effective intervention. In the USA, even when materials consistently meet the quality test for high-throughput processing, this absence of shop-floor skills and initiative often means that defective materials are not detected in the production process but are built into the final product.

The Japanese have been much more adept than the Americans at materials innovation because of relations with workers and suppliers that integrate their activities into the learning process of the organization. This organizational integration enables the Japanese to produce materials of more consistent quality, and hence enhances their ability to utilize high-throughput machinery with a minimum of materials wastage. As the Japanese have demonstrated in the implementation of just-in-time inventory systems, processed materials of consistent quality permit higher throughput without constant human interventions and without requiring large buffer inventories of these materials.

The engineering capabilities required to make the Japanese production system work rely on not only the analytical skills of professional engineers but also, as in the case of statistical quality control, the complementary, organizationally integrated, analytical skills of workers both on the shop floor and in vertically related enterprises. It is this lack of organizational integration in the USA that has inhibited the effective utilization of computer programmable machinery in American industry, in sharp contrast with its flexible use in Japanese industry (Jaikumar, 1986).

Especially in the more capital-intensive industries where high through-put is more critical to achieving low unit costs, the American system permitted competitive advantage during the first half of the century, de-spite the high wages of even unskilled American workers. Among man-power organized within the management structure, the Americans had developed the organizational capabilities to develop and utilize high-throughput machinery. American management then combined these high-throughput machines with abundant supplies of high-quality (but expensive) materials and unskilled immigrants, and then, increasingly, African-American labor.

Over the past few decades, however, the American system has been unable to sustain its competitive advantages of the past. Through indigenous innovation in the combination of labor, machines and materials, Japanese management generated a concentrated, continuous, cumulative and collect-ive learning process that, as it developed, increasingly challenged the Ameri-can system in terms of productivity and cost. To be sure, lower wages and interest rates in Japan helped their enterprises to capture markets before they had achieved the high levels of productivity of the Americans. But, as recent years have shown, the continuous development of productive capabilities in Japan, compared with relatively stagnant productivity growth in the USA, has enabled the Japanese to gain competitive advantage over the Americans even with similar factor prices.

Well into the twentieth century, the USA used tariff protection to enable its domestic industries to substitute for cheaper foreign products. Throughout the twentieth century, Japan has done the same, although it has supplemented tariff protection with many other trade barriers ranging from restrictions on the size of retail outlets to content requirements to quotas (Prestowitz, 1988). In the cases of both the USA and Japan, this import substitution strategy permitted enterprises and industries to engage in indigenous in-novation, and thereby ultimately replace import substitution with export expansion.

The principle of privileged access to markets has also been used within national economies to foster indigenous innovation. Dominant enterprises can restrict demand for products to particular firms, thus giving these firms the incentive to invest in innovation. In Japan, such privileged access to markets has been integral to the operation of enterprise groups. A prime example of such privileged access in the USA during the 1980s was IBM's relations with Intel in microprocessors and Microsoft in software that gave these suppliers greater resources and incentives to invest in innovation. The main difference between the two nations is that in the USA the ideology of ownership has created fissures between the vertically related enterprises when the innovative strategies of the upstream enterprises—in this case Intel and Microsoft—have achieved success, whereas in Japan the ideology of membership means that, within the enterprise group structure, the success of the innovative strategy is used to strengthen the position of the vertically related partners in competing for markets with domestic and foreign rivals (Ferguson, 1990).

Ultimately, however, whatever the source of privileged access to markets, the ability to capture these markets depends on the building of organizational capabilities within enterprises and industries. These organizational capabilities can in turn enable enterprises and industries to shift from old markets to new. In the USA, this capability was the essence of the multidivisional organizational structure that major industrial corporations put in place from the 1920s. These multidivisional structures permitted these companies to generate economies of scope to complement economies of scale (Chandler, 1962). Within the enterprise group structure, Japanese companies typically set up distinct enterprises to service markets in new industries. Given that these new firms maintain membership in the enterprise group, the Japanese can attain the same benefits of the multidivisional structure by sharing certain organizational capabilities (e.g. research or marketing facilities) across firms.

Where the Japanese differ markedly from the Americans, however, is in pushing economies of scope down to the shop floor. The Japanese system of production, with its integration of engineering and shop-floor skills, has made it possible to use the same plant to manufacture products for a number of different market segments of an industry. Speedy ('single digit' for less than ten minutes) changeovers allow Japanese industrial plants to shift flexibly from one product variety to another. In some industries, such as automobiles, engineers have structured the production process so that, in conjunction with shop-floor skills, many different product varieties can be produced simultaneously on the same machines. American companies, with their traditional segmentation between management and workers, have been unable to generate such shop-floor economies of scope (Best, 1990; Fruin, 1992).

5. Corporate Strategies: From First Movers to Removers

For any given industry, the organizational integration hypothesis contends that those enterprises that are first movers or fast movers already have in place an organizationally integrated structure that is appropriate to the current demands of innovation in that industry. Conversely, the hypothesis predicts that enterprises that have organizational structures that are inadequately integrated to respond to innovative competitive challenges will pursue no mover or remover strategies. A corollary of the hypothesis is that enterprises that transform their organizational structures to put in place the organizational integration required to respond to competitive challenges will be slow movers. Within this framework of the interaction of strategy and structure in the innovation process, a particularly important research challenge is to determine why some companies in an industry are slow movers while others are no movers, since neither type of enterprise possesses the appropriate organizational integration when the innovative challenge first manifests itself.

At the company level, the research agenda inherent in the organizational integration hypothesis requires data generated from a large number of comparative case studies of enterprises within particular industries and within particular nations. That systemic research lies ahead. In what follows, we shall illustrate the organizational integration hypothesis at the level of the enterprise through brief examples of American companies that have been first movers, fast movers, slow movers, no movers and removers.

First Mover

The case of Motorola provides substantial evidence that supports the hypothesis that organizational integration encouraged and permitted the company to choose a first-mover strategy. From its early base in mobile electronics, Motorola built a tradition of first-mover innovation. It had carried through three major shifts in its core business: in the 1960s from car radios to televisions and audio equipment, in the 1970s from consumer electronics to semiconductors and in the 1980s from commodity semiconductors to specialty semiconductors and telecommunications devices.

Motorola grew out of the Galvin Manufacturing Company, founded in 1928 by Paul V. Galvin, father of current Motorola executive committee chairman Robert Galvin. For the first four decades of its history, Motorola focused on consumer electronics. The Chicago-based firm's earliest products were alternating electrical current converters and automobile radios (in 1930 Motorola introduced the world's first car radio). Paul Galvin dubbed the radio he developed the 'Motorola' (from motor and victrola), and in 1947 that became the company's name.

In later decades, Motorola went on to develop an array of consumer products, including home audio equipment and television sets. Then, in the early 1970s, as it met mounting Japanese competition, Motorola deliberately migrated from consumer electronics markets to high-technology industrial electronics. Today, it sells $16 billion worth of electronic devices, including two-way private radio equipment, cellular telephones, pagers, microprocessors and other semiconductor devices, integrated networking systems, microcomputers, and automotive and industrial electronics. It leads world markets in several product lines: its cellular telephones are number one worldwide; it is the world's leading supplier of pagers, two-way radios and advanced dispatch systems for commercial fleets. It has also accumulated a portfolio of radio frequencies, operating paging services in Brazil and Hong Kong, cellular systems in Chile and Israel, and taxi-dispatch frequencies in the USA (where it is the largest operator) and Japan (where it is the second-largest operator).

To achieve these innovative transitions, Motorola had to become an accomplished self-cannibalizer. Its early car radio used the amplitude modulation (AM) system. In 1940, however, founder Paul Galvin enticed University of Connecticut professor Daniel Noble, a pioneer of a new transmission technique called frequency modulation (FM), to the company. As soon as possible, Motorola introduced FM across its product line, and FM became a strong competitor for AM.

But Motorola took FM much further. Mastery of FM technology allowed Motorola to enter the two-way radio business, and the firm sold millions of Handie-Talkies to the Army during World War II, enabling US soldiers to communicate without stringing wires in the field. After the war, Motorola expanded the uses of two-way radios by installing them in police cars and taxis.

More recently, again under pressure from Japanese competition, Motorola has moved from commodity semiconductors to higher-value microprocessors, used by Apple in its PCs, and specialized chips, which control everything from car engines and airbags to home appliances. Motorola is currently tackling Intel's PC-microprocessor monopoly with its PowerPC chip, designed jointly with IBM. In addition, its pager business is experiencing explosive growth. In 1991, Motorola sold 100,000 pagers to China; in 1992, 1 million; and in 1993, about 3 million, many manufactured in a new plant in Tianjin.

These transitions were not merely reactions to changing external circumstances, nor were they forced on Motorola by desperate competition. Business analyst James O'Toole (1985, 1991) commented on the proactive character of one of the most critical of these shifts, that out of consumer electronics:

> What must be appreciated is that Galvin made his shift proactively. There was no crisis at Motorola; the company and industry appeared to be in good shape. Galvin did something highly unusual for an American executive — he anticipated the need for future change even though the company was not in any imminent trouble.

In the early 1970s, Robert Galvin decided to 'bet the company' in the drive to make Motorola number one in semiconductors and retain the top spot in two-way communications over the coming ten years. Along with a new business mix, Motorola decentralized management while simultaneously building up internal controls, established a long-term-oriented New Enterprise operation, introduced new personnel programs and committed employees to very high quality standards (the formal goal was zero defects).

Several unusual features of Motorola's business practice account for its ability to innovate so aggressively, according to company leaders. First, almost every top executive is a trained engineer. Chief executive George Fisher, himself a PhD in applied mathematics, recently noted, 'As fast as technology moves today, there's an advantage that the leadership of the company is comfortable with the technology . . . You have to have a basic love of [technology]' (quoted by Slutsker, 1993).

Second, Motorola offers its entire workforce—including shop-floor workers —virtually lifetime employment, after a suitable qualifying period. This policy reflects more than a corporate-welfare philosophy, although under the leadership of two Galvin generations, Motorola's management had worked to build a humane and democratic work environment. For example, Motorola long ago replaced the time-clock system, and in 1947 instituted an employee profit-sharing program for its 2000 employees. Motorola's management believes that this commitment from the company allows Motorola and its workers to accumulate the experience and skills needed to master complex manufacturing technologies and stay on top of quality-improvement techniques. According to Motorola's corporate vice president for training and education, and president of Motorola University, William Wiggenhorn (1990, p. 75):

> When Motorola hired people in the old days, we hired them for life. People grew up in their jobs, acquired competencies and titles, moved from work force to management. All employees became members of our Service Club at the end of ten years, which meant we wouldn't terminate them except for poor performance or dishonesty. We never gave anyone an absolute right to lifetime employment, but we did provide an unmistakable opportunity to stay. This was the employment model that built the corporation and made it successful, and we believed the loyalty it inspired gave us added value.

Third, Motorola coupled its permanent employment practices to an extensive program of internal training. The company did not simply recruit fully trained workers to fill the slots created as it entered new businesses; it trained workers and retrained its own workforce. Eventually, it established its own substantial in-house training facility, the Motorola University. Again, Wiggenhorn (1990, p. 75) explained:

> We hadn't yet realized in the early 1980s that there was going to be a skill shortage, but we clearly needed to upgrade our training. A lot of our competitors, especially in the semiconductor business, hired people, used their skills, terminated them when their skills were out of date, then hired new people with new skills. But we had plants where 60% to 70% of the workers were Service Club members.

> We didn't want to break a model that had worked for 50 years, but we had some people who thought that if they made that ten-year mark they could mentally retire, and that was an attitude we have to fix. In the end, we had to let people know that 'poor performance' included an unwillingness to change. We had to abandon paternalism for shared responsibility.

This extra training enabled Motorola to develop new businesses and to introduce new quality- and productivity-enhancing techniques that relied on extensive shop-floor responsibility. Workers at the Arlington Heights former radio-assembly plant outside Chicago, for example, were retrained to build cellular telephones and to assume responsibility not just for one or two assembly functions but also for quality control, flexible manufacturing and mentoring the several thousand new hires needed for the new product lines. To persuade newer workers to make the learning commitment necessary to make the transition, Motorola mobilized the involvement of older workers. According to Wiggenhorn (1990, p. 78),

> We videotaped older employees within a few years of retirement and had them say to others their own age and younger: 'Look, we're not going to get out of here without learning new skills. We need to go back to class. Back in 1955, we had another moment of truth when we had to move from tubes to transistors. We did it then; we can do it now.'

Fourth, Motorola moved much earlier than other US electronics firms to involve its suppliers and customers in company programs, and to build long-term relationships with them. Suppliers and customers are encouraged to participate in company training programs, including the most advanced programs at Motorola University. In the same vein, Motorola insists that all of its suppliers either apply for, or have plans to apply for, the Baldridge quality awards.

Fifth, and probably as a consequence of the above practices, Motorola has been willing and able to plan for the long-term, especially in research and development. Sony chairman Akio Morita, a frequent critic of US business practice, and especially of US management's short-term focus, is an admirer of Motorola. In particular, Morita congratulates Motorola for its long-term emphasis: 'It has kept up a strong emphasis on R&D, and it is willing to invest in research for the long term'.

This long-term emphasis paid off at the beginning of the 1990s with the launch of Motorola's acclaimed MicroTac cellular telephone, which was much smaller and lighter than any rival's product, and won back the lead for Motorola in an extremely competitive market. No competitor has so far copied Motorola's product. But Motorola invested more than $100 million over 10 years to develop MicroTac, before it delivered any return. Such investments are the hallmark of a first-mover innovator. In summary, there is substantial evidence that organizational integration of strategic decision-makers, technical specialists, shop-floor employees and suppliers was a basis of Motorola's success.

Fast Mover

By contrast to Motorola, IBM did not usually take the lead in introducing new products but did respond rapidly to innovative competitive challenges. As the technological and market leader in computers for most of the post-war period, IBM frequently confronted the problem of being forced to cannibalize its own established sales base to maintain its dominance. That is, to introduce new generations of technology, IBM was compelled to undermine its own sales of previously successful products. Not surprisingly, therefore, IBM was often not the first to introduce new technology or to precipitate a shift to new generations of computers. Nevertheless, at least until the 1980s, IBM usually moved rapidly to dominate those fields as they opened.

By the 1970s IBM's sales were larger than those of all other computer companies in the world combined. At the end of World War II, however the world's leading computer company was not IBM, but Rand. Rand's most famous machine, UNIVAC, was the very image of computers and high technology for most Americans in the 1950s. IBM's founder, Thomas J. Watson, was determined, however, to push his company to leadership of the rapidly expanding computer industry. IBM began selling electronic business calculators in the 1940s, and in 1952 introduced its first vacuum-tube-based scientific computer, the 701. This machine was followed two years later by the 702, an electronic computer designed to replace accounting-department punch-card machines.

IBM did not gain technological leadership in the computer industry until the late 1950s, after Tom Watson Jr became chief executive. Watson Jr recruited Emanuel Piore, former head of the Office of Naval Research, to become IBM chief scientist. He also increased research spending from about 15 per cent of net income in the 1940s to 35 per cent in the 1950s, and then to a staggering 50 percent by the 1960s and 1970s (Ferguson and Morris, 1993). This extraordinary and sustained commitment to research propelled IBM to scientific leadership of the field, and enabled IBM to respond effectively to several waves of challenge from potential entrants.

Perhaps the most striking example of IBM's fast-mover strategy was its decision in 1965 to launch the System/360 series mainframe computers. These machines cemented IBM's position as the industry's dominant player for almost two decades. The firm's objective with the 360 series was to achieve a breakthrough that at a single stroke would make all other computers obsolete, including the thousands of its own machines leased to hitherto-contented customers.

IBM's decision to launch the 360 called for prodigious technological and financial resources. IBM leaders believed, however, that the risk was essential if looming competition was to be forestalled. A growing number of companies, including Philco, GE, RCA, Rand and Control Data, were selectively targeting niches in which IBM's products were becoming outdated, even though IBM had pioneered most of the computer technologies then on the market. In addition, the growing role of software in product development (up from 8 percent of the value of a system to 40 percent) meant that substantial advantages could be gained from introducing a machine that offered compatibility across a wide range of functions. The 360 allowed IBM to do just that. With the 360, customers were able to use compatible software on any IBM machine, from a small $2500-per-month calculator up to an $115,000-per-month monster. For the first time, moreover, customers could transfer software to new hardware when they upgraded.

These benefits were not gained easily. The 360 was a corporate gamble almost without precedent. Its engineering alone required investment of $750 million, IBM had to add 60,000 new employees to build it and five major new factories had to be opened at a cost of $4.5 billion. Ferguson and Morris (1993, pp. 8–9) describe the magnitude of technical difficulties IBM encountered:

> The technical challenges were stupendous, and worse, were layered one on top of the other. The 360 was the first computer to use a hybrid integrated circuit—a way station to full integration—as a base technology. But no one had ever manufactured integrated circuits on the scale and at the quality level the 360 demanded. There was no recourse but for IBM, which had always bought almost all its electronic components, to create its own integrated circuit factories—at three times the cost of any previous computer factory—and create brand-new process technologies for the manufacture of integrated circuits on a mass scale.
>
> Every peripheral component in the IBM product line had to be redesigned to assure the target compatibility throughout the series. More important, the software for the 360 series had to be consistent up and down the entire line. But that required millions of lines of code, the largest

software program that had ever been written, and all under terrible time pressures. The cost overruns were appalling. At one point, when $600 million of inventory had been 'lost', seemingly unfathomable metallurgical problems were shutting down the integrated circuit factories, and the huge software project was hopelessly bollixed, Watson admitted being close to panic, beset by fears that he had destroyed his father's company.

But the project worked. Indeed, it eventually became an enormous success, and devastated IBM's competitors. For years to come, no other firm could muster the resources needed to duplicate, let alone better, IBM's effort. The story of how IBM amassed and focused those immense human and financial resources is the key to understanding how it built its decades-long dominance of the industry.

First and foremost, management had to be able to commit the overwhelming majority of all corporate earnings, as well as most accumulated assets, to the project. That commitment had then to be sustained over several years, in spite of a growing uncertainty, at times bordering on despair, about the project's potential for success. This reinvestment of earnings meant that shareholders had to be denied immediate dividends and the comfort of steadily rising returns.

On top of financial commitment, IBM had to call upon extraordinary effort from its legions of engineers and scientists. It also had to create an entirely new manufacturing organization, both to supply parts and to assemble the finished products. The fact that IBM had gone further than almost any other company in its day toward what was to become known as the Japanese ideal of 'permanent employment' for all employees was vital to securing the commitment of the scientists and engineers as well as shop-floor workers. At IBM, the tacit promise of lifetime employment extended beyond management circles to virtually all members of the company. It was organizational integration that enabled IBM to undertake an innovative project of this enormous magnitude, by bringing, for example, virtually all component manufacturing in-house.

The result was almost total control of the world's fastest-growing industry for 20 years. Most competitors, having fallen behind and lacking the organizational integration needed to catch up, were reduced to manufacturing clone products or peripheral devices that could be plugged into IBM's machines. IBM's annual sales soared to $7 billion by 1970, and continued to grow by an average of more than 15 percent each year. IBM became the largest and most profitable industrial enterprise in history.

By comparison, IBM's entry into personal computers in the early 1980s was a much smaller undertaking. Nevertheless, that move too followed a similar fast-mover pattern. Smaller, entrant firms had opened a new market

—one in which IBM did not yet offer any product—and were beginning to gain share. The basic technology needed to compete, however, was easily within IBM's reach, and its organizational capabilities allowed it to respond quickly to the challenge. In August 1981, within a year after deciding to enter the personal-computer industry, IBM launched its PC. This machine, like the 360 in mainframes, soon established itself as the dominant architecture. Other firms were again forced to compete for almost a decade by offering clones or add-on products. Our contention is that, as in the 1960s, organizational integration permitted IBM's fast-mover response.

Slow Movers

The recent history of the automobile industry in the USA stands in sharp contrast to the determined innovation seen in computers. It is a tale of slow, or no, response to innovative challenges, and consequent loss of competitiveness. Yet it was not always so. As late as the end of the 1960s, the USA enjoyed an export surplus in automobiles, and imports accounted for a negligible proportion of cars sold on the home market. By the late 1980s, however, more than 30 per cent of automobiles sold in the USA were produced overseas, and the nation suffered a substantial trade deficit in the industry. The experience of the US auto makers in attempting to respond to the rise of foreign competition, especially from Japanese producers, provides instructive examples of the contrast between 'slow mover' and 'no mover' strategies. Ford Motor Company can be classed as a 'slow mover', while General Motors responded so inadequately for most of the 1980s that it was effectively a 'no mover'. Their divergent reactions to competitive challenges underscore both the limits imposed by lack of integration on the choice of corporate response and the vital importance of appropriate integration of shop-floor workers, engineers and suppliers in an industry.

Automobiles are extraordinarily complex products. A typical new model will include 15,000 parts, many (if not most) produced by external suppliers. Manufacturing automobiles in volume calls for the development and coordination of a wide range of skills, teams and technologies. General Motors, the world's largest automobile company, employs about 1 million workers worldwide, including roughly 300,000 in supplier companies.

The American manufacturers' problems first surfaced in the mid-1970s in the form of cost disadvantages in smaller vehicles, but soon spread to widening lags in quality and product design. In the 1980s the American industry as a whole suffered a shrinking market share as Japanese manufacturers successfully enticed nearly one in every three American car buyers to its products, and at one or other time during the decade all of the US companies faced heavy losses.

Ford's problems reached a crisis point at the end of the 1970s. During the three-year period beginning in 1980, Ford Motor Company lost $3.3 billion, an amount equal to 43 percent of its total net worth. These were the largest losses ever by a US corporation. For the industry as a whole, the crisis deepened in the 1980s. Between 1982 and 1992, North American employment at GM, Ford and Chrysler fell by 18 percent, from 717,000 to 593,000. The three companies together closed fifty-four assembly, engine or components plants. In 1991 they lost a total of $10 billion in their North American businesses.

Even by the early 1980s, however, the signs of impending crisis had been apparent for almost a decade. Yet until the crisis of 1980, the Big Three had chosen to continue as if business would soon return to 'normal'. Only after its near collapse between 1980 and 1983 did Ford resolve to change course. Billions of dollars in unnecessary costs were cut from overhead; but billions more were committed to capital spending. The workforce was reduced from 500,000 to 370,000; but at the same time Ford's management strove determinedly, and ultimately successfully, to end its traditionally acrimonious labor relations. Shop-floor quality and productivity were pushed to the forefront. Slowly but surely, Ford's automobiles improved and costs were whittled down. At the end of the decade, Ford's position looked hopeful. After 1982 Ford's share of the US car market grew from 17 percent to 20 percent, and by 1994 the cost-efficiency of its operations was reported to be within striking distance of Toyota and Honda.

How did Ford achieve this turnaround? Part of the explanation lies in the fact that Ford deliberately learned from Mazda, its Japanese partner (in which it has a 25 percent stake). In his chronicle of Ford's recovery, *Turnaround: The New Ford Motor Company*, Robert L. Shook (1990, p. 83) notes that Ford's management went to Japan to study how that country's car makers succeeded:

> To their surprise, they discovered that the superiority of the Japanese auto makers was not achieved by higher levels of automation and advanced technology. *It was not machines but people that made the difference in quality and productivity* [emphasis in original]. It also became obvious that the Japanese workers were not superior to American workers. The difference was how the Japanese workers were managed.

Ford moved to the Japanese-inspired principles of continuous improvement, just-in-time, total quality management, quality circles and employee involvement (Ingrassia and White, 1994, pp. 137–142). But to make these practices effective, Ford's managers had to transform radically their relationship with the company's workforce. Shook (1990, p. 84) describes Ford's traditional approach:

> For years a pervasive 'us' and 'them' syndrome had existed in Ford. In fact, it had been nurtured. A well-defined line between management and labor prevailed. The segregation between white- and blue-collar workers was clearly intentional. Workers considered managers uncaring and callous. And to the managers, workers were people who lacked motivation and took no pride in their work, who could contribute with their backs only, never with their brains. Little if any responsibility was delegated to workers.

These attitudes had to be abandoned if Japanese continuous improvement techniques were to be given a chance to succeed. Ford initiated what it called 'employee involvement'. Through the 1980s, Ford's top management began to include shop-floor workers in decision-making, and to seek their input into productivity improvement. These initiatives represented the first steps toward integrating the shop-floor workforce into the firm.

Similarly, Ford moved to integrate its suppliers more into its operations. Management shifted away from arm's-length relationships with its suppliers toward longer-term contracts and more trusting interactions. Susan Helper (1991) described the change as a move from 'exit-based' to 'voice-based' relationships. This transformation allowed Ford to lean more on its suppliers for new technology, shortening lead times in product development and raising the capabilities of just-in-time operations. By the end of the decade, Ford made only 50 percent of the content of its cars internally, whereas GM continued to produce 70 percent in-house.

Another part of the explanation for Ford's turnaround lies in the fact that its management retained substantial control over the firm's financial resources and used them to support the major capital investment programs needed to upgrade Ford's manufacturing technology. Fortunately, Ford did not follow financial economist Michael Jensen's advice that 'for a company to operate efficiently and maximize value, free cash flow must be distributed to shareholders rather than retained' (Jensen, 1989, p. 66). Indeed, Jensen singled out Ford as a 'vivid example' of the failure of management to 'disgorge' cash to its shareholders. He pointed to Ford as a company in which

> the senior management . . . sits on nearly $15 billion in cash and marketable securities in an industry with excess capacity. Ford's management has been deliberating about acquiring financial service companies, aerospace companies, or making some other multibillion-dollar diversification move —rather than deliberating about effectively distributing Ford's excess cash to its owners so they can decide how to reinvest it.

Rather than follow Jensen's advice, Ford management safeguarded the company's future by using the cash it accumulated during the few good years of the mid-1980s to upgrade its technological and organizational capabilities and to make provision for future competitive battles in the 1990s. New machines, new training programs and support for suppliers all cost money. So, too, in the automobile industry, does ensuring that potential customers can gain access to credit to buy the final product and ensuring that the firm can ride out future downturns, while implementing new-product-development programs. Ford not only committed its financial resources to invest for the future, but also transformed relationships within its organization to ensure that these investments would yield innovative results.

No Mover

General Motors' reaction to rising Japanese competition was quite different to that of Ford. Of the US Big Three, General Motors made the least fundamental alterations to its organizational arrangements in the 1980s. It did not move to integrate its shop-floor workforce into significant continuous-improvement programs and continued arm's-length relations with its suppliers. The consequence was an inability to raise productivity and quality. By the early 1990s GM was in the weakest position of the Big Three. In spite of the fact that it entered the 1980s as the low-cost American producer (largely a result of its superior scale), by the end of the decade GM was the highest-cost producer. In the decade following 1982, GM lost nine points of domestic market share—the equivalent of $13 billion in retail sales in a normal year. In 1991 GM lost $4.5 billion, after a $4.1 billion write-off in the previous years. In 1992 GM began to delay new-model programs to conserve cash, further undermining efforts to produce innovative new products that could win back alienated customers.

GM's underlying problem, however, was not simple complacency. During the 1980s, GM was a virtual maelstrom of feverish activity: new technology programs, the acquisition of Ross Perot's EDS, large acquisitions of overseas producers, a dramatic reorganization in 1984 and the start-up Saturn division. Yet, unlike Ford, GM did not move substantially to innovate in its core operations—to change the way it competed. Rather, it exerted ever more effort to compete in the same basic way it had in the past. It did not move toward greater organizational integration. Perhaps its more secure cash position going into the 1980s, and its greater reserves, allowed GM to choose a path not available to the more desperate Ford.

Under CEO Roger Smith, GM sought to spend its way out of its problems with advanced technology purchased on the market. Ultimately, Smith's vision was the traditional one: automating around the shop-floor workers and fighting suppliers, rather than integrating either group into the company's investment programs. Outside of the spin-off Saturn project, GM did not move broadly to adopt the key elements of the Japanese model of workforce involvement and continuous improvement. In short, little or no serious effort was devoted to improving quality, and the workforce continued to be treated as an obstacle to, rather than the source of, productivity improvement.

Even the Saturn project, which achieved marked quality improvements on the basis of organizational integration, remained largely isolated from the rest of the firm, and its lessons have not as yet successfully been injected back into the mainstream of GM's operations. In order to adopt the more integrated organizational structure required to compete against Japanese manufacturers, GM's management was forced to remove the Saturn project entirely from the rest of the company's operations. Saturn has been a success in the marketplace, and has used Japanese manufacturing techniques to improve quality and reliability. GM, however, established the manufacturing plant for Saturn at a greenfield site well away from the traditional hub around Detroit, the division recruited only workers without experience in the auto industry and it recruited many new suppliers who were offered extended contracts.

The Saturn experience has demonstrated the extent of organizational change needed to compete effectively, and in the process has highlighted just how far GM as a whole must still travel to make such organizational integration central to its core operations. All indications in the 1990s are that GM is not about to embark on the journey from adaptation to innovation. For example, under the much-publicized but short-lived reign of José Ignacio Lòpez de Arriortùa in 1992, GM's attempts to shift the burden of cost cutting onto its suppliers helped limit the company's losses but may well have undermined the supplier relations required for investment in higher quality, lower cost components (Ingrassia and White, 1994, Ch. 17). More generally, draconian plant closings, lay-offs and cost-cutting under CEO Jack Smith enabled GM's North American operations to go from a $10.7 billion loss (before interest and taxes) in 1991 to $362 million profit in 1993. Accompanying what *Fortune* has called 'the biggest turnaround in American corporate history', however, GM has seen its share of US car sales drop from 35.5 percent in 1993 to 33.4 percent in 1994 and its US truck sales fall from 31.5 percent in 1993 to 28.4 percent in 1994 (Taylor, 1994, p. 54). There is no indication that GM is making the transition from a no-mover to a slow-mover strategy, and there is even the danger that by continuing to live off the past it may be forced at some point to become a remover.

Remover

A remover strategy is one that eschews reinvestment in a company. Strategic decision-makers run the company for the benefit of shareholders by 'disgorging the free cash flow', and in the process run the company down. Strategic decision-makers may view the company's organizational capabilities as inadequate for generating a 'reasonable' rate of return in the current lines of business or for providing a foundation for moving into new lines of business. The more strategic decision-makers are disconnected from the organizational structure of the enterprise—as has often been the case in US conglomerate structures (see Ravenscraft and Scherer, 1987)—the less will they be capable of understanding the enterprise's existing and potential organizational capabilities. The more strategic decision-makers are oriented toward short-term profitability, the more attracted will they be to a remover strategy (Porter, 1992; Lazonick, 1994). In contrast, the more strategic decision-makers are integrated into the organizational structure of their enterprises, the less likely are they to pursue a remover strategy.

Max Holland's 1989 book, *When the Machine Stopped: A Cautionary Tale from Industrial America*, revealed how a remover strategy ensured the fall of Burgmaster, a well-known manufacturer of machine tools. Burgmaster closed its doors in October 1985. Its closure followed a drawn-out decline that began in the 1970s when the company became part of the conglomerate, Houdaille Industries. Through the 1980s, the company became a *cause célèbre*, as it waged a high profile campaign to gain governmental protection from Japanese competition (it was featured on CBS's *60 Minutes*, among other places). Its exertions were ultimately futile, but many politicians and media commentators portrayed Burgmaster as a victim of unfair Japanese trading practices. Holland painted a different picture; he saw the company's demise as the outcome of a long process of willful disinvestment and mismanagement by a succession of owners.

In its heyday, Burgmaster exemplified US industrial strength. From its beginning in 1946, Joe and Fred Burg had built Burgmaster into a model manufacturer. By 1965 its products were widely respected as among the foremost machine tools made in America, then the home of the world's finest instruments. In that year, sales climbed 29 per cent to $9.6 million, their eighth consecutive new high.

In October 1965, however, the Burgs sold their firm to Houdaille Industries, an industrial conglomerate based in Buffalo, NY. The Burgs were seduced by the promise of Houdaille's greater financial resources, which they hoped would allow them simultaneously to upgrade their machine-tool line and to construct a new, state-of-the-art plant. In effect, the plant had outgrown the resources of its owners.

True to its word, Houdaille did initially invest to upgrade Burgmaster's plant. A new factory was constructed and new tools were purchased. The company's new line was featured on the front page of the machine-tool industry's trade journal, and Burgmaster was attracting worldwide attention as a leading-edge manufacturer.

But Burgmaster's stock price and profit were not living up to the hopes of its new owners. Houdaille made two moves to improve Burgmaster's performance. Both proved to be mistakes. First, Houdaille shifted Burgmaster's new production from California to Tennessee, substituting a cheaper, but much less skilled, workforce for Burgmaster's existing staff. The skills of Burgmaster's California employees could not be transferred to those in Tennessee. The products made in Tennessee soon undermined Burgmaster's reputation; buyers began to inspect Burgmaster tools to see where they were made, carefully avoiding those built in Tennessee. Second, Houdaille sold some of Burgmaster's technology to a Japanese competitor, Yamazaki Machinery Works in Nagoya. The sale brought a quick windfall, but strengthened Burgmaster's future competition. Holland (1989, p. 107) summarized the effect of the two moves: 'Although not exactly cosmetic, neither of these redeployments promised to bring the machine tool group out of its doldrums. The motive was simply to become more efficient and maximize profits, to eke the last dollar out of the machine tool group at a difficult time.'

By 1978 Houdaille had become disillusioned with Burgmaster and machine tools altogether. It was not alone. Other conglomerates that moved into machines tools in the 1960s were beginning to divest.

At the same time, Houdaille itself was coming to the notice of potential buyers. Between February and April of 1978, Houdaille's stock rose from $14.50 per share to $22. By July it had shot up to $28, compared with a book value of about $20. Houdaille was clearly the target of takeover speculation. As Houdaille's management cast around for a friendly suitor, they received a call from a small Wall Street investment banking boutique called Kohlberg, Kravis, Roberts & Co. KKR (as the firm later became known) offered Houdaille's management a means for the firm to remain independent. The current owner, Jerry Saltarelli, could liquidate his stake at a substantial profit. What is more, Houdaille's management could potentially reap a substantial profit for themselves under KKR's scheme. Houdaille's management was interested.

In May 1979, Houdaille became the largest-ever leveraged buyout (LBO) to that time. Houdaille's stock was purchased for the unprecedented sum of

$335 million by the management group, using debt raised against Houdaille's own future cash flow. The key was a clever tax scheme. Houdaille's assets would be generously reappraised to inflation-increased levels and then rapidly depreciated, slashing Houdaille's tax liability. These manipulations would sharply reduce Houdaille's tax bill and lift up the available cash flow. That cash flow would in turn be used to repay the LBO debt, after which Houdaille would again be taken public, returning a handsome profit for the buyout group. Or so the theory went.

Like all LBOs, this scheme placed enormous pressure on the management group to maintain and raise cash flow to meet its debt obligations. The steps taken by Houdaille's management to increase tax flow initiated the dynamic that ultimately killed Burgmaster. During the 1980s, after over a decade of emphasizing short-run profits over long-run investments, Burgmaster became the victim of a full-fledged remover strategy. Rather than invest to improve Burgmaster's long-term innovative capabilities—and enhance its growth prospects—Houdaille opted simply to milk Burgmaster of all possible cash. In the end, Houdaille exited from the machine tool business. Quoting Burgmaster president Allan Folger, Holland (1989, p. 163) commented on the transformation of Houdaille's strategic posture wrought by the LBO:

> 'After the buyout, Houdaille per se changed . . . It seemed to lose its equilibrium.' Financial expertise became the single most valued resource, and understandably so. 'Accounting hires grew faster than manufacturing hires' because managing the cash flow 'to service the debt became the whole end', said Folger.

An early signal of Houdaille's new approach came with the firing of Folger himself. He had proposed expanding Burgmaster's plant to meet a surge in demand. Folger wanted to modernize and expand the machine shop by building a third manufacturing aisle on an adjacent lot of 53,000 square feet. Houdaille's management claimed that he had become 'too content' and did not understand the demands of the new era the business was entering.

Many further measures to maintain cash flow at the expense of Burgmaster's long-term competitive position followed during the 1980s. Bills were left unpaid or paid late, eroding supplier confidence and cooperation. Quality was compromised in a desperate attempt to get production out of the door. Extravagant promises were made to win sales, then forgotten. The best and most skilled machinists and other senior employees were let go. Eventually, Houdaille attempted unsuccessfully to partner with Yamasaki, the firm to which it had sold its technology a decade earlier.

By early 1985, Burgmaster was losing almost a million dollars a month. Its technological and organizational capabilities had been so severely depleted that customers lost all confidence in its product. On September 24 Houdaille announced a 'restructuring' aimed at 'reducing its interest expense and enhancing its future'. Seven divisions would be split off from Houdaille, of which three would be sold to a private investor, three would undergo further leverage buyouts, and one, Burgmaster, would be liquidated. On October 1 Burgmaster employees at the once-leading California factory were informed that their plant would close.

How did Burgmaster end up in this ignominious position? One part of the explanation may be Houdaille's lack of organizational integration in key respects and at critical times. When Burgmaster was acquired by Houdaille, control of Burgmaster's investment strategy passed from the hands of those who had founded the firm, knew its needs and capabilities intimately, and were unshakably committed to its future, to a distant group who were forced to 'manage by the numbers'. Because Houdaille's conglomerate managers were not organizationally integrated into Burgmaster, they made critical errors of judgement (attempting to enter the CNC business and forcing Burgmaster to buy controls that did not work; shifting plant to low-cost, but low-skilled, Tennessee; selling key technology to Japanese competitors) that undermined Burgmaster's long-term ability to compete.

These misjudgements proved critical, since with even the best possible strategy and most far-sighted management Burgmaster (like all US machine-tool manufacturers) would still have faced a very difficult business environment in the 1970s and early 1980s. Rising Japanese competition, a gyrating dollar and cyclical downturns in the domestic economy all combined to jeopardize the future of any US machine-tool maker. But Burgmaster's problems were exacerbated by a management that neither understood its needs nor was committed to its future. The consequent weakening of Burgmaster and Houdaille precipitated the situation that tempted Houdaille's managers to undertake a leveraged buyout.

The interests of Houdaille's new owner-managers were no longer tied to the long-term fate of either Houdaille or Burgmaster. That is, Houdaille's post-LBO managers were no longer in any way organizationally integrated into their company. The management group then sought only to make their gamble pay off, which meant bleeding a division such as Burgmaster. The first and dominant loyalty of Houdaille's strategic decision-makers had shifted from the business organization to the capital markets.

6. *Implications of the Organizational Integration Hypothesis*

The examples of corporate strategies from first movers to removers illustrate, although they certainly do not prove, the organizational integration hypothesis.

The most successful innovation described here was certainly IBM's 360 series computers. An enormously ambitious project, it required broad integration of its workforce, with promises of lifetime employment, and almost total integration of its component supplies, through bringing all component production in-house. Similarly, Motorola carried through its innovative programs by committing earnings to invest not only in new plant and equipment but also in new skills and relationships. Motorola and IBM had evolved over the previous decades as integrated organizations that, in retrospect, approximate much more to what we now consider to be the Japanese model than to the American model.

In contrast, Ford and General Motors epitomized the American model in the 1970s when they were confronted head-on by the Japanese challenge. Competitive success in the automobile industry called for tight linkages between employees on the shop-floor and in design, and of suppliers with assembly. The Japanese form of organization allowed them to achieve considerably greater integration of all these groups. Ford, the US company that most boldly pushed to integrate its workforce and suppliers—in effect adopting significant aspects of the Japanese model—emerged as the most successful American automobile producer by the end of the 1980s. GM, which sought merely to compete through more spending yet without transforming the American model, lost ground.

Finally, in the 1970s and 1980s success in the machine-tool industry demanded ever increasing financial commitment and organizational integration. As innovative as it had been in the past, a company like Burgmaster needed to remain continuously innovative to compete against Japanese producers. Yet, in seeking the financial commitment that was a necessary condition for continuous innovation, Burgmaster as a business came under the strategic control of decision-makers who did not have the intimate knowledge of machine-tool technology and Burgmaster's organizational capabilities to commit to an innovative strategy. Rather, when Houdaille's initial investments in Burgmaster did not yield quick returns, the conglomerate's strategy turned from innovation to adaptation. Successful innovation is virtually impossible without the organizational integration of strategic decision-makers into the enterprise.

We are by no means alone in arguing for the importance of organizational integration for industrial innovation. Over the past decade or so, analysts of international industrial competition have become increasingly aware that 'organizational capabilities' matter. The type of innovation that makes an impact in global competition is not the work of individuals, or even small teams of individuals. Increasingly, innovation is the work of highly complex divisions of labor that must be planned and coordinated to develop and

utilize new technology. Characterizing as they do the organizational requirements of technological change, these divisions of labor differ across industries
and evolve over time. As in our distinction between Japanese and American
models of organizational integration, these divisions of labor can also differ
across nations because of the impacts of social institutions that reflect the influence of different histories on the social organization of business enterprises.

In this paper we have argued that, notwithstanding distinct national patterns
of the social organization of the business enterprise, different companies
within a national industry can have, at any point in time, different organizational structures. The degree of organizational integration inherent in these
structures, combined with the degree of organizational integration required
by the evolution of a particular industry, is critical for understanding the
speed and effectiveness with which these different companies respond to
competitive challenges.

The most general implication of this perspective on the relation between
competitive strategy and organizational structure is that the structures that
implemented an innovative strategy in the past may be inadequate for doing
so in the present. Conversely, for reasons that in themselves require historical
explanation, some enterprises may have inherited from the past organizational
structures that differ markedly from the national norm but that enable these
particular enterprises to remain innovative in the future. Still other companies, also for reasons that must be explained, learn how to make investments in integrated relationships that put in place organizational structures
that can respond to competitive challenges.

The perspective that we have presented builds on the strategy–structure
approach to business history of Alfred Chandler (1962). His analysis of the
relation between strategy and structure, however, has not gone beyond the
notion that structure follows strategy. He has not analyzed either how structure constrains strategy or the conditions under which strategic managers
decide to confront structural constraints for the purposes of transforming
them.

Despite his recognition of the distinction between innovative and adaptive
strategies in his 1962 book, *Strategy and Structure*, Chandler has not subsequently sought to analyze the determinants of the types of strategies that
enterprises pursue. He does not ask why some companies undertake and
implement strategies that change structures and why some companies do
not. What determines whether a company is a first mover, fast mover, slow
mover, no mover or remover? Our perspective argues that a critical determinant of corporate strategy is the extent of organizational integration in
general, and the extent to which strategic decision-makers are integrated
into the organizational structure in particular.

If Chandler has argued that structure follows strategy, Richard Nelson and Sidney Winter (1982) have in effect argued that strategy flows from structure. Specifically, they have argued that what differentiates firms are organizational capabilities based on tacit knowledge and organizational routines. Unlike machines and blueprints, tacit knowledge and organizational routines cannot easily be transferred to other enterprises, and indeed can exist and create value only in the companies in which they have evolved. From this perspective, even investment strategies become organizational routines that derive from the tacit knowledge of strategic decision-makers.

From our perspective, the activities and relationships that constitute organizational integration generate the tacit knowledge that enables the enterprise to function as a coherent and cohesive system—that is, that make organizational routines productive. A focus on organizational integration as a prime determinant of competitive advantage asks where within the specialized division of labor this tacit knowledge resides and who within the specialized division of labor is able and willing to participate in organizational routines. Our focus also asks why and under what conditions strategic decision-makers might choose to engage in innovative investment strategies that confront and alter organizational routines, in part by extending the right to possess and utilize tacit knowledge from the managerial organization to shop-floor employees and suppliers. The issue is not only how structure determines strategy but also how strategy determines structure.

Whatever the causal relation between strategy and structure, common to the approaches of Chandler and Nelson and Winter is a predominant concern with structure rather than strategy. In adopting this focus, they differ from the business academicians (and management consultants) whose overriding concern is strategy. Such analyses tend to portray competitive strategy as a function of the mindset of the strategic decision-maker. In effect, they attempt to analyze competitive strategy in abstraction from its specific organizational context.

Yet when the analysis of competitive strategy is pursued seriously, it inevitably leads to a consideration of organizational structure as both cause and effect of strategic decisions (e.g. Hayes *et al.* 1988). Recently, important work in the areas of operations management and new product development has emphasized the competitive power of organizational integration (Hayes and Wheelwright, 1984; Clark and Fujimoto, 1991).

If valid, the organizational integration hypothesis has important implications for both business and government policy. In undertaking competitive strategies, business decision-makers must know which forms and types of organizational integration—vertical relations with suppliers, distributors and employees, horizontal relations with industry competitors—are most effective in the industries in which they intend to invest. They must also know how these characteristic relationships are evolving over time and across different social environments. For companies that want to remain first movers or fast movers rather than no movers or removers, strategic decision-makers must know what types of management methods can ensure that the relevant forms of organizational integration are put in place and, when necessary, transformed. In short, to gain and sustain competitive advantage, strategic decision-makers must know what types of investments in organizational relationships are required to develop and utilize new technologies. The organizational integration hypothesis provides a focus for generating the knowledge about the organizational determinants of competitive advantage that strategic managers require.

Enterprises do not, however, operate in a social vacuum. Within a particular sector of a national economy (for example, automobiles or consumer electronics), strategic decision-makers of the constituent firms must know when to cooperate and when to compete. To foster innovation, under what circumstances and in what respect must the strategy of an individual corporation become subservient to the strategy of a group of companies acting in concert? To support the innovation process, policy-makers in government must know what roles the social environment can play in encouraging effective organizational integration. Specifically, how can the financial, educational and legal systems that service and regulate a national or regional economy encourage rather that deter appropriate organizational integration?

If the organizational integration hypothesis is valid, it also undermines the policy positions of those who believe that market coordination of economic activity alone is the route to industrial success. In our view, an acceptance of the organizational integration hypothesis necessitates a major rethinking of government policies on education and training, labor relations, corporate governance and inter-enterprise cooperation. The organizational integration perspective, however, suggests that the research agenda must begin at the level of the strategy and structure of business enterprises as a prelude to a consideration of the roles that government policy might play.

To develop and test the organizational integration hypothesis further will require case studies of the dynamic evolution of business enterprises in high-value-added and high-growth industries. Only through careful case studies can we discover just what are the key relationships within business organizations that influence the choice of competitive strategy and that generate competitive advantage, and how these relationships vary across industries. Is it relations with production workers that are the key? Or with suppliers? Or with other enterprises engaged in cooperative research or other types of collective investments? What accounts for the variation in the relations between organizational integration and competitive advantage across industries? What constraints or opportunities on the appropriate transformation of organizational structures of enterprises derive from the national environment? Why and how does the need for organizational integration change over time?

Just to ask these questions indicates the intellectual task that lies ahead to gain an understanding of the causes and extent of American economic decline, and the incentives and abilities residing in the American economy to respond to global competitive challenges. Indeed, because our approach focuses on comparative industrial development, we would contend that it is broadly applicable to understanding the rise and decline of industrial economies more generally. As for the specific agenda of understanding American economic decline, our claim is not to have done the necessary research but to have outlined a theoretical perspective that yields a testable hypothesis that cuts to the core of industrial innovation and economic development.

References

Baumol, W. J., S. A. B. Blackman and E. N. Wolff (1989), *Productivity and American Leadership: The Long View*. MIT Press.

Best, M. (1990), *The New Competition: Institutions of Industrial Restructuring*. Harvard University Press.

Chandler, A. D., Jr, (1962), *Strategy and Structure: Chapters in the History of the American Industrial Enterprise*. MIT Press.

Clark, K. and T. Fujimoto (1991), *Product Development Performance: Strategy, Organization, and Management in the World Auto Economy*. Harvard Business School Press.

Dertouzas, M. L., R. K. Lester and R. M. Solow (1989), *Made in America: Regaining the Productive Edge*. MIT Press.

Dollar, D. and E. N. Wolff (1993), *Competitiveness, Convergence, and International Specialization*. MIT Press.

Dore, R. (1990), *British Factory—Japanese Factory: The Origins of National Diversity in Industrial Relations* (second edition). University of California Press.

Ferguson, C. H. (1990), 'Computers and the Coming of the U.S. Keiretsu,' *Harvard Business Review*, 68, 50–70.

Ferguson, C. H. and C. R. Morris (1993), *Computer Wars: How the West Can Win in a Post-IBM World*. Times Books.

Ferleger, L. A. and J. R. Mandle (1994), *A New Mandate: Democratic Choices for a Prosperous Society*. University of Missouri Press.

Fruin, M. (1992), *The Japanese Enterprise System*. Oxford University Press.

Galbraith, J. K. (1967), *The New Industrial State*. Houghton Mifflin.

Gerlach, M. (1992), *Alliance Capitalism: The Social Organization of Japanese Business*. University of California Press.

Graham, B. W. (1986), *RCA and the Videodisk: The Business of Research*. Cambridge University Press.

Hayes, R. H. (1981), 'Why Japanese Factories Work,' *Harvard Business Review*, 60, 56–66.

Hayes, R. H. and S. C. Wheelwright (1984), *Restoring our Competitive Edge: Competing through Manufacturing*. Wiley.

Hayes, R. H., S. C. Wheelwright and K. B. Clark (1988), *Dynamic Manufacturing*. Free Press.

Helper, S. (1991), 'Strategy and Irreversibility in Supplier Relations: The Case of the U.S. Automobile Industry,' *Business History Review*, 65, 781–824.

Holland, M. (1989), *When the Machine Stopped: A Cautionary Tale from Industrial America*. Harvard Business School Press.

Hounshell, D. (1984), *From the American System to Mass Production, 1800–1932*. Johns Hopkins University Press.

Ingrassia, P. and J. B. White (1994), *Comeback: The Fall and Rise of the American Automobile Industry*. Simon & Schuster.

Jaikumar, R. (1986), 'Post Industrial Manufacturing,' *Harvard Business Review*, 64 69–76.

Jensen, M. C. (1989), 'Eclipse of the Public Corporation,' *Harvard Business Review*, 67 (September–October).

Keller, M. (1993), *Collision: GM, Toyota, Volkswagen and the Race to Own the 21st Century*. Doubleday.

Lazonick, W. (1986), 'Strategy, Structure, and Management Development in the United States and Britain,' in K. Kobayashi and H. Morikawa (eds), *Development of Managerial Enterprise*. University of Tokyo Press, pp. 101–146. [reprinted in W. Lazonick (1992), *Organization and Technology in Capitalist Development*. Edward Elgar.]

Lazonick, W. (1990), *Competitive Advantage on the Shop Floor*. Harvard University Press.

Lazonick, W. (1991), *Business Organization and the Myth of the Market Economy*. Cambridge University Press.

Lazonick, W. (1992), 'Controlling the Market for Corporate Control: The Historical Significance of Managerial Capitalism,' *Industrial and Corporate Change*, 1, 445–488.

Lazonick, W. (1993), 'Learning and the Dynamics of International Competitive Advantage,' in R. Thomson (ed.), *Learning and Technological Change*. Macmillan, pp. 172–197.

Lazonick, W. (1994), 'Creating and Extracting Value: Corporate Investment Behavior and American Economic Performance,' in M. Bernstein and D. Adler (eds), *Understanding American Economic Decline*. Cambridge University Press, pp. 79–113.

Lazonick, W. and W. Mass (1993), 'Indigenous Innovation and Economic Development: Is Japan a Special Case?' photocopy Center for Industrial Competitiveness, University of Massachusetts Lowell.

Lazonick, W. and M. O'Sullivan (1995), 'Big Business and Corporate Control,' in Malcolm Sawyer (ed.), *International Encyclopedia of Business and Management*. Routledge, in press.

McKinsey Global Institute (1993), *Manufacturing Productivity*. McKinsey and Company.

Miyajima, H. (1994), 'The Privatization of ex-Zaibatsu Holding Stocks and Emergence of Bank-Centered Corporate Groups in Japan,' photocopy Harvard University.

Morikawa, H. (1992), *Zaibatsu*. University of Tokyo Press.

Nelson, R. R. and S. G. Winter (1982), *An Evolutionary Theory of Economic Change*. Harvard University Press.

O'Toole, J. (1985), *Vanguard Management: Redesigning the Corporate Future*. Doubleday.

Porter, M. E. (1992), *Capital Choices: Changing the Way America Invests in Industry*. Council on Competitiveness.

Prestowitz, C. V., Jr. (1988), *Trading Places: How We Allowed Japan to Take the Lead*. Basic Books.

Ravenscraft, D. J. and F. M. Scherer (1987), *Mergers, Sell-Offs, and Economic Efficiency*. Brookings.

Shook, R. L. (1990), *Turnaround: The New Ford Motor Company*. Prentice-Hall.

Slutsker, G. (1993), 'The Company That Likes to Obsolete Itself,' *Forbes*, 13, 139–144.

Taylor, A., III (1994), 'GM's $11,000,000,000 Turnaround,' *Fortune*, 17 October, pp. 54–74.

Thomson, R. (1989), *The Path to Mechanized Shoe Production in the United States*. University of North Caroline Press.

Wiggenhorn, W. (1990), 'Motorola U: When Training Becomes an Education,' *Harvard Business Review*, 68, 71–83.

Uneven (and Divergent) Technological Accumulation among Advanced Countries: Evidence and a Framework of Explanation*

PARIMAL PATEL and KEITH PAVITT
(Science Policy Research Unit, University of Sussex, Falmer, Brighton BN1 9RF, UK)

We present evidence for the advanced OECD countries of uneven and divergent patterns of technological accumulation. We show that 'global' firms will not smooth out the differences, since their technological activities are strongly influenced by conditions in their own countries. We suggest that—in addition to diversity in cumulative technological trajectories—the divergent patterns reflect international differences in the capacities of management, financial and training institutions properly to evaluate— and exploit—the learning benefits of technological investments. For these reasons, we conclude that technological gaps among the advanced OECD countries are here to stay.

1. The Persistence of Technology Gaps

The renewed interest over the past 10 years in the nature and determinants of international patterns of economic growth has confirmed that international 'catch up' in technology and productivity is neither automatic nor easy, since it depends on investment in tangible capital, and intangible capital in the form of education and training and—at least in the industrially advanced countries —of business expenditures on R&D and related activities (Fagerberg, 1987, 1993). These factors explain why some developing countries have been successful in reducing the technology and productivity gap, while others have not.

* This paper draws heavily on the results of research undertaken in the ESRC (Economic and Social Research Council)-funded Centre for Science, Technology, Energy and the Environment Policy (STEEP) at the Science Policy Research Unit (SPRU), University of Sussex. We are grateful to two anonymous referees for comments on an earlier draft.

This is because the international diffusion of technology is neither automatic nor easy (see Bell and Pavitt, 1993). Both material artifacts and the knowledge to develop and operate them are complex involving multiple dimensions and constraints that cannot be reduced entirely to codified knowledge, whether in the form of operating instructions, or a predictive model and theory. Tacit knowledge—underlying the ability to cope with complexity—is acquired essentially through experience, and trial and error. It is misleading to assume that such trial and error is either random, or a purely costless by-product of other activities like 'learning by doing' or 'learning by using'. Tacit (and other forms of) knowledge are increasingly acquired within firms through deliberately planned and funded activities in the form of product design, production engineering, quality control, education and staff training, research, or the development and testing of prototypes and pilot plant. Differences among countries in the resources devoted to such deliberate learning—or 'technological accumulation'—have led to international technological gaps. which, in turn, have led to international differences in economic performance.

But while uneven and divergent development is readily acknowledged among the developing countries, the same is not true for the advanced (OECD) countries. Until recently, it was commonly assumed that the open trading system would allow the rapid international diffusion of technology, so that the catching up of Western Europe and Japan to the levels of technology and efficiency of the world's leading country (the US) would be relatively smooth. In fact, there has also been uneven development among industrial countries. Some (e.g. the UK, see Pavitt, 1980) have caught up only very partially, while others (e.g. FR Germany and Japan) have actually overtaken the world's technological leading country—the US—in certain important sectors (Nelson, 1990). At a more aggregate level, Soete and Verspagen (1993) have shown recently that productivity convergence in the OECD countries stopped at the end of the 1970s.

Thus, technology gaps among the industrial countries have not been eliminated. Hence the continuing relevance of the 'neo-technology' theories of trade and growth, that were pioneered by Posner (1961) and Vernon (1966), and confirmed by Soete (1981) and Fagerberg (1987, 1988), as well as by the company-based analyses of Cantwell (1989), Franko (1989) and Geroski *et al.* (1993) Hence, also, the growing interest in the implications of international technology gaps for policy (Ergas, 1984) and for theory (Dosi *et al.*, 1990).

We shall now present statistical evidence of uneven and divergent technological accumulation in the 1980s, and shall argue that technological gaps among the OECD countries will not be eliminated in the 1990s. Given that the activities contributing to technological accumulation are complex and varied, all statistical measures are bound to be imperfect. However, as a result of the growing demands from public and private policy makers for better data, progress has been made in both measurement and conceptualization. The advantages and drawbacks of the various measures have been reviewed extensively elsewhere (Freeman, 1987; van Raan, 1988; Grilliches, 1990; Patel and Pavitt, 1994a). In particular, we have shown in our earlier work that the combined use of data on R&D activities, and on patenting in the USA by country of origin, gives a plausible and consistent picture of technological activities at the world's technological frontier. [1]

2. The Evidence of Uneven (and Divergent) Technological Accumulation

Among Countries in the Volume of Technological Activities

The data on R&D and US patenting activities show no evidence of convergence in national capacities for technological accumulation since the early 1970s, and some evidence of divergence in the 1980s.

Table 1 presents trends in the percentage of gross domestic product (GDP) spent by business on R&D activities in 17 OECD countries since 1967. [2] These show a certain stability in the rankings throughout the period at the two ends of the spectrum: Switzerland has remained with the highest share, and Ireland, Spain and Portugal with the three lowest shares. Otherwise there are countries who started near the top but have moved down the rankings: Canada, The Netherlands and—above all—the UK, there are also countries that have improved their positions: FR Germany, Sweden, Japan and—above all—Finland. In general, stability in the rankings of the countries is confirmed by a statistically significant (positive) correlation between their ranks in 1967 and in 1991. [3]

Overall, there are no statistical signs of convergence in the industry-

---

[1] R&D is a better measure of rates of change in real resources over time, but it measures technological activities in small firms only very imperfectly. US patenting is a better measure of technological activities in small firms and can be broken down quite finely by specific firms and specific technical fields. Neither measure is satisfactory for software technology, but no alternative yet exists. And neither measure captures all the activities that lead to product and process innovations, such as design, management, production engineering, marketing and learning by doing.

[2] Government funded R&D performed in industry is excluded. This is concentrated in defense-related activities, and in few countries: principally the US, UK, France and FR Germany, where it has clearly stimulated accumulation in defense-related technologies (see Tables 5, 9 and 10 below). Its wider effects on technological accumulation are a matter of debate. Our own conclusion is that defense R&D has considerable opportunity costs, particularly in electronics, where leading-edge technologies and markets have shifted to civilian applications.

[3] The correlation coefficient for the 17 countries is 0.82, which is significant at the 5% level.

TABLE 1. Trends in Industry Financed R&D as a Percentage of GDP in 17 OECD Countries: 1967 to 1991

	1967	1969	1971	1975	1977	1979	1981	1983	1985	1987	1989	1991
Belgium	0.66	0.64	0.71	0.84	0.91	0.95	0.96	1.02	1.09	1.16	1.14	1.16
Canada	0.40	0.39	0.38	0.33	0.32	0.39	0.49	0.45	0.56	0.57	0.54	0.59
Denmark	0.34	0.39	0.41	0.41	0.41	0.42	0.46	0.53	0.60	0.66	0.71	0.85
Finland	0.30	0.32	0.44	0.44	0.49	0.53	0.62	0.72	0.89	0.98	1.07	1.07
France	0.60	0.64	0.67	0.68	0.69	0.75	0.79	0.88	0.92	0.92	0.98	0.99
FR Germany	0.94	1.03	1.13	1.11	1.12	1.32	1.40	1.48	1.65	1.80	1.78	1.57
Ireland	0.19	0.23	0.30	0.23	0.22	0.23	0.26	0.27	0.35	0.40	0.45	0.58
Italy	0.33	0.38	0.44	0.43	0.37	0.40	0.43	0.42	0.49	0.49	0.56	0.61
Japan	0.83	1.00	1.09	1.12	1.11	1.19	1.38	1.59	1.81	1.82	2.05	2.13
The Netherlands	1.12	1.04	1.02	0.97	0.87	0.86	0.83	0.89	0.96	1.11	1.07	0.91
Norway	0.35	0.39	0.41	0.49	0.49	0.50	0.50	0.61	0.80	0.88	0.81	0.77
Portugal	0.04	0.06	0.09	0.05	0.04	0.09	0.10	0.11	0.11	0.11	0.14	0.14
Spain	0.08	0.08	0.11	0.18	0.18	0.18	0.18	0.22	0.25	0.29	0.34	0.38
Sweden	0.71	0.69	0.80	0.96	1.07	1.11	1.24	1.45	1.71	1.74	1.68	1.71
Switzerland	1.78	1.78	1.67	1.67	1.71	1.74	1.68	1.67	2.16	2.13	2.07	2.07
UK	1.00	0.92	0.81	0.80	0.80	0.82	0.91	0.86	0.95	1.02	1.04	0.94
US	0.99	1.03	0.97	0.98	0.98	1.05	1.17	1.31	1.42	1.37	1.36	1.36
Standard deviation:												
All countries	0.46	0.46	0.43	0.43	0.45	0.47	0.48	0.52	0.61	0.61	0.60	0.58
Excluding US	0.47	0.46	0.43	0.44	0.45	0.47	0.48	0.52	0.62	0.62	0.62	0.59

Source: OECD.

funded shares over time, since the standard deviation of the distribution has not decreased over time. On the contrary, it has increased markedly in the 1980s, suggesting technological divergence among countries. In this context, it is worth noting that the US share began slipping progressively below that of FR Germany, Japan, Sweden and Switzerland in the 1970s, and that the gap grew much larger in the 1980s.

Table 2 shows trends in per capita national patenting in the US for the same 17 OECD countries. At first sight the evidence about divergence is more ambiguous. When the US is included, the standard deviation of the population increases between the late 1960s and the early 1970s—thereby suggesting divergence—but then decreases until the mid-1980s, after which it increases again to its original level. However, there are well-known reasons for excluding the US from such a comparison, since for firms in the US, we are measuring domestic patenting, whereas for firms in other countries we are measuring foreign patenting. Given the propensity of firms to seek patent protection more intensely in their home country (Bertin and Wyatt, 1988), the rate of technological accumulation in the US is overestimated. At the same time, given the tendency of firms to give increasing attention to patenting in foreign markets, trends over time will tend to overestimate any

TABLE 2. Trends in Per Capita Patenting in the US from 17 OECD Countries

	1963–68	1969–74	1975–80	1981–85	1986–90
Switzerland	138.0	197.1	207.1	179.2	193.6
US	236.6	244.7	181.3	156.7	177.9
Japan	9.9	38.9	56.0	82.5	139.4
Germany	54.7	86.6	91.8	97.7	122.2
Sweden	64.2	94.7	100.9	87.1	99.6
Canada	41.3	55.8	49.0	45.8	63.1
The Netherlands	35.9	48.8	46.8	47.0	60.4
Finland	5.1	14.8	22.3	30.8	50.4
France	26.1	41.0	39.7	38.8	49.6
UK	43.3	55.8	46.6	40.1	47.8
Denmark	18.4	31.9	29.7	27.9	35.7
Belgium	16.3	29.3	26.4	23.8	30.4
Norway	12.7	20.3	23.0	19.4	27.2
Italy	7.8	13.1	13.0	14.0	20.2
Ireland	2.0	6.5	5.1	6.7	12.9
Spain	1.2	2.1	2.3	1.6	3.1
Portugal	0.3	0.6	0.3	0.4	0.6
Standard deviation					
All countries	60.56	67.56	59.44	52.05	59.26
Excluding US	35.05	48.91	51.44	46.13	53.58

Source: Based on data supplied to SPRU by the US Patent and Trademark Office.

decline in US performance (Kitti and Schiffel, 1978) and thereby show a spurious degree of convergence.

When the US is excluded, the evidence in Table 2 on the whole confirms that in Table 1. Throughout the period, Switzerland stays at the top and Ireland, Spain and Portugal at the bottom. Britain's relative position declines, while Finland, FR Germany and Japan improve. In general, stability in the rankings of the countries is confirmed by a significant and positive correlation between their ranks in 1963–68 and 1986–90.[4] At the same time there is an indication of international divergence in that the standard deviation increases over the period. The one anomaly is the reduction in the standard deviation in 1981–85, but this may reflect the reduction in the overall number of patents granted, following a reduction in the number of patent examiners (see Grilliches, 1990).

Finally, Table 3 presents recent trends in patenting in the US by a number of developing countries. We are very much aware of the inadequacies of US patenting as a measure of the largely imitative activities in technological accumulation that are performed in developing countries. Studies using other approaches have shown the superior performance of East Asian countries, compared to those of Latin America and to India (see for example Dahlman *et al.*, 1987). Table 3 simply shows that, while most of the developing countries have continued with a very low level of US patenting, Taiwan and South Korea have both seen massive increases. This indicates that technology in Taiwan and South Korea is now attaining world best practice levels in an increasing number of fields—a striking example of technological catch-up compared to the advanced countries,[5] and of technological divergence compared to other developing countries.

Among Countries in Workforce Education and Training

International comparisons of education and training over the past 10 years have moved well beyond the average numbers of years of schooling that used to be common usage. Greater attention is now paid to the distribution of education levels among different groups in the working population, and to quality as measured through educational attainment. One of the main pioneers has been Prais (together with his colleagues) at the National Institute of Economic and Social Research in London.[6] Some of the major results

---

[4] The correlation coefficient for the 17 countries is 0.80, which is significant at the 5% level.

[5] If the level and rate of increase of US patenting is a reliable guide to technology levels, South Korea and Taiwan are now at the level of technology in Japan about 35 to 40 years ago.

[6] See, most recently, Prais (1993).

TABLE 3. US Patenting Activities of Selected Developing Countries: 1969–1992

Country	1969	1970	1971	1972	1973	1974	1975	1976	1977	1978	1979	1980	1981	1982	1983	1984	1985	1986	1987	1988	1989	1990	1991	1992
Taiwan	0	0	0	0	1	0	23	28	52	29	38	65	79	88	65	97	174	208	343	457	592	732	904	1000
South Korea	0	3	2	7	5	7	11	7	5	12	4	8	15	14	26	29	38	45	84	97	159	225	402	538
People's Republic of China	5	6	15	8	10	22	1	6	1	0	2	1	3	0	1	2	1	9	23	47	52	47	52	41
Hong Kong	7	8	19	7	15	9	10	20	9	21	13	27	33	18	14	24	25	30	34	41	48	52	50	60
Mexico	67	43	63	43	42	51	66	78	42	24	36	41	43	35	32	42	32	37	49	44	39	32	28	39
Brazil	18	17	14	16	18	21	17	18	21	24	19	24	23	27	19	20	30	27	34	29	36	41	61	40
Venezuela	6	3	13	7	5	7	0	0	0	2	11	11	12	10	5	11	15	21	24	20	23	17	16	20
Argentina	17	23	22	29	27	24	24	24	20	21	24	18	25	18	21	20	11	17	18	16	20	23	—	—
Singapore	2	0	4	4	7	6	1	3	3	2	0	3	4	3	5	4	9	3	11	6	18	—	—	20
India	18	16	10	19	21	17	13	17	13	14	14	4	6	4	14	12	10	18	12	14	14	23	22	24

Source: Based on data supplied to SPRU by the US Patent and Trademark Office.

TABLE 4. Vocational Qualifications of the Workforce in Britain, The Netherlands, Germany, France and Switzerland

Level of qualification	Britain 1988	The Netherlands 1989	Germany 1987	France 1988	Switzerland 1991
University degrees	10	8	11	7	11
Higher technician diplomas	7	19	7	7	9
Craft/lower technical diplomas	20	38	56	33	57
No vocational qualifications	63	35	26	53	23
Total	100	100	100	100	100

Source: Prais, 1983.

of their work are summarized in Table 4, which uses census data to compare the vocational qualifications of the workforce in five European countries.

It shows striking similarities between countries in the proportion with university degrees (7–11%) but even more striking differences in the proportions with intermediate qualifications (66% in Switzerland–27% in the UK) and with no vocational qualifications (63% in the UK–23% in Switzerland). Although there had been some improvement in the UK position in the 1980s, the qualifications gap between Germany and France, on the one hand, and the UK, on the other, actually widened (Patel and Pavitt, 1991b). These skill levels in the workforce are reflected in productivity differences resulting from differences in machine maintenance, consistency in product quality, workforce flexibility and learning times on new jobs.

These studies have been supplemented by comparisons of educational attainment across countries, and which tend to confirm their findings: thus, Dutch adolescents are 2–3 years ahead of their English counterparts in mathematical attainment (Mason *et al.*, 1992). Similar differences are found over a broader geographical area, with adolescents from Japan, the four East Asian 'tiger' countries, and continental Europe (including Hungary) clearly outperforming their counterparts from the US (and often the UK) in mathematics (Newton *et al.*, 1992).

Among Countries in the Sectoral Composition of National Technological Activities

So far, we have compared countries' aggregate technological performance. Table 5 shows the sectoral patterns of technological advantage of 19 OECD countries. On the basis of the US patent classification, technologies have been divided into 11 fields. The content of most of them will be clear from their titles: technologies for extracting and processing raw materials are related mainly to food, oil and gas; defense-related technologies are defined as aerospace and munitions. For each country–region and technological field, we have calculated an index of 'Revealed Technology Advantage' (RTA) in 1963–68 and 1985–90.[7]

Table 5 shows markedly different patterns and trends among the three main, technology-producing regions of the world—US, Europe and Japan—in their fields of technological advantage and disadvantage. The US has seen rapid decline in motor vehicles and consumer electronics; growing relative strength in technologies related to weapons, raw materials and telecommunications; and an improving position in chemicals. In Japan, almost the opposite has happened: growing relative strength in electronic consumer and capital goods and motor vehicles, together with rapid relative decline in chemicals, and continued weakness in raw materials and weapons. In Western Europe, the pattern is different again, and very close to that of its dominant country—FR Germany: continuing strength in chemicals, growing strength in weapons, continued though declining strength in motor vehicles, and weakness in electronics.

Table 6 examines the similarities and differences among countries' technological specializations in greater and more systematic detail.[8] It uses correlation analysis to measure both the stability over time of each country's sectoral strengths and weaknesses in technology (first row), and the degree to which they are similar to those of other countries (correlation matrix). The first row shows that, with five exceptions (Australia, Ireland, Italy, Portugal and the UK) most OECD countries have a statistically significant degree of stability in their technological strengths and weaknesses between the 1960s and the 1980s: 10 at the 1% level, and a further four at the 5% level, thereby confirming the path-dependent nature of national patterns of accumulation of technological knowledge.

The correlation matrix also confirms the differentiated nature of technological knowledge, with the very different strengths and weaknesses in Japan, the US and Western Europe: each is negatively correlated with the other two; and significantly so in two cases out of three (the USA with the other two regions). More generally, it confirms that countries tend to differ markedly in their patterns of technological specialization.[9] Of the 171 correlations among pairs of countries in Table 6, only 31 (18%) are positively

---

[7] RTA is defined as a country's or region's (or firm's) share of all US patenting in a technological field, divided by its share of all US patenting in all fields. An RTA of more than one therefore shows a country's or region's relative strength in a technology, and less than one its relative weakness. These measures correspond broadly to the measures of comparative advantage used in trade analyses.

[8] For this analysis we use a more detailed breakdown than that used in Table 5. Again on the basis of the US Patent Classification we have divided technologies into 34 fields.

[9] Archibugi and Pianta (1992) also show that OECD countries' degree of technological specialization is increasing over time.

TABLE 5. Sectoral Patterns of Revealed Technological Advantage:* 1963–68 to 1985–90

		Fine chemicals	Industrial chemicals	Materials	Mechanical engineering	Vehicles	Electrical machinery	Electronic capital goods	Telecommunications	Electronic consumer goods	Raw material related	Defense related
USA	1963–68	0.89	0.93	1.04	1.01	0.89	1.00	1.02	1.03	0.94	1.08	0.99
	1985–90	0.97	0.98	0.95	0.99	0.55	1.01	0.97	1.04	0.65	1.28	1.15
Europe**	1963–68	1.34	1.29	0.86	0.99	1.48	1.00	0.92	0.91	1.26	0.61	1.14
	1985–90	1.33	1.19	0.83	1.13	1.02	0.92	0.61	0.94	0.59	0.83	1.40
Japan	1963–68	2.95	1.62	1.02	0.77	0.83	1.17	1.47	1.06	1.99	0.44	0.36
	1985–90	0.72	0.92	1.42	0.85	2.21	1.08	1.65	0.97	2.50	0.37	0.09
Australia	1963–68	1.05	0.69	0.80	1.16	1.44	0.74	0.19	0.72	1.48	1.02	0.31
	1985–90	0.80	0.65	0.42	1.21	1.35	0.59	0.30	0.54	0.34	1.82	1.63
Austria	1963–68	1.41	0.80	1.13	1.25	1.21	0.62	0.28	0.38	1.69	0.39	0.26
	1985–90	0.84	0.73	0.68	1.39	1.94	0.82	0.32	0.43	0.41	0.90	1.96
Belgium	1963–68	1.23	1.38	3.99	0.71	0.44	0.92	0.69	1.02	3.97	0.42	0.78
	1985–90	1.85	1.79	2.21	0.77	0.19	0.98	0.21	0.50	1.24	1.10	0.80
Canada	1963–68	0.71	0.81	0.75	1.11	1.35	0.78	0.56	0.85	0.36	1.43	0.71
	1985–90	0.68	0.74	0.67	1.15	0.65	0.83	0.40	1.38	0.47	1.69	1.13
Denmark	1963–68	3.05	0.77	0.97	1.11	0.39	0.87	0.47	0.59	1.17	0.92	0.12
	1985–90	2.38	0.91	0.49	1.19	0.20	0.90	0.21	0.46	0.54	0.82	0.39
Finland	1963–68	0.00	0.62	0.00	1.30	2.17	0.72	0.00	0.31	0.20	1.45	0.47
	1985–90	0.88	0.76	0.76	1.54	0.71	0.68	0.10	0.51	0.15	1.13	0.82

France	1963–68	1.86	1.02	1.05	1.02	2.11	1.23	0.84	1.15	0.81	0.49	1.11
	1985–90	1.34	1.03	0.88	1.04	0.57	1.17	0.85	1.56	0.49	1.03	1.55
Germany	1963–68	1.12	1.49	0.68	0.96	1.43	0.78	0.92	0.74	1.88	0.54	1.04
	1985–90	1.14	1.37	0.85	1.18	1.42	0.87	0.52	0.79	0.54	0.61	1.58
Ireland	1963–68	0.00	0.39	0.00	1.29	3.00	0.00	0.00	0.65	0.00	0.55	0.00
	1985–90	1.57	1.18	0.55	0.87	0.63	1.38	0.94	0.72	0.99	1.66	0.00
Italy	1963–68	1.29	1.93	0.51	0.93	1.26	0.68	0.87	0.69	0.53	0.71	0.78
	1985–90	1.77	1.10	0.62	1.15	1.21	0.73	0.76	0.85	0.41	0.78	0.92
The Netherlands	1963–68	1.71	1.46	1.24	0.75	0.15	1.34	1.90	1.11	1.95	1.15	0.15
	1985–90	0.54	1.13	0.89	0.87	0.26	1.27	1.24	1.25	1.82	1.07	0.33
Norway	1963–68	0.94	0.63	0.00	1.25	0.36	1.16	0.65	0.47	0.29	0.91	0.46
	1985–90	0.83	0.62	0.27	1.14	0.33	0.70	0.24	0.92	0.43	2.30	1.79
Portugal	1963–68	10.58	1.41	0.00	0.99	0.00	0.67	0.00	0.00	0.00	0.98	3.46
	1985–90	1.90	1.66	0.00	1.11	0.00	0.43	0.00	0.00	0.00	2.97	0.00
Spain	1963–68	0.84	0.56	0.48	1.20	3.00	0.86	0.13	1.02	0.47	0.47	1.93
	1985–90	1.93	0.76	0.37	1.22	1.84	0.75	0.12	0.55	0.07	0.85	2.72
Sweden	1963–68	0.94	0.44	0.44	1.22	1.16	1.14	0.72	1.37	0.38	0.68	2.35
	1985–90	0.72	0.57	0.58	1.43	0.93	0.89	0.33	0.79	0.23	0.99	1.86
Switzerland	1963–68	2.60	2.01	0.27	0.90	0.56	0.85	0.56	0.73	0.63	0.47	1.45
	1985–90	1.81	1.48	0.63	1.12	0.51	0.78	0.41	0.64	0.43	0.72	1.16
UK	1963–68	0.88	1.03	1.09	1.02	1.99	1.22	1.04	1.03	0.93	0.70	1.28
	1985–90	1.83	1.05	0.92	1.04	0.86	0.88	0.71	1.07	0.73	0.99	1.37

Notes: * For the definition of the Revealed Technology Advantage Index see foonote 7 in the text.
    ** Europe is defined as the 15 European countries included in this table.
Source: Based on data supplied to SPRU by the US Patent and Trademark Office.

TABLE 6. Stability and Similarities among Countries in their Sectoral Specializations:

	Australia	Austria	Belgium	Canada	Denmark	Finland	France	Germany	Ireland
Stability: correlations over time: 1963–68 to 1985–90									
	0.28	0.76*	0.54*	0.67*	0.47*	0.59*	0.82*	0.35*	0.05
Similarities: correlations among countries: 1985–90									
Austria	0.36*								
Belgium	−0.09	−0.14							
Canada	0.52*	0.47*	0.05						
Denmark	0.18	−0.03	0.33*	0.32					
Finland	0.47*	0.45*	0.20	0.54*	0.45*				
France	−0.27	−0.16	0.10	−0.14	0.10	−0.15			
Germany	0.27	0.05	0.22	−0.18	0.21	0.32	0.29		
Ireland	0.07	−0.10	0.09	0.21	0.14	0.03	−0.09	−0.31	
Italy	0.28	0.28	0.06	0.34*	0.30	0.53*	−0.23	0.22	0.28
Japan	−0.43*	−0.07	0.06	−0.44*	−0.22	−0.26	−0.44*	−0.20	−0.13
The Netherlands	−0.24	−0.18	−0.03	0.06	−0.04	0.07	−0.33*	−0.38*	0.27
Norway	0.36*	0.36*	−0.20	0.62*	0.22	0.28	0.02	−0.12	0.02
Portugal	0.32	0.48*	0.17	0.31	0.11	0.43*	−0.09	0.15	0.11
Spain	0.32	0.13	−0.11	0.34*	0.68*	0.38*	0.00	0.28	−0.07
Sweden	0.25	0.46*	−0.05	0.38*	0.40*	0.53*	0.36*	0.26	−0.07
Switzerland	0.35*	−0.12	0.11	−0.21	0.01	0.07	0.06	0.72*	−0.07
UK	0.08	−0.15	−0.04	−0.10	0.40*	0.03	0.23	0.30	−0.02
US	0.22	−0.03	−0.20	0.42*	−0.02	−0.01	0.23	−0.37*	0.25
Western Europe	0.26	0.04	0.21	−0.08	0.33*	0.34*	0.49*	0.93*	−0.19

Notes: For the definition of the Revealed Technology Advantage Index see foonote 7 in the text.
Europe is defined as the 15 European countries included in this table.
* Denotes correlation coefficient significantly different from zero at the 5% level.
Source: Based on data supplied to SPRU by the US Patent and Trademark Office.

and significantly correlated at the 5% level. Among these we find FR Germany similar to Switzerland (chemicals and machinery), and Canada similar to Australia, Finland and Norway (raw material-based technologies). Japan has a unique pattern of specialization, with no significant positive correlations with other countries but plenty of negative ones.

Implications

The above comparisons show some striking differences—even divergences— in the rate and direction of technological accumulation in the industrial countries. Those related to fields of technological specialization reflect inevit- able diversity in stages of economic and technological development, or a desirable diversity in fields of national scientific and technological specializa- tion. Those related to differences in the overall volume of investment in

Correlations of Revealed Technology Advantage Indices across 34 Sectors

Italy	Japan	The Netherlands	Norway	Portugal	Spain	Sweden	Switzerland	UK	US
0.32	0.45*	0.66*	0.35*	0.25	0.53*	0.73*	0.83*	0.23	0.56*
−0.13									
0.08	0.24								
−0.03	−0.50*	−0.23							
0.35*	−0.20	−0.04	0.06						
0.38*	−0.23	−0.28	0.41*	0.20					
0.19	−0.38*	−0.35*	0.30	0.30	0.45*				
0.17	−0.19	−0.26	−0.14	0.04	0.13	−0.04			
−0.03	−0.34*	−0.20	0.17	0.00	0.32	0.10	0.20		
−0.09	−0.81*	−0.03	0.50*	0.06	−0.02	0.13	−0.26	0.11	
0.27	−0.41*	−0.37*	−0.02	0.17	0.35*	0.39*	0.73*	0.45*	−0.19

technological accumulation should be causes of disquiet because—if allowed to persist—they are likely to reinforce any uneven and divergent rates of national technological and economic development in future.

The most striking international differences and technological divergencies in the overall rate of accumulation are in the core, namely, in the volume of change-generating (including R&D) activities supported by business firms, and in the skills of the workforce that they employ and that they (unequally) train.[10] Japan and FR Germany are the major countries with high company R&D and workforce skills, with the UK (and probably the US) among the major industrial countries at the other end of the spectrum.

[10] National differences in basic research also exist but appear—in the long term—to adjust to the level of demand for skills and knowledge from the business sector. For further discussion see Patel and Pavitt (1944b).

3. The Effects of 'Global Corporations'

The Importance of Home Countries for Technological Activities

The unfettered behavior of large corporations is unlikely—in and of itself—to smooth out these international differences in technological accumulation, for three sets of reasons.

First, large firms do not play a major role in the development and control of some significant fields of technology: in particular, capital goods, components, and measuring and control instruments (Patel and Pavitt, 1991a). As the recent experience of the Japanese automobile industry shows, large firms can stimulate technological accumulation in these fields through their supplier networks, including those outside Japan. But this depends on the autonomous development of skills and technological capabilities among the suppliers themselves.

Second, technology-generating activities remain among the most domesticated of all corporate activities.[11] Table 7 shows that, in the second half of

TABLE 7. Geographic Location of Large Firms' US Patenting Activities, According to Nationality: 1985–90

| Firms' nationality | Percentage shares | | | | | |
| | Home | Abroad | Of which: | | | |
			US	Europe	Japan	Other
Japan (13)	98.9	1.1	0.8	0.3	–	0.0
US (249)	92.2	7.8	–	6.0	0.5	1.3
Italy (7)	88.1	11.9	5.4	6.2	0.0	0.3
France (26)	86.6	13.4	5.1	7.5	0.3	0.5
Germany (43)	84.7	15.3	10.3	3.8	0.4	0.7
Finland (7)	81.7	18.3	1.9	11.4	0.0	4.9
Norway (3)	68.1	31.9	12.6	19.3	0.0	0.0
Canada (17)	66.8	33.2	25.2	7.3	0.3	0.5
Sweden (13)	60.7	39.3	12.5	25.8	0.2	0.8
UK (56)	54.9	45.1	35.4	6.7	0.2	2.7
Switzerland (10)	53.0	47.0	19.7	26.1	0.6	0.5
The Netherlands (9)	42.1	57.9	26.2	30.5	0.5	0.6
Belgium (4)	36.4	63.6	23.8	39.3	0.0	0.6
All firms (587)	89.0	11.0	4.1	5.6	0.3	0.9

Note: The parentheses contain the number of firms based in each country.
Source: Based on data supplied to SPRU by the US Patent and Trademark Office.

[11] We use data on the address of inventors patenting in the US as a proxy measure of the international location of large firms' technological activities. These data are consistent with the available (but less comprehensive) studies based on corporate R&D expenditures. See Patel (1994).

the 1980s, 89% of the technological activities of the world's largest firms continued to be performed in their home country—a 1% increase over the previous five-year period. Not unsurprisingly, the share performed in foreign countries by large firms based in smaller countries tends to be higher, although the proportion for Finnish firms (18.3%) compared to that for British firms (45.1%) shows that factors other than size are at work.

In particular, Cantwell (1992) has shown that the share of foreign in total production is the most important factor explaining differences among firms in the location of their technological activities, but that foreign patenting shares are smaller than foreign production shares. In other words, the technology intensity of foreign production is consistently and significantly less than that of home production and concerned mainly with product and process adaptation to local conditions.

Third, Table 7 also shows that the foreign technological activities of large firms are not globalized but are concentrated almost exclusively in the 'triad' countries—especially the US and Europe (and, more specifically, Germany). More detailed data shows that the largest proportionate increases in foreign technological activities in the 1980s were in British and Swedish firms—especially in the US, and in a number of smaller European countries outside the EC—Switzerland, Finland, Norway—all increasing their share within the EC. The firms based in countries with the largest technological activities—the US, Japan and FR Germany—had among the lowest proportionate increases in foreign technological activities. Most of any increase in foreign technological activities came as a by-product of take-overs and divestitures, rather than an explicit relocation of technological activities.

Finally, this pattern suggests that, globalization of markets and (increasingly) production notwithstanding, there remains at least one compelling reason for companies to concentrate a high proportion of their technological activities in one location. The development and commercialization of major innovations requires the mobilization of a variety of often tacit (person-embodied) skills and involves high uncertainties. Both are best handled through intense and frequent personal communications and rapid decision making—in other words, through geographical concentration (see Porter, 1990). In this context, it is worth noting that the rapid product development times in Japanese firms (Clark *et al.*, 1987) have been achieved from an almost exclusively Japanese base, while the strongly globalized R&D activities of the Dutch Philips company are said to have slowed down product development.

This is consistent with the inter-industry differences in Table 8, which shows that firms making products with the highest technology intensities are among those with the lowest degrees of internationalization of their

TABLE 8. Geographic Location of Large Firms' US Patenting Activities, According to Product Group: 1985–90

Firms' nationality	Percentage shares				
	Abroad	Of which:			
		US	Europe	Japan	Other
Drink and tobacco (18)	30.8	17.5	11.1	0.4	1.8
Food (48)	25.0	14.8	8.5	0.1	1.7
Building materials (28)	20.6	9.1	9.8	0.1	1.6
Other transport (5)	19.7	2.0	6.8	0.0	10.9
Pharmaceuticals (25)	16.7	5.5	8.3	1.1	1.7
Mining and petroleum (47)	15.0	9.7	3.5	0.1	1.6
Chemicals (72)	14.4	8.0	5.1	0.3	1.0
Machinery (68)	13.7	3.5	9.1	0.1	1.1
Metals (57)	12.8	5.4	5.7	0.1	1.6
Electrical (58)	10.2	2.6	6.8	0.3	0.4
Computers (17)	8.9	0.1	6.6	1.1	1.1
Paper and wood (34)	8.1	2.4	4.9	0.1	0.7
Rubber and plastics (10)	6.1	0.9	2.4	0.4	2.4
Textiles etc. (18)	4.7	1.4	1.8	0.8	0.6
Motor vehicles (43)	4.4	0.9	3.2	0.1	0.2
Instruments (20)	4.4	0.4	2.8	0.5	0.8
Aircraft (19)	2.9	0.3	1.8	0.1	0.7
All firms (587)	11.0	4.1	5.6	0.3	0.9

Note: The parentheses contain the number of firms in each product group.
Source: Based on data supplied to SPRU by the US Patent and Trademark Office.

underlying technological activities: those producing aircraft, instruments, motor vehicles, computers and other electrical products are all below the average for the population of firms as a whole. In all these products, links between R&D and design, on the one hand, and production, on the other, are particularly important in the launching of major new products and benefit from geographical proximity. [12]

By contrast, we see in Table 8 a high proportion of foreign R&D in industries, where some localized technological activities are required, either to adapt products to differentiated local tastes, or to exploit local natural resources: food, drink and tobacco, building materials, mining and petroleum. All in all, these data suggest a general theorem: localized 'low-tech' products require globalized R&D; global 'high-tech' products do not.

[12] The one technology intensive exception is pharmaceutical products, where the share of foreign R&D is high, but where R&D and production are unimportant compared to the links with high quality basic research, and with nationally based agencies for testing and validation.

Uneven Development among Firms Reflects Uneven Development among Countries

They also suggest that conditions in the home country remain preponderant in the technological performance of large firms. This is confirmed in Table 9, which presents evidence of uneven technological development since the late 1960s among the world's largest firms.[13] It shows, in the same 11 technological fields as in Table 5, trends in the total US patenting of the world's top 20 firms in the period 1985–90. Two major conclusions emerge from this table.

First, the technological strengths and weaknesses of each region, shown in Table 5, are in general reflected in the number of nationally based large firms appearing in the top 20 in Table 9.[14] Thus, as summarized in Table 10, Japanese firms make up 11 of the top 20 firms in motor vehicles and 14 in consumer electronics and photography, US firms make up 16 of the top 20 in raw materials and 15 in defense, while European firms have their largest numbers in chemicals.

Second, in addition to uneven development of large firms in each technological field according to their nationality, there has also been an uneven degree of stability (or instability) in the firms' shares and rankings within each technological field. A casual reading of Table 9 shows that in some fields, the leaders of the early 1970s continued to be so into the late 1980s, while in others new leaders emerged during the period. This is shown statistically in the final column of Table 10, which presents the correlation of the shares of the top 20 firms in 1985–90 with their shares in 1969–74.

Thus the low (and statistically insignificant) correlations in motor vehicles and in electronic consumer goods, mainly reflect the emergence of Japanese firms as technological leaders in these fields, while the high (and statistically significant) correlations in electrical machinery and telecommunications reflect mainly a re-enforcement of the dominance of established US and some European firms. The more stable shares in industrial chemicals reflect the continuing strength of mainly European firms.

4. *Possible Causes of Uneven Development*

The above evidence suggests that the behavior of large firms will not, in and of itself, lead to a wider international spread of R&D and related activities.

---

[13] It is based on data that we have compiled on more than 600 of the world's largest, technologically active firms, as measured by their patent activity in the US (see Patel and Pavitt, 1991a).

[14] For a more systematic statistical proof, see Patel and Pavitt (1991a).

TABLE 9. Shares of US Patenting for Top 20 Firms in 11 Technical Fields: Sorted According to Shares in 1985–90

	Nationality	1969–74	1985–90
Fine chemicals			
1 Bayer	FRG	2.84	3.70
2 Hoechst	FRG	1.61	2.53
3 Merck	US	2.57	2.44
4 Ciba-Geigy	Switzerland	4.33	2.27
5 Imperial Chemical Industries	UK	1.98	1.98
6 E. I. Du Pont De Nemours	US	1.48	1.79
7 Warner-Lambert	US	0.71	1.58
8 Eli Lilly Industries	US	1.67	1.46
9 Dow Chemical	US	1.21	1.24
10 BASF	FRG	0.58	1.19
11 Pfizer	US	1.17	1.09
12 American Cyanamid	US	2.43	1.04
13 Johnson + Johnson	US	0.36	1.03
14 Boehringer Mannheim	FRG	1.00	1.01
15 Hoffmann-La Roche	Switzerland	1.59	0.96
16 SmithKline Beckman	US	1.40	0.96
17 Monsanto	US	2.87	0.88
18 Squibb	US	1.03	0.88
19 Takeda	Japan	1.21	0.88
20 Beecham	UK	0.23	0.82
Other chemicals			
1 Bayer	FRG	2.57	2.77
2 Dow Chemical	US	2.40	2.67
3 Hoechst	FRG	2.37	2.45
4 BASF	FRG	1.40	2.31
5 Ciba-Geigy	Switzerland	2.54	1.92
6 General Electric	US	1.39	1.86
7 E. I. Du Pont De Nemours	US	3.29	1.68
8 Imperial Chemical Industries	UK	2.14	1.16
9 Shell Oil	The Netherlands	0.85	1.09
10 Eastman Kodak	US	1.33	1.03
11 Union Carbide	US	1.11	0.86
12 Exxon	US	0.79	0.84
13 Allied-Signal	US	1.62	0.81
14 Henkel	FRG	0.35	0.80
15 Rhone-Poulenc	France	0.63	0.69
16 Phillips Petroleum	US	1.46	0.66
17 Sumitomo Chemical	Japan	0.55	0.65
18 Texaco	US	0.41	0.64
19 3M	US	0.52	0.62
20 Monsanto	US	2.22	0.61
Materials			
1 3M	US	1.36	2.26
2 Fuji Photo Film	Japan	0.31	2.24
3 Ppg	US	2.72	1.81

TABLE 9. *(continued)*

	Nationality	1969–74	1985–90
Materials (continued)			
4 General Electric	US	2.32	1.76
5 E. I. Du Pont De Nemours	US	3.48	1.57
6 Hitachi	Japan	0.20	1.43
7 Corning Glass Works	US	2.77	1.13
8 Dow Chemical	US	1.26	1.11
9 Hoechst	FRG	1.01	1.08
10 Saint-Gobain Industries	France	0.96	0.95
11 Emhart	US	0.46	0.93
12 TDK	US	0.10	0.91
13 Owens-Corning Fiberglas	US	1.83	0.89
14 Allied-Signal	US	0.65	0.86
15 Toshiba	Japan	0.38	0.80
16 Sumitomo Electric Industries	Japan	0.06	0.75
17 Kimberly-Clark	US	0.61	0.75
18 W. R. Grace	US	0.69	0.71
19 Bayer	FRG	0.59	0.69
20 GTE	US	0.28	0.65
Non-electrical machinery			
1 General Motors	US	1.23	0.91
2 Hitachi	Japan	0.18	0.88
3 General Electric	US	1.22	0.80
4 Canon	Japan	0.05	0.71
5 Toshiba	Japan	0.08	0.69
6 Siemens	FRG	0.29	0.65
7 Philips	The Netherlands	0.39	0.54
8 United Technologies	US	0.47	0.54
9 Nissan Motor	Japan	0.12	0.52
10 Westinghouse Electric	US	0.56	0.51
11 Honda	Japan	0.03	0.51
12 Allied-Signal	US	0.78	0.50
13 Toyot Jidosha Kogyo	Japan	0.10	0.50
14 Fuji Photo Film	Japan	0.09	0.41
15 Mitsubishi Denki	Japan	0.03	0.38
16 IBM	US	0.46	0.38
17 ITT Industries	US	0.35	0.35
18 Robert Bosch	FRG	0.24	0.34
19 ATT	US	0.56	0.34
20 Aisin Seiki	Japan	0.10	0.31
Vehicles			
1 Honda	Japan	0.91	9.12
2 Nissan Motor	Japan	1.74	5.73
3 Toyota Jidosha Kogyo	Japan	0.76	4.84
4 Robert Bosch	FRG	3.79	4.27
5 Mazda Motor	Japan	0.78	2.93
6 General Motors	US	5.21	2.79
7 Mitsubishi Denki	Japan	0.21	2.78

TABLE 9. (*continued*)

	Nationality	1969–74	1985–90
Vehicles (continued)			
8 Nippondenso	Japan	1.27	2.57
9 Fuji Heavy Industries	Japan	0.06	2.20
10 Hitachi	Japan	0.38	1.91
11 Yamaha Motor	Japan	0.32	1.85
12 Daimler-Benz	FRG	2.71	1.50
13 Ford Motor	US	2.41	1.50
14 Brunswick	US	0.42	1.10
15 Aisin Seiki	Japan	0.34	1.10
16 Lucas	UK	0.95	0.87
17 Porsche	FRG	0.42	0.86
18 Outboard Marine	US	0.70	0.84
19 Caterpillar	US	1.99	0.76
20 Kawasaki Jukogyo	Japan	0.08	0.76
Electrical machinery			
1 General Electric	US	5.77	2.99
2 Westinghouse Electric	US	3.22	2.68
3 Philips	The Netherlands	1.44	2.15
4 Amp	US	1.10	2.02
5 Mitsubishi Denki	Japan	0.20	1.97
6 Hitachi	Japan	0.53	1.91
7 Siemens	FRG	1.47	1.85
8 Toshiba	Japan	0.41	1.53
9 General Motors	US	1.81	1.30
10 GTE	US	1.20	1.29
11 Motorola	US	0.51	0.97
12 Matsushita Electric Industrial	Japan	0.85	0.88
13 Asea Brown Boveri Ab	Switzerland	0.83	0.80
14 United Technologies	US	0.93	0.67
15 NEC	Japan	0.22	0.63
16 ATT	US	1.25	0.53
17 Robert Bosch	FRG	0.49	0.53
18 Allied-Signal	US	0.72	0.52
19 Honeywell	US	0.76	0.51
20 Canon	Japan	0.07	0.51
Electronic capital goods and components			
1 Toshiba	Japan	0.53	5.29
2 IBM	US	8.83	5.25
3 Hitachi	Japan	1.71	4.79
4 Motorola	US	2.15	2.88
5 Texas Instruments	US	1.97	2.88
6 NEC	Japan	0.97	2.75
7 Mitsubishi Denki	Japan	0.13	2.73
8 Fujitsu	Japan	0.38	2.59
9 General Electric	US	6.77	2.50
10 Philips	The Netherlands	2.81	2.43
11 ATT	US	6.05	2.09

TABLE 9. (*continued*)

	Nationality	1969–74	1985–90
Electronic capital goods and components (continued)			
12 Siemens	FRG	1.75	1.79
13 Honeywell	US	2.23	1.08
14 Unisys	US	3.47	1.03
15 Sharp	Japan	0.05	1.03
16 Canon	Japan	0.04	0.97
17 General Motors	US	1.36	0.92
18 Tektronix	US	0.26	0.89
19 Thomson-Csf	France	0.32	0.81
20 Sony	Japan	0.43	0.79
Telecommunications			
1 ATT	US	5.97	4.24
2 Siemens	FRG	2.22	3.25
3 General Electric	US	4.29	2.89
4 Philips	The Netherlands	1.54	2.55
5 Motorola	US	1.02	2.55
6 NEC	Japan	0.61	2.43
7 Westinghouse Electric	US	3.30	1.79
8 Toshiba	Japan	0.26	1.64
9 Mitsubishi Denki	Japan	0.21	1.49
10 ITT Industries	US	3.55	1.41
11 Hitachi	Japan	0.43	1.41
12 General Motors	US	1.57	1.30
13 Thomson-Csf	France	0.82	1.26
14 GTE	US	1.49	1.21
15 IBM	US	1.19	1.12
16 Northern Telecom	Canada	0.54	1.02
17 Fujitsu	Japan	0.20	0.86
18 Rockwell International	US	0.63	0.77
19 CGE	France	0.58	0.75
20 Alps Electric	Japan	0.13	0.74
Electronic consumer goods			
1 Canon	Japan	0.95	6.51
2 Fuji Photo Film	Japan	2.12	6.21
3 Eastman Kodak	US	6.24	3.32
4 Toshiba	Japan	0.42	3.27
5 General Electric	US	3.97	3.06
6 Philips	The Netherlands	2.38	3.04
7 Sony	Japan	1.02	2.94
8 Hitachi	Japan	0.62	2.89
9 Minolta Camera	Japan	0.88	2.47
10 Xerox	US	3.79	2.29
11 Konica	Japan	0.52	1.95
12 Ricoh	Japan	1.00	1.87
13 Matsushita Electric Industrial	Japan	1.20	1.61
14 Sharp	Japan	0.00	1.60
15 IBM	US	2.92	1.44

TABLE 9. (*continued*)

	Nationality	1969–74	1985–90
Electronic consumer goods (continued)			
16 Pioneer Electronic	Japan	0.18	1.44
17 Olympus Optical	Japan	0.14	1.22
18 Mitsubishi Denki	Japan	0.07	1.11
19 NEC	Japan	0.36	1.05
20 Siemens	FRG	0.59	1.01
Technologies for extracting and processing raw materials			
1 Mobil Oil	US	2.17	4.91
2 Exxon	US	3.00	2.25
3 Halliburton	US	0.60	1.62
4 Chevron	US	2.66	1.47
5 Philip Morris	US	1.32	1.42
6 Baker Hughes	US	0.41	1.38
7 Texaco	US	2.49	1.36
8 Phillips Petroleum	US	2.35	1.36
9 Nabisco Brands	US	0.32	1.29
10 Amoco	US	0.18	1.28
11 Shell Oil	The Netherlands	2.13	1.26
12 Allied-Signal	US	3.00	1.17
13 Atlantic Richfield	US	0.89	1.10
14 Deere	US	1.04	0.89
15 Union Oil Of California	US	0.57	0.83
16 E. I. Duk Pont De Nemours	US	0.87	0.67
17 Nissan Motor	Japan	0.03	0.61
18 Schlumberger	US	0.85	0.55
19 British-American Tobacco	UK	0.19	0.55
20 Nestle	Switzerland	0.15	0.55
Defense-related technologies			
1 Boeing	US	1.06	4.29
2 MBB	FRG	1.18	2.50
3 General Electric	US	1.58	1.44
4 Oerlikon-Buhrle Ag	Switzerland	0.89	1.35
5 British Aerospace	UK	0.66	1.28
6 Morton Thiokol	US	0.93	1.11
7 Feldmuhle	FRG	1.56	1.08
8 General Dynamics	US	0.29	1.08
9 Imperial Chemical Industries	UK	1.33	0.95
10 Honeywell	US	0.31	0.93
11 United Technologies	US	1.04	0.82
12 Aerospatiale	France	0.35	0.82
13 General Motors	US	0.54	0.80
14 Westinghouse Electric	US	0.15	0.80
15 Olin	US	1.16	0.71
16 Lockheed	US	0.79	0.69
17 Grumman	US	0.02	0.66
18 Ford Motor	US	0.08	0.51
19 Sundstrand	US	0.02	0.51
20 Rockwell International	US	0.83	0.46

Source: Based on data supplied to SPRU by the US Patent and Trademark Office.

TABLE 10. Nationalities of the Top 20 Firms in US Patenting: 1985–90

	Japan	US	Western Europe	Correlation of shares of the top 20: 1969–74 to 1985–90
Defense related technologies	0	14	6	0.37
Fine chemicals	1	12	7	0.54
Industrial chemicals	1	11	8	0.66*
Raw materials based technologies	1	16	3	0.45
Materials	4	13	3	0.41
Electrical machinery	6	10	4	0.68*
Telecommunications	6	10	4	0.70*
Electronic capital goods	8	9	3	0.51
Non-electrical machinery	9	8	3	0.41
Motor vehicles	11	5	4	0.15
Electronic consumer goods	14	4	2	0.27

Note: *Denotes a correlation coefficient significantly different from zero at 5% level.
Source: Based on data supplied to SPRU by the US Patent and Trademark Office.

On the contrary, our statistical analysis confirms Porter's conclusion (1990) that the conditions in large firms' home countries have a major impact on the rate and direction of their technological activities. We shall now propose a framework of analysis that might eventually explain international differences in the rate and direction of technological accumulation. At this stage, it does not lend itself to rigorous modelling and statistical analysis, although it is consistent with the conclusions of a wide range of more qualitative analyses, as well as with our own data.

International Differences in the Volume of Technological Activities: 'Institutional Failure' in the Competence to Evaluate and Benefit from Technological Learning

Some of the observed international differences in the volume of technological activities may reflect differences in the degree of market failure.[15] However, we would also stress the importance of institutional failures in the competence to evaluate and benefit from investments in technology that are increasingly specialized and professionalized in nature (e.g. industrial R&D laboratories employing highly qualified specialists in a variety of fields of science and engineering), and are long term and complex in their economic impact (e.g. from research on photons, through the laser, to the compact

[15] In particular, the effects of labor mobility on the incentive on business firms to train their workforce; and the effects of intellectual property rights on the incentive to invest in innovative activities.

disc, over a period of 25 years). For purposes of exposition, we have found it useful to distinguish between national systems of innovation that we define as 'myopic', and those that we define as 'dynamic' (Pavitt and Patel, 1988).

Briefly stated, 'myopic' systems treat investments in technological activities just like any conventional investment: they are undertaken in response to a well-defined market demand, and include a strong discount for risk and time. As a consequence, technological activities often do not compare favorably with conventional investments. 'Dynamic' national systems of innovation, on the other hand, recognize that technological activities are not the same as any other investment. In addition to tangible outcomes in the form of products, processes and profits, they also entail the accumulation of important but intangible assets, in the form of irreversible processes of technological, organizational and market learning, that enable them to undertake subsequent investments, that they otherwise could not have made.[16] The archetypal dynamic national systems of innovation are those of FR Germany[17] and Japan, while the myopic systems are the UK and the US. The essential differences can be found in three sets of institutions:

(i) First, in the financial system underlying business activity: in Germany and Japan, these give greater weight to longer-term performance, when the benefits of investments in learning begin to accrue. And they generate both the information and the competence to enable firm-specific intangible assets to be evaluated by the providers of finance (Hu, 1975; Corbett and Mayer, 1991).

(ii) Second, there are the methods of management, especially those employed in large firms in R&D-intensive sectors: in the UK and US, the relatively greater power and prestige given to financial (as opposed to technical) competence is more likely to lead to incentive and control mechanisms based on short-term financial performance, and to decentralized divisional structures insensitive to new and longer term technological opportunities that top management is not competent to evaluate (Abernathy and Hayes, 1980; Lawrence, 1980).

(iii) Third, there is the system of education and training: the German and Japanese systems of widespread yet rigorous general and vocational education provide a strong basis for cumulative learning. The British and US systems of higher education have performed relatively well, but the other two-thirds of the labor force are less well trained and educated than their counterparts in continental Europe and East Asia (Newton *et al.*, 1992; Prais, 1993).

---

[16] In other words, investments in technology nearly always have an 'option value'. See Myers (1984) and Mitchell and Hamilton (1988).

[17] Sweden and Switzerland have many 'dynamic' institutional characteristics similar to Germany.

International Differences in Fields of Technological Specialization: Local Inducement Mechanisms and Cumulative Trajectories

Further, we propose that the observed international differences in the sectoral patterns of technological accumulation emerge from the localized nature of technological accumulation, and the consequent importance of the local inducement mechanisms that guide and constrain firms along cumulative technological trajectories. We know from earlier debates about the relative importance of 'technology push' and 'demand pull' that these inducement mechanisms are numerous, and that their relative importance varies among sectors. It is nonetheless possible to distinguish three mechanisms.

Factor endowments.   Examples include the stimulus of scarce labor for labor-saving innovations in the US; and the different technological trajectories followed by the automobile industries of the US, and of Europe and East Asia, as consequence of very different fuel prices.

Directions of persistent investment.   Especially those with strong inter-sectoral linkages: examples include the extraction and processing of natural resources (North America, Australia and Scandinavia), defense (US, France, UK), public infrastructure (France) and automobiles (Japan, Germany, Italy).

The cumulative mastery of core technologies and their underlying knowledge bases.   Examples include Germany in chemicals and machinery, Sweden in machinery, Switzerland in fine chemicals, The Netherlands in electronics; Japan in electronics and automobiles; the US in chemicals and electronics; the UK in chemicals.

The relative significance of these mechanisms change over time. In the early stages, the directions of technical change in a country or region are strongly influenced by local market inducement mechanisms related to scarce (or abundant) factors of production and local investment opportunities. At higher levels of development, the local accumulation of specific technological skills itself becomes a focusing device for technical change. At this stage, firms become less dependent on the home country for creating the appropriate market signals, and more so for its provision of high quality skills and knowledge bases that local firms can exploit on world markets.

5. *Conclusions*

In their essay on the rise and fall of US technological leadership, Nelson and Wright (1992) conclude that two sets of factors—both related to the increasing interdependence of the world economy—led to the erosion of the massive US technological (and productivity) lead held before and immediately after World War II.

(i) Together with massive social changes, increasing international openness of markets after World War II eroded the US advantages in market size, natural resource availability and more egalitarian income distribution, that were of central importance to the US lead in mass production.

(ii) The highly educated and increasingly international nature of technological communities has eroded the US lead in 'high-technology' product groups.

If these mechanisms are dominant and can be generalized internationally, we could expect technology gaps to disappear among the industrially advanced countries. But both our data and our proposed framework of explanation suggest otherwise.

First (as Nelson and Wright themselves recognize), there exist international disparities in education that will influence (and for a long time to come) the 'human capital endowments' from which firms can benefit. Countries with a strong endowment of science and engineering graduates, but a badly educated workforce are likely to be constrained to specialize in fields like drugs and software, where the skills of the general workforce are not critical. Countries with a skilled general workforce will have a wider range of opportunities, including assembly and process industries, where production-related skills are of central importance.

Second, our evidence suggests that the distinction between myopic and dynamic systems of finance and management does matter, and influences not only the size of the overall commitment of resources to technological accumulation, but the capacity to maintain and develop competences in core technologies that open a range of potential future product opportunities. Thus, relative overall decline in the US has been accompanied by a major loss of competence in automobiles and in the UK in automobiles and electronics.

The UK decline is of long standing, and its nature and causes have been widely documented and debated elsewhere. For the US, Chandler (1992) identifies a number of factors changing US corporate behavior toward technology and innovation since the 1960s. In particular, the growing influence of business school graduates with universal recipes for management problems, the difficulties facing corporate management in making informed entrepreneurial judgments over a large number of often disparate product divisions, and the changing role of the investment banks from underwriting long-term corporate investments to trading in corporate control, all conspired to change the bases of strategic decisions:

> ROI data were no longer the basis for discussion between corporate and operational management as to performance, profit and long-term plans. Instead, ROI became a reality in itself—a target sent down from the corporate office for division managers to meet . . . ROI too often failed to incorporate complex, non-quantifiable data as to the nature of specific product markets, changing production technology, competitor's activity and internal organizational problems—data that corporate and operating managers had in the past discussed in their long person-to-person evaluation of past and current performance and the allocation of resources. Top management decisions were becoming based on numbers, not knowledge (Chandler, 1992, pp 277–278).

The same features exist in other OECD countries, and there is no reason to believe that they will diminish in future. In our view, uneven and divergent technological development among the industrially advanced countries is here to stay.

References

Abernathy, W. and R. Hayes (1980), 'Managing Our Way to Economic Decline,' *Harvard Business Review*, (July/August) pp. 67–77.

Archibugi, D. and M. Pianta (1992), *The Technological Specialisation of Advanced Countries*. Kluwer Academic Publishers: Dordrecht.

Bell, M. and K. Pavitt (1993), 'Technological Accumulation and Industrial Growth: Contrasts between Developed and Developing Countries,' *Industrial and Corporate Change*, 2, 157–210.

Bertin, G. and S. Wyatt (1988), *Multinationals and Industrial Property*. Harvester-Wheatsheaf: Hemel Hempstead.

Cantwell, J. (1989), *Technological Innovation and Multinational Corporations*. Blackwell: Oxford.

Cantwell, J. (1992), 'The Internationalisation of Technological Activity and its Implications for Competitiveness,' in O. Grandstrand, L. Hakanson and S. Sjolander (eds), *Technology Management and International Business*. Wiley: Chichester.

Chandler, A. (1992), 'Corporate Strategy, Structure and Control Methods in the United States in the 20th Century,' *Industrial and Corporate Change*, 1, 263–284.

Clark, K., T. Fujimoto and W. Chew (1987), 'Product Development in the World Auto Industry,' *Brookings Papers on Economic Activity*, 3.

Corbett, J. and C. Mayer (1991), *Financial Reform in Eastern Europe*. Discussion Paper No. 603, Centre for Economic Policy Research (CEPR): London.

Dahlman, C., B. Ross-Larsen and L. Westphal (1987), 'Managing Technological Development: Lessons from Newly Industrialising Countries,' *World Development*, 15, 759–775.

Dosi, G., K. Pavitt and L. Soete (1990), *The Economics of Technical Change and International Trade*. Wheatsheaf: Hemel Hempstead.

Ergas, H. (1984), *Why Do Some Countries Innovate More Than Others?* Paper No. 5, Centre for European Policy Studies: Brussels.

Fagerberg, J. (1987), 'A Technology Gap Approach to Why Growth Rates Differ,' in C. Freeman (ed.), *Output Measurement in Science and Technology: Essays in Honour of Y. Fabian*. North-Holland: Amsterdam.

Fagerberg, J. (1988), 'International Competitiveness,' *Economic Journal*, 98, 355–374.

Fagerberg, J. (1993), 'Technology and International Differences in Growth Rates' (mimeo), Norwegian Institute of International Affairs (NUPI): Oslo.

Franko, L. (1989), 'Global Corporate Competition: Who's Winning, Who's Losing, and the R&D Factor as One Reason Why,' *Strategic Management Journal*, 10, 449–474.

Freeman, C. (ed.) (1987), *Output Measurement in Science and Technology: Essays in Honour of Y. Fabian*. North-Holland: Amsterdam.

Geroski, P., S. Machin and J. van Reenen (1993), 'The Profitability of Innovating Firms,' *RAND Journal of Economics*, 24, 198–211.

Grilliches, Z. (1990), 'Patent Statistics as Economic Indicators: A Survey,' *Journal of Economic Literature*, 28, 1661–1707.

Hu, Y.-S. (1975), *National Attitudes and the Financing of Industry*. Political and Economic Planning, Vol. XLI, Broadsheet No. 559, London.

Kitti C. and Schiffel, D. (1978), 'Rates of Invention: International Patent Comparisons,' *Research Policy*, 7, 323–340.

Lawrence, P. (1980), *Managers and Management in W. Germany*. Croom Helm: London

Mason, G. S. Prais and B. van Ark (1992), 'Vocational Education and Productivity in the Netherlands and Britain,' *National Institute Economic Review*, (May), 45–63.

Mitchell, G. and W. Hamilton (1988), 'Managing R&D as a Strategic Option,' *Research-Technology Management*, 31, 15–22.

Myers, S. (1984), 'Finance Theory and Finance Strategy,' *Interfaces*, 14, 126–137.

Nelson, R. (1990), 'US Technological Leadership: Where Did It Come From, and Where Did It Go?' *Research Policy*, 19, 117–132.

Nelson, R. and G. Wright (1992), 'The Rise and Fall of American Technological Leadership: The Postwar Era in Historical Perspective,' *Journal of Economic Literature*, 30, 1931–1964.

Newton, K., P. de Broucker, G. McDougal, K. McMullen, T. Schweitzer and T. Siedule (1992), *Education and Training in Canada*. Canada Communication Group: Ottawa.

Patel, P. (1995), 'Localised Production of Technology for Global Markets,' *Cambridge Journal of Economics* (in press).

Patel, P. and K. Pavitt (1991a), 'Large Firms in the Production of the World's Technology: An Important Case of 'Non-Globalisation', *Journal of International Business Studies*, 22, 1–21.

Patel, P. and K. Pavitt (1991b), 'Europe's Technological Performance,' in C. Freeman, M. Sharp and W. Walker, *Technology in Europe's Future*. Pinter: London.

Patel, P. and K. Pavitt (1994a), 'Patterns of Technological Activity: Their Measurement and Interpretation,' in P. Stoneman (ed.), *The Economics of Innovation and Technical Change*. Basil Blackwell: Oxford, (forthcoming).

Patel, P. and K. Pavitt (1994b), 'National Innovation Systems: Why They Are Important and How They Might be Measured and Compared,' *Economics of Innovation and New Technology* (forthcoming).

Pavitt, K. (1980), *Technical Innovation and British Economic Performance*. Macmillan: London.

Pavitt, K. and P. Patel (1988), 'The International Distribution and Determinants of Technological Activities,' *Oxford Review of Economic Policy*, 4, 35–55.

Porter, M. (1990), *The Competitive Advantage of Nations*. Macmillan: London.

Posner, M. (1961), 'International Trade and Technical Change,' *Oxford Economic Papers*, 13, 323–341.

Prais, S. (1993), *Economic Performance and Education: The Nature of Britain's Deficiencies*. Discussion Paper No. 52, National Institute for Economic and Social Research: London.

van Raan, A. (ed.), *Handbook of Quantitative Studies of Science and Technology*. North-Holland: Amsterdam.

Soete, L. (1981), 'A General Test of Technological Gap Trade Theory,' *Weltwirtschaftliches Archiv.*, 117, 638–666.

Soete, L. and B. Verspagen (1993), 'Technology and Growth: The Complex Dynamics of Catching Up, Falling Behind, and Taking Over,' in A. Szirmai, B. van Ark and D. Pilat, *Explaining Economic Growth*. Elsevier: Amsterdam.

Vernon, R. (1966), 'International Investment and International Trade in the Product Cycle,' *Quarterly Journal of Economics*, **80**, 190–207.

The Co-evolution of Technology, Industrial Structure, and Supporting Institutions

RICHARD R. NELSON

(School of International and Public Affairs, Columbia University, 420 West 118th Street, New York, NY 10227, USA)

There is a large intellectual discrepancy between most formal growth models described by economists and descriptions of growth in economic history. This paper draws on an evolutionary theory of economic growth that brings together appreciative theorizing regarding growth and formal theorizing. It aims to piece together a relatively coherent appreciative theoretical account of economic development at a sectoral level by laying out a story of the growth, and development, of a manufacturing sector, from birth to maturity, and perhaps until death, that seems to fit many cases and which can serve as a target for formalization. The paper first describes and tries to link two broad bodies of appreciative evolutionary theoretic writing. The first proposes that a new technology develops along a relatively standard track from the time it is born, to its maturity, and that firm and industry structure 'coevolve' with the technology. The other is concerned with the development of institutions in response to changing economic conditions, incentives, and pressures. The paper then considers 'punctuated equilibrium' before concluding with a consideration of two economic developmental implications that appear to flow from the analysis. One concerns the pattern of change of productivity, of capital intensity, and relative variables associated with economic growth, as a technology and industry structure develop. The other is concerned with implicitly cross-country comparisons, and is focused on how 'comparative advantage' develops in a new industry.

1. Appreciative and Formal Theorizing About Economic Growth

There is a large intellectual discrepancy between most of the formal growth models economists have devised, and descriptions of growth that take the form of economic history. Contemporary formal growth theories treat economic growth as almost all 'quantitative'. They aim to explain why various magnitudes, like per capital income, the real wage rate, and capital intensity, rise over time. Other magnitudes like the savings rate, or the share of labor in national income, or the rate of return on capital, tend to stay constant in these models, either because they are assumed to be constants, or because of various mechanisms built into the models. In any case, in economic growth as it is thus depicted, nothing much happens qualitatively. On the other hand, in the historical accounts, lots of qualitative things are happening. New technologies are emerging, and so also are new forms of business organization, and new institutions. Put another way, development is moving forwards and not simply things getting bigger or smaller or staying the same size.

Some economists would be wont to say that the discrepancy here is simply between theories which are by their nature abstract, and historical analyses which by their nature involve relatively detailed description of what has been going on. This explanation surely is partly correct. However, there clearly is a lot of 'theorizing' in the historical accounts. Certain kinds of developments and mechanisms are highlighted, and others ignored. Most economic histories are full of casual arguments.

Some years ago, Sidney Winter and I (Nelson and Winter, 1982) called this kind of economic analysis, which stays relatively close to the data and is expressed mostly in words but which, nonetheless, involves theorizing—appreciative theory. We argued that when the economic research enterprise was going well, appreciative theory and formal theory were in basic tune with each other. And we proposed that a dissonance between appreciative and formal theorizing was an indication of analytic troubles.

The central reason we began to develop an evolutionary theory of economic growth was our belief that such an approach had promise of bringing appreciative theorizing regarding growth, of which historical accounts are an example, and formal theorizing closer together. The language of evolutionary theory seems so natural to employ to describe, and explain, the detailed historical accounts of growth. While that language certainly abstracts and simplifies the picture painted by historians, it does not seem to distort it greatly, nor does it force one to ignore large parts of it. On the other hand, evolutionary theorizing is amenable to powerful formal modeling.

However, while the promise may be there, the fact remains that the formal evolutionary models that Sidney Winter and I, and others, have developed, while arguably much closer to appreciative theorizing in some aspects, still depict growth as largely quantitative (see e.g. Metcalfe and Gibbons, 1986; Metcalfe and Saviotti, 1991; Silverberg *et al.*, 1988; Soete and Turner, 1987). The statement about the failure of formal theories to capture the developmental aspects of growth holds for both formal neoclassical and formal evolutionary growth theory, as these intellectual vehicles have been developed to date.

The purpose of this essay is to sketch out how I think the gaps can be significantly reduced, at least when the analysis is concerned with economic growth at an industry or sectoral level. The reason for this qualification is that, at the economy wide level, economic growth is an extraordinarily complex and variegated process. The economy as a whole comprises many different sectors which, at any time, are developing differently. Further, a central part of the economic growth process as we have experienced it involves the shifting of resources from one sector to another. It is not surprising, therefore, that different historical accounts tend to focus on different things. And while a number of the pieces do seem to fit together, at this stage our understanding of economic growth, in the sense of development, seems more a collection of pictures of 'pieces of the elephant', with large gaps in the overall picture, than a coherent appreciative theory of economic growth at the national level. There certainly are opportunities for building formal models of growth at a national level that have more of a developmental flavor, but it seems inevitable that such efforts can aim to capture only small parts of the picture.

On the other hand, as a result of a variety of recent research, it now seems possible to piece together a relatively coherent appreciative theoretical account of economic development at a sectoral level (at least if one limits oneself to manufacturing sectors). That is, one can now begin to lay out a story of the growth, and development, of a manufacturing sector, from birth, maturity, and perhaps until death, that seems to fit many (but not all) cases, and which can serve as a target for formalization. And this is the aim of the essay.

I shall proceed as follows. In Sections 2 and 3 I describe and try to link two broad bodies of appreciative evolutionary theoretic writing. The first proposes that a new technology develops along a relatively standard track from the time it is born, to its maturity, and that firm and industry structure 'coevolves' with the technology. The other is concerned with the development of institutions in response to changing economic conditions, incentives, and pressures. Section 4 will be concerned with 'punctuated equilibrium'.

Then, in Section 5, I will consider two economic developmental implications that appear to flow from the analysis, although my argument is not yet as clear as I would like. One concerns the pattern of change of productivity, of capital intensity, and related variables associated with economic growth, as a technology and industry structure develop. The other is concerned with implicit cross-country comparisons, and is focused on how 'comparative advantage' develops in a new industry.

Finally, a reprise on formal modeling.

2.   The Co-evolution of Technology and Industry Structure

Much of the motivation behind my early work with Winter was to try to incorporate in an economic growth theory a characterization of technical advance that squared better with what was known about that process than its treatment in neoclassical growth theory. In particular, we treated technical advance as an evolutionary process, in which new technological alternatives compete with each other and with prevailing practice, with *ex post* selection determining the winners and losers, usually with considerable *ex ante* uncertainty regarding which the winner will be.

However, while we highlighted the elements of uncertainty in technological evolution, we stressed as well the strong systematic selection that many market environments provide. We also argued that the generation of alternatives often was highly focused. In most modern fields of technology there is a considerable body of technological understanding that provides guidance as to what kinds of projects are likely to be technologically successful and what are not, as well as understanding of user needs, which provides strong guidance as to what advances would have value. Thus the technological 'mutations' offered to the market selection environment are far from strictly random. This, as well as systematic selection, provides direction to technical advance.

We observed that in many fields technological advance was 'cumulative' in the sense that today's technological advances tended to proceed from yesterday's, building on and from what previously had been achieved, and improving it in various directions. In many cumulative technologies what we called 'natural trajectories' tend to appear, with the cumulative improvements proceeding along particular lines of advance that reflect both what technologists understand they likely can achieve, and what entrepreneurs believe customers will buy. We discussed the cognitive aspects of such dynamics, introducing the term 'technological regime' to refer to that cognitive structure, and to the group of individuals and organizations working with it. Later, Dosi (1982) called this cognitive structure a 'technological paradigm'.

Winter and I briefly mentioned the fact that technological development often seemed to change in character as a particular technology 'matured', but we did not make much of that proposition. We also noted that industry structure often seemed to change over the life of a technology, but did not follow through on that either. Our failure to do this partly reflected the limited scope of research in these subjects at that time. Since then research has exploded, and I believe that what has been learned is highly relevant to an evolutionary theory of growth, at a sectoral level.

Almost all of the research I report here has as its unit of observation a particular broad technology or industry, or a connected group of these, as contrasted with being focused at the level of the overall economy. A good portion of this research effort is concerned with developing generalizations that hold across technologies or industries, and that will be the orientation here, although an important open question is how widely these generalizations hold.

It is analytically convenient to begin by discussing a body of research that purports to identify a 'life cycle' through which many technologies seem to go. At the present time a number of scholars, including both economists and organization theorists, are doing work that I would put in this category. However, much of the contemporary formulation was offered over 15 years ago by Abernathy and Utterback (1978) who had been working on automobiles. The basic starting argument is that when a new technology comes into existence there is considerable uncertainty regarding which of a variety of possible variants will succeed. Different ones are tried out by different parties. However, after a period of time and competition one or a few of these variants come to dominate the others, and attention and resources become concentrated on these at the expense of the others. In the parlance of several of the workers in this field, a 'dominant design' emerges.

There are several different stories about how a dominant design comes into existence. In the most straightforward of these, one variant simply is better than the others and, with time and experimentation, the best basic design comes to be identified and widely recognized. However, there are other more complex stories.

If the competing technologies are cumulative, an early advantage, which could have been simply a matter of chance, of one over the others may lead to the race ending very shortly. If one technology gains an advantage over its competitors, there are strong incentives for resources to be drawn away from trying to advance its rivals, since major advances may be needed to make them competitive. And once resources come to be largely focused on the leader, further improvements may soon make it and its further development the only economic way to proceed because competing designs are left so far behind. Winter and I suggested this as a possibility some time ago, and some of Arthur's recent modeling (1988, 1989) can be interpreted this way. In such a context there is no reason to believe that the dominant design society fixes upon is the best one. It could well be that other broad configurations would have turned out better had resources been allocated to advancing these in the technological race.

Still a third story, or rather a family of stories, has some commonalities with the second, but stresses systems aspects. In particular the focus is on interaction economies that may occur when the number who own and use a particular variant grows, as skills develop that are particular to a certain variant, or through investments in complementary products designed to fit with a particular variant (see e.g. David, 1985, 1992; Arthur, 1989; Katz and Shapiro, 1985). While sometimes used more generally, the special term 'standard' tends to be used to denote the key mechanism or configuration that defines and delineates the dominant 'system' when it emerges. As the authors writing in this field argue convincingly, there is no reason why the standard that emerges and, in effect, 'locks' in the system, need be optimal.

In the original Abernathy and Utterback story, once a dominant design comes into existence, radical product innovation slows, and product design improvements become incremental. There may, however, be a considerable period of time where there is substantial improvement of process technology. If the advancing process technology is specific to a particular product design, cumulative process innovation further locks in that design and makes it even more difficult for different designs to compete. This story line is quite consistent with that being spun by economists interested in systems technologies and standards.

When Abernathy and Utterback first spun out the dominant design story, they based it on detailed observation of only one industry—automobile manufacturing. Since that time the basic story line has been tried, and found fitting, in a wide range of industries (see in particular the work of Tushman and colleagues, 1986, 1992, and by Utterback and Suarez, 1993). Some writers clearly believe it is universal. I confess some skepticism about that. The story seems to fit best industries where the product is a 'system', and where customers have similar demands. It is not at all clear if the notion of a dominant design fits the experience of the chemical products industry where often a variety of quite different products are produced for similar uses, or pharmaceuticals where customer needs are divergent and specialized. Some time ago Pavitt (1987) argued that the domain of dominant design theory was far more limited than its advocates allowed. Nonetheless, dominant design theory certainly has proved illuminating in a wide range of industries.

Where it does seem applicable, that theory raises very interesting, and troubling, questions about the nature of economic explanation, about whether one can presume market forces generate efficient outcomes, and even about what one means by market forces. In the first 'story' economic logic prevails. But in both the second and third story of how a dominant design emerges, there are stochastic forces at work that can be decisive. Particularly in the third, there also may be processes of coalition building that can nudge the outcome one way or another, which may have little to do with projections of long run economic efficiency (see e.g. David 1985, 1992, and Tushman and Rosenkopf, 1992). Some writers have gone so far as to argue that it is power, or social consensus, rather than economic efficiency which determines which broad path ultimately is followed (see e.g. Bijker *et al.*, 1989). This raises the question of how far economic selection arguments can take one in an evolutionary analysis of economic change, and the extent to which political and social forces need to be taken explicitly into account not simply in influencing transient or short term developments but in determining the broad paths along which technology proceeds. More on this later.

There is another body of research which uses concepts similar to those employed in the technology life cycle literature, but with a different focus— in particular, what happens to firm and industry structure as a technology matures. Abernathy and Utterback (1978) were interested in this question, but it was not the central focus of their earlier articles. Indeed until recently, the bulk of the research in this area has been done by economists, who made little reference to the above technology cycle literature. A number of economists have contributed to this line of research and 'story telling'. Mueller and Tilton (1969) wrote a pioneer piece along these lines. Recently Gort and Klepper (1982), and Klepper and Graddy (1990) have developed the empirical and theoretical argument further. Over the past few years there has been convergence. Utterback and Suarez (1993) coming from the technology life cycle tradition have discovered the industrial organization literature. Klepper (1993) coming from the latter has found the former.

In any case, the basic propositions tend to be these. During the early period of experimentation and flux, before a dominant design emerges, there are no particular advantages to incumbency. Market demand is fragmented across a number of variants. Firms producing particular designs tend to be small. Model change may be frequent. There is a considerable amount of exit from and entry into the industry.

However, after a dominant design becomes established, firms that do not produce a variant of it tend to drop out of the industry, or into small niche markets. With product design more stabilized, learning by incumbent firms becomes more cumulative, and potential entrants increasingly are at a disadvantage. With the market less fragmented and more predictable, firms try to exploit latent economies of scale, and advances in process technology both reflect and enforce this. Generally scale intensive technology is capital intensive as well, and so the cost of entry rises for this reason too. There is 'shake out' in the industry and structure becomes more concentrated, with the surviving firms tending to be relatively large.

As with the theory about dominant designs, there is a question about how universal is the proposed pattern of industry evolution. The empirical work by Gort and Klepper (1982) and Klepper (1993) show that the basic story does seem to fit a wide range of industries in the USA. Utterback and Suarez (1993) similarly claim widespread applicability. However, there certainly are exceptions. The companies that got into the (then) new pharmaceuticals business in the 1930s and postwar were, by and large, the old strong chemical products companies, rather than new entrants.

Even where the empirical facts seem to fit the theory, it is important to recognize that other theories may fit the facts just as well. Thus in Klepper's 1993 model, the reason why innovation shifts away from the creation of new products and towards the improvement of process technology as an industry matures has nothing to do with tendencies inherent in technological development. Rather, in his model, product innovation depends on the number of firms, and process innovation depends on their size. As the industry evolves firms get larger, and there are fewer of them. Thus the shift in the character of innovation is driven by changes in market structure, rather than the other way around.

Finally, it should be noted that almost all the empirical research on the topic has been on patterns in the United States. At least in the post World War II era, there is reason to believe that new products that were pioneered by new firms in the United States, were pioneered (somewhat later) by established firms in Europe and Japan. If so, these international differences seem interesting to explain.

The story about changing firm and industry structure contained in the literature described above is tied to the notion of organizational learning. That part of the story can be enriched considerably, I believe, by tapping into another body of research associated with the proposition that successful firms develop a complex of 'core capabilities' that enable them to be effective in the context in which they operate. (For a representative set of articles see Teece *et al.*, 1992; Prahalad and Hamel, 1990; Dosi *et al.*, 1992). The basic argument is that firms have (at best) a limited number of things they can do well, which include operating and advancing the particular technologies they know well, their particular approaches to marketing and purchasing, their ways of identifying and responding to environmental changes, etc. Further, ability to do even a limited number of things will usually take a considerable amount of learning by experience, and significant financial investments in those 'core capabilities'. Chandler (1990) has stressed the investments in production, marketing, and management that are needed for a firm to become and remain competitive in an area.

The research described above on 'dominant designs' suggests that these capabilities and investments cannot be developed when a technology still is in flux, but only after broad orientations have become clear. On the other hand, the proposition that a firm's core capabilities have a limited domain of applicability suggests a tailoring of firms to the requirements of prevailing dominant designs. In turn, this suggests that established firms may have considerable difficulty in adjusting, in gaining control of needed different capabilities, when important new technologies that have the potential to replace prevailing ones come into being. I will pick up this issue later.

Firms do not stand by themselves, of course, but rather in a context in which they compete with rivals, are served by suppliers, sell to customers, and draw on particular talents and skills. For an industry with special input and skill needs, growth and effectiveness is strongly conditioned by how rapidly and effectively a support structure grows up. Recently several scholars—Piori and Sabel (1984), Lazonick (1990), and Krugman (1992) quickly come to mind—have resurrected Marshall's notion of an 'industrial district' which includes most of the firms in the industry itself, specialized suppliers, and concentrations of workers with the particular needed skills. These latter may be associated with the presence of training institutions and programs.

3. The Evolution of Supporting Institutions

By and large, the evolutionary processes discussed above proceed in a market setting, and involve competition among firms, with selection determined to a good extent by market forces. One can see a route toward formal modeling drawing ideas from various industry models Winter and I have developed, from Arthur and colleagues, and from Klepper. A society's institutions— both general and specific to the broad sector that contains the developing industry—will influence the parameters of the model, and perhaps even its broad shape. Thus the ability of a firm with a better product to eliminate its competition may depend on its ability to attract funds to exploit its advantage.

However, a number of detailed historical accounts document that various features of the institutional environment themselves tend to adapt and change in response to pushes and pulls exerted by the development of a new industry. The processes involved here are not market processes, at least not of the standard variety, but involve the forming of collective bodies, decisions of voluntary organizations, government agencies, and political action.

One important development that almost invariably occurs as a new industry develops is that the people in it become conscious that there is a new industry, and that it has collective interests and needs (see Granovetter, 1985). Industry or trade associations form. These may be active in the standard setting discussed earlier. More generally, they give the industry a recognized organization that can lobby on its behalf for regulation to its liking, for protection from competition from outside the group, for public programs to support it, etc. This is another feature of an industry's evolution that can lock in the status quo.

If the technology on which the industry is based has novel characteristics, new technical societies and new technical journals, tend to spring up. In some cases whole new fields of 'science' may come into being.

Research by Nathan Rosenberg and myself (Nelson and Rosenberg, 1983) has called into question certain popular notions about the relationships between science and technology. Conventional wisdom has it that the sciences, in general, do not aim to solve practical problems but rather to advance basic understanding of nature, but that enhanced basic understanding makes technological advances possible even if the work is not aimed to do that. Thus the work of Maxwell on electromagnetism, which was an exercise in pure science, ultimately led to radio. The case of Sadi Carnot, who launched the field of thermodynamics largely because he wanted to understand what was going on in steam engines, is recognized but generally considered something of an exception.

Our research suggests that these kinds of 'exceptions' may well be the rule. Quite often when a new technology comes into existence, there is very little scientific understanding relevant to it. However, the appearance of that new technology then induces scientific research to understand it, and lay the basis for its subsequent development. The result may be the creation of a new scientific field related to that technology. Thus the field of metallurgy came into existence because of a demand for better understanding of the factors that determined the properties of steel. Computer science is the field that was bought into existence by the advent of the modern computer. Chemical engineering and electrical engineering rose up as fields of teaching and research because of industry demand for them that occurred after the key technological advances that launched the industries.

The appearance and development of these technology oriented sciences tend to tie industries to universities, which provide both people trained in the relevant fields, and research findings which enable the technology to advance further. The development of these sciences naturally tends to lend extra strength to prevailing technologies. On the other hand the presence of university research tends to dilute the extent to which firms in being have knowledge advantages over potential entrants. Also, research at universities may just become the source of radically different technological alternatives.

Recognition of the role of technical societies and universities in the development of modern technologies opens the door to seeing the wide range of institutions that may co-evolve with technology. Often legal structures need to change. Thus there may be intellectual property rights issues that need to be sorted out—bio-technology is a striking contemporary case in point. There almost always are issues of regulation, as was prominently the case in radio and, in a different manner, biotechnology again. Hughes (1987) has described in great detail the wide range of legal and regulatory matters that had to be decided before electric power could go forward strongly, and how the particular ways they were decided affected the evolution of the technology and the industry.

In many cases new public sector activities and programs are required. Thus mass use of automobiles required that societies organize themselves to build and maintain a system of public roads. Airplanes required airports. The development of radio required mechanisms to allocate the radio spectrum. Development of commercial television required that as well, and also depended on governmental decisions about standards.

These examples indicate that the evolution of institutions relevant to a technology or industry may be a very complex process, involving not only the actions of private firms, but also organizations like industry associations, technical societies, universities, courts, government agencies, legislatures, etc. The 'new institutional economics' started with a broad theoretical stance that, somehow, institutions changed optimally (if perhaps with a lag) in response to changes in economic circumstances that called for those changes. Recently, however, scholars in that field are beginning to highlight the interest group conflict often involved in public responses, and the strong sensitivity of outcomes to political structures and processes (see e.g. North, 1990; Shepsle and Weingast, 1981; Cohen and Noll, 1991). Not only is there an abandonment of the assumption of 'optimality' of institutional response. There is now strong recognition that one needs a process model to predict and understand what the institutional accommodations will be.

4. Punctuated Equilibrium

This leads me to another set of strands I want to gather here: those concerned with what happens in a mature industry when radical new developments come about that call for significant change. An example would be the effect of the advent of transistor and later integrated circuit technology on the mature electronics industry which had been dedicated to vacuum tubes. Another would be the advent of biotechnology on the mature pharmaceuticals industry.

Perhaps the largest body of writing addressing this issue has been concerned with who adopts and brings to practice such a new technology. In particular, do incumbent firms adopt it, or does its adoption depend on new entrants? The proposition advanced by this literature is that the answer depends on whether the new technology employs roughly the same kinds of understanding and skills as does the old. If so, firms in the industry tend to be able to switch over to it. If not, new firms will tend to enter the industry, and the failure rate among incumbents may be very high. Work along these lines has been done by Tushman and Anderson (1986), Tushman and Romanelli (1985), Hannan and Freeman (1989), and Henderson and Clark (1990), among others. However, as with the empirical literature on the evolution of firm and industry structure described above, virtually all of this work has been based on the United States. As I noted earlier, there is reason to believe that in Europe and Japan, new firms do not seem to enter the picture so readily, and incumbent firms thus have more time to adjust.

A broader question, of course, is whether the larger set of institutions supporting the established technology and industry are able to adapt, or whether their conservatism makes it difficult for established firms to shift away from old practices, or for new firms to enter and to take over. Lazonick (1990), among others, has elaborated the theme that the broad organization of work and institutions for training labor that worked so well for British industry in the late 19th century became a handicap in the 20th. Veblen's famous essay (1915) on the rise of Germany as an economic power stressed more generally that British industry was in effect sorely handicapped in adopting the new technologies that were coming into place around the turn of the century by an interlocking set of constraints associated with her institutions and past investments, whereas Germany could work with a relatively clean slate.

The most sweeping of the propositions along these lines has been made by Perez (1983) and Freeman (1991), who have developed the concept of a 'techno-economic paradigm'. Their argument starts along lines developed by Schumpeter many years ago: different eras are dominated by different fundamental technologies. They then propose that to be effective with those technologies a nation requires a set of institutions compatible with and supportive of them. The ones suitable for an earlier set of fundamental technologies may be quite inappropriate for the new. Their arguments clearly are similar to those of Veblen, in the particular case he addressed. Thus while Britain lagged, Germany and the USA had or quickly adopted institutions that could support the rising chemical and electrical industries that were the basic ones in the era from 1910 to 1960 or so. Perez and Freeman propose that the period since 1970 or so has seen the rise of 'information technologies' as the new basis of economic effectiveness, and argue that effective accommodation requires a very different set of institutions than those required in the earlier era. Japan they see as coming closest to having them.

One can be skeptical about these propositions simply because they are so grandly stated. However the basic point, that new technologies often are not well accommodated by prevailing institutional structures, and require institutional reform if they are to develop effectively, I think, squares with the historical record.

5. *Economic Growth and the Formation of Comparative Advantage at a Sectoral Level*

In the Introduction, I stressed that virtually all formal growth theory focuses on the quantitative aspects of growth and captures little either of the developmental or the qualitative features of the detailed historical accounts.

Regarding the quantitative aspects, the appreciative theory sketched above certainly does suggest a 'developmental' flavor to the time paths of measured worker productivity, capital intensity, and total factor productivity as an industry matures, and also some interesting connections between these variables and firm size and industry structure. In particular, the argument leads one to expect that rising capital intensity and the development of large scale units are phenomena that go together and occur after a dominant design or mode of production has been established. One might suspect that these developments also would be associated with an acceleration of growth both of labor productivity and of total factor productivity. However, particularly if effective use of the potential latent in a new technology requires significant institutional accommodation, it might take a long time before there is much effect on productivity. David's study (1991) of electric power is consistent with this story.

For me, perhaps the most intriguing implications of the life cycle appreciative theory concern the factors it suggests may lie behind the establishment of comparative advantage in a new industry. The 'new trade theory' recognizes, in stylized form, that comparative advantage in certain fields is created rather than being innate in broad country level variables, and that both private and public actions may be needed for comparative advantage to be built. However, the stories sketched above provide a much richer and variegated account of how comparative advantage is built.

Among other things, they suggest that different factors may be operative early in an industry's history than those important later. Regarding the determinants of comparative advantage when an industry is new, the technology cycle story calls attention to the fact that countries clearly differ in the ease with which new firms can form and get funding and in the degree to which markets are open to new sources of supply. They also differ in the speed with which universities are able to adopt new sciences, in how adaptable legal structures are to changing demands put on them by new technologies, in how supportive public sector programs are of the new as contrasted with protective of the old, etc. On the other hand, once a dominant design is established, different features of a nation's institutional environment become important. Ability to finance large scale investment, for example. Ability to train labor for the specifics of the jobs, for another.

6. A Reprise on Formal Theorizing

This essay has been on appreciative theorizing. It is my conviction that it is important to get appreciative theory reasonably well worked out, before one gets into the business of building formal theory. Otherwise there are few restraints preventing formal modeling from going amuck, and little that pulls the enterprise towards being about real phenomena. On the other hand, given the existence of a reasonably well worked out appreciative theory, formal theorizing can be a very helpful part of the intellectual enterprise.

There is, centrally, the problem that the informality of appreciative theorizing makes it difficult to check out the logical completeness and correctness of the 'causal' arguments in that theory. The exercise and discipline of formalizing the argument can reveal a lot about what is incomplete or problematic in the appreciative causal story. As someone who has played this game a number of times, I can attest that much is learned even before a formal model is fully developed and capable of serving as an analytic engine, for example through the process of discovering that various appreciative theoretic causal propositions or 'predictions' won't go through formally unless one makes certain ancillary assumptions. In turn, one might be quite willing to make these, or one might go back and reconsider the appreciative theoretic logic. Once a formal model gets up and running, the same dialectic between appreciative and formal theorizing continues, as one discovers that the hypothesized conclusions hold only for certain sets of parameter values, or that the model is generating certain kinds of outcomes regarding which the appreciative theory was mute. Again, one is forced to revise or qualify or extend the appreciative theory, or at least learn to interpret it differently in terms of how it can be appropriately formalized.

In that spirit, what are the key issues that I, right now, would like to explore with a carefully constructed formal model? (Above I indicated that I am sure that once one is up and running I will discover a lot of matters that I have not thought about.) First of all, I think the logic of the various processes that have been argued to lead to the emergence of a dominant design ought to be worked through in the context of a complete evolutionary model, with diverse firms, whose growth or decline is tied to their profitability, and who are locked in varying degrees to particular technologies. The model certainly should contain diverse customers, who have various degrees of rigidity in their preferences, and who may or may not want to buy what others have bought. The model should build in various mechanisms that generate different forms and degrees of dynamic increasing returns. The Polya urn scheme (see e.g. Arthur, 1988) that, up until now, has been virtually the only way the dominant design question has been formally analyzed, strikes me as possibly missing a number of interesting complications.

Second, the relationships between the evolution of a technology and the evolution of firm and industry structure surely can be illuminated by formal modeling. How much difference does it make, for example, if the broad technology is available to new entrants, because, say, much of it is codified in a scientific discipline? How does the diversity of customers affect how industry structure evolves? etc.

As I indicated earlier, I think I see a reasonably clear road towards modeling these kinds of things, drawing from early Nelson–Winter and related models, from Arthur, and from Klepper. I think it will be far more difficult to model the coevolution of institutions.

There are two reasons. One is that it is not clear exactly how various institutions ought to be represented. Thus how should one model an 'industry association' or a 'technical society'? How should one treat MIT and Stanford as parts of the institutional structure supporting the American semiconductor industry? What activities do they perform? How do they affect the behavior and performance of firms in the industry? We have 'appreciative theory' about this. It will not be easy to translate that theory into formal theory, however. That is exactly the reason why it is important to try to do so.

The second reason is that the 'evolutionary processes' through which new academic disciplines get formed, or get blocked, or the ways in which new law gets created, or old law modified, are very different from the processes built into extant formal evolutionary models. We have 'appreciative theories' about these matters, but virtually no work trying to formalize those theories. It should be fun, but not easy, to try to do so.

References

Abernathy, W. and J. Utterback (1978), 'Patterns of Industrial Innovation', *Technology Review*, 41–47.

Arthur, B. (1988), 'Self-Reinforcing Mechanisms in Economics', in P. Anderson, K. Arrow and D. Pines (eds.), *The Economy as an Evolving Complex System*, Addison Wesley Publishing Co.

Arthur, B. (1989), 'Competing Technologies, Increasing Returns, and Lock-In by Historical Events', *Economic Journal*, March.

Bijker, W., T. Hughes and T. Pinch (1989), *The Social Construction of Technology Systems*, MIT Press: Cambridge.

Chandler, A. (1990), *Scale and Scope: The Dynamics of Industrial Capitalism*, Harvard University Press: Cambridge, MA.

Cohen, L. and R. Noll (1991), *The Technology Pork Barrel*, Brookings: Washington.

David, P. (1985), 'Clio and the Economics of QWERTY', *American Economic Review*.

David, P. (1991), 'Computer and Dynamo: The Modern Productivity Paradox in a Not-too-Distant Mirror', *Technology and Productivity*, OECD: Paris.

David, P. (1992), 'Heroes, Herds, and Hysteresis in Technological History: Thomas Edison and the Battle of the Systems Reconsidered', *Industrial and Corporate Change*, 1, 129–180.

Dosi, G. (1982). 'Technological Paradigms and Technological Trajectories: A Suggested Interpretation of the Determinants and Directions of Technical Change', *Research Policy*.

Dosi, G. (1988), 'Sources, Procedures, and Microeconomic Effects of Innovation', *Journal of Economic Literature*.

Dosi, G., D. Teece and S. Winter (1992), 'Towards a Theory of Corporate Coherence: Preliminary Remarks' in G. Dosi, R. Giannetti and P. Toninelli (eds.), *Technology and Enterprise in Historical Perspective*, Clarendon Press: Oxford.

Freeman, C. (1991), 'The Nature of Innovation and the Evolution of the Productive System', in *Technology and Productivity*, OECD: Paris.

Gort, M. and S. Klepper (1982), 'Time Paths in the Diffusion of Product Innovations', *Economic Journal*.

Granovetter, M. (1985), 'Economic Action and Social Structure: The Problem of Embeddedness', *American Journal of Sociology*, November.

Hannan, M. and J. Freeman (1989), *Organizational Ecology*, Harvard University Press: Cambridge, MA.

Henderson, R. (1991), 'Underinvestment and Incompetence as Responses to Radical Innovation: Evidence from the Photolithographic Alignment Equipment Industry', *Mimeo*, MIT, October.

Henderson, R. and K. Clark (1990), 'Architectural Innovation: The Reconfiguration of Existing Product Technologies and the Failure of Established Firms', *Administrative Sciences Quarterly*.

Hughes, T. (1987), *Networks of Power: Electrification in Western Society 1880–1930*, Johns Hopkins Press: Baltimore, MD.

Katz, M. and C. Shapiro (1985), 'Network Externalities, Competition, and Compatibility', *American Economic Review*.

Klepper, S. (1993), 'Entry, Exit, Growth, and Innovation Over the Product Cycle', Carnegie-Mellon University, unpublished manuscript.

Klepper, S. and E. Graddy (1990), 'The Evolution of New Industries and the Determinants of Market Structure', *The Rand Journal of Economics*.

Lazonick, W. (1990), *Competitive Advantage on the Shop Floor*, Harvard University Press: Cambridge, MA.

Metcalfe, J. and P. Saviotti (eds.) (1991), *Evolutionary Theories of Economic and Technological Change*, Harwood Publishers: Reading, PA.

Metcalfe, J. S. and M. Gibbons (1986), 'Technological Variety and the Process of Competition', *Economic Applique*.

Mueller, D. and J. Tilton (1969), 'Research and Development as Barriers to Entry', *Canadian Journal of Economics*.

Nelson, R. and N. Rosenberg (1983), 'Technical Innovation and National Systems', in R. Nelson (ed.), *National Innovation Systems: A Comparative Study*, Oxford University Press: New York, NY.

Nelson, R. R. and S. G. Winter (1982), *An Evolutionary Theory of Economic Change*, Harvard University Press: Cambridge, MA.

North, D. (1990), *Institutions, Institutional Change, and Economic Performance*, Cambridge University Press: Cambridge, MA.

Pavitt, K. (1987), 'On the Nature of Technology', Inaugural Lecture given at the University of Sussex, 23 June.

Perez, (1983), 'Structural Change and the Assimilation of New Technology in the Economic and Social System', *Futures*.

Prahalad, C. and G. Hamel (1990), 'The Core Competences of the Corporation', *Harvard Business Review*.

Shepsle, K. and B. Weingast (1981), 'Structure Induced Equilibrium and Legislative Choice', *Public Choice*, Fall, pp. 503–520.

Silverberg, G., G. Dosi, and L. Orsenigo (1988), 'Innovation, Diversity, and Diffusion: A Self-Organizing Model', *Economic Journal*.

Soete, L. and R. Turner (1987), 'Technological Diffusion and the Rate of Technical Change', *The Economic Journal*.

Teece, D., G. Pisano and A. Shuen (1992), 'Dynamic Capabilities and Strategic Management', manuscript Berkeley, June 1992.

Tushman, M. and D. Anderson (1986), 'Technological Discontinuities and Organizational Environments', *Administrative Sciences Quarterly*.

Tushman, M. and E. Romanelli (1985), 'Organizational Evolution: A Metamorphosis Model of Convergence and Reorientation', JAI Press: Greenwich, CT.

Tushman, M. and L. Rosenkopf (1992), 'Organizational Determinants of Technological Change: Towards a Sociology of Technological Evolution', *Research in Organizational Behavior*, 14.

Utterback, J. (1974), 'Innovation in Industry and the Diffusion of Technology', *Science*, February.

Utterback, J. and F. Suarez (1993), 'Innovation, Competition, and Market Structure', *Research Policy*,

Veblen, T. (1915), *Imperial Germany and the Industrial Revolution*, MacMillan: New York, NY.

Vincenti, W. (1990), *What Do Engineers Know and How Do They Know It?*, Baltimore: Johns Hopkins Press.

Williamson, O. (1985), *The Economic Institutions of Capitalism*, New York: Free Press.

INDEX